War

Controlling Escalation

War

Controlling Escalation

Richard Smoke

Harvard University Press

Cambridge, Massachusetts
and
London, England
1977

Library of Congress Cataloging in Publication Data
Smoke, Richard.
   War: controlling escalation.

   Bibliography: p.
   Includes index.
   1. War.   2. Military history, Modern.   I. Title.
U21.2.S63   355.02'15   77-6248
ISBN 0-674-94595-6

For E. C., with gratitude

Preface

This study springs from a deep concern with the limitation and mitigation of warfare. I begin from two convictions: the likelihood of war is not lessening as we move deeper into the nuclear age, and the dangers that war may pose are growing.

In the thirty years between 1945 and 1975 there were some hundred wars around our planet, an average of more than three a year. There is no reason to suppose that the future will be less warlike than the past; indeed there may be reason to think that it could be more so. Conflicts over economic issues, running roughly North-South, are being added to the traditional East-West competition concerning social order. There is some grim evidence that the seeds of wars in the coming decades already lie incubating in the grinding destitution of many peoples and their growing desperation to meet even their simplest material needs.

Such new conflicts would occur, furthermore, at just the moment in history when advancing and proliferating technology is placing quantities of highly destructive weapons into more and more hands. Very probably the next few decades will see the spread of atomic weapons to additional nations, and perhaps to terrorist and criminal groups. Almost certainly there will be a similar proliferation of exotic conventional technology like hand-carried missiles and precision-guided munitions (the so-called one-shot/one-kill weapons). The sober observer must reluctantly conclude that wars in the final decades of the twentieth century are likely to be at least equally frequent, and more destructive, than previously.

By far the best way of limiting and mitigating warfare is not to allow it to begin. But moderating influences and enlightened impulses toward reasonable accommodations sometimes will fall short. Some wars are going to begin. When they do, the possibilities of their escalating alarmingly are greater than ever before in human history.

Many complexities present themselves to anyone concerned about this prospect. Wars have the potential of widening in geographic scope and involving additional nations (sometimes called horizontal escalation) or of becoming more intense in the tempo of events and the violence of weapons employed (vertical escalation). At no time have there been so many independent and semi-independent centers of decision upon the world stage, and at no time have there been so many layers of national interests to be considered—political, economic, ideological, territorial, tribal, and others. By now these intertwining interests form a single, highly complex planetary web, along and around which the ramifications of major events ripple, react, and reverberate. It is hard to think of any area on the globe where a spark might not be struck that could ignite a spreading fire of interests, fears, and involvements.

Should war begin, the ever more numerous options provided by advancing military technology will create a perplexing profusion of ways in which the fighting can intensify. As the belligerents escalate, the process may prove harder and harder to control and in time threaten to soar toward higher levels of violence than anyone may have intended. Lurking in the background will be the horrifying possibility that atomic weapons may be employed. If and when they are, the great inhibition that has slowly built up over thirty years will dissolve; use of *all* the many tens of thousands of nuclear weapons now in existence will suddenly become much more plausible—in that war and in any subsequent wars. Furthermore, most ways of using atomic weapons invite some form of immediate nuclear retaliation, perhaps a chain of very rapid escalations capable of leading even to thermonuclear Armageddon.

If it is true that war is likely to be at least as frequent an occurrence in the future as in the past, and if it is true that it will pose more complicated and more dangerous escalation possibilities, then it is vital that we learn as best we can not only how to prevent the outbreak of war, but also how to control escalation after war has begun. It is astonishing how little attention has been given to this task. Active and retired military officers and government officials agree almost uniformly that escalation is a dimension of warfare for which few reliable guidelines exist. The large body of literature that has grown up since the mid-1950s in the field of study variously known as national security affairs, defense studies, war and peace research, and the like contains very little that is directly concerned with practical ways to control escalation. For that matter, even theoretical questions about the dynamics of escalation have received little attention from analysts and scholars of foreign policy and international affairs.

Much of this book therefore must be concerned with escalation as well as with escalation control. Our understanding is so inadequate that the analyst cannot take up the question of controlling escalation immediately and systematically. He must first try to understand better what it is that he is trying to control.

Incidentally, although the distinction cannot be an absolute one, it is useful to distinguish between the escalation of military operations on the one hand, and the escalation of objectives on the other. Except as otherwise noted, the term *escalation* as used in this book refers to operations; other phrases will be employed to describe heightened objectives, stakes, threats, or other intangibles. This distinction and its limitations will be discussed again later.

The escalation of warfare is a subject full of the sort of paradoxes that create opportunities for "reverse psychology." One of these is that it is hard to study and write about escalation without the hazard of convincing someone that he *could* control escalation; and hence that he could, after all, fight or intensify some particular war at only modest risk. I can merely register my uncomfortable awareness of this paradox, for there is no possible escape from it. The things we want to know *after* a war begins, to try to keep it under control, are inevitably the very things which, to the extent they are known *before* the war begins, might allow people on one or both sides to believe they could start a war without too much danger. (The same is true, during an apparently stable ongoing war, of the temptation to expand it "just a little.") The best the analyst can do is to emphasize again and again that, even to the extent that a few useful ideas about controlling escalation may eventually be developed, these can never be counted upon too heavily in any particular situation. War is one of the most unpredictable phenomena known to man.

If we embrace this unpredictability as the first axiom of all theory and all practice, then it is permissible and desirable to attempt to study the problem of escalation control. Since *escalation* is a term with many meanings and many components, I have sharpened the focus of this study in a couple of ways. It does not try to deal with the intensification of diplomatic crises, nor with the transition from crisis to open fighting (although it may subsequently turn out that some of what is said here applies, *mutatis mutandis,* to those situations as well). By and large, I deal only with the escalation of actual warfare. The study also focuses mainly on escalation that gets "out of control" as the belligerents counter each other's immediately preceding move, the process as a whole moving "inexorably" to a much larger war, often general war. Many analysts point out that, strictly speaking, phrases such as the quoted ones have little meaning. After an initial description of this kind of escalation, I shall use such phrases without quotes or repeated reservation, as a shorthand for the processes this book tries to analyze.

While control of such escalation is not the only problematical part of escalation control, it is the part that seems to me to be the most important at the present time. The dynamics of this sort of escalation also lend themselves to analysis. There is little to be said in advance about the wartime situation where one side sees pretty clearly that it can get away with one or two escalations of the conflict without much danger of setting off a sequence. We may, or in some circumstances we may not, regret this decision. We may, or we may not, find specific reasons in a particular situation to think that the decision will be too costly, in casualties or in other ways, for what it is likely to achieve. But probably we are not going to determine ahead of time many generalizations about the overall politico-military dynamics of such occurrences.

What we may hope to derive with appropriate research, however, are some ideas about how an apparently inexorable series of escalations begins, and how it seems to get out of control. While such ideas can never lead to a sure formula for controlling escalation, they could conceivably be helpful to decision-makers trying to prevent a chain reaction during some future war. They could, that is, if they are drawn from past situations that resemble the likely future ones in truly significant ways. This brings us to the problem of finding the most useful historical material.

The desirability of utilizing case histories from before World War II to try to shed light on situations plausible for coming decades can be argued pro and con. (The arguments are sketched in Chapter 3.) There is a compelling reason for using such material in this particular investigation: it is only before 1945 that concrete cases exist where escalation *did* mount "uncontrollably" all the way to general war. For that matter there has been only one occasion since then when, it is widely agreed, an international conflict *almost* escalated this way (a category we shall also consider). This was the Cuban missile crisis of October 1962, which has already produced a large literature—in fact, it is undoubtedly the most studied crisis of recent times. For these reasons and others mentioned later, I have chosen to employ pre-World War II case histories, and to analyze them somewhat selectively for aspects that seem particularly germane to the current era.

The resulting book is intended both for decision-makers and working-level civilian and military officers, and for scholars specializing in international relations, foreign policy, and related fields. Reconciling the quite different needs and demands of these two communities is not easy. For ease of reading, much of the scholarly apparatus of the study and some technical elaborations have been relegated to footnotes and to the second and third appendixes. The first appendix, "Operational Questions for Decision-Makers," is intended for the practical convenience of governmental audiences.

Acknowledgments

Among the many who have provided assistance and support to this effort, three individuals in particular are owed a deep debt of gratitude.

In its earliest phases as a fledgling Ph.D. thesis, the project was nurtured in many important ways by William W. Kaufmann of the Massachusetts Institute of Technology. Surpassing the usual definition of a dissertation chairman's responsibilities, Professor Kaufmann provided a wealth of wise advice about the topic, valuable suggestions about research directions, kindly corrections of numerous errors both methodological and substantive, and—not least appreciated—benign patience vis-à-vis a rate of progress that at times seemed glacial.

While still in an early phase, the dissertation was much strengthened through my work with Alexander L. George of Stanford University. Professor George had undertaken a major project on the theory and practice of deterrence in American foreign policy and already done a great deal of research and writing thereon, when he generously invited me to join him in what eventually became a book on that topic. His conceptualization of the research method of "focused comparison" of historical case studies enormously clarified my understanding of appropriate methodology for the present investigation and was carried over wholesale into it. Professor George then redoubled his kindness by twice criticizing drafts of the first part of the dissertation, and by sponsoring my presentation of a paper based on two of its chapters to a panel of the Western Political Science Association in April 1971.

Additional assistance was provided subsequently by Thomas C. Schelling of Harvard University. Professor Schelling gave me a detailed and comprehensive critical analysis of the theoretical portions of the dissertation, including a cornucopia of ideas and suggestions for conceptual improvements. Then and later, Professor Schelling was equally generous in offering repeated encouragements that a revised version of the study should be published.

The Helen Dwight Reid Award of the American Political Science Association for 1971 and 1972 also encouraged a grateful recipient to believe that further work might be worthwhile, as did Ernest R. May's selection of the study for attention in one of his seminars at Harvard in 1973. At other stages of the project, Graham Allison and Robert Jervis provided hefty measures of good advice and good ideas, including the latter's detailed critique of the dissertation. Others who have made thoughtful suggestions at one time or another include Lincoln Bloomfield, Robert Coulam, Larry Finkelstein, James Foster, Ole Holsti, Amelia Leiss, Uwe Nerlich, George Quester, and Larry Weiler.

A political scientist who attempts to use history as I have tried to here runs many risks. Mine were much reduced by the kindness of a number of historians who consented to review the dissertation's historical chapters. Gordon Craig of Stanford graciously took on not one but two chapters, on the German wars, and suggested colleagues who were expert on the other periods treated. Very helpful criticisms and suggestions on particular chapters were received not only from Professor Craig but also from Thomas Bailey and Patrice Higonnet (Seven Years War), Gabriel Jackson (Spanish Civil War), and Kenneth Rock (Crimean War). More general readings of the historical part of the study were offered by Ruhl Bartlett, Ernest May, and Sam Williamson. I must emphasize that many changes have been made in all the historical chapters in the several years since these solicitous reviews were received, and errors of omission or commission may have crept in. Any and all are entirely my responsibility.

This project has also been fortunate in its institutional friends. In its early stages it was supported directly and indirectly by the Center for International Affairs and the John F. Kennedy School of Government, both at Harvard. Plans for the dismantling of the dissertation, for a new phase of research, and for the study's resurrection in book form were laid while I was a postdoctoral fellow in psychology at the Institute of Personality Assessment and Research, University of California at Berkeley. The research and the bulk of the writing were done at the Center for Advanced Study in the Behavioral Sciences in Palo Alto. In the environment, support, and other qualities it offers scholars, the center is little short of celestial, and I am thankful that a year's fellowship there provided a fortunate opportunity to bring the project to completion. Some final rewriting and editing were done at the Wright Institute in Berkeley. I am grateful to all these institutions for their support.

Vivian Wheeler of the editorial staff at Harvard University Press, and Susan Green and Mary Tye, typists, all made contributions well beyond the call of obligation, and made them with grace and good humor. Considering a history of assistance such as that recorded here, all the inadequacies of the final product must be laid squarely at the door of the author.

Contents

Tables

Maps

Part One
The Problem of Escalation

1

Introduction

Ballistic missiles are being installed by the Soviets in Cuba; we could destroy them with air strikes, but mightn't this create a military confrontation that could lead to World War III?

The Viet Cong are attacking our bases in South Vietnam; we could launch air attacks against the North, but mightn't this bring the Communist Chinese into the Vietnam conflict?

Nazi Germany is preparing to invade; we could launch RAF bombing raids on industrial targets, but mightn't this trigger major Luftwaffe attacks on England?

The British economy is faltering; we could complete our blockade around Britain by having our U-boats sink neutral shipping, but mightn't this cause President Wilson to bring the United States into the war?

The Poles are rebelling again; we could suppress them with extra troops presently stationed at home in Russia, but mightn't this raise the risk of a clash with Austria-Hungary over Galicia?

Our friends the Corcyraeans are being defeated by the forces of Corinth; we could save them by committing our Athenian navy, but mightn't this cause the Spartans to come to the aid of their Corinthian allies?

All these, and many others that might be given, are instances where individuals responsible for determining governmental policy have had reason to take some new and stronger action during a war or military crisis, but have wondered whether doing so might not lead directly or indirectly to a bigger and more violent war—something neither they, nor frequently anyone else, really wanted.

Escalation: Why So Poorly Understood?

Escalation is a relatively new word. It does not appear in diction-
aries, in military or scholarly literature, or in the public statements
of government officials, before about 1960. Still, the idea that the
word names must be as old as man's thought about war. There is an
early stage in almost any conflict when neither side has yet committed itself and its resources fully and when, therefore, escalation
is a possibility or likelihood. For that matter, in most conflicts
neither side ever commits itself totally. Virtually all the wars we
know of, even those that have escalated almost as much as possible, have included some aspect of restraint throughout. In modern
times especially, most wars have been fought within very important restraints and limits. Even World War II, often thought of as a
total conflict, was fought throughout within the important con-
straint that none of the belligerents employed their ample stocks of
poison gases and nerve gases. In its most general sense, then, escalation is a feature—either actual or possible—in all conflict. In its
breadth of applicability and its omnipresence, escalation ranks
with any concept in the taxonomy of violence.[1]

It can also be among the most complex of the ideas spawned by
war. One may attempt, as I do in this book, to distinguish escalation in operations from escalation in intangibles, but these factors
are closely intertwined and it is not always clear which diplomatic
messages, which public statements, which delegations of authority
to military commanders are part of an escalation, and which are
preparatory to an escalation or part of its context. A decision to
escalate leads to important and sometimes difficult tactical issues,
such as the choice between gradualist escalation or a quick and decisive stroke.[2] The basic decision to escalate, however, is a strategic
issue, involving not only assessment of the immediate advantage to
one's own side, but also difficult and often painfully uncertain calculation of the possibilities for counterescalation by the enemy.

Many escalation decisions, too, have diplomatic and international political aspects that complicate the military questions.
Violating the limits within which a war is being fought carries the
danger that the escalation process will get out of control and mount
to levels of extreme violence. On the other hand, some escalations
turn out to be readily reversible. A decision to escalate may reflect
a change in policy-makers' objectives; or it may reflect merely a
fresh urgency or determination to achieve the same objectives. And

in the decision-making process a myriad of bureaucratic, institutional, political, and psychological factors can play important roles. "There are many ways," one analyst has written, "in which a limited war can become less limited and many reasons why, during a war, governments change the level of effort they devote to bargaining, fighting, and deterrence. Today, all this is tucked under the label 'escalation.' "[3]

The omnipresence of escalation as a fact or possibility in warfare, and its complexity, make it hard to study. An additional discouragement has been the fact that most of the analytical questions one might wish to investigate are heavily *context dependent*. For instance, decisions to escalate, or not to escalate, or to de-escalate, all of which the United States made during the Vietnam conflict, depended substantially upon U.S. policy-makers' immediate perceptions of the situations of the moment, and only very marginally upon generalizations, ideas, or theories of how escalation dynamics work. The analyst studying these decisions retrospectively and comparing them, say, with equivalent decisions made during the Korean War, must be struck by the extent to which the similarities and differences are *not* explained by different doctrines, theories, "rules," or ideas about escalation, but by the concrete similarities and differences in the surrounding contexts—military, international, and domestic—of the two wars. Planners for a hypothetical U. S. military action in Europe in defense of NATO would have to consider very different possibilities for escalation (including, perhaps, the use of atomic weapons) as a result of the very different circumstances and significance of a European war. Some other U. S. action—in the Mideast, say—would be very different again. Other escalation situations, perhaps not involving the United States, would present decision-makers in the various countries involved with still other factors to consider. In sum, the analyst of escalation cannot escape the fact that the consequences of any escalation decision, and the entire pattern of belligerents' actual or potential escalations in the midst of a war, are heavily dependent upon the specifics of the situations.

All these features have tended to discourage the systematic study of escalation. Its omnipresence in warfare makes it difficult to isolate for scrutiny. Its complexity subsumes many variables of many different kinds, including subjective and psychological factors that make it hard to examine rigorously. Its dependence on context, its habit of altering its appearance to fit each situation, make it hard to pin down. One result is that few studies of escalation exist—surprisingly few in light of the important dangers that escalation poses. There are other problems and topics in national security affairs that enjoy a sizable literature, sometimes a whole body of theory. Not so with escalation.

This is not to say that escalation goes unmentioned. It is mentioned often. But most of the time it remains an ancillary aspect of an analysis focused upon deterrence, crisis management, decision-making processes, or something else. In formal, scholarly terms one might say that escalation appears often in the literature as a parameter, an independent variable, or a mediator variable, but rarely as the dependent variable.[4]

Another result of the difficulty in studying escalation is that the studies that do exist tend to concentrate on some aspect of the subject other than the central problem of how the escalation process in war works. Existing studies are of two general varieties. There are a few hypothetical models that try to explore conjecturally the levels, steps, or thresholds, as they are variously called, through which escalation can proceed. And there are a few empirical, concrete case studies of past instances of escalation.

Herman Kahn's book, *On Escalation: Metaphors and Scenarios,* is a well-known example of the first variety. It is certainly the premier conceptual "framework" study to date of the various thresholds through which escalation might proceed in a future war. Kahn constructs a now-famous escalation ladder of forty-four rungs, thirty of them involving some kind of nuclear warfare. He does not focus upon the process of escalation as such, nor does he explicitly define and examine what escalation is. Rather, most of the study is devoted to detailed discussions of these rungs (for example, the constrained force-reduction salvo rung, the slow-motion countercity war rung, and so forth).[5]

A variation on this approach is the study of escalation possibilities in a *specific* hypothetical conflict. A substantial number of such "scenarios" and contingency analyses are classified; the open literature includes some, but not many. In the United States the majority, both classified and open, concern U. S. and NATO planning for a hypothetical East-West conflict in Central Europe. Of the literature of this sort, Bernard Brodie's *Escalation and the Nuclear Option* most emphasizes general conclusions of research interest. Yet

Brodie suggests observations about the nature of escalation dynamics and processes as such only in one three-page section. Most scenario-building is not research oriented at all and employs apparently commonsense notions of what escalation is—usually without explanation, and often only implicitly.[6]

Analysts of escalation processes enjoy a great advantage that analysts of the widely discussed problems of strategic nuclear warfare lack: mankind has had a great deal of actual experience of escalation but none, mercifully, of strategic nuclear war. Nevertheless, it is astonishing how few empirical studies of real escalation in past wars there are. Frederick M. (Fritz) Sallagar's *The Road to Total War* is an analysis in detail of the growth of the air war in Europe in the period 1939 to 1941. George Quester's *Deterrence Before Hiroshima* contains chapters on the same topic. Articles about how escalation occurred in one historical case or another have been written by Daniel Ellsberg and a handful of others. All of these "single-case" studies attempt primarily to explain, often in depth, the progression of events in a particular crisis or war. They rarely try to offer more than fragmentary observations of general significance about escalation itself. In formal terms we might identify these studies as configural or idiographic, and observe that they have not yet "cumulated" general research findings.[7]

Another empirical approach to escalation is the comparative assessment of some number of case histories. Ole R. Holsti's *Crisis Escalation War;* Lincoln P. Bloomfield and Amelia C. Leiss's *Controlling Small Wars;* and Richard E. Barringer's *War: Patterns of Conflict* are three studies that take this approach and reach conclusions about escalation. The most important of these concern, respectively, the role of stress and time pressure in reducing the rationality of decision-making, the importance of halting developing conflicts at an early stage by use of multilateral diplomacy, and a typology of four kinds of escalation situations.[8] None of these studies attempts a comprehensive approach to the general problem of escalation *processes* in war. (On the other hand, each of them is concerned with more than escalation.) They are not primarily configural or idiographic, and unlike most single-case studies they do achieve an inductive form of theory-building. But the theoretical results are in no sense synoptic, at least with respect to escalation. To the contrary, the results—although of greater general significance than those of conjectural exploration and of single-case

7

studies—are fragmentary from the viewpoint of the general problem of escalation processes.

Studies of escalation are few, then, and do not add up to a comprehensive and adequate understanding of the subject. In the roughly fifteen years since the term has come into general use, escalation processes simply have not received sustained empirical research. Even the range of meanings and implications of the concept itself have not been systematically explored, as the next chapter will show. There is a great deal we do not yet know about the intimately intertwined questions of how escalation dynamics work, and how they may be controlled.

It is the purpose of this book to pose *How do we control escalation?* as one of the central operational problems that face governmental decision-makers contemplating the reality or possibility of war—and to try to make a contribution, from one viewpoint and employing one approach, toward coping with this operational problem. The subject is sufficiently amorphous and sufficiently ill-understood that we should begin by clarifying what "the problem of escalation" is. Only then can we try to isolate the more important portions of this complex topic from the less important portions, and develop one way of studying what is significant. This is my goal in Part One of this book.

The Genealogy of an Idea: Escalation and Limited War

Contemporary images and attitudes about escalation are derived from diffuse and intuitive notions of how wars grow, from officials' direct and vicarious experiences of wars in the current era, and, in the English-speaking world especially, from a body of thought and literature about so-called limited warfare. This literature grew up in the wake of the Korean War and represented, in its early phase, an attempt by analysts and scholars to capture the implications of that conflict. [9]

The United States entered the Korean War with almost no experience of military conflict less violent than total war for total victory, and hardly any plans or doctrine about how to fight any other kind of war. The nation came out of that conflict with many officials and analysts convinced that Korea was likely to be a pattern for the future. The fear of atomic war, they argued, would continue to keep the superpowers from using nuclear weapons in the small wars that would be bound to flare up from time to time, and might also encourage them to impose some other restraints upon their involvement in these wars. As a result, small wars would probably remain limited and might drag on for some time, as Korea had, beneath a fairly stable relationship of mutual nuclear deterrence. In the mid-1950s and for about a decade thereafter, a literature about this new, limited war flowered in the United States and, to a much lesser degree, in other Western nations.

As time passed, the range of meanings of *limited war* tended to expand, as did the range of plausible conflicts that could reasonably be called by that name. Comparatively small-scale wars, geographically remote from the superpowers and involving mainly their minor allies or neutral nations, came to be called *local wars*. By the mid-1960s, analysts interested in this kind of limited war were fixing their attention more and more on events in Southeast Asia. At the time of this writing, however, there has not yet emerged a stream of literature on the lessons of Vietnam comparable to the literature of the 1950s on the lessons of Korea. Many and contradictory conclusions about the U. S. experience in Vietnam can be drawn—and in different quarters are. They are not yet widely published and debated, however, perhaps because to do so would be to reawaken the agonizing, but presently sleeping, controversies of the war itself. Theorizing about local wars is presently quiescent.[10]

However, since the 1950s kinds of conflicts other than local wars have been discussed in the United States, and to a lesser degree elsewhere, under the heading of limited war. As the amount of damage that an all-out strategic war between the superpowers would inflict has become ever more extreme, the spectrum of conceivable wars has widened, wars "limited" when compared to that ultimate possibility. From this country's perspective, wars short of a strategic nuclear exchange with the USSR seem limited in another way too: it is hard to think of plausible ways such wars could reach into American home territory. However destructive, however close to home, however "strategic" in their consequences Mideast wars or hypothetical European wars might be for other nations (including U. S. allies), from the American point of view such wars seem at least somewhat limited.

The special American geographic perspective, and the United States' success in keeping two sizable wars in Asia limited, have not been the only factors that have encouraged Americans in particular to emphasize limited-war thinking. American officials and analysts, probably more than their counterparts among U. S. allies, have perceived potential challenges to national security throughout the globe and have concerned themselves with many kinds of contingencies in many corners of the planet. Even the Soviet Union has only recently begun to acquire capabilities for projecting military power to any portion of the globe. With a handful of exceptions, the USSR to date has been careful to avoid direct military involvements outside its border areas. The same is true of China.

In addition, the United States, more than its allies and more than the USSR or China, possesses sophisticated transportation and communication technologies. These have encouraged an American belief in the possibility of relatively flexible applications of force even at great distances. Finally the United States, more than its allies (or China) and until recently more than the USSR, has had at its disposal a great range of nuclear weapons. The diversity of their explosive power and of their means of delivery has seemingly filled the gap between large conventional wars and the all-out strategic exchange with many possibilities for using a relatively few atomic weapons in a so-called limited nuclear war.

By reason, then, of historical experience, of geography, of global perspective, and of transportation, communication, and nuclear technologies, Americans more than their friends and more than their enemies have found the possibilities for limited warfare to be numerous and plausible. This in turn has had its impact upon the American attitude about escalation.

The characteristic U. S. attitude seems to have two components that are related in a paradoxical way to each other. On the one hand, the whole idea of limited war implies that escalation in warfare need not be mindlessly automatic. If a war has been successfully limited, the pressures toward its escalation have been successfully halted and contained. The prevalent belief in limited war tends to carry with it, consciously or unconsciously, a parallel belief that *the threat of escalation can be controlled*, at least under many circumstances.

On the other hand, the habit of imagining, analyzing, and planning for many levels of limited warfare has generated a belief that under many circumstances one may deliberately shift up and down among the different possibilities. Particularly in the absence of much literature about escalation dynamics, the limits of this kind of strategy have been little explored. Rather, analysts have articulated widely their hope that by varying the scope or tempo of military operations, by varying the kinds of weapons used, by combining various "signals" to the opponent with one's tactics, the level of ongoing violence can be somewhat precisely differentiated and manipulated. The prevalent postulation of many levels and kinds of limited war tends to carry with it a belief that *escalation and de-escalation can often be deliberate, controlled strategies.*

Neither of these beliefs is necessarily wrong. Historical experience has shown that under some circumstances both can be quite valid. So far, however, only modest attention has been paid by officials or analysts to *what* circumstances favor or disfavor these possibilities. (A few basic ideas that have emerged will be taken up in a moment.) And it is almost certainly true that American officials, analysts, and scholars are more optimistic about the general validity of these beliefs, and extend them to a wider range of situations, than many of their counterparts abroad.

A couple of concrete examples of these attitudes at work might be useful. Let us glance briefly at the two issues that have received the greatest attention in the literature on limited war.

One major issue, around which there has been an ongoing policy debate in the West almost continuously since the 1950s, has been the question of when (if ever) to begin using nuclear weapons in a limited war. The problem is most often posed in the context of an East-West clash in Europe, because it is there that U. S. and allied conventional forces seem most likely to be inadequate. Generally believing over the last several decades that NATO conventional forces in Europe have been moderately inferior to their Warsaw Pact counterparts, Western planners have usually concluded that in the event of a major European conflict, NATO might find itself having to resort to the "first use" of nuclear weapons to avoid defeat.

Nonetheless, they have often disagreed about how and at what stage atomic arms might be employed. The Americans have tended to argue for a comparatively late use of nuclear weapons, against tactical targets on and near the battlefield, employing some form of "sophisticated," relatively fine-tuned "escalation strategy." Most Europeans, whose homelands unavoidably would be the battlefield, have tended to argue for a very early threat, followed if necessary by a comparatively early use, of nuclear weapons against strategic targets in East Europe and the Soviet Union. A number of European specialists tend to regard the whole idea of controllable, deliberate escalation as a dubious theoretical invention of the

Americans, conceived and propagated to justify policies the United States prefers for what, they suspect, are actually political and technological reasons. The Europeans also point out correctly that the Soviets do not seriously plan on a limited nuclear engagement in Europe and that their military doctrine has always denied the possibility of limiting one. If the Soviets do not try to keep such a war limited, it is asked, how could NATO do so?[11]

A second and more general issue in the literature about limited war, which can be seen as subsuming the nuclear question, concerns the number and flexibility of the military options the West should hold in readiness. During the 1950s this issue took the form of a debate on whether the United States could or should try to deter the outbreak of communist-inspired limited wars like Korea by threatening to retaliate with nuclear attacks on the Soviet and Chinese homelands. This seemed to be the intention of the Eisenhower administration's declared policy of Massive Retaliation, announced in 1954 and accompanied by a program aimed at greatly reducing U. S. capabilities for fighting conventional wars.[12] But the hazards of a policy of bluff—and the obviously even greater hazards if the policy was not a bluff—inspired a stream of critical literature from national security specialists. Arguing that as the Soviet nuclear arsenal grew, this kind of deterrence would be less and less credible and hence less and less effective, the critics of Massive Retaliation put forward an alternative approach called Flexible Response, which was subsequently adopted by the Kennedy administration and its successors down to the present.

Although not a unified, precise doctrine, Flexible Response in all versions prominently includes the idea that the United States and its major allies should maintain multiple options for responding to the outbreak of different kinds of conflicts, with forces and strategies appropriate to each kind. If a low-level or medium-level war breaks out, the West should not have to resort to a tremendous nuclear escalation in order to avoid losing it. Before such a war breaks out, the West should not have to resort to threatening such an escalation, a threat so extreme that potential enemies might not believe it would ever be carried out. Such, encapsulated, is the attractive argument for Flexible Response.[13]

On the other hand, the Flexible Response policy, by creating forces and strategies for all levels of conflict, has made it easy for planners to imagine shifting up and down the various levels of violence. Flexible Response wisely rejected the policy of building into U. S. strategy and forces the *necessity* for *drastic* escalation, but substituted for this the creation of seemingly numerous *possibilities* for *controlled* escalation, in deliberate gradations through an extended range of violence. This implication of the national policy has influenced American beliefs about the nature of contemporary war itself. It has become a standard assumption that many possibilities for controlled manipulation of the level of violence *would actually exist* in most situations. Again, the number and kinds of situations in which this is not likely to be true have not been investigated, and the many preconditions that must be met before this kind of controlled manipulation is really possible have not been identified.

To sum up: A variety of historical, geographic, technological, and doctrinal factors have combined to encourage American officials and analysts to believe somewhat more than most of their foreign counterparts in the controllability of escalation. This faith takes the form both of believing that escalation processes in war can be restrained and halted and wars kept limited, and of believing that escalation can be deliberately managed to manipulate the ongoing level of violence. Although some American specialists are skeptical that either of these ideas would apply to nuclear warfare, many others extend them to warfare of this sort as well. Meanwhile, the preconditions and tasks that must be fulfilled before escalation can be controlled in either sense have not really been examined.

The Structure of Limited Warfare

During the time that these various factors have been shaping attitudes about escalation, academic and other theorists have been trying to conceptualize some more general questions that the limited warfare of the current era seemed to raise. To some extent they have addressed themselves to the basic issues of the nature of limited war, and of the limits that operate in such wars.

Some analysts recognized very early (although not until later was there widespread agreement) that atomic weapons are not "just another weapon," but are qualitatively different. Nuclear weapons, even those of relatively small explosive power, are generally considered to be more like chemical and biological warfare in their strangeness and horror than they are like chemical explosives. Because they are felt to be bizarre and special, politically they *are*, no matter how limited their strictly military effects might be in

13

some cases. Gradually it was recognized that the deliberate nonuse of nuclear weapons is the most obvious, most certain, and most important firebreak, as it came to be called, for keeping a war contained.

For analysts the concepts of a war arena and of geographic sanctuaries were clear from the Korean experience where these had provided, in a sense, another kind of firebreak. The Korean experience also suggested the value of firm civilian control at the highest level of the basic decisions that would determine whether a war remained within its intended limits. And theorists realized in a general way that the maintenance of limits in a war requires some cooperation from both sides.

Finally, it was not difficult to arrive at the distinction between the *objectives* of war and the *means* of war (weapons, categories of targets, troop levels). The *scope* (geographic or numbers of participating nations) was sometimes considered a third category and sometimes included under means. The ends-means differentiation proved troublesome in practice, however, because it was discovered that comparatively unlimited wars could be and had been fought, at least at first, for quite limited objectives. World War I was the obvious example.[14] In Korea too the belligerents had ended up committing great resources for what were, especially on the United Nations side, relatively minor objectives. Later, the United States war in Vietnam would be another example. There turned out to be no simple one-to-one correspondence between extent of purpose and extent of method.

Indeed, theorists came to realize that the ends-means relationship is dynamic, not static: objectives tend to shift with ongoing events. For instance, one may increase one's own effort either because the enemy's strength has grown or because it has weakened. Further, as the war ebbs and flows, previously unchallenged interests or values may become jeopardized, or previously undreamed-of goals may become achievable. Then too, as the costs one is paying become greater and greater, the prospective reward that one believes will justify the price tends to grow also. In short, whereas the expansion of means and the elevation of objectives are readily distinguishable concepts, the relationship between the actualities is ambiguous, complicated, and dynamic. It seems to lie near the heart of what after a few years came to be known as escalation.[15]

Analysts thus were able to identify some aspects of how wars might be kept limited. But for some years there was no general theoretical framework for these and related ideas. This framework, and with it the single most significant intellectual advance in our understanding of limited warfare, was contributed at the end of the 1950s in a series of articles by Thomas C. Schelling. Gathered into a book (*The Strategy of Conflict*) in 1960 and expanded in a subsequent book (*Arms and Influence*) in 1966, Schelling's ideas now dominate the literature on limited warfare and escalation and have undoubtedly been absorbed into government thinking also, in the United States and to some extent abroad. Because of their influence, as well as their intellectual merit, they require brief summation.

The fundament of Schelling's analysis is the distinction between those aspects of action that are oriented toward gaining direct goals in a conflict, and those aspects that are oriented toward "bargaining" with one's opponents over the nature of the conflict, including its "ground rules." Since explicit communication between the two sides is mostly or entirely absent, the bargaining is essentially by moves—by each party's actions. "Communication is by deed rather than by word." Hence the mutually recognized limits in any war "are generally found by a process of tacit maneuver."[16]

Schelling begins his analysis with the case where a war is beginning and each side, faced with a potentially chaotic situation, is searching for a set of limits that both can agree on. He points out that "the best choice for either depends on what he expects the other to do, knowing that the other is similarly guided." Schelling calls this "the problem of coordinating expectations," and he suggests that belligerents should, and usually do, pick out salient aspects of the objective situation to highlight by their actions. "Because the bargaining tends to be tacit, there is little room for fine print." Each side picks points of uniqueness in the situation, which because they are objective and noticeable, each can reasonably hope the opponent will also notice and appreciate. "The proposals have to be simple; they must form a recognizable pattern; they must rely on conspicuous landmarks; and they must take advantage of whatever distinctions are known to appeal to both sides."[17]

Geographic physiognomy is the most obvious kind of saliency. Holding one's actions within an area bounded by a range of mountains, a river, or a minor political boundary clearly signals a new limit that is being offered for both sides to observe. In Korea, for instance, the United Nations conspicuously halted all operations (including air operations) at the Yalu River; the communists did not attack U.N. forces or their supporting logistic systems outside the Korean peninsula and its immediate air and water environs.

A saliency does not have to be geographic, however. Whether the weapons employed are nuclear or not is a particularly obvious saliency. Traditional conventions of war, and other conventions of a legal, historical, cultural, or intellectual nature, can also be used. The critical conditions establishing saliencies are, first, that they be in some sense "objective," so that both sides know that each is aware of them or can easily be made aware of them; and second, that they be in some sense discrete or discontinuous—"qualitative and not matters of degree."[18]

Schelling then goes on to the case where one side seeks, for whatever reason, to escalate the war—but only by a certain amount, keeping the situation under control. He calls this the problem of "demarcating the limits of one's intentions." In principle, he suggests, the solution is the same: by escalating only up to another saliency, one communicates one's intention to keep the war controlled. For instance, if one side has been bombing up to a certain latitude, then escalates by bombing beyond this but very blatantly halts at the next obvious place to do so, a new limit or ground rule has been offered. The enemy, while he may take a discrete retaliatory step of his own, is not likely to breach all the limits of the war, out of fear that his opponent is doing so or is about to do so.[19] There is nothing inherent in this escalation process that causes all the limits of a war to disappear; rather, certain limits become discredited and irrelevant and new limits appear. Sometimes the new limits, although roomier, are stronger than the old ones.

Schelling's third step is to bring into his theory the possibility of what is sometimes called uncontrolled escalation. He notes that "the danger of all-out war is almost certainly increased by the occurrence of limited war; it is almost certainly increased by an enlargement of limited war." Each side knows this, and each side can use any such enlargement as a tool in the bargaining over the war. "Deliberately raising the risk of all-out war is thus a tactic that fits the context of limited war." Any specific escalation threatens to trigger a rapid chain reaction of uncontrolled escalation, but the exact degree of risk cannot be calculated. This is a "threat that leaves something to chance." By escalating, and thereby raising the danger of all-out war for both itself and the opponent, one side puts pressure on the other to de-escalate its activities, or perhaps to seek negotiations, or at a minimum to be chary of counterescalating in reply. Of course, both sides can play the same game, and thereby heighten at each step the risk for all. Schelling calls this a "competition in risk-taking."[20]

The applicability of Schelling's theory does not appear to be restricted to wars like Korea, or even to twentieth-century wars. It is a general theory, in which limited war means, in principle, *any* war in which the belligerents are fighting less than absolutely all out. (Herman Kahn applies the theory without strain to nuclear warfare in his book *On Escalation: Metaphors and Scenarios.*) Its applicability is, however, restricted in another way: Schelling's approach is focused much more upon limits in warfare than upon escalation processes. Exploring this idea for a moment may help clarify the current status of the escalation problem.

If limited war is meant in Schelling's sense—any war at a level less than all out—then we may say that the concept of limited war and the concept of escalation mutually imply, and intermesh with, each other. Escalation is the process by which the previous limits of a war are crossed and new ones established (or, in the end, the last limits crossed). Conversely, the (expanding) limits of a war are the barriers or thresholds or stages of the escalation process. From this point of view, limited war and escalation are coextensive: neither is "larger" as an idea, or encountered more frequently in reality, than the other. But *limited war* is the static term; *escalation* is the dynamic term.

It is easier to develop ideas and to theorize within a static framework than a dynamic one. This is one major reason why there is a considerable literature about limited war, comparatively little about escalation. Also, some form of static theory must normally precede, and provide the basis for, work on dynamic aspects of the problem. Schelling's is such a theory. He starts, in effect, with the pure static case: the problem of finding limits by coordinating expectations, which is achieved by means of saliencies. Then he successively relaxes a couple of aspects of the static quality. The task of "demarcating the limits of one's intentions" is the problem of finding *new* limits. Competition in risk-taking is a possible strategy, for one or both sides, in *accomplishing* the task of finding a superior set of new limits. First the problem is to get limits at all; then it is to change their particulars while keeping limits in general; then it is to use the risk of losing "limits in general" as a strategy in getting still other and more advantageous limits in particular.

17

Throughout, the essential focus is upon the limits, not upon the motives or forces that strain against the limits. Schelling presupposes such forces in assuming that belligerents may want to find new limits. But his question remains where the new limits will come from and how they may be established. He does not inquire into the dynamics of the war, or how these may affect the recognition or use of salient limits.

This is not a criticism of the Schelling theory, merely an explication of what it does and does not attempt to do. Schelling himself makes a somewhat similar point when he remarks that "if the analysis provides anything, then, it is not a judgment of the probability of successfully reaching tacit agreement but a better understanding of where to look for the terms of agreement."[21]

His theory, however, provides a great deal of useful intellectual material for clarifying the issues that have gotten "tucked under" escalation. So many and so ramifying are these issues that the very term *escalation* has come to have a number of meanings. In the next chapter we shall try to identify the more important of the various ways the word and idea of escalation are used. Doing so will allow us to narrow the focus of the inquiry to the most significant aspects of escalation and its control.

2

The Many Meanings of Escalation

The word *escalation* comes originally from the Latin word for *ladder* and is etymologically related to the English verb *to scale*. Evidently inspired by the moving stairway already called an escalator for some decades, *escalation* suggested at the time of its introduction at the end of the 1950s two specific attributes of the process it named. Unlike such possible terms as *intensification* and *expansion*, it carried the implication of step-by-step, qualitative growth rather than homogeneous, quantitative growth. And unlike such possible terms as *stairway* or *ladder*, it suggested a built-in, active thrust upward rather than a mere framework with no intrinsic bias.

In the literature of the 1950s on limited war, it had been usual to say that the conflict might *expand* or *spiral upward*, terms that do not seem clearly to suggest either of these two implications.[1] The exceeding rapidity with which the earlier terms fell into disuse after *escalation* was introduced may indicate that the implications of the new word were very widely felt to catch true and important aspects of the process. (I shall argue shortly that, indeed, so they do.)

However, so wholly did escalation capture the verbal terrain and drive out all competitors that its meaning has tended to enlarge and, in the process, become more vague. The word has become too popular, and it is now used promiscuously in almost any war context to describe any change in a situation involving "more" of any of its qualities or variables. The result is a kind of semantic inflation: the verbal currency has been cheapened. Today one or both of its original implications of an innate and step-by-step upward thrust seem sometimes to be intended and sometimes not, and rarely is either intention made explicit. There are other important dimensions of what escalation means that are generally left unarticulated, implicit, and ambiguous. The result is that there are different senses in which the term is used, some of which conflict with others. (The widespread recognition among analysts of this multiplicity of meanings has added to the perception of escalation as a slippery, amorphous problem and has further discouraged its study.)

These competing meanings are not just a verbal issue or a matter of semantics. Corresponding to them are conflicting *images of the real nature of escalation.* To give an elementary example, the expansion of a war along an almost homogeneous curve of growth, or by a sequence of readily distinguishable steps, are two images of the escalation process, each widely employed, that mutually contradict each other.

Differences like this matter. These images, separately and in various possible combinations, amount to primitive implicit models of the escalation process. Like models in general, each of these is based upon assumptions about its subject and context, and each suggests implications for policy as well as for theory. If we continue with the same example, the homogeneous curve and the discrete-steps models of escalation are clearly founded on different assumptions about the nature of escalation and of warfare, and they tend to suggest different implications for policies of escalation and escalation control.

This chapter will attempt to do two things. First, it will try to identify briefly the most important of these images of escalation and indicate, very succinctly, the reasons why each image exists and seems important. (Only widely used images, not technical inventions of theorists for special applications, will be discussed.) No a priori judgments will be made about how valid any particular image may be. The aim of the exercise is simply to clarify the subject of escalation by pointing out alternative meanings of the word —in other words, alternative images people have of what the escalation process is.

Second, this clarification will be used to narrow the focus of this book to something manageable. Just as *escalation* can mean many things, so too can *controlling escalation.* Not all can be taken up in one book, nor are all equally important in the world of the late twentieth century. Without trying to establish a single "correct" image or definition of escalation, we need to select and focus on the most significant aspects of the subject. At the end of the chapter, the aspects of escalation thus flagged will be pulled together into a single concept, to be employed as a working definition of escalation for the purposes of this book.[2]

Two Popular Images of Escalation

Let us begin with two simple images of escalation that are especially frequent in general discourse about escalation and war. I shall call them the *actor image* and the *phenomenal image* of escalation. The actor image presents escalation as being a unilateral *act* of specifiable individuals and institutions, an independent and conscious decision to commit a certain kind of action and the deliberate execution of that decision. The phenomenal image presents escalation as being a natural *phenomenon* of war, a process that seems to get started and keep going on its own, partly outside the control of any participant. In other words, wars "naturally" tend to expand.

Each image has a number of implications which, if followed consistently, add up to an *implicit model* of escalation. The phenomenal model includes the concepts that escalation tends to happen automatically in war; that it is almost a kind of force; that this tendency or force is constantly present; and that it may get out of control, and indeed is likely to do so. The actor model includes the ideas that escalation is a neutral possibility, which may be decided upon and may not; that it sometimes is decided upon and carried out, and otherwise is absent; and that control is a tangential or nonproblematical issue. The phenomenal model is a continuous model, focusing on a process that works over time. A sequence of events is the paradigm case. The actor model is a discontinuous model, focusing on a decision that is made (or not made) in a particular moment. A single situation at a given point in the war is the paradigm case.[3]

An implicit phenomenal model is commonplace in popular discussions of escalation, such as newspaper editorials and columns of opinion. Antiwar polemics nearly always rely heavily upon an implicit phenomenal model. An implicit actor model is frequently found in strategic analyses performed by military and national security specialists; it is also common in accounts written long after a war by diplomatic and military historians. During an ongoing war, polemics that urge an aggressive strategy and emphasize the prospects of victory almost always rely heavily upon an implicit actor model.

Wartime arguments over policy, in fact, often use a fairly extreme version of one or the other model, and sometimes castigate a deliberately extreme version of the opposing one. Even more sober literature concerning escalation sometimes tends very strongly in one direction or the other.[4] Unarticulated and implicit, these two simple models underlie much of the popular and professional discussion of escalation issues, particularly in wartime. Together they pervade the conventional wisdom.

Yet the difference between the two models, if each is followed through consistently, is fundamental. In the phenomenal model, escalation is something that *happens*, in which the participants are caught up. In the actor model, escalation is something that some government unilaterally *does*.

Indeed, these two basic images of escalation seem to exist because *escalate* is both a transitive and an intransitive verb. To say "we shall escalate the war" tends to imply the actor image; to say "the war will escalate" tends to imply the phenomenal image. Naturally, one must choose either the transitive or the intransitive form at any one time. However, a consistent or nearly consistent use of one form or the other throughout a whole discussion of escalation tends to raise up and favor the substantive implications of the corresponding image. In fact, one can have a strong advance clue about the conclusions of a speaker or writer simply by observing whether he makes fairly consistent use of one form or the other![5]

In most real situations, though, a consistent appeal to either the actor or phenomenal image will distort the discussion, by communicating too simple an idea of what escalation is. A simple or "pure" model of either variety is utterly unsatisfactory as a general model of escalation. Neither image by itself is adequate or true. Neither should we settle, somewhat vaguely, on thinking that the truth lies somewhere in the middle.

This book will take the viewpoint that *both* perspectives are true and valuable, as long as they are accepted *together*. Although the fully elaborated implications of each idea—taken separately as abstract, isolated theories—are mutually contradictory, the basic actor and phenomenal images supplement each other by describing two different aspects of the same problem. The intimate and dynamic interplay between the actor *aspect* and the phenomenal *aspect*, as they should properly be called, seems to be part of why the problem of escalation is such a difficult one. No one can reliably tell just when or how or to what degree an escalation "phenomenon"—a sequence of more and more violent actions—may get going, and it is obvious that no matter what occurs in a war someone, even if it is a preprogrammed computer, is giving orders and taking actions. Yet everyone who has thought much about nuclear war (or even some kinds of intense nonnuclear war) feels the danger of seemingly uncontrollable processes somehow taking over. The intimate tension between the actor aspect and the phenomenal aspect of escalation contributes to escalation's being a confusing problem, both intellectually and in the making of policy.[6]

Within this complicated interplay are other important images of escalation that have barely been touched on so far. Let us proceed to the assessment of these.

Images of Escalation: Is There an Upward Dynamic?

Some treatments of escalation, which emphasize the actor aspect almost exclusively, suggest that there are no greater forces that favor escalation than favor de-escalation. "No movement" is the natural state of a conflict. Escalation in this image is without causes. The *reasons* for making decisions to escalate will be as many and as various as the tactical situations in which escalation can appear useful.[7]

Nevertheless, the majority of contemporary discussions adopt the image of escalation that includes some degree of innate upward dynamic. This presupposition is not limited to discussions that heavily emphasize the phenomenal aspect of escalation, but is found in more balanced treatments as well.

There are several reasons why this assumption is popular and plausible. Of course, there are a great many reasons why an upward thrust might be found in particular wars. But there seem to be six general sources for an upward dynamic that are likely to be relevant to *all* wars and to be, in fact, part of the nature of war. They do not conflict with one another, but are mutually reinforcing.

The first and most obvious source of an upward dynamic is the desire to take a step that will contribute greatly to winning the war, perhaps even win it. As William Kaufmann has written, "Because of its competitive character war places a heavy premium upon the attainment of an advantage, however fleeting; and this in turn invites imitation. As the belligerents strive to gain a comparative advantage, the conflict undergoes an expansion."[8]

A second general source of escalation is the desire not to lose. This is not the same thing as the desire to win, but is almost equally basic. A nation trying to stave off complete defeat is likely to seize on any feasible way of escalating the war—perhaps to spin out the conflict in the hope that circumstances will change for the better, perhaps to attain some kind of stalemate, perhaps to convert a developing disaster into only a modest loss. If a way can be found to do it, a nation with declining hopes of winning may be very highly motivated to commit an escalation that promises some outcome other than a disastrous defeat.

A third source of an upward dynamic supplements the first two with an analogy drawn from poker: as the stakes rise, so does the desire to do more to win the whole pot (and so does the fear of losing the whole pot). There is a kind of escalation of the stakes— which is distinguishable from, but is one of the causes of, decisions to escalate operations. For example, after the death or maiming of millions of young men and after colossal economic costs, neither side in World War I was able to settle for the modest objectives with which it had begun. After Great Britain in World War II realized its extreme peril, it found itself escalating its means of warfare to include a punitive weapon, terror bombing of cities, which it had previously considered horrible and immoral.[9] As the stakes rise, the costs one is willing to pay and the risks one is willing to run also tend to rise. So do the objectives one wants to set as the appropriate reward for incurring these costs and risks.

Yet the mere fact that nations by this time are warring violently tends to threaten larger stakes than were in dispute at the outbreak of hostilities. Kaufmann observes that "the interests that become jeopardized once a war starts . . . are numerous and complex, and their protection and/or enhancement may seem worth very considerable sacrifices."[10] In sum, belligerents' *motivation* to win, and not to lose, is a *variable* that is almost sure to rise after actual war has broken out and begun to jeopardize additional interests. It may rise still higher as the war drags on, imposing ever-higher casualties and costs, and if the war escalates, threatening still greater values. Thus escalation can feed on itself: earlier escalations threaten wider and deeper interests, which heighten the motivation on both sides to win—and hence the motivation on both sides to escalate.

A fourth and related source of escalation concerns the personal motives and psychology of high-level decision-makers. In wartime it is normal for decision-makers to set aside other policy goals they may have entertained for their country and concentrate upon winning. Achieving victory becomes the perceived prerequisite for nearly all other policy objectives. (For example, President Lyndon Johnson in 1966 and 1967 believed that resuming his effort to create a Great Society demanded a victory in Vietnam first.) High-level decision-makers and their immediate staffs may also feel that victory, or at least the clear prospect of victory, is necessary if they are not to be thrown out in the next election—or, in nondemocratic countries, in a coup or revolt. Decision-makers in wartime also usually conclude that, whatever their other achievements or other goals, their place in history will be importantly determined by whether or not they won their war.

For these and other similar reasons, policy-making individuals and groups tend in wartime to identify their own personal position, success, and the like with the success of their nation in the war. This conscious and unconscious identification with victory creates a psychological and political climate at the upper levels of governments that is receptive to escalation options that seem to promise a quicker and more certain victory (or a less likely or less serious defeat). Organizational and bureaucratic incentives reinforce this, for in wartime it tends to be the military services (and other agencies whose mission is victory) that move to the center of the policy-making process.

A fifth source of an intrinsic upward bias concerns the tactical or purely military requirements of war. In most war situations there will seem to be military reasons for crossing whatever salient barriers may exist, particularly if one does not try hard to be imaginative about possible enemy countermoves. For instance, the enemy may be receiving very important support from sanctuaries just across the border in Cambodia or coming down the trails in Laos, which apparently can be interdicted and destroyed easily. Or enemy aircraft may be impudently flying from air bases just north of the Yalu River, which could easily be attacked. Or it would only take a period of unrestricted submarine warfare to greatly reduce the opponent's merchant marine and effectively blockade his island homeland. Or it would mean much lower casualties among one's own men if one could just flush enemy troops out of their caves with poison gas.[11]

The desired military action need not seem decisive, although it may. This motive for escalation is not the same as the hope of winning. Rather the action may simply seem (like wiping out the Cambodian sanctuaries) important if not critical, very tempting, and frustrating to forgo.

25

There is another aspect of the tactical situation that may be seen as a corollary to this. It moves fast. In the heat of battle there may be compelling and urgent reason to take some step to avoid a serious tactical loss. Or a tactical opportunity may present itself which, if not quickly seized, will probably disappear. There may not seem to be time to clear the move with all the relevant departments and policy-makers—who anyway might maddeningly refuse permission to act. Yet in fact, a novel "defensive" maneuver, a hot pursuit, or some other quick action may appear to the opponent as a real escalation of the war—a saliency crossed, a new pattern established.

These are five rationales that seem to offer a persuasive basis for a study like this one to adopt the image of escalation as an innate tendency, a built-in upward dynamic. Adopting this image also preserves one of the original, and evidently appealing, implications of the word *escalation:* an escalator, unlike a ladder, carries its riders up. Furthermore, to acknowledge this tendency provides a more significant and realistic challenge to those who seek to control escalation than to disavow most of the problem by denying any inherent upward tendency. There is a sixth rationale, though, which comprises the most intriguing, and from one point of view the most fundamental, source of escalation's upward dynamic. It is worth discussing in a little more depth.

Images of Escalation: Is There an Action-Reaction Effect?

Many discussions impute to warfare a kind of "action-reaction effect," in which an escalation by one belligerent triggers a counterescalation by the other as a reaction, which may then trigger another counterescalation by the first as its reaction, and so on. It is this reciprocal feature that gives escalation much of its complexity and that provides a compelling reason for postulating an upward dynamic. (It is reminiscent of the action-reaction effect that many specialists have thought to be one of the causes of arms races.)

Certainly escalation does not have to have a back-and-forth character. There are many historical instances of a single escalatory act by a belligerent, which went unanswered by the opponent. Indeed, there are instances of repeated escalations by the same power, all of which failed to call forth a significant response, often because of simple incapability on the part of the opponent. The Spanish-American War was like this. Once it became clear, as it very quickly did, that Spain's frantic diplomatic efforts to find

European allies would come to nothing, the Americans could escalate the war as much as they pleased.[12]

But in most situations, particularly in the contemporary world, both sides in a war retain options for escalating the conflict. Or one side may be able to appeal to a powerful ally if it is in danger of losing too heavily (as Egypt, for instance, did in the 1973 Yom Kippur War).

There are two main images of action and response in escalation. One presents a two-step process of action and reaction—tit for tat. One belligerent escalates to achieve an advantage, whereupon the opponent counterescalates in reply.[13] Let us call this *reciprocal escalation*.

The reciprocal-escalation image tends to arise in two situations. One may be contemplating a specific step oneself, and wonder what specific response the opponent may make. "If I do x, what will he do?" Or one may be making a kind of prediction about one's own response to a possible escalation by the opponent. "If he does x, I shall do y in response." In both cases use of the reciprocal-escalation image will carry the implication, often unexamined, that the process will stop after two steps rather than continue. The essence of the image is a presumption of stability in the war, after the action and counteraction have been taken.[14]

The other main image emphasizes the improbability of stability; it posits that escalation can go on indefinitely. An original escalation triggers a reaction, which in turn leads to a counterreaction, and so on, with no clear, necessary, or definite end to the cycle. Let us call it *cyclical-sequence escalation*.

This extremely common image of escalation has several important features. It is associated at least loosely with the phenomenal model of escalation: a partially automatic process, having in some sense an existence of its own, is imputed to war. The cyclical-sequence image is continuous image, in which an indefinitely lengthy series of steps is the paradigm case.

Escalation in this image is *interactive* in nature. The consequences of the original escalation and its reply create a new situation, which has two important qualities. First, it is likely to encourage additional escalations. Second, the new situation is not entirely foreseeable in advance because the consequences of different players' moves have interacted. For these reasons players are likely to underestimate how much the situation, after a few escalations back and forth, is likely to encourage still further escalations.

The essence of this image of escalation is that the action-reaction phenomenon interactively creates situations which cannot be fully calculated before embarking on the process, and which typically will involve unexpected new pressures (or unexpectedly strong pressures) for further escalation.

Certainly decision-makers realize, to a greater or lesser degree, that these postescalation situations are really incalculable. Those who employ this image of escalation often presume, though, that their realization of this is not very clear, or that policy-makers underestimate how much pressure they will feel later to escalate again. In any case, decision-makers in this image usually *are* confronted after the second, fifth, or *n*th event with unexpected and undesired circumstances presenting strong incentives or pressures to escalate further.

Conceivably policy-makers may understand in advance that this outcome is very likely and embark upon the cyclical sequence anyway. This is Schelling's "competition in risk-taking." Either or both sides may deliberately raise the risk to both parties of a very much more violent war, which neither wants, in the hope that the opponent may get frightened first and come to terms, or at least scale down his objectives. "To share such an increase in risk with an enemy may provide him with an overpowering incentive to lay off." Of course, recognition (to whatever degree) of the risk does nothing to reduce it. The heart of this image of escalation is the interaction of events generating unpredictable situations that favor further escalation. The conscious recognition and strategic employment of this likelihood is a derivative issue.[15]

Another important feature of the cyclical-sequence image is its strong emphasis upon escalation's *potentially open-ended* character. This feature distinguishes it sharply from the reciprocal-escalation image. One could construct variations on the two-step theme wherein the expectation in a given case might be that escalation would go three, or four, or any small number of steps; these would be only variations on the theme, because they would still employ its essential premise—that after a specific number of events, a plateau of stability will be reached and the process will halt. The cyclical-sequence image differs sharply from this in its implication that the process may not halt, but continue indefinitely. To be sure, the cyclical-sequence image presents escalation only as *potentially* open-ended: unless the phenomenal aspect of escalation is being emphasized very heavily, there is no necessary implication that escalation must actually continue to the limit of the belligerents' capabilities. Uncertainty plays a large role in this image. The emphasis, however, is upon the probability of additional escalation.

The potentially open-ended cyclical sequence is a more important escalation image for a study of this kind than the alternatives of no reaction or simple reciprocal escalation. It is also the broader image, since the potentially open sequence can be interpreted as including no reaction or reciprocal escalation as two very limited possibilities—"sequences" of one or of two events. This book will focus upon the *potentially* open-ended cyclical sequence.

One way of illuminating why this is the more important image is to observe how uninteresting, analytically, are the rather rare cases where this potential is, in fact, not present. It occasionally happens that adversary powers are so completely disparate in their capabilities that the much stronger side perceives no significant cost or risks involved in escalating. By no means are all conflicts between strong and weak powers of this nature; weak powers often possess important nonmilitary advantages. Still, it can happen that a strong power finds itself free to increase its commitment with no danger of serious countermeasures by a weak opponent who is already fighting all out and who lacks nonmilitary advantages. We may speak in such cases of the strong power "just deciding to escalate." That side makes the obvious calculations, steps up its commitment, finishes the war promptly, and that is that. As noted earlier, the Spanish-American War is an example. Such cases tend to be analytically uninteresting precisely because an open-ended action-reaction potential is absent.[16]

This study will also focus upon the potentially open-ended cyclical sequence for another reason. As noted in the preface, there is not a great deal to be said in advance about the kind of war situation where policy-makers recognize that they can escalate, if they wish to, with little danger of setting off a chain reaction. In such cases, a decision to do so or not will turn upon the policy-makers' estimation of the costs and benefits of taking a specific action, and such estimates are almost totally derived from the particulars of the immediate situation at hand. These particulars differ from one case to another.

But cyclical escalation sequences at different times and places may bear some points of similarity to one another: in governmental decision-making processes, in the logic of the interactions back and forth among the warring nations, in the effects of earlier decisions on later ones, and so on. It is possible that there are identifiable dynamics at work in escalation *sequences*. This study aims to explore that possibility.[17]

Images of Escalation: Stepped versus Homogeneous

There are two final images of escalation to be discussed which are particularly important. Each is very common, and they are in direct conflict with each other. Highly significant in their analytic implications, they are a confusing ingredient in much debate. The issue is, Does escalation proceed gradually and homogeneously, or in steps? And if in steps, how big a step must one take to be really escalating?

Some analysts restrict the meaning of escalation to steps that are very large indeed. One is escalating only if one changes the character of the war in a very gross way. Thus, for instance, at the outset of his book *On Escalation*, Herman Kahn suggests that an escalation is a step big enough to win a war: "Either side could win by increasing its efforts in some way, provided that the other side did not negate the increase by increasing its own effort."[18] It might be argued that by sharply restricting the meaning of escalation in this way, one has succeeded in reducing the scope of the problem. Gross alterations in the character of the conflict are likely to be simpler, more comprehensible in their consequences, and of greater significance than lesser expansions.

Nevertheless, I believe that for all but special purposes, this is too narrow and undifferentiated an image of escalation. It seems likely to encourage the analyst to fasten upon the particular attributes of very large escalatory steps. It excludes a great many cases where lesser escalatory actions are taken that seem similar enough in their logic and in the general pattern of their consequences to be reasonably called escalation. And it excludes many instances where decision-makers on both sides themselves believe that escalation is occurring.

Toward the opposite pole is a frequently recurring image of escalation, often called gradualist or graduated escalation: escalation proceeding in a very large number of indefinitely small steps. In its logically extreme form, this image presents escalation as a homogeneous, undifferentiated process—a continuous curve with infinite gradations in the level of violence.[19]

Much of the basis for this rather popular image may be the suspicion that escalation is dangerous precisely because it comes as the cumulative effect of many small acts, rather than as the predictable consequence of a deliberate decision. Certainly this image tends to be found in polemic antiwar speeches and literature, and in its extreme form can easily be married to an extreme phenomenal model of escalation. Somewhat paradoxically, a homogeneous image of escalation probably also tends to be the image held by many professional military officers, who often seem to have little objection to describing almost any new battlefield operation or any introduction of new weapons as an escalation.

I believe that for most analytic purposes this is also too narrow an image, and one freighted with many difficulties. It retards analysis by falsely suggesting that there is little that can be observed, pinned down, and identified. It tends to overlook the many known historical instances where a single identifiable step or set of steps had definable consequences, clearly different from the consequences of any other new battlefield action. It contradicts the decision-makers' frequent perception that when escalating, they are making serious, meaningful decisions of high policy. And, if it includes the idea of inevitability, it is intrinsically pessimistic with respect to controlling escalation.

For clarity of exposition I have presented these images in their extreme or pure versions. Between the pole of infinite gradation and the pole of a very few giant steps lies a range of images where escalation is seen proceeding in a larger or smaller number of smaller- or larger-sized actions. In fact, history provides instances of wars expanding in steps of virtually all sizes. In a sense this is the source of the conceptual difficulty: instances of escalation can actually be found to exemplify every image. Real and consequential examples range from the single giant step (the German sweep through Belgium in either World War), and even the dramatic, war-winning step (the Hiroshima and Nagasaki bombs), through the entire range down to very small gradations (the early months of the U. S. air campaign against North Vietnam).[20] The first point to be made, therefore, is that a general inquiry cannot *begin* by defining escalation exclusively in terms of either pole or of any arbitrary point along the continuum.

However, neither dare we begin by adopting laissez-faire and letting escalation mean any or all of these images simultaneously or according to convenience. To do so would help perpetuate the verbal and theoretical confusion. The solution to this seeming

31

dilemma is to cease defining escalation in terms of the absolute magnitude of the action.

The Schelling theory of limited war provides a different kind of criterion, which can accomplish what the moot debate over magnitude cannot. This criterion concerns the nature of limits. We recall that for Schelling, by no means can anything at all be an effective limit to a limited war. Rather, limits are saliencies that are objective, hence noticeable by all parties in the situation, and that are in some fashion discrete or discontinuous. For Schelling, to escalate is to cross such a saliency.

A major advantage of this criterion is that it is entirely contextual. It dispenses with any attempt to find an a priori, noncontextual size for escalations. According to circumstances, a step may or may not need to be "big" to cross a salient limit. This corresponds to a commonsense appraisal of the matter.[21] Let us adopt this criterion. *Escalation* here will mean crossing the limits of any less-than-all-out war, *limits* being defined in Schelling's way. Escalation as the term is used in this book is not a homogeneous growth curve, nor a step of any foreordained magnitude, but *a step of any size that crosses a saliency.*

Because of the complications and confusions—intellectual and verbal as well as operational—that surround escalation, the rationale and implications of this criterion are not, I think, as obvious as they might seem at first blush. Let us therefore take a little care with them.

In the first place, escalation is *not*, in fact, invariably viewed as the crossing of the current limits of a limited war. It is perfectly possible to say that even very minor actions, which clearly cross no limits, are escalations. (Adding one squadron of helicopters to a war the size of the U. S. conflict in Vietnam in 1967 might be an example.) I reject this usage simply because I do not think it is helpful in coping with the difficult and troublesome problems, analytical and operational, that escalation poses.

Generally speaking, for instance, the main reason people find an act of escalation interesting or important is precisely because they feel that such an act has consequences and meaning for the overall pattern or nature of the ongoing war: its ground rules or limits. It seems interesting or important because it noticeably intensifies or widens the arena of the violence, and because, as discussed earlier, it may carry the possibility of sparking an open-ended action-reaction cycle. Thus in common usage escalation is a meaningful and significant concept insofar as it means a change in the limits or ground rules. To refer indiscriminately to any battlefield action as an escalation smudges that meaning and significance. (Some people may *want* to smudge it: prowar polemicists to suggest that a minor battlefield action shows that "our side" has a proper aggressiveness and will to win; antiwar polemicists to suggest that a minor battlefield action shows that "our side" is headstrong and oblivious to the danger of a far larger war.)

Pointing out that escalation is interesting because—and when—it means crossing limits would not be very helpful if almost anything could be a limit or ground rule. But there is an intuitive and commonsense notion prevalent, if a somewhat vague one, that not just anything is. Schelling's ideas, percolating through the governmental and research communities, probably have strengthened this impression and crystallized it around the concept of saliency. I want to adopt the saliency idea here for several reasons: because I am convinced that the commonsense notion is basically right; because of the influence of Schelling's ideas on contemporary literature on this subject, at least in the English-speaking world; and because the saliency criterion, as opposed to either a homogeneous image of escalation or an image of some arbitrary-size step, can provide us with a basis for a flexible yet careful working concept of escalation. (We shall formulate this in a moment.)

The saliency criterion has some other advantages. It corresponds closely to the distinction between strategic and tactical decisions, and to the perceptions and beliefs of high-level decision-makers in wartime. Such people usually are not concerned with minor shifts in tactics or operational deployments, nor with minor additions to or subtractions from the opposing forces or their own; these are matters for field or theater commanders. What high-level decision-makers normally concern themselves with are steps by their own or the opposing side that expand (or contract) the general pattern of perceived limits of the conflict.

Employing saliency-crossing as one's criterion of escalation can also accomplish some clarifications on the spot. Consider again the matter of infinite gradations. More is said about this later, but one point is worth making now. The image of escalation proceeding in a multitude of very small steps can easily be resurrected by pointing out that sometimes saliencies are crossed precisely by breaking up the step into many lesser actions. This can be done deliberately:

Kahn reminds us that "the distinct quality of a rung . . . can be blurred, particularly if a participant . . . wishes." Or, as Sallagar observed of one phase of World War II, it can happen accidentally: "The very slowness of the transition to indiscriminate air warfare eased its ultimate acceptance as official policy, for each escalatory step seemed so small as to require no explicit policy decisions."[22]

The possibility of blurring a saliency in these ways might be raised as an objection to the validity of saliencies, and might seem to be a basis for accepting an infinite-gradations image after all. But this would miss the point. The infinite-gradations image in itself contains nothing that can distinguish between interesting cases of blurring and many other cases of insignificant, imperceptible steps—like, say, the sequential addition of several more helicopter squadrons in Vietnam. It seems to be the fact that it is a *saliency* being blurred that makes the case interesting. Not just any blur is. Saliency, then, is still a criterion that distinguishes the important cases from the unimportant ones.

A Working Concept of Escalation

This chapter has tried to illuminate a number of conflicting images of escalation that are currently prevalent. Certain selections have also been made among them, in an attempt to find images that are the most significant for the problem of controlling escalation. Let us now draw the various threads together into a single coherent conception, which will then serve as a working definition of escalation for the remainder of this study.

The working concept, or model, to be employed has the following main features. It presents escalation as consisting in the crossing of saliencies, which are taken as defining the limits of a conflict. As a war escalates, it moves upward and outward through a pattern of saliencies that are provided situationally. What defines a saliency is that it is objective, and hence noticeable by all parties, and that it is in some way discrete or discontinuous.

The model assumes that war by its nature favors escalation. The analytically most distinctive reason for this is the potential, usually present in war, for an open-ended action-reaction sequence, where the consequences of the various steps interact to create situations that cannot be fully foreseen. Because of this potential for *cyclical-sequence escalation,* and for other important reasons that have been discussed, there is an inherent upward tendency in warfare. Escalation is not a mere possibility—something that may happen or may not, like a rainstorm over the battlefield. It is an ever-present "pressure" or temptation or likelihood, something that requires more deliberate thought and action to stop and reverse than to start. It is certainly not inevitable, however, nor do we assume that an automatic, uncontrollable process leading to all-out war can be triggered easily.

All this should now be encapsulated into a working concept, stated formally. For the purposes of this study, escalation is an action that crosses a saliency which defines the current limits of a war, and that occurs in a context where the actor cannot know the full consequences of his action, including particularly how his action and the opponent's potential reaction(s) may interact to generate a situation likely to induce new actions that will cross still more saliencies.[23] A war expansion that crosses a saliency where the actor does have reliable foreknowledge of the consequences technically may also be called escalation, but such cases are rare and analytically uninteresting.

3

Understanding Escalation Control

Up to this point the intellectual problem posed by escalation has been the focus of our attention. A working concept of escalation has been found that highlights those aspects of the subject that seem to be the most pressing and important from the standpoint of controlling escalation. From here study of a subject as complicated and rich as escalation control could proceed in many directions. We must choose one.

The choice made in this book has been guided by two principal elements. First, my goal is results that might be *operationally* useful to civilian and military officials during wartime. The research therefore should be primarily directed, not at the creation of an abstract theory about escalation control, but at the uncovering of concrete factors and issues that might prove relevant and applicable in practice. (Theory that might be useful for this purpose should not be ignored.) Second, I am struck by the small amount of *empirical* study of escalation to date, despite modern man's vast experience of it; I want to make a contribution toward filling a very large gap. Thus, research results should be derived from known or discoverable facts about the way escalation has actually worked in past wars, and how it has been controlled or failed to be controlled during those conflicts.

A great variety of methods and approaches for empirical research in politico-military matters has been created by political scientists and other specialists. This book takes an approach that I think is particularly appropriate to the search for operationally useful results, and also particularly appropriate to "exploratory research," as it could be called, on a topic as little-studied and conceptually undeveloped as escalation. The approach may be viewed as a variation on the case study method. Instead of analyzing one war in great depth, however, the researcher develops a number of case studies—because of limited time and resources, generally a small number—and then compares the pattern of events from one to another. He looks for similarities among the patterns, of course; but he also looks for significant differences.

A comparison of this kind would not work if there were not some way of standardizing the various case studies. They all must look at similar aspects of each war, and they all must come up with variables and relationships that are similar enough to permit realistic comparisons. (Because single case studies have often been undertaken by different specialists with different interests and goals, the results have been hard to compare and general conclusions hard to draw.[1]) The comparability of the case studies in this book is ensured by asking a limited number of specific research questions of each of the cases, and asking the same questions each time. By this device only certain aspects of each war are explored, and each of the case studies remains focused upon the particular problem at hand, defined in a particular way. *Focused comparison* is a technical term sometimes employed for this approach.[2] (For scholarly purposes, more must be said about this approach. Detailed attention to the rationale and assumptions of the methodology used in this book, and an elaboration of its theoretical context, are found in an appendix.)

Some Research Questions about Escalation

Six research questions have been posed about the wars considered in this book. To make the case studies more readable, I have not used a routine question-and-answer format. Instead, I shall introduce and briefly explain the research questions in this chapter, and leave it to the reader to observe the way in which they are woven into the design of the case studies.[3] Shortly I shall explain the rationale for selecting the particular cases studied.

The research questions are derived almost entirely by logical development of the working concept of escalation. A line of logic is preserved, therefore, from the initial analysis of prevalent images of escalation, through the selection of certain images and their combination into a working concept, and now by the disassembly of that concept into a form—the research questions—that can be applied directly to empirical case study material.

Each question is actually a package of several tightly related questions on essentially the same topic. (Not all the elements in each package will be relevant to every situation.) The package questions are oriented primarily toward the interactions *between* two or more states in a war situation. However, a parenthetical query is attached to each one about different groups or individuals *within* each state. In many of the situations to be analyzed, it is the dynamics between nations that require primary attention, and the governments involved may be taken as single entities, a reasonable approximation not doing too much violence to reality. Still, in some situations divergences among decision-makers, departments, or agencies may be central to an explanation of events. It is reasonable to suppose that bureaucratic politics, and the perverse outcomes that the standard operating procedures of large organizations sometimes lead to, may play an important role in escalation processes.[4] Therefore research questions are needed that can detect both the intergovernmental and intragovernmental aspects of events.

Since cases will be studied where there was "already" ongoing warfare within some set of salient limits, the first question to be asked concerns what those limits were and how they were perceived.

> (1) What were the *salient limits* of the conflict as perceived by decision-makers in each government? Were some limits more visible or apparently more certain than others? How in the perception of the decision-makers had the situation been defined? (Were there important differences in their perceptions, or limitations in the governmental processes through which these perceptions had developed—that is, were there what we shall call process limitations?)

Before asking what decision-makers thought would be the consequences of escalating, we need to know their expectations about the likely future course of the conflict in the absence of escalation.

> (2) What were the expectations and uncertainties of decision-makers in each government concerning the *future development* of the conflict, presuming the current set of limits was maintained? What was their estimate of their opponents' expectations in this regard? (Were there important differences or process limitations in their expectations or estimates?)

Naturally, policy-makers' war objectives must be specified.

(3) What were the *goals* of decision-makers in each government? What were their perceptions of other nations' objectives? (Were there important differences or process limitations in their goals or perceptions?)

A factor in some decisions will be policy-makers' estimates of the likelihood that the opponent may escalate, and what effect this might have.

(4) What expectations and uncertainties did decision-makers have concerning the probability of an *escalation by the opponent* and the likely consequences thereof? How did they evaluate these risks? (Were there important differences or process limitations in these expectations or evaluations?)

Only in the context of the foregoing are we in a position to ask about policy-makers' decisions for or against escalation.

(5) What were policy-makers' expectations and uncertainties concerning the *consequences of escalation:* military consequences, the opponent's reactions, the new situation thus created and its potential to alter players' perceptions and objectives? (Were there important differences or process limitations in their expectations?)

Finally, in those instances where escalation did take place, a comparison of prior expectations and actual results is of interest.

(6) What were the *actual consequences* of escalation, and how did they differ from the expectations among decision-makers in all the governments?

The reader will have noted that this cycle of research questions must be applied anew at each step of an escalation sequence.

The Selection of Case Studies

These research questions are moderately wide in scope and fairly demanding in the amount and kinds of factual detail they seek to evoke in the case studies. In turn, these features have implications

39

for the selection of cases to be studied using this approach. Cases are required where a substantial amount of information is available about policy-makers' perceptions, expectations, goals, and calculations, and also about how top decision-makers went about making their decisions. In particular, cases are required where this information is available about all major parties to a war.

This last requirement is a major reason why I have chosen in this book to employ case studies dating from before the beginning of the Cold War era. They possess a perhaps deceptively obvious advantage: in general, specialists working in the Western world do have access to the records of both sides. This is not true of cases from the present era. Studies by Westerners of Cold War conflicts and crises, as well as more recent ones, are continually thwarted by the fact that we do not really know what either the calculations or the decision-making processes on "the other side" were. We can make some estimates—sometimes, doubtless, good ones. Nevertheless, the lack of knowledge imposes a serious limitation on analytical results.

The information advantage of pre-Cold War cases is especially germane to an empirical study of escalation, because escalation is so much an *interactive* process between sides in a conflict. Many other topics in national security affairs put less demand on the researcher for detailed information about other parties. Some topics, like the study of U. S. foreign-policy-making processes, put almost none. But where the interactions between one side and the other are as much the essence of the subject as they are in escalation, having a substantial amount of information about both sides of a war becomes vital to the investigator.

Despite the importance of this consideration, a legitimate question may be raised whether case study research findings dating from a time before nuclear weapons existed in quantity can be applied to an era when they are very numerous.[5] My belief is that the answer depends strongly upon what sort of empirical findings are sought, and upon how they are applied to the contemporary era. It would certainly be possible to perform a mechanical analysis of various pre-Cold War events and to derive results which, although perhaps historically valid and interesting, would be likely to have little operational applicability in the late twentieth century. A mechanical analysis is not the purpose here, however. And I have tried to reduce the danger of slipping into it accidentally by designing research questions that de-emphasize such factors as technology, kinds of military force employed (such as air cavalry or horse cavalry), and the like; and instead emphasize political and decision-making factors which, arguably, might be more similar across time. I have also tried to reduce this danger in another way: by unhesitatingly *selecting* aspects and elements of the pre-Cold War cases used in this book which, in my judgment, are most similar to many possible situations in the contemporary world. Other aspects and elements of the wars discussed, even if they seem to have something to do with escalation, will be excised whenever they appear to depend too heavily upon the particulars of pre-Cold War technology, old-fashioned diplomatic practice, or other elements that are now obsolete. A *discriminating* use of pre-Cold War cases, I argue, can definitely yield conclusions of contemporary relevance.

Now a word specifically about nuclear weapons. The possible objection that information from the preatomic era for the most part is irrelevant to the present breaks into two pieces. One is the assertion that a nuclear escalation process whereby both sides used atomic weapons in quantity (for example, in Europe) would be unlike anything the world has ever experienced. This is undoubtedly true. Nonetheless, a few useful things can be said even about nuclear escalation, drawing on pre-Cold War information, as Ole Holsti has shown with his analysis of the outbreak of World War I. If psychological stress, time pressure, and information overload can have as serious an effect on policy-makers' ability to make rational decisions as they did in 1914, over a period of nearly a month and with less at stake than there would be today, enormous doubt is cast on the plausibility of nuclear escalation as a deliberate strategy.[6]

The other piece is the assertion that in *all* recent military conflicts policy-makers have had in the back of their minds the possibility that sometime, somehow, the war might "go nuclear," and that this has made a difference in their decisions, even in low-level conventional conflicts. This is true, I think, yet I am uncertain how much difference it has made—and in what direction(s) the implications point. On the one hand, it can be argued that the nuclear possibility makes everyone more cautious; on the other, it can be argued that it makes the scope much greater for brinksmanship, for calculated efforts to make gains by appearing irrational ("playing chicken"), and for other ways of deliberately manipulating a shared risk as part of one's strategy. Which is it? In my opinion, probably some of both.

In any case, neither tremendous risk nor awareness of the possibility of using risk strategically is anything new. Thomas Schelling, who has carefully analyzed the strategic manipulation of shared risk, makes this clear and gives an illustration from classical Greece.[7] And the possibility that an originally small conflict can get out of control and end up wreaking tremendous devastation was certainly discovered by the leaders of Troy and Carthage, to give two examples much more remote than any in this book. I conclude that it is probably worth exploring some carefully selected cases dating from before the Cold War and seeing whether it seems to get us anywhere.[8]

How can we make an appropriate selection from the tremendous number and variety of escalation situations of modern times? Some ideas already set forth can provide help here. The decision to focus on the potentially open-ended cyclical sequence and the working concept of escalation developed earlier can yield a couple of fairly sharp criteria for choosing cases. We shall see that they also yield another important reason for employing pre-Cold War cases.

For a moment, consider four abstract possibilities—four hypothetical kinds of situations involving war and escalation. First, there might, in principle, be situations where a cyclical sequence of escalations goes out of control, and where a hypothetical observer concludes that it was almost inevitable that it do so: the chances of controlling it clearly are very poor. Second, there might be situations where it goes out of control, but the observer concludes that it was not at all inevitable that it do so: there are possibilities for controlling it that are never seized upon. Third, there might be situations where escalation stays under control, even though our hypothetical observer is surprised that efforts to control it are successful: the conflict seems very likely to escalate to a much larger war. Finally, there might be situations where escalation stays under control, but there is nothing surprising about it: the war never really seems to threaten to take off in an uncontrollable way. Most wars in history, incidentally, do not fall clearly into any one of these categories, but somewhere in between.

If ever there has been a real-world candidate for the first category, it is the ever-possible war in Europe between the NATO and Warsaw Pact countries in which nuclear weapons would probably be employed. While one cannot be sure in advance that escalation to all-out war would be inevitable (or almost inevitable) in such a conflict, it is certainly the case where this possibility is most likely. It is also a hypothetical case, which—fortunately—cannot be researched empirically, only imagined and thought about.

Let us jump for a moment to the fourth category. Cases of this sort exist in history and can be studied. They are wars where, for systemic and structural reasons imbedded deeply in the international situation of the day, an uncontrolled escalation sequence was very unlikely. Such cases are not very interesting to the researcher looking for *operational* aspects of escalation control, precisely because policy-makers in those situations did not have to grapple with the difficult aspects of controlling escalation.

From the operational viewpoint the most interesting cases are those that belong to the two middle categories—the situation where the hypothetical observer is "surprised." How does a war which looks as if it ought to be controllable nevertheless get out of control? Or how does a war which looks as if it ought to lead to some much larger conflict nevertheless stay under control? Cases of these two kinds, if we can find them, can lead to the most significant operational conclusions. Evidently these are the cases where background factors, inherent in the situation and outside the immediate control of policy-makers, have relatively the least impact on the final outcome. They are the cases where the factors that decision-makers can get their hands on, to exert real leverage on the situation, have relatively the greatest impact.

These, then, are our criteria for the selection of cases. We want to find cases in which the control of escalation has strikingly failed where it might well have succeeded, and cases in which it has strikingly succeeded where it would be very understandable for it to have failed.

Mankind is fortunate that the nuclear era has seen few wars that fit clearly in these categories. Perhaps only two: there is a general consensus that the Cuban missile crisis of 1962 (although it remained an acute diplomatic crisis, not a shooting war) seriously threatened to spiral into a nuclear war. And the U. S. war in Vietnam got out of control in the very meaningful sense that the United States ended up fighting a vastly larger and longer war than was originally intended. Probably no American policy-maker of the early and mid-1960s would have wanted to pursue the war policy, had he been able to foresee the ultimate length and size of the Vietnam conflict. But I have felt that these cases are unsuitable for detailed study in this book, although a few of their ramifications will be mentioned in the concluding chapters. The Cuban missile crisis is already the most amply studied crisis of modern times[9] (and also was not, technically, a case of escalation of an ongoing war). The research method used in this book cannot yet be applied to Vietnam: that conflict is still too close to be seen objectively, and there is a great deal about the decisions, strategies, and motives of policy-makers in Hanoi that is not yet known in the West.

Instead, I have located four wars from the earlier twentieth century and the second half of the nineteenth century which fit the two criteria unusually well. In addition, I have included one case from the mid-eighteenth century; although somewhat further removed from us in time, it also fits the criteria dramatically well and contains ingredients that are unusually relevant to the contemporary era.

It was widely feared that the Spanish Civil War (1936-1939) might lead to a second world war, particularly as Nazi Germany, fascist Italy, and the USSR became increasingly embroiled in the military events in Spain. Nevertheless, escalation was contained, and the Civil War did not lead to World War II. The two wars that jointly unified Germany—the Austro-Prussian War of 1866 and the Franco-Prussian War of 1870-1871—drastically upset the European balance of power. Despite widespread anxieties at the time about the possibility of a major war, and despite the fact that what was at stake was greater both times than at the outbreak of World War I, neither of the German conflicts triggered a general European war. The Crimean War (1854-1856) began as another minor war between Russia and Turkey, similar to a number of earlier ones. It escalated—contrary to the intentions of decision-makers among the great powers—into a vastly larger conflict involving almost all the major powers of Europe. The Seven Years War (1756-1763), generally known in the United States as the French and Indian War, began as a low-level battle between English and French colonists in North America. It escalated—again contrary to the intentions of decision-makers—into an all-out war between Britain and France, which promptly spread to the Continent and involved all the great powers of Europe.[10]

Three wars will be taken up, then, which strikingly did not escalate into much greater conflicts, where it was widely feared at the time and still seems very plausible in retrospect that they might have. And two conflicts will be discussed which strikingly did escalate into vastly greater wars despite the intention of most or all policy-makers that they not do so, and despite, in both cases, substantial efforts to control escalation.[11] Part Two of this book contains these case studies; conclusions are offered in Part Three.

One more word, for historians, political scientists, and other scholars, about this way of using history. I have tried to make the case studies fully comprehensible in themselves, with little prior knowledge required for the reader to derive a balanced perspective on the aspects of each war that are covered. Each study is intended to offer an explanation of why the conflict did or did not escalate, as the case may be. I have not hesitated, therefore, to give attention to background, contextual, and idiosyncratic features of each case, where it is necessary to do so to construct an adequate explanation. But the studies are intended primarily to generate analytic findings that may lead toward research conclusions about escalation control. Hence I have also not hesitated to interrupt the historical flow to strike strategic themes, and otherwise sculpt the history in any way that can serve the politico-military analysis. Strategic and analytic observations offered in the course of historical narrative are printed in italics to highlight them for the reader.

This investigation is in no way intended as primary research from the viewpoint of the professional historian. Indeed, I have taken advantage of the fact that all the wars studied are already documented in a huge historical literature. In some instances I have resorted to primary materials, but for the most part I have simply relied upon the secondary literature, incorporating alternative or competing explanations of events into the body of the politico-military analysis. (Formally, this study may be viewed as a test of the methodological hypothesis that the secondary literature of diplomatic and military history can be relevant and useful to the analysis of contemporary politico-military problems.)

Part Two
Case Studies in Escalation and Its Control

4

The Spanish Civil War

The first case to be taken up, and analytically perhaps the most straightforward one, is the Spanish Civil War. This conflict did not escalate into a much larger war even though at one time or another every major power in Europe had forces fighting in Spain, or stationed nearby as part of escalation control efforts.

Historical Overview

The Spanish Civil War began on 18 July 1936 with a military uprising against the constitutional republic.[1] The great majority of the military caste—supported by the church, landowners, traditional monarchists, most of the business community and bourgeoisie, and several fascist groups—believed that the leftist results of the democratic elections of 16 February, and the Popular Front government subsequently installed, represented an intolerable threat to traditional Spanish social order and values. The new cabinet comprised only moderate democrats, but was dependent upon the support of the Socialist and Communist parties in the Cortes (parliament); important Socialist leaders seemed likely to be included in the government later. During the spring the Popular Front government appeared unable to control a rapidly rising wave of open political violence perpetrated both by extreme rightist elements and by militant Communist and anarchist workers' groups. Spaniards who valued Catholicism, tradition, and order in varying proportions came to see the new government as comparable to Alexander Kerensky's in the Russia of 1917 and feared that it would soon be followed by an October Revolution that would impose extreme anticlerical, egalitarian, and proletarian measures. Indeed, radical left elements held exactly the same expectations, had supported the Popular Front in the elections partly to further these goals, and were openly boasting in the spring that the "revolution" was near.

49

The military preempted the leftist revolutionaries with a general uprising on 18 and 19 July from their garrisons and bases scattered around the country; they intended a rapid seizure of state control on the lines of the classic putsch model. Their action was only a partial success, however. Most of the small navy and air force, and most police and militia units, remained loyal to the government. By 20 July only some 40 percent of the country was effectively under the control of the Nationalists (as the traditionalist side, led by the army, came to be called). The government, rallying its militia and other forces, retained the capital, the industrial cities and districts, and more than half (though the poorer portion) of the countryside.

There followed over two and a half years of war between the Nationalists, led by a junta of generals (General Francisco Franco gradually assuming supreme power), and the Loyalist forces, supporting the government and led by shifting coalition cabinets increasingly dominated by the Communists. With very few exceptions these years witnessed the steady, although rather gradual, progress of the Nationalist cause and the diminution of the territory and resources controlled by the republic. An ill-considered counterattack along the Ebro River in the summer and fall of 1938 so exhausted Loyalist forces that they were unable to resist rapid Nationalist advances that winter. Barcelona fell in January, Madrid in March, and the republican regime fled into exile.

The Analytic Pattern of Escalation

Almost from the hour that Nationalist troops marched out from their bases, the Spanish belligerents fought each other with all the resources they could muster. From the viewpoint of the analyst of escalation, the significant and interesting questions concern not their actions, but the increasingly violent roles played in the Spanish arena by major outside nations. Foreign powers involved themselves in Spain from the beginning. When by the second day it had become clear that the revolt would not succeed immediately, the Nationalists wanted to transfer the Spanish foreign legion and the Moroccan troops—the only hardened and disciplined Spanish army forces available to either side—from North African bases to the Spanish mainland. The republic, however, was in control of the navy and hence the straits. Franco appealed to the Germans for assistance, and Hitler dispatched thirty transport aircraft. A similar appeal to Mussolini yielded Italian fighter aircraft to escort ships crossing the straits with equipment and more troops. The rapid arrival of the veterans, starting on 27 July, gave the Nationalist cause a critical advantage from the very outset.[2]

Almost simultaneously the republic, finding itself with many men willing to fight, but few arms, appealed for materiel to France, where Léon Blum's Popular Front government was an ideological cousin. Blum was eager to assist. Indeed, for nearly the whole course of the war a succession of French governments of the left were tempted to help the Loyalist cause and sometimes did so covertly in small ways. But Blum discovered at once that the British, then close allies, intended to be neutral in the Spanish conflict, wanted France to be neutral too, and were greatly concerned that the civil war might spread to a more general conflagration. Furthermore, major elements of French domestic opinion and some members of Blum's own coalition cabinet were worried that France might get drawn into the Spanish war. After some initial arms shipments, therefore, the French began approaching other capitals with the suggestion of a general nonintervention agreement, an idea the British instantly accepted and soon made their own. Early in August the French were informed that if they became embroiled in Spain and a war with Germany followed, Britain would consider itself absolved of the Anglo-French military alliance. Reluctantly, the Blum cabinet halted aid to the republic and closed the Pyrenees border to military commerce, even though the nonintervention agreement had not yet been effected.

These first weeks represented what analytically might be termed a *definitional phase*, one that determined the initial roles of outside powers in the war. No additional escalations were undertaken for some two months.

The British took advantage of this time to try to ensure that there would be no more significant escalation of the war at all. At London's instigation, the various states that had consented in principle to a nonintervention agreement formed at the end of the summer a Nonintervention Committee, intended to draft an agreement and see to its implementation. Besides Britain, France, and a number of the smaller European states, Germany and Italy promptly joined the committee. Policy-makers in Berlin and Rome thought it potentially dangerous diplomatically to be left out; they expected (accurately) that as members they could impede its operation and give pro forma cooperation while actually violating the agreement; and they feared that if they failed to subscribe to "nonintervention" France might go to the aid of the republic openly and massively.

The USSR also joined promptly. Stalin thought the committee might succeed in halting German and Italian help to the Spanish fascists and, hoping to achieve a diplomatic alliance with Britain and France, wished to be generally cooperative.[3] Through the autumn and winter the Nonintervention Committee deliberated— as slowly as its fascist representatives could manage—and did not come up with a "control plan" to put to the Spanish belligerents until early in 1937.

Meanwhile, the next phase in the escalation sequence had gotten under way: a *reciprocal escalation* initiated by the Soviet Union and answered by Germany and Italy.

In September Stalin began receiving reports that the republic was in growing danger. Its forces were retreating before the foreign legion, and an attack on Madrid loomed. Earlier he had limited Soviet assistance to nonmilitary goods, mainly food; now, in violation of his agreement to nonintervention, he began sending the republic modern Soviet aircraft, pilots, good tanks and tank crews, small arms and ammunition, and military advisers. (These last were important: the Loyalists lacked experienced military specialists, who were nearly all on the Nationalist side.)

Simultaneously the Communist International (Comintern), controlled by Moscow, began funneling quantitites of open-market and black-market military supplies to the republic and organizing the so-called International Brigades. A small number of individual foreigners had already begun volunteering to serve in Spain with the Loyalist forces, of whom the most famous was André Malraux with his squadron of flyers. The Comintern's propaganda, finances, and organization eventually sent some forty thousand volunteers from many countries, most of them with military experience, to fight with the Loyalist militia. The Brigades, and the Comintern and Russian materiel, were credited with saving Madrid (and probably the republic) from a November offensive.[4]

With Madrid firmly in Loyalist hands, the Nationalists' hope for an early end to the war was frustrated. Indeed, it now seemed that the republic had the edge. The Germans and Italians decided to answer the Soviet intervention. In great secrecy, Hitler sent Franco eight combat aircraft squadrons, eight tank companies, and related units comprising 6,500 men in all—called the Condor Legion. Mussolini, who had already established a base for Spanish operations on the island of Majorca, now secretly committed an infantry division of "volunteers."[5]

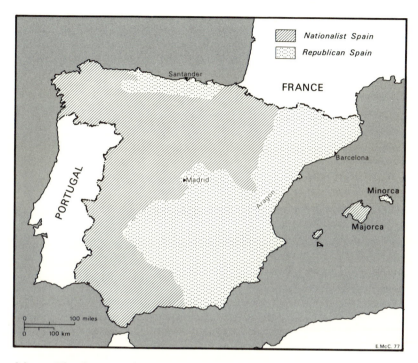

Map 1 The division of Spain in the spring of 1937.

While Mussolini's action was the largest, and from the point of view of escalation the riskiest, to date, the Italians took a number of steps to lower the risks. Their soldiers arrived in Spain wearing Spanish uniforms, carrying Spanish identification, and being paid partly in Spanish money. And the division was transported gradually to Spain, in a series of small, fractional units. Thus the first units to arrive could test whether any sharp reaction might be forthcoming from either the Western democracies or the USSR. Furthermore, the division was not committed to battle until months after it had begun to arrive.[6]

There was no sharp reaction. Policy-makers in both democracies and especially Britain wished to avoid an open diplomatic breach with Italy, and could not bring the matter before the Nonintervention Committee without legally admissible evidence, unobtainable until after Italian soldiers had been captured in battle by republican forces. The Soviet Union did not counterescalate for several reasons. Stalin wished to limit his commitment; indeed, he was never again as generous to the republic as he was that first autumn. Still hoping that the Nonintervention Committee could become an effective policy instrument, he did not wish to violate its precepts further himself, at least until it had had a full chance. Perhaps most important, he was wooing the Western democracies and did not want to offend them.[7] This phase in the Spanish escalation pattern therefore ended after one reciprocal escalation.

In March agreement was finally reached within the committee, and with the two Spanish governments, on a so-called control plan. Implementation began in May. The principal features were multinational observers on the Spanish frontiers and on merchant ships going to Spanish ports, and a multinational naval patrol of Spanish waters. But there was no provision for the inspection of arriving aircraft, or of merchant ships flying either Spanish flag, or of merchant ships flying the flag of any nation not party to the Nonintervention Agreement. Aid could continue to flow to Spain.[8] Meanwhile the presence at the Spanish front of organized Italian units had come to the attention of the Nonintervention Committee, but to achieve even minimal agreement the committee had been obliged tacitly to overlook all interventions prior to adoption of the control plan. The French, British, and Soviets hoped to remove the Italian and German forces by means of an additional agreement on the "withdrawal of foreign volunteers" from each side. But negotiations on this point among the powers, and between the committee and the Spanish belligerents, dragged on and on, and agreement on this issue never was reached.[9]

The control plan, too, soon broke down. Germany and Italy withdrew from the plan (but not from the committee) after alleged republican attacks on the German warships *Deutschland* and *Leipzig*. The *Deutschland*, officially part of the German contribution to the naval patrol, was in a Nationalist harbor when it was bombed by Loyalist aircraft. This was a legal attack, therefore, but the Germans retaliated with a naval bombardment of the republican seacoast town of Almeria. Shortly thereafter, the Germans claimed that the *Leipzig* had been attacked by a Loyalist submarine, although this was never proved.

Meanwhile the third major phase in the Spanish escalation sequence had begun. In November of 1936 the Spanish Nationalists began to choke off Soviet and other aid to the republic by declaring a blockade of the republic-controlled seacoast, enforced with air and sea units supplied in part by Italy. For the British and French, this precipitated another exigency; legally, their navies were obliged to protect their flag merchantmen from any attack, the Nationalists not having "belligerent" standing in international law. Britain, however, enacted legislation forbidding the use of British ships to carry arms to Spain, and the French government ordered its navy not to protect French merchant ships running the blockade. (The blockade issue was to recur on subsequent occasions, as British ships in particular continued to visit republican ports. Negotiations between Franco and the Conservative government in London always prevented that issue from reaching crisis proportions, however.[10])

Then, on 4 January, British and Italian diplomats signed an accord, generally known as the Gentlemen's Agreement, which recognized Rome's sovereignty over recently conquered Abyssinia and asserted that the status quo in the Mediterranean would be maintained. Prime Minister Stanley Baldwin, Foreign Secretary Anthony Eden, and the cabinet in London viewed this agreement as part of a general diplomatic strategy to keep Mussolini out of alliance with Hitler. In Rome it was understood as an implicit sanction of Italian activity in Spain.

A series of unilateral escalations by Italy through the winter, spring, and summer of 1937 included deployment to the Spanish front of four full infantry divisions. Table 1 gives additional details. We could term this phase one of *exploratory gradualist escalation.* As the table suggests, policy-makers in Rome waited to see the reaction to each step before taking another. Each time there was no response.[11]

Then the Italians tried something that challenged British and French interests directly. During the summer of 1937 the Nationalist blockade of the republican coast was extended. In all parts of the Mediterranean, merchant ships headed toward Spain began to be sunk by "unknown pirate" submarines. Although a pretense was attempted that the pirates were Spanish Nationalist, it was generally known that in fact they were Italian. Aircraft and surface vessels also carried out a few attacks. During August and early September, no fewer than eighteen merchant ships were hit; seven were sunk. After a submarine attack on the Royal Navy destroyer *Havock*, the British and French called an international conference of the riparian powers. The conference, held in Nyon, Switzerland,

Table 1 Unopposed escalations by the Italians and the Spanish Nationalists, and related events: winter, spring, and summer 1937.

Approximate date	Event
November 1936	Nationalist blockade of the republican coast begins.
December 1936	First Italian division arrives piecemeal in Spain.
Winter of 1936-1937	Britain and France tolerate the clearly dilatory tactics of fascist representatives on the Non-intervention Committee.
4 January 1937	Anglo-Italian Gentlemen's Agreement is signed.
January and February	Three more Italian divisions committed to Spain arrive rapidly—a total of more than sixty thousand men.
3-8 February	Battle of Malaga, in which for the first time Italian ground troops are committed in force.
8-18 March	Battle of Guadalajara, in which all four Italian divisions are committed. The republic wins and gains extensive evidence of Italian involvement.
Late March, April, May	Britain and France fail to take significant action on the above evidence, either in the Nonintervention Committee or outside. The League of Nations also fails to take action.
June	Rome lifts her secrecy on the presence of Italian forces in Spain and begins to boast of them openly. The British, as well as the French and Soviets, express concern.
June	Preliminary campaign by Italian submarines begins against only ships flying the flag of the Spanish republic. Western naval powers do not react.

July	Mussolini and Prime Minister Chamberlain exchange letters; Chamberlain stresses his desire for friendly relations with Italy.
August	Rome publishes an exchange of telegrams between Mussolini and Franco congratulating each other on the joint Nationalist/Italian capture of the city of Santander. Western democracies fear that Rome's boastful declarations may portend a lifting of all restrictions on Italian activities in Spain.[a]
August	Italian submarine campaign is extended to all ships of all flags in the Mediterranean that appear to be involved in supplying republican Spain.

[a] Between the beginning of the Nationalist blockade and 1 August 1937, forty-one merchant ships other than those flying Spanish republic or Soviet flags were stopped, searched, and in some cases seized by the Nationalists. In this period eighty-four Soviet ships were similarly treated, not all of them in transit to or from Spain. In addition, eight ships of miscellaneous flags were attacked by Nationalist aircraft.

early in September, resulted in a scheme for destroyer patrols of the Mediterranean that effectively halted the attacks, and with them the sequence of exploratory gradualist escalations by Italy. Except for a brief flurry of renewed submarine activity the following January, there were no further escalations of the civil war for many months.[12]

The next major phase in the Spanish escalation sequence witnessed significant new moves by both sides. The two sets of actions, however, were only indirectly related to each other. They were undertaken not to counter some move by the opponent, but to meet perceived strategic and tactical needs and opportunities. This was a phase of *nonreciprocal opportunistic escalation*.

On 12 March 1938 German troops marched into Vienna to complete the Austrian anschluss. Throughout the Austrian crisis, the Western democracies had never seriously threatened military action, nor did they after this unexpected climax. The leaders of the fascist powers concluded that they had overestimated the willingness of the British and French to run risks in defense of national interests that were less than utterly vital, and Rome quickly found a new option for escalating in Spain, one that did not directly threaten French and British use of the Mediterranean. On March 16th the Italian air force began the strategic bombing of Barcelona.

The bombing of cities and their civilian populations was not yet an accepted part of warfare, and the attacks on Barcelona brought a storm of popular indignation in the democracies, as had the earlier isolated incident of the bombing of the republican town of Guernica. The bombing was temporarily stopped. Still the governments in Paris and London took no official action; indeed, the British at this time were accelerating their policy of trying to keep Mussolini from making a firm alliance with Hitler. On April 16th the new Conservative Prime Minister, Neville Chamberlain, signed an Anglo-Italian Mediterranean Pact, which again guaranteed the status quo in the Mediterranean; and the Italians promised under this treaty to remove their forces from Spain—at the end of the war.

After the Mediterranean Pact was signed, decision-makers in Rome felt they could escalate further with impunity. Air attacks began on all merchant ships found in or near republican ports and waters (and in May the Italian air force resumed the bombardment of Barcelona, which was extended shortly to other Republican seacoast cities and towns). Between mid-April and mid-June some twenty-two British merchantmen were attacked and half of them sunk or badly damaged. Yet the government in London would not act, arguing that no counterescalation could be effective unless Britain was prepared to escalate to the point of war against Franco, which presumably would mean war against Italy and Germany as well. This was something Chamberlain was unwilling to contemplate. The criticism in Parliament and the popular outcry in England against this inaction became so intense that the Conservative government for a period was in danger of falling. Since a Labor government would have been a disaster for Italy, Mussolini called off the shipping attacks for six weeks, and the Conservatives retained power.[13]

From a strictly military viewpoint the various Italian air actions were rather ineffective, and it was not because of them that the Soviet Union and France renewed massive aid to the republic the same spring. Rather it was because the overall strategic position of the republic was now slipping rapidly. The Nationalists on March 9th had begun a major offensive in the Aragon region, which threatened to drive all the way to the Mediterranean and thereby split republican Spain in two. (In fact it did, a month later.) On March 13th Léon Blum returned to power in France and formed a new Popular Front government (the fourth in two years). Immediately the prime minister of the Spanish republic flew to Paris to beg for help. For about three months, under the governments of Blum and his successor, Edouard Daladier, the frontier was held open and quantities of military supplies flowed across, including 300 aircraft sent from the USSR. This aid was critical in staving off republican defeat for almost another year. In June the frontier was closed again under British pressure, and since the Nationalist blockade around what remained of republican Spain was quite effective by this time, little additional assistance got through for the remainder of the war.[14]

After the opportunistic escalations represented by the Italian air actions and the new Soviet and French aid, the limits of the war again stabilized for a period of some months. The diplomatic debacle of Munich came at the end of September. Afterward Hitler again scaled sharply downward his assessment of the willingness of the democracies to risk war; he concluded that nothing Germany might do in Spain would generate any violent Western response.

But the clouds of a general European war were lowering, and Hitler wanted Franco to wind up his campaign and be fully in control in Spain when the storm broke.

The final phase of escalation in Spain came with Hitler's decision to strike for victory there, with a *decisive escalation*. In exchange for some important mining rights in Spain for German firms, he sent Franco enormous new quantities of arms and ammunition and refurbished the Condor Legion. His expectation that this would suffice proved correct. Without this rejuvenating injection, the Nationalist armies would have been as exhausted by the summer's lengthy battle of the Ebro as were the Loyalist armies. With it, Franco launched the tide of a new offensive that flowed on nearly without interruption until the whole of the republic had sunk beneath it.[15]

Table 2 summarizes this analysis of the pattern of escalation in the Spanish Civil War.[16]

The Sources of Escalation Control

As this narrative suggests, the Spanish Civil War was rich in actual and potential escalations by intervening outside powers. Too rich, in fact, for all of its significant escalation aspects to be fully analyzed by the method employed in this study. The submarine campaign was the single most dramatic escalation of the war, and it may have been the one most threatening to the peace of Europe. Certainly it is the most interesting theoretically and the richest in analytical nuance. For these reasons it is scrutinized in detail in Appendix C.

The civil war as a whole, however, is meaningful to the contemporary analyst mainly because it did *not* escalate uncontrollably into a second global war. There were many fears at the time that it would. On a number of occasions during the two and a half years of warfare, an escalatory act by the fascist or communist powers, unilaterally or with their respective Spanish allies, seemingly threatened to trigger a new world war and sent a war scare through Europe. In retrospect, too, it is far from obvious how it happened that all these escalations, these fears, these thirty-two months of hard fighting on the European continent, never ignited a bigger war.

Unlike the other wars to be taken up later, the bulk of the explanation comprises a fairly small number of elements. Some ten

Table 2 The pattern of escalation in the Spanish Civil War.

Phase	Character of phase	Approximate date	Activity
First	Definitional	July–August 1936	Initial small but significant German and Italian assistance. Some French aid, followed by closing of the border.
		About two months of no new escalation	
Second	Reciprocal escalation	Autumn 1936	Large shipments of Soviet aid to the republic, followed by arrival of the Condor Legion from Germany and new equipment plus one infantry division from Italy to aid the Nationalists.
Third	Exploratory gradualist escalation	Winter, spring, and summer 1937	Sequence of escalations by Italy and the Nationalists (detailed in Table 1), culminating in the submarine campaign. Sequence halted when Britain and France effectively counter this campaign.
		More than six months of no new escalation	
Fourth	Nonreciprocal opportunistic escalation	Spring 1938	Italian air force bombardment of Spanish republican towns and of merchantmen in republican waters. Major new shipments of supplies to the republic from the USSR via France, to cope with deteriorating strategic situation.
		About four months of no new escalation	
Fifth	Escalation aimed at victory	Autumn 1938	In exchange for mining rights and with the conviction that counterescalation is highly unlikely, the Germans give the Nationalists sufficient aid to win the war rapidly.

factors, in combination, seem to explain why escalation remained under control.

(1) The most essential factor is that, with two exceptions, decision-makers in all the participating governments clearly recognized the grave danger that escalation in Spain could trigger a general European war, which they ardently wished to avoid. They all therefore avoided taking steps that seemed to seriously risk igniting a quick sequence of escalations that could lead to total war.

One of the two exceptions was Hitler's conclusion after Munich that this hazard was no longer real—that no great power would react to anything he was likely to do in Spain in a fashion that might lead to war. Subsequent German actions in Spain did not trigger any major escalation sequences because this estimate of the wider situation then existing was correct.

The other exception was a general belief within the Spanish republican government, from at least the spring of 1938 on, that only a general European war could save the republican cause. This conviction had been growing for some time, in tandem with the percentage of Spanish territory held by Franco. Some leaders in the shifting government coalition, for instance Indalecio Prieto, firmly held this belief much earlier. [17]

Republican policy-makers, however, never translated their growing conviction that total escalation was the only hope of victory into any positive policy that would attempt to generate escalation, despite the fact that they did have possible options for such a policy. A systematic and unprovoked attack on German merchant or naval vessels—or, less probably, on Italian vessels—might have done so. Significant air and/or naval attacks on military bases in Italy would have been a possible generator of wider war; an even more likely one would have been air raids on Italian cities in reprisal for the Italian air force's strategic bombing of republican cities. These tactics, while within Loyalist capabilities, were not attempted. Appeals for assistance, and for the right to purchase arms abroad, invariably had been based on the standing of the republic in international law as the legal government of Spain. Even toward the end of the war, such appeals and claims were not hopeless, as manifested by the major French aid in the spring of 1938. In any case, the claim of the Madrid government to legitimacy and moral superiority over its foe rested upon its status as the legal, responsible, and constitutional government of Spain, which acted within the framework of international law. Any overt effort to escalate the localized civil war into a general European war would have endangered the moral and legal foundations of the republic.

Partly for this reason, any such effort might also have proved counterproductive even from a strictly military viewpoint. A strategy of deliberate escalation depended for its success upon the affiliation of France and/or Britain with the republic in the event of wider war, but tactics such as those just mentioned might easily have caused the leaders of the democracies to break off all support to the republic, or at least to stand aside while it suffered reprisals. Had the Germans or the Italians been able to demonstrate systematic, deliberate Loyalist "aggression" against them, the republic might well have been left to face alone their major counterescalations. Thus republican policy-makers avoided taking the steps that might have triggered a rapid escalatory sequence—even though they hoped for exactly that.[18]

Still, a general intention of the participants to avoid taking steps that might start a small war escalating into a larger one is not any guarantee that it will not do so. Other important factors were at work in the Spanish Civil War to assist in the control of escalation.

(2) A set of sharp territorial limits to the war, visible to all, was supplied by Spain's peninsular geography. Save only for the Portuguese and French borders, the latter a mountain range, Spain is surrounded by water. Spanish Africa and all other Spanish possessions (with one minor exception) were held securely by the Nationalists from the first, so the conflict was confined to the peninsula.[19]

The French border was closed from the French side for most of the war. Even when open it was avoided by the Nationalists, who feared French intervention beyond all other possible intercessions from the outside world and scrupulously sought to prevent any incident that might trigger it. The Loyalists did not feel a similar compunction with respect to the Portuguese border, over which flowed supplies to the Nationalists that had been unloaded in secure Portuguese ports. Yet almost from the very beginning of the war there was a wide belt of Nationalist-held territory around the border that the Loyalists could not penetrate. Largely because of geographic and military circumstances, then, the arena of warfare was sharply delimited, and these clear saliencies helped to contain escalatory pressures throughout the war.

Of the various escalations that did occur, only the submarine campaign significantly violated these salient boundaries, a fact that did much to make it so dramatic—and so necessary to respond effectively to it.

(3) A vital factor in controlling escalation in Spain was the fact that decision-makers of two of the three principal intervening powers, Germany and the USSR, for most of the war held the *negative objective* of avoiding the defeat of their Spanish allies, rather than the positive objective of securing victory for them. They had no reason to escalate their involvement whenever their allies were not clearly losing.

In Berlin, the Nazi leaders expected an eventual Nationalist victory and saw no reason to accelerate it at any great cost to Germany. Furthermore, they wanted to obtain German rights to Spanish mineral wealth, which Franco was somewhat reluctant to grant. This interest was best served not by the Nationalists' winning a quick victory but by their discovering that they wanted German help badly enough to pay well for it. Also, a long war in which Germany and Italy were effectively allies would help cement the growing friendship between Berlin and Rome into a real axis—a treasured policy goal in Berlin. Finally, in 1936 and 1937 Hitler did not wish to provoke France or Britain unnecessarily, so he played along with their Nonintervention Committee and held his own interventions to a lower level than those of either Mussolini or Stalin. Late in the war he felt he could dismiss that consideration and began to desire a Nationalist victory, particularly when Franco finally was willing to grant the mining rights. But for the first two years he was content simply for the Nationalists to progress slowly with a modest level of German aid.[20]

The view from Moscow was somewhat complicated. As far as Spain itself was concerned, the Soviets were alert to the possibility of moving the Popular Front government toward a Moscow-aligned regime using Soviet and Comintern aid as a lever; and in fact the role of Moscow-line communist elements within the coalition government in Madrid did increase proportionately with the arrival of Russian material, pilots, and other specialists and advisers. Stalin also felt that he needed to take action to try to prevent the defeat of the republic as part of the struggle against Trotskyism, against which he was waging relentless war, both abroad and at home, in this period. And the Russians like the Germans saw Iberia in the late thirties as an opportunity to test their new planes and tanks, and tactics for them, in a real war—at Spanish expense. All Soviet and Comintern military assistance to the republic was well paid for in Spanish gold.

More significant than these considerations, however, was the relation of the Spanish problem to broader Soviet foreign-policy objectives. At this time the Kremlin, deeply concerned about the rise of powerful fascist states in both Europe and Asia, was vigorously seeking to draw Britain and France into some form of mutual collective-security arrangement with the USSR. A degree of Soviet involvement on the antifascist side in Spain would encourage this in several ways, including demonstration of the seriousness of Moscow's concern. However, the French and British at least for the time being were championing "nonintervention" in Spain; so Stalin early in the war sought not to offend them, by keeping his involvement reasonably limited. He also hoped at first that the Western nonintervention effort might actually prevent serious German and Italian intercession in Spain. Finally, the USSR was not prepared for a general European war and dared not risk triggering one by taking action in Spain that was too militant.

The sum of all these vectors was, for much of the war, a policy of Soviet involvement only to the extent needed to prevent a republican defeat. Yet aid to the republic from Russia gradually declined, and after the renewed burst in early 1938 fell off to almost nothing. In part this resulted from the increasingly effective Nationalist blockade which, when combined with a closed French border, choked off more and more of the flow of supplies. In part it also resulted from decisions in Moscow to disengage the Soviet Union from the Spanish problem. Stalin apparently resigned himself to the eventual defeat of the republic; and the none-too-plentiful Soviet materiel was needed at home. What could be spared was increasingly being sent to Chaing Kai-shek to aid in China's war against Japan, assessed in Moscow as more directly serving vital Soviet interests.[21]

Since any war that does not end in stalemate or negotiated compromise ends in the defeat of one side, the existence of negative objectives could not have been counted on to control escalation indefinitely. By the time it was clear that the Spanish republic was losing the war, however, policy-makers in the USSR were less motivated than earlier to try to prevent its defeat, and because of the blockade were less capable of doing so.

Early in the war the Italians' positive objective of victory for the Nationalists might possibly have interacted with the Soviets' negative objective to generate an escalation sequence—except that the Italians also wished to avoid uncontrolled escalation. True, Mussolini wanted dramatic victories that would cover his "legions" with glory and make the decisive contribution to the Nationalists' prompt victory. Nonetheless, he was obliged to increase his commitment in Spain slowly in the period prior to the Anglo-Italian Gentlemen's Agreement for fear of possible actions the British or French, or conceivably the Soviets, might take in response. Even thereafter his escalation sequence was gradual and exploratory. As it advanced, Soviet involvement was already shrinking. Furthermore, at no time were the Italian forces in Spain tremendously effective. At sea, the USSR lacked the naval capabilities in the Mediterranean to challenge the various Italian and Nationalist attacks on and seizures of Soviet shipping. The positive Italian and negative Soviet objectives did not intersect to generate escalation, then, for a combination of reasons of timing and of military weaknesses on both sides.[22]

(4) The existence of negative objectives in Berlin and Moscow may be seen as part of a larger theme. Escalation control in Spain was greatly assisted by the fact that there was a significant compatibility among the *range of objectives* pursued by policy-makers of all the great powers involved in the situation. In no capital, save perhaps in Rome toward the end, did decision-makers embrace a single goal as "the" objective, or identify their own national interest substantially with that of their respective Spanish comrades. Rather, they recognized and coped with the somewhat more difficult task of accepting a tension among several different and partially competing goals—goals that prominently included, as we have noted, controlling the danger of escalation. (Later in this book we shall find instances where this task was not recognized as a necessary one by policy-makers in similar situations.)

Thus while there was a powerful element of competition among the perceived national interests of the involved great powers, it was not permitted to dominate policy-makers' definitions of the situation. Let us glance now at the perceptions and calculations of the French and British, to whom this generalization applies especially.

French society in the late 1930s, like Spanish although not to as extreme a degree, was polarized along the left-right dimension. Each wing of French public opinion ardently supported its Spanish counterpart. A major French intervention in Spain would have perpetrated a severe domestic political crisis, and this was one factor that discouraged the succession of governments in Paris from interceding. Another was the report of the French general staff that any significant armed intervention in Spain would require general mobilization, which would have been an intensely unpopular decision. Additionally, the French people in this era deeply hoped to avoid the national agony of a second major Continental war in twenty years; this introduced into French foreign policy the profound motive of avoiding risk-taking, as the Austrian anschluss and the Munich crisis were to demonstrate. Yet another reason for caution was a running difference of opinion even within the succession of Popular Front cabinets, where for various reasons some ministers strongly favored and others distinctly opposed French intercession in Spain. The revolving-door governments of this period were unstable enough as it was without exacerbating their internal divisions unnecessarily by constantly reopening the Spanish question.[23]

Against these motives for eschewing any major intervention in Spain was set the wide range of options Paris possessed for minor diplomatic and political intercessions, for various forms of overt military aid to the Spanish republic short of committing the regular French forces, and for many kinds of covert activities. Also set against the arguments for caution was a deep ideological and emotional sympathy between the government of the Front Populaire in France and the Frente Populare in Spain. Furthermore, a friendly Spain would help protect—but a hostile one would threaten—the utterly vital communication link between France and French North Africa. For these reasons the French role in Spain would almost certainly have been significantly greater than in fact it was, had it not been for Great Britain.

The military alliance with Britain was the bedrock of security-conscious France's foreign policy in this period; and when on August 8th Sir George Clerk, the English ambassador in Paris, informed the French cabinet that if French involvement in Spain led her into a general war, Britain would abrogate the alliance, French policy at once became extremely cautious.[24] At the outset of the civil war the French had expected the republican government in

Madrid to put down the rebels promptly, and assisting it to do so was not so much calculated as felt to be axiomatic. The British message chilled these feelings by invoking a far deeper axiom.[25] Thereafter covert French assistance to republican Spain continued at a modest level, but overt policy aimed at helping her by negative means: trying to halt aid to her enemy through the Nonintervention committee, while overlooking Soviet intervention on her behalf.

This policy continued for over eighteen months until the threat of the Nationalists' Aragon offensive, on top of previous republican losses, reduced expectations in Paris that the republic could survive without some new level of outside help. The combination of this altered expectation and the installation of a new cabinet somewhat further to the left led to the March 1938 decision to reopen the frontier, and in various other ways to assist in a flow of major fresh supplies, mostly Soviet in origin. Throughout the war the Nationalist forces had clearly been avoiding incidents along the frontier, and this reassured the new Blum government that allowing supplies to cross (without permitting any French forces to enter Spain) would be unlikely to trigger an unwanted or dangerous incident. Yet even this modest action was opposed in London and in June Daladier, Blum's successor, bowed to the pressure and again closed the frontier.[26]

Popular opinion in Great Britain was very nearly as divided as in France on the Spanish question. The Labor Party, the intelligentsia, and about half of the newspapers supported the republic, while much of the business community—some of which had commercial interests in Nationalist Spain—and the other half of the newspapers supported Franco. The official policy of the Conservative government, under both Baldwin and his successor Chamberlain, was neutrality. However, as Franco's cause prospered this neutrality came gradually to have a pro-Nationalist tinge. In particular there were substantial British mining and industrial interests in the Basque area of Spain, which fell to the Nationalists in 1937. London's actions, as opposed to its declaratory policy, then took a somewhat pro-Franco tack. Furthermore, from early in the war, the expectation within the British government (unlike the French) was of an eventual Nationalist victory, and Britain's interest in the vital sea lanes through the Mediterranean and to the Cape argued against alienating the probable future government of Spain.[27]

Hence the policy of overlooking the huge Italian and substantial German violations of the Nonintervention Agreement was not quite so ingenuous as it might seem. To make an issue of them might only weld Franco more tightly to his friends. It might also cause the fascist great powers to denounce the agreement and resort to much greater intervention in Spain. The most vital purpose of the agreement and committee was not to prevent all intervention (an objective thought to be impossible) but to prevent the kind of gross and/or public intervention that would make a general war much more likely. Prime Minister Chamberlain told the House of Commons that "the policy of nonintervention was designed to prevent the conflict spreading beyond the borders of Spain, and . . . it has been a complete success."[28]

The policy objective embodied by the Nonintervention Agreement thus contained a dilemma for British and French policy-makers. They had to chart a path between tolerating greater and greater infringements on the agreement, which might at some point advertently or inadvertently ignite a wider war, and attempting to deter those infringements through explicit and implicit threats of counterescalation by the British and French themselves—which if executed also might ignite a wider war. By and large, they resolved this dilemma in favor of nonprovocative implicit threats and by tolerating the violations. The Western governments thus found themselves in the paradoxical and difficult position of trying to forestall total escalation by winking at moderate escalations—and thereby in fact subtly encouraging them, as prorepublicans bitterly pointed out. The anterior premise of this general policy was that Spanish Nationalist and overall fascist aims were limited, and if appropriately appeased, needed not conflict irreconcilably with Britain's or France's most vital interests. However wrong this premise may have been when applied to Nazi Germany, applied to Nationalist Spain it was correct: Franco did not join Hitler in World War II and never seriously harmed British or French interests.

De facto, the British also encouraged Italian escalation in Spain by their broad policy in these years of attempting to keep Mussolini out of the arms of Hitler, and if possible to woo him into closer relations with the West. The diplomatic universe was therefore not a perfect tripolar one of two fascist, one communist, and two democratic great powers, all three groups mutually hostile. Rather the most powerful democratic power was attempting a détente with

Italy, and this presented decision-makers in Rome with greater opportunities to escalate in Spain than they would have had in a pure tripolar context. An additional unbalancing factor in their favor was an Italian spy in the British Embassy, who for most of the duration of the Spanish war was forwarding to his masters copies of the British ambassador's secret cable traffic with London.[29] On the basis of this intelligence, Mussolini could be considerably more confident than he might otherwise have been of the strength of the British desire to court Italy and attract her into closer relations.

The result was somewhat ironic from an escalation control viewpoint: policy-makers of the one nation (Italy) that most highly valued a rapid victory in the Spanish Civil War found it much easier to escalate because they knew that the leaders of the one nation (Britain) most capable of controlling escalation were simultaneously pursuing a conflicting objective: trying to woo Italy to the West.

(5) Important to escalation control in the Spanish Civil War was the fact that decision-makers not just in Britain and France but in all the major powers were not only highly *aware* of the risk of inadvertent general war, but took positive policy *measures* to avoid it. Leaders of the USSR and Germany controlled risk by holding their interventions to a fairly low level, by maintaining secrecy, by employing (in the case of the USSR) the proxy of the Comintern, and by partially cooperating with the Nonintervention Committee. The Italians, who eventually ran the greatest risks, intervened at first only modestly and secretly. Their expectations concerning what they could get away with in Spain became steadily more sanguine as the British détente effort progressed. Even with confident expectations that Britain would not react violently to their escalations in Spain, they employed a "testing strategy," discussed in part earlier, by which major steps were taken only after the reaction to previous steps could be assessed.[30] The fact that policy-makers of each of the great powers interested in Spain could observe others calculating their measures to control escalation encouraged them to do so as well, and reduced pressure for preemption.

(6) The definitional phase of the escalation pattern seems to have been highly significant. The actions taken during this period suggest that policy-makers in the nations involved did not contemplate drastic escalations early in the conflict. On the contrary, during the period in which the initial limits were crystallizing, the low-lev-

el actions taken suggested that the initial limits would be likely to remain stable, at least for awhile, hence generated *expectations* that the conflict was likely to proceed within fairly stable limits.

These expectations meshed with the negative objectives of the Germans and Soviets, because the expected stability suggested that their proxies were unlikely to lose quickly. However, the image of stability established in the definitional phase may have acted in the contrary direction as encouragement to the Italians, with their positive objective of victory, to proceed a few months later with their sequence of unilateral escalations.

Expectations during the definitional phase were also significant in another, more subtle way. French and British policy-makers were initially optimistic about the probable effectiveness of their planned Nonintervention Agreement. Soviet officials were hopeful but doubting; the Germans and Italians were confident that the agreement could be evaded. During the early weeks of the conflict, these perceptions intersected with the diverse expectations in the various capitals about the likely outcome of the civil war. The French and Soviets, anticipating an *early Loyalist* victory, thought that little prompt action of their own would be necessary because nonintervention would prevent outsiders from aiding the Spanish Nationalists. The Germans and Italians, anticipating an *eventual Nationalist* victory, thought that little prompt action of their own would be necessary because nonintervention would not prevent them from involving themselves later when and as they wished to. In this odd and ironic way, opposing expectations about nonintervention and about the likely outcome of the war combined to discourage escalation by all parties early in the conflict.

(7) Until late in the war the principal policy-makers of all the powers intervening in Spain were uncertain at what points actions of their own might trigger a strong escalatory response by an opponent (points known technically as response thresholds). This uncertainty, which tended to inspire caution and thus discourage escalatory actions, in turn was a product of ambiguity in the declaratory policies of the various governments about response thresholds.

The historical record gives no indication that the French and British made specific deterrent threats to try to keep any of the intervening nations' activities from going beyond a certain level. They tried in various ways to stabilize, and if possible to lower, the level of violence in Spain; but they did not signal, either publicly or (it appears) privately, any specific hypothetical interventions that they would counter with force. It would be incorrect to presume that this ambiguity was a deliberate policy and ascribe it to a sophisticated appreciation of the analytic argument against such threats—that if you are too specific in saying "I'll react to such-and-such a level of escalation," you may implicitly be inviting the opponent to escalate up to a little below that level. Probably some decision-makers in Paris and London thought of this, but the ambiguity was mainly a product of broader foreign-policy attitudes and bureaucratic processes. The increasingly embraced doctrine of appeasement was hardly consistent with making deterrent threats. And it would have been very difficult for either cabinet to command an internal consensus, or the genuine concurrence of its bureaucracy, on a definite response threshold.

Stalin for his part could make no credible escalation-deterrent threat without the backing of the democracies. In fact policy-makers among all the totalitarian powers (except Italy later in the war) were somewhat handicapped in making such threats to one another, both by the secrecy they maintained about their involvement in Spain and by the policy objective of not provoking the French or British too gravely. In addition, some decision-makers among the totalitarian powers probably appreciated the analytic argument against such threats.[31]

The image of ambiguity presented by leaders of each of the powers concerning their response thresholds led to mutual uncertainty, and since all of them sought to avoid uncontrolled escalation to general war, the sense of caution undoubtedly increased all around. However, it must also be recognized that some of the Italian escalations in Spain might have been avoided by a vigorous deterrence strategy carried out by the British and French acting together. Such a strategy could only have been executed, though, as part of a foreign policy fundamentally different from the appeasement policy these countries were pursuing.

(8) In the absence of confidence about probable risk-acceptance and response thresholds, policy-makers of the great powers involved in Spain, except for those of the USSR, overestimated one another's willingness to run risks and underestimated one another's response thresholds. Officials of the fascist powers and the democ-

racies guessed their opponents to be more willing to run hazards and more ready to react to minor provocations than in fact they were, and these mutual misestimates intersected in a curious way. The Germans and Italians kept the Nonintervention Committee alive and did not wholly obstruct it, for the specific purpose of keeping France out of the Spanish war. Simultaneously, the French and British were overlooking the many violations of Nonintervention for the specific purpose of keeping Italy and Germany from leaving the committee, denouncing Nonintervention, and intervening in great force openly. Thus each side felt that it was the fiction of the committee, which *it* saw through, that was keeping the other side in hand—and for that reason wanted to sustain the fiction!

In short, both sides were deluded as to the real readiness of the other to run a grave risk of general war. Neither side incurred some risks it might have, had it known the other side's true degree of risk aversion. The interests of escalation control were thereby served.

The democracies also got the better of this odd bargain, since their real readiness to run risks was less than the fascists' real readiness to. The restraint that Hitler and especially Mussolini showed early in the war was substantially a product of their erroneous expectation that more significant escalations would draw a vigorous, perhaps military, response from the West. The Italian gradualist exploratory escalation sequence in early 1937 somewhat lowered the fascists' estimate of the Western willingness to run risks in Spain. And their final escalations in the closing phases of the war were a direct product of their lowering this estimate further on witnessing the meek Western reaction, first to the Austrian anschluss, and then to Munich.[32]

(9) A natural path for escalation to general war to take, from a geographically isolated arena in which outside powers are involved, is along the routes by which outside forces and assistance arrive in the arena. But between Spain and the involved European powers there were discontinuities or "firebreaks" of several kinds.[33]

Had the USSR possessed air or naval forces in the Mediterranean, it is not unlikely that these forces would have been used to protect the constant stream of Soviet merchant vessels en route to and from republican Spain. In that event, it is plausible that clashes might have occurred between such units and the Nationalist and Italian naval and air elements imposing the blockade. Significant Russo-Italian air/sea battles might have touched off a general war escalation sequence. In actuality, the USSR had no military forces in the Mediterranean, and the Soviet merchant vessels were totally at the mercy of Italian and Nationalist forces, which attacked the ships with impunity. The absence of commensurate Soviet forces generated a discontinuity on this possible escalation sequence path.

During the two brief periods of the war when supplies to the republic were flowing over the French border, the Nationalists and their allies deliberately introduced a firebreak by their own self-imposed prohibition on any border area attacks that might generate an incident. If the border had been open for a much longer time and the effect of the supplies coming across it had been much greater, this policy might have been reconsidered. To complete the blockade, the Nationalists might have begun to attack the supply routes in the vicinity of the French border, and an escalation sequence involving France might have been triggered. Something like this, of course, was precisely the concern of decision-makers in London; hence their pressure on the French to keep the border closed. The combination of the British pressure, the French acquiescence to it, and the Spanish Nationalists' restraint on the brief occasions when the border was open, created a major discontinuity along the possible escalation sequence paths leading out of the Spanish arena toward France.

France's connection with the war arena along her Spanish border had another implication: paradoxically, her contiguity to Spain may actually have inhibited her Spanish policy. Had France been geographically situated where, say, Germany is, the strong ideological comradeship felt by most members of her succession of governments for the Spanish republic might have led the French to a more militant policy—sending numbers of "volunteers," perhaps. (This much, after all, was done by the leaders of Nazi Germany, who felt less of an ideological bond with the Spanish Nationalists than most members of the French Popular Front did with the Spanish Loyalists.)[34] But any kind of force commitment from a contiguous country would have presented direct pathways by which a sequence of military actions and counteractions could have escalated to military events within France herself. German, Soviet, and Italian forces in Spain clearly were based in Spain, but French forces there could not be obviously and unambiguously based there. Even if they had been, it would have been difficult to establish the *appearance* of "no connection" between French forces in Spain and French forces in southern France. This posed an escalatory hazard that decision-makers in Paris could not tolerate, at least without firm assurance of the British alliance in all contingencies.

The substantial risk of escalation to general war would have been further increased if French forces in Spain had come into action against Italian or German forces there, and it is hard to see how they could have avoided doing so anytime after the first few months of the war. France borders on both Italy and Germany, and these additional contiguities would have presented many possible paths for dangerous escalations that perhaps would have cycled rapidly to general war. Thus France was necessarily somewhat deterred from military intervention in Spain after the Italian and German forces there reached substantial levels. The French therefore had fewer options for interceding later in the war, as it was becoming clear that the republic was losing, than they possessed at the outset before the fascists committed their forces. (Of course, earlier it was also expected in Paris, as in Madrid, that the republic would put down the revolt promptly.)[35]

The lines of connection between Nationalist Spain and Italy and Germany represented another set of possible pathways for escalation out of the arena; with minor exceptions these paths were avoided through a mixture of deterrence by Italy and Germany, self-deterrence by all the antifascists, and simple military incapability. The French and British were not about to attack these pathways, except when the Italian submarine campaign threatened their own use of the Mediterranean. On this occasion they found an option for counteraction that did not involve any attacks on Italian bases or naval units. The Soviets did not have the capability to attack the lines of connection between Spain and Italy or Germany, even in the unlikely event that Stalin would have been willing to run the risk. The Spanish republicans lacked the naval and air capabilities even to consider a counterblockade against the Nationalist coast (which would have had to include Portugal); the substantial escalatory potential of such an attempt therefore never became relevant.

In the absence of military options for these kinds of direct measures, republican policy-makers had to fall back on considering escalation threats and/or reprisal actions to attempt to cope with threats coming from outside Spain. As noted earlier, they in effect "deterred themselves" from this kind of strategy, out of concern for legal implications and out of a justified fear that the republic's friends among the great powers would not back the strategy, leaving them open to potentially grave counterreprisals. Mussolini's eagerness to indulge in the bombing of cities, and a notable German irritability and willingness to respond violently to any incursions on German privileges, indicated that fascist counterreprisals might be severe. The perfectly legal attack on the *Deutschland* called down a heavy German reprisal on the Loyalist seacoast town of Almería. And on the one occasion during the war when the Loyalists followed their opponents' common practice of capturing merchant vessels by seizing the German freighter *Palmas*, Berlin made it into an immense diplomatic imbroglio accompanied by German reprisal seizures of republican ships and threats of further German military action. All these events and other lesser indications helped deter the republicans from exercising what capabilities they had against the lines of connection to Italy and Germany. As the war continued, an increasing number of republican leaders began to hope for an uncontrolled escalation sequence that would lead to a major European war; but they were unwilling to try to initiate one. ("Turning the problem around" in this way suggests just how hard it can be under some circumstances to get escalation going "out of control.")

Despite the complexity of the Spanish Civil War and the deep involvement in it of outside powers, on only two occasions did an actual or potential belligerent take serious measures against some line of connection between the Spanish arena and an outside power that was capable of responding with major counterescalation. One of these was the Italian submarine campaign, considered in detail elsewhere; the other was the joint Nationalist-Italian blockade of the republic, which affected French shipping mildly and British shipping more seriously and which generated a series of diplomatic crises of varying gravity. Franco and Mussolini backed down when serious British action threatened, as when they abandoned a blockade of Bilbao in the spring of 1937, and when they called off the air strikes on merchantmen in the spring of 1938 to save the Conservative government.

(10) A final significant factor in explaining why the Spanish Civil War did not escalate into a general European conflict was the absence (with certain exceptions) of highly public and provocative

escalations—the kind that national leaders often find it hard not to reply to, even if the provocations are not especially significant in military terms. This was partly a result of the awareness of all parties of the possible risks and their efforts to calculate their moves from the viewpoint of escalation control. And it was partly fortuitous. The British especially were concerned that, whatever military steps were actually taken in Spain, the public *appearance* of escalation there not become too dramatic. Their strategy in the Nonintervention Committee and in much of their related diplomacy had its genesis in this perspective. There seems to have been an awareness in other capitals, too, that if Spanish escalations impacted too excitingly on the public consciousness, policy-makers might be driven toward decisions that would heighten the risk of general war.

Mussolini and his advisers, peculiarly secure as the objects of London's special diplomatic attentions, seem to have been alone in dismissing this consideration after most of a year had passed, although they paid close heed to it earlier. The dispatch of four infantry divisions, the subsequent lifting of secrecy about them, and several later Italian actions advertised the fact that Rome was simply no longer much concerned about public provocation. It was helpful, perhaps essential, for controlling escalation that no opposing power's decision-makers took the same attitude and entered into a provocative sequence of cyclical actions with Italy. And it was significant (perhaps slightly fortuitous) that no power opposed to Italy had committed substantial forces to Spain by that time.

The distinction between infantry and tank or air crews became important here. The infantry inherently involves numbers of combatants; a battle between an Italian division and a Soviet division, or even an Italian regiment and a Soviet regiment, would have been hard to hide and once known would almost certainly have aroused strong popular feeling in the two homelands. Infantry men are also less professional and could not be expected to operate long in secrecy. On the other hand, the Soviet and German tank and air crews operating in Spain were exotic professionals. They engaged their opposite numbers in a relatively detached spirit and were relatively discreet about it afterward. Furthermore, in tank and air warfare individuals do not see themselves as confronting individuals, but as confronting machines. All the machines in Spain were painted the colors of one of the Spanish belligerents; so the combatants could not always know that the opponents they were engaging were not Spaniards. The elite specialists sent to Spain by Germany and the USSR therefore did not represent a threat of public provocation in the way the Italian infantry did (although, ironically, they were much more destructive to their enemies than the infantry was).[36]

Other Italian actions were also provocative: the bombardment of republican cities and the air attacks on British merchantmen aroused outcries in England and elsewhere, although neither threatened vital interests of Great Britain. More provocative was Italy's launching of a general submarine war in the Mediterranean. That action, and the response the riparian powers fashioned at the Nyon Conference, had a number of unusual features that combined to reduce considerably the danger of a much larger war that they might otherwise have posed. These features are assessed in some detail in Appendix C.

Analytic Summary

The pattern of escalation in the Spanish Civil War is summarized in Table 2. Some ten factors seem to explain, in combination, why the conflict did not escalate uncontrollably into a second global war, despite widespread and recurring fears that it might:

(1) All major parties recognized this danger, which with minor exceptions they all strongly desired to avoid. They therefore eschewed taking steps that clearly risked igniting an uncontrollable escalation cycle.

(2) The conflict had well-defined, highly salient territorial limits.

(3) The primary objective for two of the three principal intervening powers was negative—that their proxy not be defeated.

(4) With one partial exception, policy-makers did not embrace a single objective, but recognized and coped with the more difficult task of accepting tensions among several partially competing goals, including that of cooperating with adversaries in controlling escalation.

(5) Policy-makers among all powers were not merely aware of the risk of uncontrolled escalation but took positive measures to

avoid it, calculating their policies with specific attention to escalation control.

(6) The definitional phase crystallized an initial set of limits and generated expectations that the limits might remain reasonably stable.

(7) Until late in the war, policy-makers among all the powers were highly uncertain about one another's risk-acceptance and response thresholds.

(8) In the context of this uncertainty, the democracies and the fascist powers mutually overestimated one another's probable risk acceptance and underestimated one another's probable response thresholds.

(9) There were discontinuities of various kinds along many of the natural lines of connection between the Spanish arena and the outside powers involved.

(10) With the exception of several Italian actions, the powers involved avoided highly public and provocative escalations.

The most dramatic and analytically interesting single escalation of the civil war, analyzed in Appendix C, was the Italian submarine campaign in the Mediterranean. For a number of reasons, most of them difficult to reproduce in other contexts, even this action did not pose serious danger of igniting a new world war.

5

The Wars of German Unification: The Austro-Prussian War

Seventy years before the Spanish Civil War, two major wars were fought in the heart of Europe; jointly they created the Second German Reich, whose kaiser was the King of Prussia. Only the second of these, the Franco-Prussian War of 1870, was launched with this end in view. But the first, the Austro-Prussian War of 1866, was essential in preparing the way for the later conflict and created some of the important prerequisites for Prussian decision-makers to consider the greater goal of 1870. For this reason, and because there are many close analytical similarities between them, we shall consider the two wars, in chronological order, in this chapter and the next. (An earlier conflict, the Schleswig-Holstein War of 1863-1864, had set the stage for the 1866 war, but because it was much smaller and posed less threat of major escalation, it will not be analyzed in this study.)

As in the Spanish Civil War, what is interesting and important about the two major Prussian conflicts, from the point of view of the student of escalation control, is the fact that both remained quite limited. Although the belligerents fought each other from the first with all the military resources at their command, neither war expanded into a wider European war.

Both policy-makers and observers feared at the time, however, that such an escalation might occur, and with good reason. The 1866 war represented by far the greatest shift in the balance of power that Europe had seen in half a century, since the close of the Napoleonic Wars; and the 1870 conflict produced a still greater change. In both conflicts the stakes were much higher than they were at the beginning of World War I. The potential implications of the Prussian wars were appreciated by policy-makers among the onlooking European powers even as events were unfolding. In both conflicts there were specific opportunities for one or more outside nations easily to have become militarily involved; in both, a chain of events could have resulted—as it did in 1914—in a general European war. Yet this never happened. Why?

A small part of the explanation may lie in the nature of international relations of that era. By the middle of the nineteenth century the balance-of-power system was reaching its zenith. Constrained by few important lasting hostilities, the European great powers— Britain, France, Austria, and Russia—and the middle powers— mainly Prussia, Italy, and the Ottoman Empire (Turkey)—mutually maneuvered among themselves, enjoying a maximum of flexibility in the pursuit of limited gains. (Prussia at this time had an ambiguous status: less than fully a great power, but more so than any other nation of the second rank.) It was also a system of cabinet diplomacy. In every nation, including democratic Britain, a small number of men controlled hierarchically organized foreign affairs establishments of limited size, communicated in secrecy with their opposite numbers abroad through ambassadors and diplomatic notes, made decisions from which (save in Britain, and not always there) there was effectively no appeal short of revolution, and presented their publics with faits accomplis which were justified after the fact if at all. The results, in principle, could come fairly close to the Weberian ideal of governmental rationality through hierarchical bureaucracy. In practice, the system often did approach nearer this hypothetical single national decision-maker than most public policy processes of more recent eras. Finally, although historians disagree about the importance of this feature, all the European cabinets shared *some* general sense of responsibility —the so-called Concert of Europe—to save civilization from another cataclysm like the Napoleonic period. Less debatably, they possessed important tools for doing so, including devices such as "compensation" to cope with individual grievances and thereby prevent them from accumulating, and the standard practice in times of crisis of calling a general congress of the foreign ministers of all powers.[1]

These background factors may provide a partial explanation, both of why there were so few wars in Europe in the period 1815 to 1914, and also of why those that were fought did not often include uncontrolled escalation. For example, in the Austro-Prussian War and in the early (but not late) phase of the Franco-Prussian War, no policy-makers among the European powers wanted a general war—and in the international relations of that day, their policy choices became reality somewhat more fully and readily than they might have if government policy-making had been more complex.

Still, such factors by themselves are not sufficient to account for the control of escalation in the two major Prussian wars. That decision-makers do not want escalation is certainly no guarantee that it will not occur. At various times during and immediately preceding these wars, both the informed European public and the highest decision-makers among the involved powers feared precisely that the conflicts might escalate into general European wars. The Crimean War, to be discussed later in this book, occurred in the same historical period, and *did* escalate, substantially out of control, into a vastly larger and more general war than anyone had either foreseen or desired. Furthermore the Crimean conflict, which shifted the European balance of power only marginally, involved smaller stakes than either of the Prussian wars, whose visible consequences and implications were not confined to the kind of limited gains and losses that the balance-of-power/Concert of Europe system was designed to handle.

The nonescalation of the Prussian wars remains, therefore, an interesting and significant question for the student of escalation control. This chapter will try to answer that question for the Austro-Prussian War; the next, for its successor four years later.

Historical Overview

The Austro-Prussian War, also called the Seven Weeks War, had as its underlying cause the historical competition between Prussia and Austria for dominant power in Germany, a competition that in varying form and intensity had been proceeding for at least 150 years. The proximate cause was the situation existing in northern Germany as a result of the Schleswig-Holstein War of 1863-1864. The outcome of that conflict had seen a victorious alliance of Austria and Prussia in joint control of the two duchies of Schleswig and Holstein, predominantly German in population but previously ruled by Denmark. The Prussians, geographically positioned not far from the duchies, wanted to annex them both. But the more distant Austrians preferred to hand the question of their disposition over to the German Confederation. This was a legally loose, and in practical terms extremely weak, union of all the German-speaking nations: the Austrian Empire, Prussia, several smaller states like Bavaria, and the mini states like Nassau. The confederation diet, which met in Frankfurt, had sanctioned in the name of all Germany the joint Austro-Prussian campaign against the Danes. From a sincere desire to maintain good relations with Prussia, the Austrians agreed to maintain "temporary" joint rulership over the duchies until a permanent solution could be found, rather than immediately submit the problem to the diet.[2]

Possessing not only irreconcilable ultimate aims, but also very different notions of what form the temporary occupation should take, Prussian and Austrian diplomats clashed repeatedly during the following two years. The details need not detain us: their essence was an effort by Otto von Bismarck, the principal minister in Berlin, to complicate and envenom all questions in the hope that the Austrians would become sufficiently wearied to surrender their half of the ownership and leave the duchies to Prussia. But Emperor Franz Joseph and his ministers in Vienna rejected this course as both disadvantageous and dishonorable. Tensions mounted. By the end of 1865 Bismarck knew he would not be able to gain Schleswig and Holstein peaceably.

Taking advantage of an already favorable European situation, he now manipulated the international constellation skillfully to generate an optimal military and diplomatic context for the outbreak of a war with Austria. Inevitably most of the small German states allied themselves with Vienna, but Berlin secured the alliance of Italy and the neutrality of all the other major powers. The crisis mounted as the Austrians, followed immediately by the Prussians and Italians, began mobilizing their armies and deploying them near the borders.

War might still have been averted, but the Austrians blundered by unilaterally turning the question of the duchies over to the confederation diet on 1 June 1866, an act which at that point violated a treaty with Prussia. In Berlin, King Wilhelm was enraged and unleashed the eager Prussian general staff, first against Schleswig-Holstein, then against the northern German states siding with Austria, then against Saxony, a buffer state between Prussia and Austria, whose forces retreated to join the Austrian armies.

Beyond the Alps the Italian army was thrown back by the defenders of Austria's southern front, but on June 22nd the advancing Prussians entered Austrian territory and proceeded to win almost

Map 2 Central Europe prior to the war of 1866.

every one of a succession of small battles. On July 3rd the Austrians committed nearly all their forces in the north, including the Saxon troops, at the battle of Königgrätz (also called Sadowa) and were decisively defeated in one of the most clear-cut field victories of modern times.

The broken remnants of the Austrian and Saxon armies retreated in the direction of Vienna to make a stand before the capital.[3] However, Bismarck was able to obtain a quick armistice by insisting that Prussian objectives remain limited. Over the vehement objections of the general staff, he succeeded in persuading King Wilhelm that Prussia dared not make demands that might induce the Austrians to fight on and that might encourage other powers to enter the war. The terms offered on July 25th in the peace preliminaries of Nikolsburg did not demand any Austrian territory for Prussia, and only one province was to go to Italy. Even Saxony escaped territorial loss. Instead, the Prussians took their gains from the lesser German states, absorbing several including Schleswig-Holstein, and combining with others in the north to form a North German Confederation completely dominated by Prussia. All formal Austrian influence was barred from the remaining South German states. Through an additional diplomatic maneuver Bismarck secured these southern states' agreement to secret annexes to the peace treaty, pledging them to defensive alliance with the North German Confederation—pacts he was to exploit fully against France in 1870.

The Escalation Dimension of the Conflict

Unlike the Spanish Civil War, the outbreak of the Austro-Prussian War was not unexpected. Officials throughout Europe recognized its likelihood several months in advance, and it was being planned in Berlin long before that. King Wilhelm was not pursuing aggressive ambitions for Prussia very actively in this period, but Bismarck definitely was. Although in wartime the king, as commander-in-chief, made all important decisions, in peacetime Bismarck personally wielded nearly absolute control over foreign policy.[4] The minister was pursuing, with a single-minded determination that Wilhelm did not fully comprehend, the goal of raising Prussia fully to the rank of a great power. He had decided to annex Schleswig-Holstein as his first step, and as his politico-diplomatic campaign against the Austrians failed to induce them to hand over their half-control, he imperturbably concluded that a war against them would be necessary. He proceeded to plan for one.

Von Moltke, the chief of the general staff, and Von Roon, the minister of war, were highly confident of victory as long as two prerequisites were met. Prussia would need some ally to draw off and engage part of the Austrian army. And of greater interest to us here, there could be no intervention by any other major European power. For Bismarck there was also another prerequisite. King Wilhelm deeply admired the ancient Austrian Empire and almost revered its ruling Hapsburg dynasty, the oldest in Europe. Against Austria he would never order a military action that he considered aggressive. Bismarck therefore needed to find or create a crisis in which Austria would take the aggressor's role, or seem to.[5] To attain all three of these preconditions simultaneously might have been extremely difficult, but Bismarck found himself aided by an unusually favorable international situation and also, as events progressed, by some unwitting help from Vienna.

Thus an important element in the nonescalation of the Austro-Prussian War into a wider conflict is that Bismarck was in fact acutely aware of precisely this danger, and did his best to see to it that the war did not begin except within a situational framework designed specifically to minimize that danger. He was entirely successful. When the war broke out, no other European power became involved immediately—and indeed major fighting proceeded for some weeks in Central Europe during the summer of 1866 without any outside nation even threatening involvement. Analytically we may say that escalation was initially controlled by Bismarck's *defining an initial war context* for that purpose.

However, the astonishingly lopsided outcome of the battle of Königgrätz completely upset expectations throughout Europe regarding the probable consequences of the war. The context that Bismarck had prepared dissolved, and immediately threats of interventions began to take shape. The minister's success, then, in terminating the war very promptly, before these dangers could materialize, was critical in forestalling escalation of the conflict.

An analysis of escalation control in the Austro-Prussian War thus divides into two distinct phases: the prewar phase in which the context was defined, and the period in July, following Königgrätz, when the conflict was quickly terminated. Each of these will receive detailed attention here. The intervening period of several weeks of minor fighting is less significant for our purposes, because the situational context in force at the oubreak was still in effect.

There was another piece to the escalation puzzle of the war that will not be taken up here. Before the outbreak Berlin had hoped that many, perhaps nearly all, of the small German states would remain neutral. Their formal accession to the Austrian cause in the early days of the war represented a policy success for Vienna and expanded the number of Prussia's enemies beyond what the general staff would have preferred (although they had hedged adequately against this contingency). This part of the war's escalation dimension proved inconsequential for the war outcome and for other more important parts of the escalation problem; its diplomatic intricacies are too peculiar to that historical era to have much analytic significance today.

Definition of the Initial War Context

Although tensions between Prussia and Austria had been gradually rising almost from the day their joint war against Denmark was concluded, in 1866 a sense of real crisis emerged in Berlin and Vienna only when Bismarck began seeking an alliance with Italy in February. Table 3 outlines the most important events as the crisis mounted thereafter,[6] including some details not mentioned in the foregoing narrative.

For Prussia this period represented a *controlled crisis:* throughout its duration and up to the very eve of war, Bismarck had options for resolving and ending it by the unilateral action of Prussia. To do so would have required him at least to postpone, and perhaps to abandon, the goal of annexing Schleswig-Holstein; in the later phases it might also have meant a diplomatic loss of face for Prussia and perhaps his own subsequent dismissal from office by the king. Yet at no time was there any serious danger that Prussia would be dragged into a war against Bismarck's will or under circumstances other than the desired ones.

However, the foreign minister did everything he could to avoid any resolution of the crisis—and indeed, everything he could to accelerate it—because he saw this crisis as likely to meet all three of his prerequisites for war. He correctly assessed the advisers to Emperor Franz Joseph as being at least temporarily caught up in internal governmental conflicts, and somewhat slow to recognize the developing pattern of events. As of early April he had achieved the Italian connection, although with a three-month time limit, which might or might not be renewable. These considerations argued for war sooner rather than later, as long as it could be isolated from the involvement of other powers. To this vital objective the Prussian foreign ministry had given much of its attention for many months, and gave more and more from early April on.

The policy of Great Britain in these years was to avoid Continental embroilments, and Berlin could reliably expect the British

Table 3 Major prewar events in the Central European crisis of 1866.

Approximate date	Event
28 February	Prussian Crown Council decides that Prussia should seek an alliance with Italy.
7 and 14 March	In Vienna, the emperor and his military council begin preliminary actions to strengthen Austrian forces on the northern front.
14 March	General Govone arrives in Berlin from Italy to begin treaty discussions.
29 March	Prussia responds to Austrian military preparations by taking similar action in the southern regions.
8 April	Berlin and Florence sign a treaty of military alliance, to be in force for three months.
Mid-April	Vienna begins to receive reports of Italian troop movements and other military preparations.
21 April	Discovering a mobilization only in the southwest to be impracticable, Emperor Franz Joseph and his advisers decide on full mobilization.
3 May	In response, Prussia begins mobilization of its army.
1 June	Austria brings Schleswig-Holstein question to the confederation diet, in violation of a treaty with Prussia.
7 June	King Wilhelm authorizes military occupation of Schleswig-Holstein and forcible ejection of small Austrian detachments there.

not to interfere in the developing situation and to declare neutrality, as they did, when war came. The Russians were another matter, as they necessarily were profoundly interested in the Central European balance of power. The czar, traditionally somewhat antipathetic toward Austria, was related to King Wilhelm by blood and was predisposed favorably toward Bismarck because of the latter's assistance in advantageous settlement of a Polish crisis in 1863. For these reasons Bismarck could hope for Russian neutrality in the war and noninterference in his preparatory maneuvers.[7]

As the crisis grew, Bismarck took measures to *reinforce the behavior* (to employ the psychologist's term) that he desired from St. Petersburg. For Russian benefit he manufactured a diversion: a rumor which went around European diplomatic circles that Vienna was covetously eyeing the Danubian Principalities, an area of eastern Europe, now in Rumania, which under Austrian control would seriously threaten Russian security. Several times he also sent a General Schweinitz, who sincerely believed that Prussian policy was to avoid war, on special missions to St. Petersburg as ambassador extraordinary, to plead the reasonableness and defensive intent of Berlin's activities. The Austrians in this period simply maintained normal diplomatic contacts and made no effort to create any comparable extraordinary communications channel. General Schweinitz also believed that Prussia would lose any war with Austria and presented this to the Russians as the general conviction of his government. Russian policy-makers did not actively use their diplomatic and intelligence instruments to check more carefully on expectations in Berlin, because they themselves shared this estimate.

Indeed it was greatly to Prussian benefit that the whole of Europe, other than parts of the Berlin government, believed that the much larger and more populous Austrian Empire was superior to Prussia in military power. On paper the Austrian army numbered three times the Prussian. Although it was generally realized that the force Vienna could actually field was smaller than this, only Prussian military intelligence had adequately appreciated the serious tactical, logistical, and other deficiencies in Austria's real preparedness for war. The general expectation in Europe, which officials in Berlin were careful *not* to refute, was that Austria was militarily superior even to a Prussia aided by Italy's modest forces.

In St. Petersburg decision-makers concluded, on the basis of this expectation as well as Bismarck's measures of reinforcement, that the Prussians could not be mainly responsible for the worsening crisis. They urged the Prussians and Austrians to try to resolve the dispute, but they did nothing that seriously interfered with Bismarck's nurturing of it. In particular the czar did not put personal as well as diplomatic pressure on Wilhelm, to which the king would have been quite vulnerable, to change Prussian policy. And the Austrians, failing to appreciate how motivated the czar actually was to prevent a Central European war, made no special effort to get him to exert this pressure.[8]

For the Prussians an even more advantageous feature of the international landscape than this *general misperception of the real military balance* was the fact that at this time the Italian-speaking city and province of Venice was part of the Austrian Empire. Except for the city of Rome, Venice was the principal territory not yet joined to emerging modern Italy, and Garibaldi and the other leaders of the *risorgimento* that was unifying the peninsula were extremely eager to obtain it. In turn, Napoleon III, Emperor of France, considered his nation and himself personally to be patrons of the Italian unification movement, which France had assisted (for a good price) in 1859 in a brief war against Austria.

While Bismarck did not create this favorable constellation, he realized that he might be able to *exploit the current international situation in designing his initial war context.* He had visited France in October 1865, and during a famous conference at Biarritz had delighted Napoleon with discussion of a possible Prusso-Austrian war. Napoleon, feeling that such a prospect would "open up to our [French] policy more than one advantage,"[9] foresaw opportunities to win Venice for Italy. He also expected that French ambitions for German territory on the Rhine would profit from a "fratricidal" and mutually debilitating war among the various German states, which he assumed would last some time. The emperor assured Bismarck that there was no formal or informal Franco-Austrian alliance or understanding, the possibility that had worried Bismarck the most. Napoleon made it emphatically clear that this would be impossible until Venice was Italy's, and Bismarck had already felt sure that Austria would not give up the rich province merely for an alliance. It was Biarritz that created the stage which Bismarck proceeded to set.

Late that winter he opened negotiations with Italy. With prodding from Napoleon (as Bismarck had anticipated), the Italians agreed secretly and somewhat reluctantly to a contingent offensive alliance. Italy was committed to go to war against Austria if Prussia did, but Prussia was committed to nothing—neither to join Italy in a war Italy started, nor to start one herself. These were extraordinary terms, but they were balanced by the three-month time limit on Italy's commitment, and the Italians were promised Venice in the event of a victorious joint war in the interim. With a hope of defeating Austria by forcing her into a two-front war, and foreseeing otherwise no opportunity in predictable international affairs to prevent the Austrians from holding Venice indefinitely, the highly nationalistic Italians signed. The agreement had two attributes important to Berlin: it gave Prussia *full control over the situation*, and it was achieved quickly.[10] Bismarck was anxious to set his stage before the Austrians fully awoke to their peril. (We shall take up decision-making in Vienna in a moment.)

To complete his definition of the initial war context Bismarck needed, besides some aggressive move by Austria that he could not produce himself, reasonable confidence that Vienna would be little aided either by the small German states or by French actions. He was not able to prevent most of the German states from eventually allying themselves with Austria, but he could and did do much that kept them from assisting the Austrian army effectively on the field of battle. Counting on their petty jealousies and parochial interests to keep them divided and in turmoil during the crisis, he exacerbated these conflicts as much as possible and exploited fully all the advantages that a single, highly organized decision-making unit has over a multitude of players with only partially common interests. The details need not concern us: with a threat to Hanover here, a promise to Bavaria there, a private message to Hesse-Darmstadt today which deliberately differed in small but important details from what he had told Württemberg's ambassador yesterday, he kept the cauldron of confusion bubbling as the crisis mounted. When war came, only adjacent Saxony was a truly useful ally to Austria. The tardily mobilized and unintegrated forces of the other states were swept up seriatim by a secondary Prussian corps.[11]

The temperamental, ambitious, and somewhat unpredictable Napoleon III posed the greatest potential hazard to Bismarck's attempt to isolate the coming Central European war. The French had many options for various kinds of bargains with the Austrians, and in fact some negotiations between them did take place. The most dangerous plausible French move, Bismarck knew, would be the mobilization of several army corps along the northeastern frontier, which would tie down equivalent Prussian forces and completely change the practical military balance with Austria. At Biarritz Bismarck had hoped to find out just what Napoleon's demands in Rhineland territory would be in return for a hands-off policy in the war. He had been somewhat disturbed when the emperor refused to name his price. But the Prussians gradually discovered that French intelligence had poorly estimated the relative strength of Prussia and Austria. Even after the Italian alliance had been joined, the French were expecting a long war of attrition that would favor Austria and did not discover or inquire into Prussian expectations to the contrary. Napoleon and his advisers believed that as the war dragged on, either or both sides might bid very high for a French alliance and intervention. He declined to name his price in advance, thinking he could probably get a better one later. Bismarck, making good policy use of a capable Prussian intelligence arm as well as extremely careful assessments by the Prussian military of its own strengths and weaknesses, was confident that Napoleon's expectations were wrong and happily let the matter slide.

Through the spring he *hedged* against Parisian policy taking a more Austrian turn by repeatedly inviting the French to discuss their Rhenish desires and by dangling various attractive possibilities, but without making any specific commitments. As the crisis approached its climax, he again *reinforced the behavior* he desired, this time by submitting to the diet of the German Confederation a "reform plan" built around Napoleon's much-touted principles of democracy and universal suffrage. As the minister expected, this very uncharacteristic proposal further confused the small German states, at the same time pleasing Napoleon and making it temporarily difficult for him to seem to oppose Berlin. The war came, naturally, before the plan could be considered seriously.[12]

What made possible the Prussian government's success in defining the intitial war context via these various actions? Certainly this success depended upon there being material at hand in the international situation (such as the Franco-Italian ambition for Venice) that could be exploited and manipulated. The Prussian success depended to some extent on Bismarck's personal diplomatic skill; but it also depended upon the superior information of the higher foreign ministry and military circles in Berlin about the diplomatic and military situation in Europe, and upon their making use of this information in ways that were both more analytic than their opponents' and more imaginative. Otherwise the material could hardly have been sculpted into the form required for the three demanding prerequisites of an advantageous war to be fulfilled simultaneously.

Successful definition of the initial war context crucially depended, in particular, upon accurate information and assessment by the Prussian general staff of the *military balance* in Europe; and upon Bismarck's superior evaluation of the *motives and expectations* of other major governments. On this basis the Prussians were able to devise and execute a strategy containing both political and military elements for fighting a war within a preplanned, and in a sense controlled, context.

Particularly important here was a sharp *asymmetry* between the Prussian decision-making system and that of the principal opponent, Austria, in the amount and quality of usable information at hand, and in the respective roles of "analysis" or "calculation" using that information. Historians have judged that Prussia's inherent position at the outset was not superior to Austria's.[13] It was an asymmetry between the crisp running analysis being performed in Berlin, and not one but a whole series of analytic failures in Vienna that was perhaps the decisive factor in establishing the initial war context the Prussians needed. Some of the most crucial of these Austrian failures should be mentioned.

In the first place it was not until February 1866, when Bismarck's plans were already well along, that policy-makers in Vienna began to consider seriously the possibility of war, and it was not until March that they realized that Bismarck was negotiating with the Italians.[14] Part of the reason they were so tardy in incorporating this contingency into their expectations was that to do so carried the penalty of trying to decide what action to take. The options were not exciting. The foreign ministry had long ago received an offer from Italy to buy Venice for cash—one billion lire, which Austria's strained treasury desperately needed—but the emperor had made it a fixed principle not to give up any of his traditional Hapsburg domains unless and until compelled to, by defeat in war. The option of finding a face-saving formula for letting Prussia have Schleswig-Holstein, with some nonterritorial compensation for Austria, also had been ruled out. As it became inescapably clear that Prussia not only *might* try to make an alliance with Italy but in actuality *was* trying to do so, attention turned slowly and reluctantly to another option, unpleasant and complicated but possibly feasible: to promise Venice to Italy and France, in exchange for neutrality from Italy and some modest assistance from France in a war with Prussia, from which the Austrians expected to gain German territory as compensation for losing Venice. They had in mind principally Silesia, a region formerly controlled by Austria and more recently by Prussia; its recovery had long been a valued objective in Vienna.

If some such scheme, which had a number of potential variations, had even been hinted in Florence and Paris, the situation might well have developed differently. Talks might have ensued during which Italy would not have allied with Prussia, and Bismarck's accelerating effort to define a favorable war context might have been derailed. However, the slow-moving Austrian governmental machinery did not investigate these possibilities during the few weeks that passed between their dawning realization of Bismarck's objectives and intentions, and the Italian commitment to Berlin.[15]

Certainly the policy dilemma of the Austrian decision-makers was, to a degree, a genuine one. As one historian puts it: "They could not gain Italy's neutrality without yielding Venice; they *would* not yield Venice without getting Silesia; they could not get Silesia without war; and they did not want war if it could possibly be avoided."[16] However, to close the circle completely, we must add that war could not be avoided without gaining Italy's neutrality! This was not adequately comprehended in Vienna, in the last analysis because Bismarck's overall goals, and the extent of his motivation to obtain them, had not been comprehended. The Austrians did not understand that Bismarck was determined to make Prussia a great power.

Overestimating Austria's diplomatic position and influence, hoping that something would turn up to rescue the situation, and overconfident of Austria's military capabilities if the worst contingency did materialize, the Viennese vacillated while Bismarck bargained. Serious diplomatic conversations about Venice were the one point in the circular fence imprisoning the Austrians' policy where their own initiative could have altered the situation. Yet in the crucial period before the Italians made their bargain with Berlin, Austrian diplomats had strict instructions not even to talk about Venice.

Ironically, by early June the Austrian policy-makers were willing, indeed eager, to sign a treaty with France promising to give up Venice for retransfer to the Italians *even in the event of Austrian victory over Prussia and Italy,* in exchange for nothing more than the French promise not to intervene against Austria in the war! Anytime before early April a far higher price could have been obtained for the same goods.

The Austrians made this agreement in June because in the preceding weeks Napoleon had threatened that if they did not, he would join the war on the Prusso-Italian side. Officials in Paris were still expecting a long war that would slowly favor Austria, realized that in such a war Italy would not be able to seize Venice, and hit upon this device for securing it. What made the irony complete was that this threat actually was a bluff. Much of the regular French army was in Algeria and Mexico at this time, and Napoleon was unwilling to take the very unpopular step of a general mobilization, at least until an Austro-Prussian war was well under way. With the comparatively small regular forces at their immediate disposal, the French could intervene with some effectiveness against Prussia, but for reasons of geography less effectively against Austria. In any case the general expectation within the military and diplomatic establishments in Paris was that as the war dragged on, the French eventually would intervene on the *Austrian* side, as they could fairly cheaply, to bring the war to a close (and in the process to take equivalent compensation in the Prussian Rhinelands for Austria's gain of Silesia). In Vienna, policy-makers did not know French military capabilities in detail, and still less French expectations, and they bit—"paying Napoleon heavily to do what he would have done in any case."[17]

After the Italians made their April bargain with Berlin, its main outlines were soon learned in Vienna. Knowing that King Wilhelm would not begin a war except in response to what he felt was aggression, the Austrians correctly concluded that avoiding all actions which could be perceived this way should now be a crucial foreign-policy objective.[18] But almost at once they proceeded to nullify this conclusion with contradictory policy decisions.

Within a few weeks military intelligence reports indicated that the Italians were mobilizing and beginning to deploy troops in the border area. These reports later were shown to be premature, alarmist, and much exaggerated, but meanwhile the Austrian policy-makers hastily decided on a partial mobilization along the southern frontier. No efforts were made to confirm through other channels the validity of this crucial strategic warning, even though the reports had been brought forward by the army which, as an organization, favored and had already been advocating mobilization.[19]

The Austrian commanders then discovered that for technical reasons a partial mobilization would be impossible: there would have to be a general mobilization throughout the empire or none at all. This striking rigidity in Austrian policy, so hauntingly similar to what Germany was to face fifty years later in the summer of 1914, is doubly astonishing when one reflects that the Austrians had fought a war on their southern front alone, only seven years earlier in 1859!

Clearly a full mobilization would be extremely provocative to Prussia, but over the objection of the foreign minister, Emperor Franz Joseph decided in favor of it; in Berlin the pleased Bismarck convinced Wilhelm that this was a sufficiently dangerous threat that Prussia must follow suit. So, now, did Italy.[20]

With the potential belligerents mobilizing, Austria finally took the decisive diplomatic action: it offered Venice to Italy and France, in return for their neutrality. But the Italians were now bound to Berlin until July 8th. At this point Napoleon could and did propose a general European congress to negotiate all outstanding issues and end the crisis. The Russians and the British, hoping to forestall war, immediately supported the proposal. Bismarck was unable to avoid agreeing to it, and had the Austrians done so too, King Wilhelm probably would have insisted that Prussia go along with the subsequent decisions of the congress. The Austrians' formal acceptance, though, amounted to a refusal: they would send a delegation only if "no territorial aggrandizements" were taken up—in other words, if Venice were not discussed. This, of course, robbed the congress of all meaning and it was not held.

Franz Joseph's motive for this reply was the knowledge that there was no way a congress could compensate Austria in territory for the loss of Venice. To gain Silesia was a plausible outcome for a war, but not for a congress. What remains difficult to comprehend is why he did not accept and then stall for time, if necessary letting the congress fail, while the Prusso-Italian treaty ran out; for he knew it carried a deadline only weeks away. Then the offer of Venice could have been renewed, for Italian neutrality and other quids pro quo. As a matter of fact, the congress idea had originally been suggested to Napoleon by the Italians, precisely as a way of running out the clock of their Prussian treaty so they would not have to fight a war for Venice! But these Italian and French motives, plans, and expectations had not been investigated by the Austrians.[21]

By the end of May the powers were approaching full mobilization and deployment of their forces and a major effort at international mediation had failed; yet even now war was not inevitable, as Bismarck for one was keenly aware. However, the Austrians failed to realize that King Wilhelm had not yet opted for war. Although they had clearly recognized earlier that the king would not commit aggression against the Hapsburg regime, Franz Joseph and his advisers now decided that Wilhelm would not have allowed the crisis, and his mobilization, to have proceeded so far unless he had secretly decided on war. They concluded this, despite the fact that *they* had done exactly the same things without having made a war decision! They therefore took the fatal step of bringing the Schleswig-Holstein question to the confederation diet. Their motive was to gain the fullet and promptest assistance from the small German states in the "inevitable" war. But these states already knew that Vienna wanted a confederation solution to the problem of the duchies, and they also knew that to bring it unilaterally to the diet would probably mean a war—conceivably an unnecessary one. For these reasons and others they did not spring to the Austrian cause. Thus the gain for the Austrians from their final policy decision was marginal at best, and trivial compared to the chance that Wilhelm was not yet set on war, as in fact he was not.[22]

In these and in other lesser errors during the winter and spring of 1866, Austrian decision-makers proved themselves to be far less sensitive than their Berlin counterparts to the motives and expectations of the principal actors in the system, and to the realities of the military balance. Nor was the chain of blunders merely the product of an improbably lengthy series of carefully thought through, but unfortunately erroneous, calculations. Rather, these decisions were made on the basis of highly inadequate, sometimes virtually non-existent, plans, information, and analysis. By Prussian standards they were *not so much "miscalculated" decisions as decisions hardly calculated at all.*

High-level Austrian officials did not possess and did not seek crucial information about expectations in Paris or about the comparative risks of going to the diet in June. In other instances just discussed the partial information at hand was not examined critically enough to uncover its limitations. Plans and analyses simply did not exist for the obvious contingency of a southern-front mobilization alone.

Beneath these specific lapses lay a *more general failure of analysis*, an endemic intellectual deficiency that infected both the military and the foreign ministry in Vienna. For years the Austrian army's intelligence, and analysis of its own capabilities, had not been entirely realistic. The assessments brought before Franz Joseph and his Crown Councils in the mid-1860s overestimated the forces Austria could actually deploy in the field and the usable power of her probable allies among the smaller German states. And they drastically underestimated Prussia's military potential in every category—quantity of trained troops, quality of leadership and tactics, military technology (firepower), and logistics.[23] Meanwhile Austrian diplomats did not clearly understand what the Prussians' basic foreign policy goals were, and did not comprehend until late in the day that an Austro-Prussian War was a realistic possibility and one that Berlin might favor under certain circumstances. They therefore failed to analyze what those circumstances might be and made it possible for them to emerge by default.

Inextricably intertwined with the pattern of analytic failure in Vienna was an equally serious pattern of institutional failure. *Dysfunctional organizational processes and bureaucratic politics*, far more severe in Vienna than in Berlin, generated an institutional asymmetry between them parallel to the asymmetry in the respective roles of analysis. So abnormally serious, in fact, were the institutional dysfunctions within the Austrian government that to do them justice would require a lengthy separate case study in itself. Their effect may be suggested, perhaps, by mentioning a few of the highlights. Top decision-making diplomatic and military positions in Austria, much more than in Prussia, were filled on the basis of aristocratic rank rather than merit; a generous seasoning of mediocrities, and even outright incompetents, was the inevitable result. In Vienna there were hardly any established procedures of coordination between the foreign ministry and the military, and not even much informal contact: each institution operated largely in ignorance of the other's activities. Similarly, most of the internal segments of each institution operated largely in ignorance of the activities of other segments. Emperor Franz Joseph turned over his foreign ministers quickly; and whoever was minister at a given time found his actions being substantially determined by the rapidly shifting internal politics of the cabinet, so that foreign policy took a new tack every six months or so. The domestic politics of the multinational, multilingual empire were intricate, especially the relation of German-speaking Austria to Hungary (a relationship soon to be transformed into the dual monarchy). Since the Hungarians favored opposite policies from the German Austrians on most foreign questions, politics contaminated and complicated nearly all issues. Finally, the emperor appointed his military commanders primarily according to what would be politically advantageous for the Hapsburg dynasty, and only secondarily on the basis of their professional ability.[24]

These and related hindrances to the decision-making process in Vienna depressed the influences of organizational processes, bureaucratic politics, and domestic politics—always somewhat dysfunctional even under the best of circumstances—to truly pathological depths. In the same period the well-coordinated Prussian military under its general staff system, and the foreign ministry under Bismarck, were approximating the "single, unitary rational actor" to a degree unusual even by nineteenth-century standards. From this viewpoint, the successful Prussian definition of the intitial war context was a triumph of smooth and "rational" decision-making over chaotic bureaucratic politics and organizational malfunctions.[25]

The institutional asymmetry and the analytic asymmetry (for which there were other deep-seated causes as well[26]) mutually exacerbated each other. Well-intentioned men found themselves unable to stay on top of accelerating events and fashion workable policy. Drift in Vienna contrasted with mastery in Berlin, and in June 1866 the Prussians found themselves in possession of all the preconditions for launching a war that they were confident would not escalate uncontrollably.

The July Phase of the Conflict

The battle of Königgrätz began at about 7:30 on the morning of July 3rd. By nightfall the broken remnants of the Austrian army were fleeing southward in wild disorder. The officers needed days to reassemble their units, and even then it was doubtful whether the units could be sent into battle again soon. In addition to suffering

99

huge casualities and abandoning much of their equipment, the men had lost all confidence in their commanders. Senior Austrian officers had given the army slow muzzleloading rifles whereas the Prussians had rapid-firing breechloaders, and they had instructed junior officers and trained their troops almost exclusively in a single battle tactic, the one tactic that was nonsensical when facing an enemy with superior firepower: the repeated mass infantry charge. In addition, the Austrian generals had committed many tactical blunders, both on July 3rd and in small battles over the previous days. The destruction of morale after Königgrätz was so complete that it was doubtful the regiments would face the Prussian army again.[27]

Franz Joseph, on learning of the lost preliminary battles even before July 3rd, had sent Napoleon a message asking him to mediate the conflict and offering to hand over Venice at once in exchange for an armistice on the Italian front. When news of the disaster came in, the emperor withdrew about half of the much smaller, but intact and so far victorious, southern army to join the remnants of the northern army in defense of the capital. This combined force, even if it would fight, would still be smaller and weaker than the army that had just been shattered; and shortly thereafter Franz Joseph contacted the Prussians to inquire about an armistice and terms for peace.

King Wilhelm, after his generals' preliminary successes, had left Berlin for the war theater. He, Von Moltke, Bismarck, and their staffs had watched the battle of Königgrätz from a nearby hilltop. They did not immediately realize the full extent of their victory, and it was some days before Prussian military intelligence discovered how badly the Austrian army had been crippled. The general staff then concluded, probably correctly, that the imperial government in Vienna simply did not have the military resources left to prevent the Prussian army from going wherever it liked inside the Austrian Empire.

Prussian decision-makers therefore found themselves, about ten days into July, in a situation that even their own confident prewar assessments had failed to anticipate. A victory big enough to give Prussia Schleswig-Holstein had been expected. One big enough to give Prussia a hegemony in northern Germany had been hoped for, as the maximum feasible goal. But no one had been prepared for a victory so large that Austria would be militarily prostrated. As the army advanced deeper into the empire, Prussian policy-makers tried to decide what to do next. Present at headquarters to advise the king were not only the generals, but also Bismarck—and their respective staffs. An intense disagreement rapidly erupted as the military and civilians drew opposite policy conclusions from their novel and unanticipated situation.

The generals, joined initially by the king, took the position that what was militarily feasible should be done. They wanted to pursue the war at least to the capture of the enemy's capital (a traditional military objective in the nineteenth century and earlier). For themselves and the troops, they wanted a triumphal march through the boulevards of Vienna. For Prussia's future they wanted annexations of German territory on a large scale: most or all of the small states, substantial parts at least of Saxony and Bavaria, and perhaps a corner of the Austrian Empire as well. Such a drastic increase in Prussian territory and resources would make her the unchallengeable master of Germany and one of the greatest powers on earth.

Precisely this prospect, Bismarck feared, would bring in other powers to prevent it, widen the war, and perhaps undo all that had been accomplished. He and his staff took the position that the war must be ended quickly, on the best terms that could be obtained on the strength of Königgrätz alone. These terms would certainly include all the objectives, including hegemony in northern Germany, to which the Prussians had aspired when they began the war.[28] To prolong the conflict would give the Russians—and even more, the French—a steadily extending opportunity to intervene and an ever-increasing motive to do so.

Bismarck's calculations revolved in essence around his perceptions and informed projections of French and Russian *expectations.* He knew that before Königgrätz they had envisioned a much longer war that would culminate in an Austrian victory of modest proportions, followed by a marginal gain for the Austrian position in Central Europe in the peace settlement. He anticipated—correctly —that they would be stunned by the news of Königgrätz, and by what they would now have to accept as a revised estimate of the power of the Prussian army and of the true military balance in Europe. They might also accept some moderate increase in Prussian territory as the appropriate consequence of Königgrätz. But he feared they would not assent to any dramatic territorial increase that would drastically upset the future balance of power on the Continent. The Prussian army therefore dared not penetrate Austria too deeply; for the more completely it seemed to be trying to destroy Austria's military position and power, the grander would be the objectives that the Russians and French would impute to Prussia; hence the greater would be their fears for their own positions in the new Europe, and the greater their motivation to enter the war.

Bismarck's fears were well founded. The French now came very close to intervening at once. Napoleon instantly accepted the Austrian invitation to mediate the conflict, an act that involved the French government officially and legally in the war and that was interpreted at Prussian headquarters as presaging a French armed intervention. Then, in Paris on the evening of July 5th, Napoleon held a conference with some of his advisers to consider what the French reaction to Königgrätz should be. One group led by the foreign minister, Drouyn de Lhuys, pointed out that the battle had been a disaster for French hopes of a drawn-out German war that would give Paris maximum leverage. But, they argued, major gains could still be made if Paris were to threaten Berlin by immediately mobilizing forces on the German border, and demand compensation to France for any Prussian annexations. Napoleon agreed and directed that the necessary orders go out the next morning.

Later that night he reversed himself. Another set of advisers had reached the emperor with opposing arguments: that Austria had collapsed so completely that France might find herself fighting almost alone against a newly powerful Prussia; that France was unprepared, as only a third the number of Prussian troops presently in the field could be mobilized soon; and that a military demonstration on the border would lead France "towards an incalculable European war."[29] Napoleon canceled the mobilization orders for the time being.

In succeeding days the emperor tried to straddle the two schools of opinion within his government. He mobilized no troops and concentrated upon mediating an end to the fighting. Simultaneously he convinced himself that after helping to bring the war to a quick close, he could appeal to Prussian gratitude and to the diplomatic principle of compensation by making a claim for some territorial gain for France after the hostilities were over. This was a mistake: Bismarck was not one to give up tangible assets out of gratitude or for the sake of traditional principles, and he was to ignore the claim when it ultimately arrived, in August, after the war was over and when the situation was no longer fluid. In any case, in July Napoleon merely postponed, but did not abandon, his objective of Rhineland territories for France in compensation for Prussia's gains.

By July 14th Napoleon and Goltz, the skillful Prussian ambassador in Paris, had worked out a set of terms for a war settlement that Napoleon thought were reasonable for both belligerents to accept and appropriate for himself as mediator to sanction, and that Goltz knew were not too different from what Bismarck personally had in mind. The emperor sent them to Vienna and to Prussian headquarters, urging the belligerents to end hostilities and accept his terms as the preliminaries for a peace treaty. Thus was his role as mediator discharged. After a delay Vienna agreed to the terms. Bismarck, under pressure from a king who held much more ambitious objectives, could accept them only as the basis for a truce. It was agreed that the fighting would halt for five days beginning July 22nd while the Austrians sent a high-level delegation to the Prussian headquarters near Nikolsburg to try to negotiate a final peace, employing Napoleon's terms as an agenda.[30]

In the end these negotiations succeeded, although for most of the five-day truce it appeared that they would not. With the benefit of long hindsight it is difficult to escape the conclusion that, if they had not, there would have been severe danger of the war's expanding markedly, perhaps into a general conflict involving all the major Continental powers.

For the Prussians to have torpedoed the negotiations by insisting on sharply elevated objectives (as the military, joined for most of this period by the king, wanted) would have been interpreted in Paris as a direct rejection of Napoleon's role and actions as mediator. The emperor would then probably have accepted the more aggressive policy urged by the foreign minister and his associates, which he had only tentatively rejected for the sake of successful mediation. (As it was, Napoleon directed that the French mediating role officially terminate with the beginning of the truce, and his first, albeit preliminary and unspecific, demand for compensatory territory arrived at Prussian headquarters the next day, July 23rd.) A French mobilization along the German border was the first step Drouyn de Lhuys had recommended, and the transmission to the Prussians of very specific territorial demands was the second.

King Wilhelm had already decided absolutely that no German-

speaking region could be given up to France under any circumstances—indeed, that had been his inflexible rule long before the
war had begun. Even Bismarck had earlier threatened that rather
than give up German land to France he would declare a liberal con-
stitution for the confederation similar to the one the radicals had
wanted in 1848; enlist the liberal, confederation-minded South
Germans under its banners; and fight a "national war" of all
Germany against France. Von Moltke, meanwhile, was already
drafting contingency plans for an invasion of France. Drouyn de
Lhuys's policy therefore would have posed, at the absolute minimum, the severe risk of a more general war. [31]

Meanwhile in St. Petersburg, the czar and his advisers were
already becoming disturbed by the potential magnitude of the
Prussian war objectives. Pointing out that the balance of power in
Central Europe had been carefully constructed by the Congress of
Vienna in 1815, the conservative Russians began to demand another grand congress to fashion a new European power arrangement. Few eventualities could have been more distasteful to the
Prussians at this point than a congress, which inevitably would
take back in the salons most of what their generalship and firepower had won them in the field. Fortunately for them, the proposal was stymied by the French, who knew that a congress would
never sanction their taking German land. The Russians, then,
would have had to resort to threats of force to influence events
significantly.

Even in the weeks *after* the mild Nikolsburg terms were agreed
upon, Bismarck took this hazard seriously. To gain Russian assent
even to *these* terms he dispatched the prestigious General Manteuf-
fel on a special mission to St. Petersburg as another ambassador extraordinary, with a package of carrots and sticks for the czar. (The
most important were an offer to soften the penalties imposed on the
conquered princes who were Romanoff relatives if the czar concurred in the peace terms, and a threat to make trouble in Poland if
he did not.)[32] Presumably the Russian reaction would have been
correspondingly more severe to greatly elevated Prussian war objectives and an extended war, and/or to an expanded Central
European war involving France. One cannot be sure that the czar's
government would have opted for military involvement; it was immersed in internal reforms at this time. The Russian security interest in a balance of military power in Central Europe was so great,

however, that decision-makers in St. Petersburg might have had difficulty avoiding involvement if, as was probable, either Prussia or Austria appeared likely to emerge from the new war in a dominant position.

Meanwhile, the Italians in late July were eager to fight on against Austria, to gain objectives beyond Venice (Trieste and the Tyrol). As events actually developed, they were prevented from doing so only by the armistice on the northern front, which allowed Austria to deploy her forces southward again. In a wider war the Italians would have had objectives at French expense also: the districts of Nice and Savoy, which had been Napoleon's price for helping Italy in the 1859 war against Austria.

The failure of the Nikolsburg negotiations and the resumption on July 27th of the Prussian invasion of Austria, then, would have generated a serious threat of the war's escalating into a much broader European conflict that would pit Prussia and Italy against Austria and France, with Russia a not improbable additional participant at some point. That this threat did not emerge is creditable to Bismarck's success in persuading the ultimate Prussian decision-maker, the king, to terminate the war promptly on terms acceptable to his opponent. The control of escalation in the final phase of the Austro-Prussian War thus turned on the outcome of the intragovernmental debate at Prussian headquarters.

After the victors of Königgrätz had realized their new military preeminence, Bismarck did not immediately provoke a confrontation in the Crown Council over the desire of the king and his officers to humiliate Austria and seize broad swathes of territory. He wanted to learn the shape of Napoleon's proposals, and the Austrians' reaction to them, before committing himself to a specific position regarding Prussian objectives. He did, however, do everything he could in the council meetings to influence military decisions in the direction of slowing down the Prussian army's advance, for he wanted no more major battles until a final decision about war objectives could be reached. Another victory like Königgrätz would confirm the king irremediably in his ambitious goals. Naturally Bismarck's "negativism" aroused the anger of the generals and completely polarized the internal debate; the generals likewise resented his intrusion into what they regarded as purely military issues. The minister did succeed, however, in preventing any official statement being issued about war goals that might affront Napoleon and cause him to break off his mediation.[33]

Napoleon's proposed terms arrived on July 17th; and on the 19th the French ambassador, who to the Prussians' irritation had succeeded in locating their field headquarters, informed Bismarck that the Austrians had agreed to the terms and that the French government expected the Prussians, at an absolute minimum, to open negotiations on that basis and to declare a few days' truce.

The Prussian Crown Council meeting later that day was a protracted and stormy one. Bismarck argued determinedly that the French demand must be met, even though Napoleon's suggested terms did not include any Prussian territorial acquisitions beyond Schleswig-Holstein, because otherwise the danger that France might enter the war was too great. He believed that Napoleon could be persuaded to accept moderate additional gains in territory for Prussia later, during the negotiations. The king and the military officers, who had in mind more than "moderate" gains in any case, felt that this was an uncertain gamble. Most of the generals were passionately convinced that total victory over the enemy was almost within their grasp. The Prussian advance guard was only one day from crossing the Danube; on the other side of the river the army could outflank Vienna's northward-facing defenses. As one general put it: "In eight days it will be all over, if the diplomats, who attach themselves to every honorable war like bugs to a bed, don't destroy the sport for us."[34] But Bismarck got Von Moltke to admit that a hasty crossing of the river might be a hazardous operation, and Von Roon argued that a short truce would actually improve Prussia's military position by allowing the overextended troops to rest, regroup, and be resupplied. In the end the king agreed to a five-day truce for negotiations. He fully expected that the talks would fail and that the attack would be resumed with renewed vigor.

It is questionable whether Bismarck would have won the first round of the policy debate had there not been good military as well as politico-diplomatic arguments for his position (and Von Roon on the military side to argue them). His voice was strengthened somewhat when on the 22nd word arrived from Paris that, as he had predicted, Napoleon would agree to substantial Prussian territorial gains in North Germany as long as the South German states and Austria herself were left intact.

The Austrian plenipotentiaries arrived at Nikolsburg on July 23rd, and that afternoon the first of two negotiating sessions was held. It ended in stalemate when the Austrians rejected Bismarck's demand for part of Saxony. Franz Joseph in Vienna was determined to remain loyal to the one ally who had actually helped him, and he had promised the Saxon leaders that he would renew the war rather than bargain away their territory. The effect of the stalemate was to reinforce the general expectation that the negotiations would fail and the war resume; it persuaded Bismarck that he could not gain more for Prussia than North Germany and would have to try to convince the king to settle for that. Later in the day he wrote a careful memorandum for Wilhelm, repeating his fears of intervention by the French and/or Russians and arguing that it would be a serious mistake "to endanger everything that has been achieved by trying to get from Austria a few square miles of territory or a few millions more indemnity."[35]

On the next day, the 24th, Bismarck discovered that the king remained adamant and continued to insist upon seizing Austrian, Saxon, and other South German territory, and upon resuming the invasion if the Austrians would not agree. A private meeting between the two men degenerated into a heated argument. Eventually Bismarck withdrew, defeated in his attempt to change the king's mind. Fearing catastrophe for Prussia in the form of a general European war, the minister considered resigning on the spot—and even, as he tells us in his probably exaggerated memoirs, committing suicide. Instead he had a talk with the crown prince, who comprehended Bismarck's viewpoint and who now agreed to present it to his father and support it himself. How he succeeded in changing the king's mind has not been recorded; only that he left the interview "exhausted." In any event Bismarck received the king's assent to terms that Napoleon and the Austrians would accept.[36]

The second negotiating session with the Austrians was held on the following day, and after some haggling over details the agreement was signed. The five-day truce was extended into a general armistice, and the following month the Nikolsburg terms were formalized in a peace treaty. Prussian territory was increased by almost half again and Prussian population by over 20 percent, by the absorption of some of the small North German states that had fought on the Austrian side. The others, and Saxony, joined a North German Confederation dominated by Prussia. Saxony and the South German states that had fought in the war remained intact, and Austria lost only Venice—to Italy.

On Terminating the War

There are several things about the post-Königgrätz phase of the war that are of interest to the escalation analyst. One is the important role that *unexpected military events* can play in creating pressures toward escalation. The astonishingly lopsided victory posed a greater danger of an uncontrolled sequence of escalations than even the outbreak of warfare had (because of the constructed context of the outbreak).

This unexpected event had at least four effects that are worth distinguishing. First, it created an extremely *fluid situation*. In fact, the days following Königgrätz witnessed the most fluid international situation that Europe had seen since the defeat and removal of the first Napoleon, two generations earlier. The battle completely dissolved the war context that Bismarck had prepared and raised up a slew of previously unanticipated possibilities. Bismarck was as surprised by Königgrätz as everyone else. He had made no plans, not even contingency plans, for such a situation and his subsequent actions, like everyone else's, were improvised. We should note that the effect of the battle was more drastic than simply altering everybody's probability estimates, as a twentieth-century observer might call them. It created a range of possibilities which, until July 3rd, no sober observer or analyst had thought of to attach a probability to, *at all*.

Second, the victory at Königgrätz added greatly to the *momentum* of the Prussian offensive. This was true physically: the Prussian forces, which in the days prior to the battle had been moving fairly rapidly, now raced toward the Danube River before halting (only briefly, as they thought). It was even more true psychologically: their great victory thrilled Prussian officers and men of all ranks, and the civilians at headquarters as well, and filled them with confidence and enthusiasm for pursuing and utterly crushing an enemy who now seemed prostrate.

Third, the consequences of Königgrätz created *new and unexpected security threats* to nations that previously had been involved only peripherally in the conflict. Drouyn de Lhuys in Paris was alarmed at the prospect of Prussian hegemony over much or all of Germany and urged the threat (and, he recognized, quite possibly the fact) of military intervention as much for defensive motives as offensive ones. In St. Petersburg, policy-makers had traditionally been more concerned about the threat of Austrian power than of Prussian, and from that viewpoint had some reason to welcome Königgrätz. However, they also had a definite security concern until they were sure that any new war objectives King Wilhelm set would mean only a moderate accretion in Prussian strength.

Finally, Königgrätz activated previously *latent objectives* of the Prussians themselves—objectives so latent, in fact, that few if any Prussian military officers or civilian officials had been aware of them before the battle. The duchies of Schleswig-Holstein were the ostensible war objective. Hegemony in north Germany was the outermost limit of what most Prussians consciously considered a possible war objective in the event of victory. Still, for generations Prussians had been duelling with Austrians—often by diplomacy, sometimes by war—for greater influence in Germany, and for generations they had dreamed of territorial conquests in Germany. The sudden and almost complete collapse of the traditional opponent revived old hopes and dreams and offered an exciting and completely unexpected opportunity to bring an ancient competition to a victorious, and very possibly final, conclusion.

Let us look a little further at the debate that now erupted at Prussian headquarters over whether these seemingly new objectives should be adopted, at the cost of extending the war. (And escalating it, in the sense that to achieve them the Prussian army would have to strike deeply into the Austrian Empire and seize the capital.) Since this debate split mostly along civilian-military lines, it would be easy to see the dispute as one between moderate, "sensible" civilians who wished to end the war for political and diplomatic reasons and stop the bloodshed, and aggressive generals who wanted a longer war for typically militarist reasons. Such an image would be thoroughly false. It was the principal civilian, Bismarck, who had gotten the war started in the first place, and for an avowedly aggressive goal. He shared the generals' expansionist aims, indeed if anything he was more aggressive in his goals than they. Before the war he had already been thinking about eventually unifying all Germany under Prussian rule, although he had not anticipated that it might be possible to do so in 1866. The generals did not advance that goal, even after Königgrätz.

It was not a case, therefore, of "military" arguments that favored escalation and elevated objectives, and "political" arguments that opposed. Nor was the group favoring escalation more aggressive in its overall intentions than the group opposed. *There was no clear relation between arguments for and against escalation and "aggressive intentions," or between these arguments and the ratio of military to political factors in the content of the argument.* Both sides shared the same aggressive intentions and both sides' arguments contained both military and political elements. In today's jargon, they were all politico-military.

The real difference between the two sides concerned the *breadth of the time-span* each group was contemplating and the *breadth of the considerations and contingencies* that accompanied the time-spans. The Prussian generals made their argument on the basis of expectations about the next several weeks or less. Bismarck made his on the basis of expectations about a substantially longer period, and his argument also embraced a substantially wider range of contingencies and possibilities. Let us dwell a moment on this theme.[37]

Understandably, the military advisers to King Wilhelm focused mainly on the issues posed by the existing threat—the Austrians' remaining military capabilities—and on the immediate implications of the final removal of that threat. For the most part, they argued that the Austrians were so weakened that continuing the war for several weeks promised almost complete destruction of the Austrian forces and the capture of Vienna. Secondarily, the generals advanced the (somewhat inconsistent) argument that enemy military capabilities were still sufficient for major operations against the Prussian army and therefore should be dealt with promptly.

Bismarck was only marginally interested in the question of the precise extent of the existing threat. He assessed the enemy's remaining capabilities as being, in any case, clearly insufficient to reverse the consequences of Königgrätz. Rather, he focused mainly on the issues posed by possible new threats of the near future—from the French or, conceivably, the Russians—and on the relatively indirect, less immediate implications of the final destruction of the Austrian army. From his point of view, there was an obvious limit to how gravely the Austrians could threaten the Prussian army. On the other hand, possible actions by the French or Russians over the next six to eight weeks, or longer if the situation remained fluid, could potentially be very threatening. He was mainly interested in the campaign against the Austrians insofar as it might contribute still more to the already distinct danger of a wider war.

At the risk of oversimplifying somewhat, we may say that the general staff was primarily concerned about the threat that was present and concretely real. Bismarck, by contrast, was primarily concerned about threats that were future and (so far) hypothetical.

More formally, we might say that the basic argument between the general staff and Bismarck was over *the locus of the most salient uncertainties*. The staff found the uncertainties posed by the remaining Austrian military capabilities to be the most obvious uncertainties, and the ones Bismarck was raising to be somewhat hypothetical. Bismarck found the uncertainties posed by the remaining capabilities of the Austrian army to be comparatively unimportant, because their outer bounds could be specified with high confidence. By contrast, the outer bounds of the uncertainties posed by a wider war could not be specified—except by placing them very far out (a general European war): a range that included great dangers to Prussia.

Let us not misinterpret the significance of this distinction. The generals, for instance, could not reasonably be called shortsighted. There was a legitimate difference in their assigned role, as well as in their professional training and orientation, which encouraged the military officers to concentrate on the existing military situation. Their assigned role and their profession also encouraged them to leave to civilians of the foreign ministry questions about other nations' possible future decisions—decisions that would emerge, if at all, from "political" policy-making processes within those governments.

Furthermore, some of the generals, certainly including Von Moltke, freely recognized that there was a real danger of early French intervention. Von Moltke argued, though, that a modest contingent could hold a defensive line against the Austrians, and the main body of the Prussian army could wheel around to the west, invade France, and defeat the French army before the bulk of it could be mobilized and properly assembled. Thus the king's chief military adviser argued that Prussia could accept the military risk that he calculated as accompanying the Austrian campaign.

Bismarck, a civilian, was not in a position to oppose frontally the Chief of the General Staff's assessment, based on military calculations, of the military risk. Instead, his opposition was to some of the implicit assumptions Von Moltke's assessment seemed to make.

He feared the Austrians might abandon their capital and retire to their ample territory to the east and south. The French too might not surrender after initial defeats of their armies, even major ones, but fight on. There were many uncertainties and dangers attached to the prospect of a drawn-out war against two major nations. On the other hand, if the Prussians should be successful against both, the Russians would feel threatened and might then intervene. In short, Bismarck argued, there were too many considerations that were too complicated and too diffuse to be calculated with high confidence. And some of the possibilities led toward a general European war, the outcome of which would be completely unforeseeable.

The essence of Bismarck's argument for terminating the war quickly, then, addressed a different level from the one the general staff was addressing. The staff could have modified substantially its estimates about military risk and its predictions about various specific contingencies involving the Austrian and even French armies, without changing Bismarck's case. His argument basically concerned the more general politico-military context that would surround any and all purely military events of the near future, if the war were continued, almost regardless of the specific scenario postulated for the near term. Almost any well-defined scenario the general staff could construct, within the realm of plausibility, about the likely events of the next several weeks would not cope adequately with the range of more general hazards that Bismarck foresaw, from that moment until the conclusion of the fighting.

Let us pursue this from a different angle. Again at the risk of oversimplifying, we might say that the general staff, in adopting expectations and making predictions about a continued war, tended to begin by assuming that the war context that had existed to that time would continue. Then, in response to Bismarck's pressure, the staff began to change the framework or parameters it was assuming, *one parameter at a time*. (Von Moltke, for instance, willingly altered the context he was assuming, to the extent of one major new scenario—a French war declaration and accompanying mobilization order, followed by the rapid defeat of the mobilized forces.)

However, Bismarck's basic argument was that *all* the parameters of the war might change, or at least a great many of them might. There were more possibilities and more uncertainties, he believed, than could possibly be pinned down by a logical process of contingency planning, in which assumptions were changed one at a time. A general war could not be excluded as a real possibility; and there was no way to plan with confidence how to conclude such a war to Prussia's benefit.

Today we may recognize that Bismarck's argument was the more sophisticated and the more realistic one, from the point of view of controlling escalation. We should also recognize, though, that in the policy debate at Prussian headquarters it suffered from an important handicap: it could not be made as concrete and specific as the opposing argument. The general staff could point to tangible dangers and readily discuss specific, easily visualized situations. Because Bismarck's argument extended farther into the future and embraced a wider range of possibilities, he was at something of a disadvantage in making a compelling case. He did not have tangibles to set against tangibles. The political judgments he feared the French and Russians might make, which were the basis of his argument, themselves lay mostly in the future and were somewhat vague and abstract compared to the generals' military scenarios.

In situations like this where the uncertainties in question lie mostly in the future, it is always easier to *leave open* the question, "How serious are these uncertainties?" (as implicitly the general staff did) than to show convincingly that they are serious. The evidence one can point to itself tends to be ambiguous and uncertain, and to lie partly in the future. There was, therefore, an asymmetry between the kind of argument the general staff was making and the kind Bismarck was making, which as a practical matter worked to Bismarck's disadvantage.

This brings us to a final observation about the decision-making process at Prussian headquarters. Because of the handicap under which Bismarck's argument suffered, it was probably fortunate that a significant amount of time was available before a final decision had to be made. If only a day or two had been available, it is less likely that Bismarck's somewhat hypothetical argument could have succeeded. His determined insistence and his constant reiteration of it over a period of ten days probably had something to do with his success in ultimately persuading the crown prince, and through him the king.[38]

Analytic Summary

Despite its upheaval of the Continental balance of power, the Austro-Prussian War did not escalate into a general European conflict. In the first instance, this was prevented by Bismarck's success in designing an initial war context that was specifically aimed at forestalling other nations' involvement. Relying on a widespread miscalculation of the actual Prusso-Austrian military balance, and employing special communications channels and other means to reinforce desired behavior by others, he manipulated a "controlled crisis" that he could have unilaterally resolved at any time. This was made possible by the overall superiority of Prussian intelligence information, military assessments, and analytic capacity, and especially by a sharp asymmetry in these areas between Prussia and Austria. Repeated failures in analysis and information management, and pathologically poor decision-making mechanisms in Vienna, mutually exacerbated each other.

The dramatic victory at Königgrätz exploded the initial war context. It created a highly fluid international situation, added greatly to the momentum of the Prussian offensive, created new and unexpected security threats to two great powers, and activated previously latent Prussian objectives. If Bismarck had not, with great difficulty, persuaded King Wilhelm to moderate his objectives, the conflict might well have escalated into a general European war. The debate at Prussian headquarters was not defined by military arguments for and political arguments against the king's initial, extended objectives. Rather, it divided along differences in the time-span and the number of considerations embraced by each group's expectations. The general staff was primarily concerned with a "threat estimate" of what was concretely real, and located the most serious uncertainties in the immediate future; Bismarck was primarily concerned with hypothetical, but he believed all too probable, threats and uncertainties located in the slightly more distant future. The general staff was prepared to make contingency plans for that time period that presupposed a changing of the character of the war in very specific respects, and that altered assumptions one parameter at a time. The essence of Bismarck's argument was that the character of the war had changed fundamentally, and that nearly all the parameters had shifted in ways that were too complicated, diffuse, and basic to be calculated with confidence.

6

The Wars of German Unification: The Franco-Prussian War

A war between Prussia and France was the logical sequel to the Austro-Prussian War and was widely anticipated after 1866, not only in France and throughout Germany but elsewhere in Europe as well. For centuries a fundamental national interest of France had been to keep the German-speaking lands fragmented and thus prevent the rise of any major power on the other side of France's one major nonnatural frontier. After Napoleon III had failed to intervene in the 1866 war to forestall the rise of Prussian power, it was widely expected that his regime would welcome any good opportunity to undo that outcome and return Germany to its previous, more splintered state. For his part Bismarck, having accomplished fully his objectives in the Austrian conflict, now aimed at joining the South German states to his North German Confederation, thereby unifying the whole of Germany under a regime which, like that of the confederation, would be dominated by Prussia. The obvious and by far the simplest way for this to occur would be in the wake of a victorious "national war" against the traditional German enemy, France, in which success would depend crucially and visibly upon Prussia's military power. Thus both Paris and Berlin had deep-lying interests in the late 1860s and thereafter that led them to welcome a war; it was because this was generally appreciated, not only in those countries but throughout Europe, that a Franco-Prussian War was so widely anticipated.

Historical Overview

The immediate cause of the war, however, concerned the succession to the throne of Spain. In September 1868 Queen Isabella II was deposed, and a regency hawked the empty throne around the royal houses of Europe. A series of highly secret off-again, on-again

115

negotiations began over the possible candidacy of Leopold Hohen-
zollern-Sigmaringen, a prince of a branch of the ruling family of
Prussia. Bismarck was later to claim that he promoted these negotiations to create a war, but it is more likely that he merely foresaw
diplomatic advantages in the candidacy. In any case, by 21 June
1870 Prince Leopold, his father, and King Wilhelm (as head of the
Hohenzollern family) had all agreed that Leopold should accept
what by now had become a firm Spanish offer of the throne.[1]

At this point occurred one of those unpredictable events that
change history. The Spanish emissary to Prussia telegraphed home
the acceptance in cipher and stated that he would return to Madrid
carrying the formal acceptance on 26 June. The plan was that Leopold's acceptance would be ratified at once by the Cortes, then sit-
ting, and the deed would be a fait accompli before the French could
object. However, an error by a cryptographics clerk produced a
message to Madrid that the emissary would not be back before 9
July. The Cortes was therefore prorogued, the summer being a very
hot one and the legislators unwilling to remain in Madrid for a purpose that could not be revealed. The returning Spanish emissary,
not knowing these developments, was indiscreet. The result was
that rumor of Leopold's candidacy appeared in a Paris newspaper
on July 2nd, and that evening the situation was officially admitted
to the French ambassador.

French public opinion was so enflamed that Emperor Napoleon
III's government, which did not mobilize its armed forces until the
14th, was in danger of being unseated for that delay. Almost unanimously, the French newspapers called for immediate war. That the
entire matter was a Prussian trick directed solely at France was
never doubted, and memories of the encirclement of France by the
empire of Charles V almost two centuries earlier were quickly
revived.

Faced with an intense diplomatic crisis, the French foreign ministry sent its ambassador in Prussia to Ems, where King Wilhelm
was vacationing, to demand that the head of the family withdraw
Leopold's candidacy. While refusing to go that far, Wilhelm agreed
to advise Leopold to withdraw. During this period Leopold's
father, alarmed by the crisis, withdrew his son's name anyway.

Had events stopped there, Napoleon III would have won a
much-needed diplomatic victory at Prussian expense. And indeed,
Bismarck in Berlin was chagrined that the king had reversed him-

self. He was saved, however, by the bumbling diplomacy of Napoleon, who decided to seal his popularity at home by demanding additionally that King Wilhelm agree never in the future to permit a Hohenzollern to apply for the Spanish throne.[2] When the French ambassador put this to King Wilhelm on 13 July, His Majesty declined to bind himself for the future; when pressed, he courteously stated that that issue was closed and he would not see the ambassador again on that subject. The king sent Bismarck a telegram from Ems to inform him of these developments and gave his permission to make them public if Bismarck so desired.

In one of his most famous actions, Bismarck released an abbreviated version of the Ems telegram to the press, a version contrived to appear to Germans that the Frenchman had insulted the King of Prussia, while appearing to the French that King Wilhelm had snubbed their ambassador. This maneuver was well-calculated to drive the French public into a frenzy. Napoleon's cabinet (partly on British advice) had held off committing itself to war. But after the Ems telegram was published, the wild enthusiasm among the legislature, the newspapers, and the Parisian public for immediate war compelled Napoleon to mobilize the army on the 14th. The next day the North German Confederation followed suit, and the South German states did so a few days later (as required by treaties with the confederation). The French declared war on the 19th.

The French entered the war supremely confident of victory. Indeed, in July 1870 almost everyone in Europe (except in Prussia) confidently expected France to win the war quickly and easily. In actuality the French army suffered an almost unbroken string of reverses from the very outset. Half the army was trapped and surrounded in the fortress of Metz by 19 August; and the other half was caught, in the battle of Sedan on 1 September, with its back against the Belgian frontier—whereupon 85,000 troops, and Emperor Napoleon, who was leading them personally, simply surrendered.

German steel-bore, breechloaded artillery manufactured by the Krupp munition works had proved devastatingly superior to the muzzleloaded French artillery. French generalship on the whole had been incompetent by Prussian standards. Perhaps most significant of all, Prussian logistics had proved a marvel of efficiency, debouching 300,000 troops and all necessary supplies according to precise plans on the French frontier in just three weeks—at that

Map 3 The Franco-Prussian War of 1870-1871.

time a shockingly short period; the French had counted on Prussia's taking six weeks. By contrast, French logistics turned into a hopeless jumble; frequently a unit would arrive at one terminus, discover that its supplies were at another, perhaps its reserves and their supplies at a third, and horses and wagons at a fourth. The Prussian generals, though confident of ultimate victory, had expected to fight the first phase of the war on the defensive in Germany. In fact, French soldiers barely set foot in Germany (they held one town for one day) before the Prussians shifted to the

118

offensive and swept the French armies before them in a rising crescendo of victory.[3]

After the surrender of Napoleon at Sedan, the war entered a second and quite different phase. In Paris a bloodless coup replaced the empire with a new Government of National Defense, which did not consider itself responsible for the French declaration of war and its causes and would have gladly terminated the conflict on the basis of the status quo before the war. The Germans, however, having won (at considerable cost) one of the most lopsided campaigns in history, now adopted specific war aims that they were in no mood to abandon, including a substantial slice of French territory. They demanded Alsace and most of Lorraine. M. Favre, the new foreign minister in Paris, declared that France would never give up "an inch of our territory or a stone of our fortresses."[4]

Accordingly, after a pause following Sedan to permit a change of players, the drama resumed. While the Government of National Defense tried desperately to raise new armies—the entire regular French army having surrendered or been trapped in Metz—the Prussians drove on Paris, surrounding and besieging it on September 19th. For four months the capital was cut off from the world; communication from the city to the south and west of France was by balloon and carrier pigeon only. In addition, the Prussians began to bombard the city with artillery in January, although this proved ineffectual; Paris surrendered on January 29th, when starvation was imminent.

The French government now requested and was granted an armistice to hold elections in the unoccupied part of the country. The delegates selected were to attend an assembly in Bordeaux to debate continuing the war. Since only a small minority of deputies who favored the war were elected, peace preliminaries were signed. Under their terms, France gave up all of Alsace (except one town) and most of Lorraine and pledged to pay a war indemnity of five billion francs, at that time an enormous sum. The occupation of France was withdrawn in stages, as the indemnity was gradually paid off.

Meanwhile the German Empire had been established in the Hall of Mirrors at Versailles on January 18th. What had previously been the North German Confederation was joined with the southern states to become the German Reich, constructed substantially according to Prussian design, and the King of Prussia became the kaiser. Among other consequences, creation of the empire completed the upset of the European balance of power begun earlier, for where there had been a multitude of competing states there now was just one—one, furthermore, that clearly was the strongest military power on the Continent. The leaders of Austria-Hungary (which had been formed in 1867) finally abandoned their centuries-old interests and involvements in Germany, and directed their ambitions into the Balkans, a shift that contributed greatly to the cataclysm a generation later. And for the first time in the modern age, the French found themselves faced with a great power of the first rank on their very doorstep, a fact which was to define the core problem of the international politics of Europe for the next seventy-five years.

The Escalation Dimension of the Conflict

A. J. P. Taylor, the English historian, has written that the Franco-Prussian War was "the last war fought solely in Europe and confined to European great powers. It was indeed confined to two powers. This was unexpected."[5] Through much of the war a number of policy-makers in France and Germany, emphatically including Bismarck, thought that the conflict might well grow into a bigger war. Similar expectations were held by officials and informed observers in other countries, who appreciated that a French victory —or even more, the great German victory that began to take shape —would seriously alter the European balance of power. In addition, on at least two occasions during the war decision-makers on the outside took specific actions, or threatened to do so, that posed substantial risk of a wider war. (These will be discussed later.) Why, despite these factors, the Franco-Prussian War did not escalate into a much larger war, even a general European war, is the central question for the researcher of escalation control.

The escalation dimension of this war resembles that of its predecessor of four years earlier, the Austro-Prussian War, in certain basic respects, although it also differs from it in a number of important ways. (I have selected these two wars, in part, exactly because of the opportunity they provide to explore variation within a basic similarity.) In both conflicts the belligerents fought all out, and the danger of uncontrolled escalation lay in the hazard that events could trigger actions by outside powers that would lead in turn to counteractions by others, and so on to general war.

The factors that prevented this during the Franco-Prussian War operated mainly during two phases. As in 1866, the first was one in which an initial war context was defined almost unilaterally by one side, the Prussian. The method, however, was somewhat different from the parallel definition of the earlier war. This phase again preceded the outbreak of fighting, but in 1870 it also extended into the first weeks of warfare.

As in 1866, there was a brief intervening period that is less significant for our purposes, followed by the second phase, which concerned the problems of terminating the conflict. In the Franco-Prussian War, this phase extended over a period of months and in various respects was different from the parallel phase in the earlier conflict. Both major phases will receive detailed treatment later in this chapter.

Minor Escalations in the War

First, though, let us glance briefly at several significant escalations that did occur—minor compared to the possibility of a general European war, but of interest nonetheless. In this respect the 1870 war resembles the Spanish Civil War. The comparatively controlled escalations during the Spanish conflict were more numerous and much more serious than were the escalations of the earlier war. On the other hand, in the Franco-Prussian War nearly all of them occurred at about the same time: during the period following the battle of Sedan. They were a consequence in one way or another of the Germans' decision to elevate their war objectives to include Alsace-Lorraine. We will discuss later the reasons for this decision, which are interwoven with the broader problem of how the war was to be terminated. At this point let us merely note several specific escalations in the level of violence that flowed from this elevation of objectives, and also note the reasons why they never posed a very great danger of igniting an uncontrolled escalation sequence.

(a) To besiege the enemy's capital city and starve it into submission was an act that had not been witnessed for some time in Europe. It pitted the German war machine, not against its French counterpart, but against civilians, particularly when the artillery bombardment began in January. Nonetheless, reducing the opponent's capital was a traditional goal of European warfare, legitimized by many comparable attacks in preceding centuries. (Napoleon I's seizure of Moscow and the English burning of Washington, D. C., were the most recent precedents.) The unpleasantness of life in Paris as starvation approached was not felt abroad as keenly as it

121

might have been, because the Prussians did not permit visitors or news reporters to pass their lines and enter the city. Furthermore, the crowds who had surged through the boulevards of Paris in July crying "À Berlin" could hardly plead very moving outrage at their own besiegement in the autumn.

(b) Just as seventy years later, when the Germans occupied northern France, guerrilla bands sprang up to harass the occupation forces. In 1870 these were called *francs-tireurs.* The Prussians improvised a ruthless counterinsurgency operation, which included summary courts-martial of captured guerrillas and their immediate execution, and the reprisal annihilation of towns suspected of harboring guerrillas. This program was sufficiently effective that the Prussians never were seriously threatened by the francs-tireurs in their control of the region, although they felt compelled to import large quantities of second-rate guard troops (*Landwehr*) for occupation duty. This new dimension of the war was not as striking at the time as it appears to twentieth-century eyes. The Government of National Defense paid the insurgents only desultory attention, and failed to publicize them abroad. The insurgency, indeed, remained mostly unorganized, local, and spontaneous in character. The Prussians regarded their counterinsurgency operations as an uninteresting, unmilitary, and insignificant sidelight to the war; they revealed little about these operations to their own home populace and, strategically, did not permit newsmen into the occupied area. The result was that the insurgency not only had relatively little effect on the military progress of the war, but also had little political impact.[6]

(c) There was a diffuse change in the character of the war following Sedan, of which the insurgency may be seen as one expression. Napoleon III's controversial imperial regime had been declining in popularity in France for years. The Government of National Defense, however, was nonpartisan, indeed almost nonpolitical. It existed only to terminate the war, had strictly defensive objectives, and plausibly could claim to speak and act for the whole French people—doubly so when it became apparent that the enemy proposed to seize almost all of two French provinces. Prussia's establishing the objective of Alsace-Lorraine transmuted France into a united "nation in arms." With such a level of deep popular support, the Government of National Defense proclaimed universal conscription in the unoccupied portions of France, and immediately new armies began to be formed. In the hope of being liberated and the even greater hope that foreign powers would intervene in the war, the people of Paris, themselves caught up in the new spirit, chose to withstand a long siege.

This change in the character of the war became more striking in retrospect, though, than it seemed at the time, particularly outside France. At its outbreak the war had been extremely popular with the French people. That this enthusiasm, inspired somewhat by aggressive designs on Germany, was shallow compared to French feelings later concerning Alsace-Lorraine and the German occupation was not clearly reported or realized abroad until the war was over. And the Government of National Defense did not succeed in translating its broader and much deeper political support into hard military advantage. The fresh forces raised in the west and south, almost of necessity, were inadequately trained and equipped, and the Germans were able with a series of spoiling operations to prevent them from approaching Paris.[7]

The creation of the nation in arms, the accompanying decisions that Paris should hold out and that fresh armies should be raised, the insurgency and counterinsurgency campaigns, and the siege of the capital were all notable escalations of the Franco-Prussian War. But they did not have much potential to trigger an uncontrolled escalation sequence that would lead to a more general war. In the perception of decision-makers abroad, each was either comparatively invisible (for example, the change in the character of the war and the insurgency/counterinsurgency campaigns) or comparatively legitimate (for instance, the siege and later bombardment of Paris). None of these events, in fact, posed the danger of uncontrolled escalation that the mere existence of the war did.

One additional point concerning these specific escalations should be made. With the exception of the bombardment of Paris, which could have begun much sooner, none of these steps conceivably could have been taken earlier or indeed under any conditions except ones similar to those under which they actually were taken. From the outbreak of the war both France and the German military alliance committed all the resources they could to the conflict. To put it differently, the two belligerents fought all out from the very beginning of the war; they later escalated against each other; afterward, they were again fighting all out.

This occurrence, which appears paradoxical from the viewpoint of any simple theory or image of escalation, derives from the fact that the meaning of *all out* is variable. It is not always a constant, even at any given level of technological and other physical resources possessed by a given number of actors; some change in the overall character of a war may, as here, activate elements that previously were wholly irrelevant to the conflict. This aspect of the Franco-Prussian War reminds us that not only can escalation occur when nations actualize possibilities previously known but forgone, but also when a change in the overall nature of the war widens the scope of the possibilities themselves.

Definition of the Initial War Context

Let us turn now to the general analytic problem: why the conflict did not escalate into a much broader, perhaps general, European war. As in 1866, this was prevented in the first instance by the careful attention the Prussians gave, prior to the war's outbreak, to this very danger. The international context existing in July 1870 by and large was *not* the product of undesigned interactions among the major powers; it emerged only by virtue of long-standing policy on the part of the Prussians.

Bismarck, now chancellor of the North German Confederation and enjoying authority even greater than he had held previously, was as determined in 1870 as four years earlier that no war should begin except within a context that minimized the probability of its expanding into a general European conflict. Throughout the period prior to June 1870, he could have withdrawn Prince Leopold's name and closed the secret negotiations with the Spanish emissaries at any time. Thus he could have forestalled any crisis with France resulting from the Hohenzollern candidacy, had the international situation developed in a manner that suggested higher risks for Prussia than he was willing to accept. The most fundamental reason why the Franco-Prussian War did not escalate in any major way, then, is that its causal crisis could feasibly have been prevented unilaterally by one belligerent.

In this basic respect the Franco-Prussian War mirrors the Austro-Prussian War. They differ greatly, however, in the form in which the defining of the initial war context proceeded. In 1870 Bismarck had to create many fewer elements of the international constellation that he needed; more were given him free of charge. His policy, therefore, could be significantly more passive and, in that sense, more subtle. The Austro-Prussian War had been the product of a controlled crisis building over a period of months, which Bismarck, with considerable effort, manipulated almost constantly to encourage all developments that tended to exacerbate tensions and to discourage various developments that might have reduced tensions. The more compressed prewar events of June 1870 represented what might be better termed an *exploited crisis*. Bismarck probably did not expect a war to emerge from the Hohenzollern candidacy, but when a crisis erupted he exploited it. Even then only one positive action of any significance on his part, alteration of the Ems telegram, was required to drive the crisis over the brink into war. Throughout the rest of the prewar period the chancellor did little actively on the international scene. (After the outbreak he became more active, as we shall see.)[8]

Bismarck exploited this particular crisis, rather than earlier ones or potential later ones, because it promised to fulfill preconditions that he recognized as essential. The chancellor's overall objective was to create a united Germany under Prussian leadership, through a victorious war against France, but several prerequisites had to be fulfilled before the prospect could be a reasonable one.

(*a*) In the first place, Prussia would have to appear to be acting defensively, and France seem to be the aggressor. This was not required to satisfy the king as in 1866, for the monarch had few scruples to inhibit him from striking at a traditional enemy of all Germans. It was required to bring the South German states reliably into the conflict. The annexes to the peace treaty of 1866 pledged the states of southern Germany (Bavaria, Württemberg, Baden, and Hesse) to place their armies under Prussian command in wartime. Bismarck knew, however, that they would not actually do so—at least not swiftly and surely—unless the war seemed clearly to be a defensive one. The southerners were not about to assist in Prussian aggrandizements.[9]

The Hohenzollern candidacy crisis presented Bismarck with an opportunity to satisfy this precondition. The alteration of the Ems telegram had the specific purpose of goading the French into being the first to mobilize armed forces. The defensive alliance between the confederation and the South German states was thereby activated, and the southerners quickly mobilized their forces and placed them under Prussian command.[10]

Indeed, in late July and August the whole world other than parts of the Berlin government believed that France was responsible for starting the war. Thereby the likelihood was reduced of any outside assistance to France, then or later, that might pose risk of a wider conflict.

(b) Bismarck had known for years that a war against France, to have the greatest probability of success should come only after the governmental institutions of the new North German Confederation had shaken down into their practical patterns of functioning. It should also come only after the Prussian military staff had completed integration on a contingency basis of the armies of the South German states into that of the confederation (that is, integration of war plans, of logistics, and so on). It took some three years, after the creation on paper of the confederation and the signing of the contingency military alliance in 1866, for planners in the general staff and foreign ministry offices in Berlin to satisfy themselves that in the event of war, the institutions of the confederation and of the military alliance would work smoothly. By 1869 or so, then, this prerequisite had been met. As more time passed, the French might begin to catch up with German technical and logistical advantages, so Bismarck had an incentive to exploit the next crisis that appeared.[11]

Earlier, however, the chancellor did not allow crises with France to mature. For example, a serious crisis over Luxembourg in 1867 was defused, with Bismarck making significant concessions to do so.[12]

(c) The final and most complicated precondition concerned specifically the requirement of escalation control: a war should not be allowed to begin except within an international constellation that minimized the hazard of the war's widening. The task of defining the initial war context was simpler in the period preceding the Franco-Prussian War, however, than in the comparable period preceding the war four years earlier. This time Prussia did not need allies among the major powers to achieve a satisfactory military balance, so Bismarck was able to concentrate on the goal of denying the enemy any allies. Nor was this as difficult as earlier, because on the whole the interests of other great powers were not likely to be as immediately engaged in any Franco-Prussian crisis as in any Austro-Prussian crisis.

Neither Italy nor Russia was geographically positioned so as to be directly affected by a Franco-Prussian crisis, or even a Franco-

Prussian war, as long as one belligerent did not emerge from it so preponderant as to upset the general European balance. British interests, by contrast, were somewhat more engaged in the theater of 1870 than they had been in the theater of 1866; but they were engaged in a way that tended to favor the Prussian cause. Britain was primarily concerned with the security of the Low Countries and especially Belgium, the principal threat to whom, in this era, was France. During the 1860s French designs on Belgium had instigated a series of diplomatic crises of which the most recent had been caused by Napoleon's moves in 1869 to take over partial control of the Belgian railways. The Prussian foreign ministry therefore could be reasonably confident that Great Britian would not easily involve herself in the war in any way friendly to France, at least at the outset. It was an increase, not a decrease, in French power that was feared in London. Indeed, the British diplomatic effort of early July to restrain the French from war derived primarily from anxiety that a French victory over Germany (which decision-makers in London, as in every other major capital except Berlin, expected) would lead Napoleon to be much more aggressive toward Belgium.[13]

Austria-Hungary remained Bismarck's most serious concern. Vienna had an obvious basis for an alliance with France, namely the objective of reversing the unhappy outcome of 1866. The same prospect that Bismarck had feared then, Paris and Vienna agreeing to balance advances by one along the Rhine with advances by the other in southern Germany, was in principle equally feasible in 1870. And in fact, many negotiations between the two capitals had taken place in the intervening years.

Austria-Hungary was not quite so plausible a candidate for the role of interventionist in 1870, however, as France had been in 1866.[14] The dual monarchy was not confident that its newly twinned institutions should yet be tested in the fires of war. The Hungarians could hardly welcome a resurgence of the power of the German-speaking Austrians within the regime, and while this was not necessarily an inevitable consequence of victory in southern Germany, it was not an unlikely one. Austria-Hungary, unlike France in 1866, had to its rear a hostile great power, Russia, which might well intervene herself should the Central European balance seem likely to emerge from the new war too heavily weighted in Vienna's favor. Bismarck, who understood these factors and whose diplomatic intelligence on Austrian perceptions and attitudes was excellent, was able to dismiss rumors of a Parisian-Viennese alliance in the period preceding the war as "conjectural rubbish"[15] and did not feel it necessary in this period to take major diplomatic action to try to keep the two countries apart.

Thus the process of defining the initial war context in one sense differs strikingly in the 1870 case from the 1866 case, although in a more general way they resemble each other. In both prewar periods the Prussians were faced with meeting several preconditions, including that of allowing a war to break out only in an international context that would minimize the danger of escalation. But in 1870 these were all met either "automatically" by the existing situation, or by Bismarck's publication of the altered telegram. Little other action was required. The case demonstrates that deliberately and carefully *defining an initial war context does not necessarily require, or reveal itself in, much action on the international scene.* From a conceptual or planning point of view, Bismarck was just as deeply and actively involved in this problem, and in meeting the other preconditions, as he had been in 1865 and 1866, but from a policy or action point of view, this time he needed to do almost nothing. When the Hohenzollern candidacy crisis broke, it met his requirements and was immediately exploited for his purposes.

The Analytic Asymmetry

Successful attainment of the Prussian preconditions depended upon the existence of an important asymmetry in the quality of analysis and information available to the highest decision-makers of the two nations. In particular the French, like the Austrians before them, suffered from a deficiency (compared to their opponent) in their ability to calculate accurately the true *military balance* and the *motivations and expectations* of policy-makers in other major capitals.

The French military, studying Prussian performance in the 1866 war, had concluded that the victory stemmed largely from the Prussian army's monopoly on one superior technology, the breech-loading infantry rifle. In contemplating a possible Franco-Prussian war, they dismissed this advantage because the French infantry was also being equipped with a breechloader (a slightly superior one). Focusing upon the most visible difference between the Prussian and Austrian forces in 1866, they greatly underestimated some less obvious features: superior Prussian generalship, other technological advantages such as the excellent Prussian railway system, and the smooth Prussian logistics. They also failed to observe something the Prussians noted carefully: that breechloaded artillery, possessed by both sides in small quantities in 1866, had been vastly more effective than muzzleloaded field pieces. In the ensuing four years the Prussians had completely equipped themselves with modern steel-bore, breechloaded artillery. The importance of this was lost upon the French, with disastrous consequences when the war came.[16]

The French military also set great store by a "secret weapon"—a rapid-fire gun, ancestress to the machine gun, called the *mitrailleuse*. To maintain its secrecy, comparatively few men were trained in its use, and in 1870 it did not come into action often enough or in sufficient numbers to make much difference. Prussian intelligence knew all about the weapon anyway, and correctly discounted its importance, given the existing French doctrine for its use.[17]

French military intelligence and self-assessment were also far inferior to Prussian in their respective estimates of the two powers' capabilities to mobilize their forces. Decision-makers in Paris expected the German mobilization to be much slowed by difficulties in coordinating the confederation's activities with those of the South German states, although in Germany it was fairly well known that integration of the northern and southern forces on a contingency basis had been thoroughly planned. Most serious of all was the French confidence in their own capacity to mobilize swiftly, a confidence ludicrously misplaced in light of the logistic shambles that actually developed. Yet a very important factor in Parisian policy-makers' rapid decision for war in June was their expectation that France was well ahead in the mobilization competition and would be able to strike while Germany was still unprepared. The English ambassador in Paris reported to the London foreign office in this period that "the French are getting more and more excited. They think they have got the start of Prussia this time in forward-ship of preparation."[18]

Behind these specific errors in intelligence and self-assessment lay a more general and diffuse French *failure to assess carefully the military balance*. While to a small degree the army had been hindered in its preparedness for war by budget cuts imposed by the legislature, the bulk of its difficulties flowed from a lack of rigor in planning and analysis, which in turn was mainly the result of complacency. France had beaten or held off most of the rest of the civilized world at the beginning of the century, and in 1859 had won a clear-cut victory over Austria, then generally regarded as the other great European land power. The French army, especially in its upper echelons, believed too well its own boast of being the best in the world. Information was not systematically sought that might challenge this assumption. Nor were analysis performed—for instance, comparing the French logistical system with what was known about the German—that might have highlighted a need for fresh and challenging questions or otherwise alerted decision-makers to their complacency. The French failed to inquire carefully into the expectation, generally held in Prussian military circles, of victory in a Franco-Prussian war. One very accurate set of secret intelligence reports warning of German military power was dismissed and not circulated within the government in Paris.[19]

Where the Austrian failure before 1866 to calculate the military balance accurately had been caused, in part, by almost medieval organizational and institutional arrangements and processes, the military arrangements and processes in France before 1870—while certainly inferior to their Prussian counterparts—were relatively less significant. More significant was the fact that the high policy-makers and military officers *chose not to challenge their own sanguine expectations.*

A similar attitude in the French foreign ministry led to comparable blunders, two in particular. One was a largely unexamined assumption that the leaders of the South German states were so hostile to Prussia, and so Francophile in their cultural attitudes, that they would decide to cooperate with Berlin in a war against France with vast reluctance and delay, and very possibly not at all. In a war in which Prussia manifestly was the aggressor, this might have been a valid estimate. In a war in which Prussia succeeded in appearing to be the defender of all Germans against a belligerent and aggressive France, it was a drastic misestimate. As one historian has written, "The unanimous enthusiasm with which the southern German states joined Prussia did not throw much weight into the military balance; but it made nonsense of the French political program, so far as they had one."[20]

What is especially remarkable is that for three years the originally secret treaties between the confederation and the South German states, which dealt with this contingency, had been public. Bismarck had published them during the 1867 Luxembourg crisis as a warning to France. Nonetheless, the foreign ministry in Paris had concluded that they were pro forma because they had been signed in the heat of the 1866 war and did not reflect real loyalties. The French overlooked the fact that actually they had been signed when Bismarck had shown the South German diplomats documentary evidence of French aggressive designs on German territory. The French did not consider the possibility that the treaties embodied a partially *latent* anxiety among the southerners—an anxiety that, to be sure, was not expressed routinely in their normal politico-diplomatic behavior, but that might be activated under certain circumstances. They therefore did not analyze what those circumstances might be and permitted them to emerge by default.[21]

Nor, indeed, did the southerners' anxiety remain all that latent, for the general Franco-Prussian tensions of the late sixties and the widespread expectation of war led to a gradual rise of national and pro-Prussian feelings in South Germany. In 1870 Napoleon and his advisers were so immersed in defending France from Hohenzollern encirclement that they failed to appreciate that their policy could seem aggressive in South Germany, or could easily be made by Bismarck to appear so.

In part this gap developed in the French perception of South German motivations and expectations because Napoleon and the foreign ministry officials had not really comprehended that Bismarck's fundamental objective was—or might be—to unite Germany under Prussian leadership. They therefore *failed to assess what preconditions* Bismarck would have to have satisfied before he could begin to reach actively for that objective. Not identifying or knowing these requirements, they permitted them to materialize in 1870.

The other major blunder was an expectation, held in many though not all parts of the French government, that Austria-Hungary would enter the war promptly as an ally. (And incidentally that Italy would also, although this was much less significant since Italy's probable contribution would be minor.) The diplomatic conversations between Paris and Vienna that had gone on in preceding months and years had been interpreted by many French officials as having created a mutual understanding that amounted to an alliance. Antoine Gramont, the French foreign minister, told the cabinet early in July that immediately upon the outbreak of hostilities, Austria-Hungary would mobilize and put a large troop concentration on the German border, thereby tying down a major portion of the Prussian forces. Policy-makers in Vienna, however, had not intended to make a specific commitment; in writing at least they had not done so. "All that Napoleon had on paper was a letter from Victor Emmanuel (King of Italy) and another from Francis Joseph (Emperor of Austria-Hungary) approving the idea of common action at some future date. He showed these letters in July 1870 to the Council at Paris that had war and peace in its hands and they profoundly influenced the decision."[22]

There was some confusion in French expectations about this matter, the result of inadequate coordination between the foreign ministry and the army. The most recent military mission to Vienna had returned in the late spring believing that Austria-Hungary would mobilize and concentrate troops on the border only after France invaded South Germany. This was closer, at least, to the truth. Policy-makers in Vienna (and Florence) did intend to intervene in the war in the wake of significant French victories, when the overall outcome would be reasonably certain. Although they expected France to win, they intended to balance their intent to cash in on French power against their motive of caution. This strategy was not much appreciated in Paris. The mistake there, particularly among civilians, was in failing to appreciate the extent to which realization of the expected alliances depended upon prior French performance. When the war broke out, "Hapsburg policy waited upon events."[23] Pending major French victories in the field, Austria-Hungary declared neutrality on 20 July. Decision-makers in Paris were stunned.

The carelessness of the foreign ministry about the specific terms of its "alliances," and its more basic carelessness about Austro-Hungarian motivations and expectations, was abetted by the other political and military misapprehensions already mentioned. Whether Vienna joined immediately or only after French victories in the field did not seem such an important question when the French were also assuming that they were ahead of their opponent in the mobilization race, that they would be virtually invited into South German territory, and that they were militarily superior to Germany as a whole in any case. Conversely, it was easier to be casual in their own military estimates when for years they had been taking for granted that Austria-Hungary would join in a Franco-

Prussian war. In this manner the French analytic failures tended to interlock and mutually reinforce one another.

There was one more reason for the analytic asymmetry between the French and the Prussians. Policy-making in Paris had been handicapped for years by a plethora of objectives. Between 1866 and 1870 Napoleon shifted his focus back and forth among Mexico, Luxembourg, Belgium, Germany, Rome (protection of the papacy), and the Near East. Neither the foreign ministry nor the military were staffed, or otherwise equipped, to cope in detail with all the important possibilities inherent in such a multitude of interests, among which the highest policy-maker vacillated somewhat unpredictably. From a planning or analytic viewpoint, France in this period simply *did not possess a coherent foreign policy* that included a systematic and reasonably stable assessment of the risks facing, and opportunities open to, the state and the costs of meeting them. Such an assessment could hardly have failed to draw attention to the serious long-term danger to France posed by the possibility of a still greater German power arising, and the possibility that creating precisely this power might be Bismarck's goal.[24]

During the same four-year period, Prussian decision-makers were concentrating almost exclusively upon France. After the close of the 1866 war there was a general conviction in the foreign ministry and among the general staff in Berlin that a war with France was both inevitable and desirable. In Paris the civilians and military also expected and welcomed a war. But Bismarck, unlike Napoleon, oriented his foreign policy around this expectation and around meeting the preconditions for a desirable war; the Prussian army planned meticulously for such a conflict and for the principal contingencies that could arise during it. The thoroughness with which this was done is perhaps best illustrated by the fact that Von Moltke, chief of the Prussian general staff, himself walked the Franco-German border from one end to the other.[25] When a crisis arose that met Prussia's requirements, everything was ready, and Bismarck exploited it unhesitatingly.

The Outbreak of the War

When the war became certain, Bismarck dropped his previously passive pose and took a number of actions to *reinforce the initial war context.* Although he calculated that intervention by Great Britain was unlikely, he took steps to ensure it by trying to redou-

133

ble London's suspicions of French intentions. First he privately informed the English ambassador in Berlin that French diplomats had, some time previously, proposed that Prussia absorb South Germany in exchange for France absorbing Belgium. Then he instructed the Prussian ambassador in London to approach the British foreign ministry with the same information. Finally, on July 25th, he leaked to the London *Times* the text of a draft treaty to this effect allegedly proposed by the French foreign ministry. Although the British cabinet guessed that this might be another of Bismarck's famous maneuvers, it had the desired effect. London spent the next three weeks proposing to the belligerents a new treaty guaranteeing Belgian neutrality once again. The Prussians signed instantly, the French with hesitation—which did nothing to allay British suspicions.[26]

More serious to Prussia was the risk posed by possible actions of Austria-Hungary. When policy-makers in Vienna decided upon neutrality on July 20th, they also announced that they were taking measures to prepare for war, including a partial mobilization of their armed forces. By this decision they were securing for themselves, at considerable expense, the option of intervening in the conflict.

The Prussians had been compelled to run a real hazard by the requirements of their contingent treaties with the South Germans. For the southerners to believe that they were fighting a defensive war required that the general European belief in French military superiority be allowed to stand. Only then would a crisis activate the South Germans' fears and ensure their prompt execution of the contingency treaties. However, this belief would also increase Vienna's incentive to join France in the war.

Bismarck's solution to this dilemma was to add one more factor, Russia, into the equation. After France started to mobilize, Bismarck suggested to Russian diplomats in Berlin, and through the Prussian embassy in St. Petersburg to the Russian foreign ministry, the possibility of a complete German collapse in a two-front war against both France and Austria-Hungary. He raised the possibility of Vienna's troops "in Berlin and Posen," a prospect that could only be frightening to the Russians, who had long been trying to defend against Austrian penetration of their Polish satellite. In response, Bismarck received the czar's promise that, should Vienna declare war, he would concentrate 300,000 troops on the Austro-Hungarian border to immobilize the forces of the dual monarchy. Bismarck hastened to communicate this to Vienna, trying to deter any Austro-Hungarian escalation of the war.[27]

The decision in Vienna for an *armed* neutrality was one of the actions by an outside power during the Franco-Prussian War that significantly increased the danger of an uncontrolled escalation sequence, and that represented a shortfall in Bismarck's strategy of defining a "safe"—that is, a reasonably escalation-proof—initial war context. The Austrian decision greatly disturbed the Russians. Over the next weeks they made a concentrated effort to induce the Austro-Hungarians to demobilize and settle for an unarmed neutrality, an effort that included threats that Russia might commence its own war mobilization. This had not yet been begun by early September, partly because of the costs involved and partly from fear that the mobilized armies facing each other for an indefinite time would be too likely to strike some spark that could very easily escalate into a war between the two traditionally hostile eastern empires. Despite this risk, as the weeks passed, decision-makers in St. Petersburg were growing increasingly anxious about the Austro-Hungarian military preparations; if the war in the west had gone on longer and more indecisively, some form of Russian mobilization might well have begun.[28]

If this judgment is correct, the ability of the Prussian military machine to deliver prompt and overwhelming battlefield victories may have been an important factor in 1870, as it was in 1866. *No initial war context can be expected to be entirely escalation proof, or to last a long time.* It will be particularly short-lived if it is grounded upon fallacious expectations in foreign capitals about the probable military outcome (as it was in both 1866 and 1870), for events inevitably will explode the illusion. In any case an initial war context almost has to begin breaking down at some point. Hence the strategy of creating such contexts must necessarily be supplemented by an ability to exploit them rapidly and to move the situation to some entirely new stage. Sedan did just that in 1870, as Königgrätz had in 1866.

Two final aspects of the war's initial context should be mentioned briefly. As in 1866 there was a relative *absence of moderate military moves* open to outside powers. Particularly after Bismarck communicated to Vienna the threat of the Russian troop mobilization, Austrian decision-makers lacked options for intervening in the Franco-Prussian War without running serious risk of a Russian counterintervention. If both nations had taken military action, even relatively low-level action at first, it would have been extremely difficult to prevent the conflict from becoming a general European war.

Secondly, the Franco-Prussian War was tightly constrained geographically. Unlike 1866, this time the Prussians did not require an outside ally. From the time the French mobilized, the South German states placed their forces under a single unified (Prussian) command. Thus the numerous battle fronts that had existed in 1866 were not replicated in 1870. The French and Germans engaged each other only in a single, fairly small area defined by the Franco-German border and the French provinces to its west.[29]

The Effect of Sedan

Sedan, like Königgrätz, was one of those dramatic and decisive events that changes a war completely. Its effect on the escalation dimension of the conflict was quite different, however. Königgrätz had raised an acute danger of rapid French intervention, which was forestalled only by Bismarck's convincing King Wilhelm to bring the war to an immediate close, and by Napoleon's bumbling. Sedan, on the other hand, had the immediate and direct effect of *reducing* the danger of a major, uncontrolled escalation (although indirectly and subsequently it raised it again).

Both London and St. Petersburg welcomed the news of Sedan, London because it meant a reduction in French power for some time to come and St. Petersburg because it made Austrian adventurism far less likely. Also after Sedan, the possibility of an Italian involvement was utterly out of the question; indeed, the Italians took advantage of the situation to seize Rome, which French power previously had been holding for the pope.

The most important direct effect of Sedan, however, was in Vienna. As the Prussian army had started to win battles during August, the likelihood of Emperor Franz Joseph's actually employing his mobilized forces dropped precipitously, and on the 22nd he defined his new objective as "averting from us" the consequences of the mounting Prussian victory.[30] After the news of Sedan came in, he decided to demobilize the army. On October 1st he said to the Prussian ambassador, "You cannot expect me to be pleased about the thing itself . . . [but] I shall not interfere at all; I shall let anything happen."[31] Policy-makers of the dual monarchy adopted a new goal—wooing Berlin's friendship—which was to become the hallmark of Austro-Hungarian foreign policy for over four decades. After the victory of 1866, Bismarck had made a great effort to mitigate Vienna's hostility and had held open the door to Austro-German friendship. The demonstration of Prussian power in the summer of 1870, culminating at Sedan, activated Vienna's interest in such a friendship and Bismarck's farsighted policy paid off handsomely.

At the outbreak of the war the British had tried to promote an understanding among all the uninvolved great powers that they would remain neutral, and in the weeks after Sedan they aired the idea of a multilateral mediation of the war. But the Austro-Hungarians had resisted neutrality in hopes they might be fighting the Prussians, and now rejected mediation in hopes they might be their friends. The Russians also were not responsive, but were more interested in deriving advantages for themselves from Prussia's victories. The British, who dared not press the mediation idea without the backing of other great powers, subsided into gentle encouragements to the belligerents to negotiate.[32]

One immediate effect of the victory at Sedan, therefore, was to reduce the probability of an uncontrolled escalation of the conflict into a much larger war. Another was to compel the German decision-makers to face the question of whether to terminate the conflict immediately or to prolong it—and if the latter, what demands to make of the French. Up to this point the principal war aim had been, ostensibly at least, to repel and defeat the French attackers. The decisive victory of Sedan accomplished this objective thoroughly and left the problem, "What now?"

One of the general paradoxes embedded in the escalation problem is that as the perceived hazard of uncontrolled escalation declines, belligerents feel more free to take some deliberate escalatory step. It was so in this case. The evident low risk of triggering an unwanted major escalation sequence, even by making relatively drastic moves, was one of the crucial conditions that allowed the Germans to decide to postpone terminating the war, and to raise their sights to new vistas. Let us turn now to this important elevation of objectives, which was to lead to several escalations and a much longer war.

The exact mix of motives that led the Prussians to demand Alsace-Lorraine has been a subject of endless dispute among historians and will probably never be known precisely.[33] The attitude among the ranking military officers at headquarters was similar to what it had been in the summer of 1866 after Königgrätz. They enthusiastically advocated significant territorial gains as the appropriate reward for a stunning victory, and as compensation for the price Germany had paid in casualties and other costs—all the more so since, as far as they were concerned, they had not begun the war. These attitudes were sanctioned by centuries of tradition. Alsace and Lorraine were the obvious choice because until the time of Louis XIV they had been part of the German confederation known as the Holy Roman Empire. More than this, there was a strong strategic argument. The two provinces formed a rough triangle with the apex pointed at Germany; in French hands they provided an advantageous position from which to launch attacks. They also contained the major fortresses of Metz and Strasbourg, which by themselves were worth, in Von Moltke's judgment, two army corps.

Bismarck almost certainly was influenced heavily by the strategic argument. Reading the history of the past couple of hundred years as one of constant French aggression (he proclaimed that Germany had been attacked "twelve or fifteen times" by France in two centuries[34]), he was determined to win the security for Germany he believed the provinces and their fortresses would provide. He had two other important motives, more subtle and more complicated.

The one that Bismarck later announced himself was that seizing Alsace-Lorraine would ensure the unity of the new German Empire and its military, Prussian character by preserving French hostility and an active French military threat indefinitely. As one prominent Bismarck scholar puts it, "A France so bled and mutilated would be an irreconcilable enemy [and] would be an incontrovertible argument for the continuance of the Empire in arms. What Germany had taken by force she could only keep henceforward by force . . . The perpetual danger would prevent Prussia from 'falling asleep' as she did after 1786 'on the laurels of victory'."[35]

This was a long-range motive for annexing Alsace-Lorraine, and there seems little doubt that Bismarck did actively seek the new objective partly for this reason. He had another, much more immediate reason, which may have been equally or even more compelling and which is more significant for us here. Elevating his objective in this way now seemed necessary in order *to protect his chances to achieve fully his central objective* in the war: the creation from the various German states of the new German Empire, a Second Reich, modeled on and led by Prussia. For the new circumstances created by Sedan presented a certain challenge to that objective, a challenge that merits discussion in a little detail.

In order to create a strong Reich, Bismarck needed the voluntary agreement, and preferably enthusiasm, of most of the ranking officials and the bulk of the public in all the German states, south as well as north. The recovery of Alsace-Lorraine was an old dream of many Germans, a deeply latent objective activated by the victory at Sedan and shared by the leaders and much of the public in the South German states. So Bismarck embraced this objective for the political support and unity it offered.

Furthermore, his plan all along had been that the new empire must be born, not sometime after the conclusion of the peace, but in the very fires of war. This was necessary if Prussia, chiefly responsible for the victory, was to be sure of gaining a dominant position in the empire, and also to give the new imperial government the military tone that Bismarck wanted. Midwifery of the Reich by war increased the influence of the generals and hence the importance that they be satisfied in their military ambition for Alsace-Lorraine.

Furthermore, during the war Bismarck himself had relatively little authority, for the king took control of decisions in wartime. Bismarck therefore had to rely heavily on his somewhat shaky personal influence with the king—who was greatly swayed by his generals, who himself acted and thought in wartime mostly as a military officer, and who personally shared in the military desire for Alsace-Lorraine. Finally, after the surprise of Sedan and after only six weeks of war, Bismarck probably was not yet fully ready to set in motion the process of creating the new Reich. The South Germans were only beginning to take seriously the prospect of union with North Germany, and Bismarck needed the conflict to continue so that he would not lose the advantages of bringing the empire to birth in the midst of the stresses of war.

It is primarily for this package of reasons that the relation between the victory at Sedan and the prompt German elevation of objectives thereafter becomes highly interesting for the analyst of escalation control. The relationship is *not* the simple one of the Germans finding themselves victorious and in an unexpectedly strong position, both military and international, and inevitably deciding to "go for more." Rather it seems to be, on the part of the main architect of the war at least, an unusual and provocative example of elevating subsequent objectives in order to protect the original objective.

Normally one expects to see this behavior on the part of a nation that is *losing* a war. It is commonplace for a belligerent, finding its original goals in jeopardy, to raise the ante in some fashion. What is so remarkable about Sedan is that the fact that the belligerent was *winning* apparently led to the conclusion that the objectives must be elevated to protect the original objective.

What made this situation possible is the orientation of Bismarck's original objective toward domestic politics, not foreign policy: toward accomplishing the unification of Germany in a particular manner, not toward increasing German territory, resources, or influence. In short, the war was intended to be instrumental in accomplishing an ulterior purpose. From Bismarck's viewpoint, any and all direct results of fighting the enemy could only be tangential and secondary. A change, even a rather major one, in the direct military outcome, and a prolongation, even an indefinite one, of the life of the instrument, would have to be accepted if they appeared necessary to preserve prospects for the ultimate goal.

The immediate occasion that brought this somewhat unusual logic to life, though, was the generals' insistence upon Alsace-Lorraine. In this sense, the elevation of German objectives after Sedan involved *an interaction between military and civilian motives.* The military demand prceded the civilian motive, and activated it, by implicitly challenging one of Bismarck's critical preconditions for achieving his main goal—that of an active and manifest unity among the major German actors, north and south, civil and military. To a degree, this interactive effect operated by way of bureaucratic politics at German headquarters: Bismarck's need not to lose influence over King Wilhelm and the progress of events generally. To a greater degree, it operated by way of domestic politics: Bismarck's need to protect the unity of the various German governments involved, both among officials at field headquarters and in capitals at home, as well as the more general unity of purpose of the various German populations.

This precondition for establishing the Second Reich was not being challenged as long as the outcome of the war was uncertain, and it might not have been seriously challenged by a moderate victory, particularly if it had arrived somewhat later. In that event, it would have been clear to all that the Germans could impose only mild terms. It was the combination of facts that Sedan was unexpected, overwhelming, and came early in the war, that generated a situation where this interaction could take place.

It may be objected that this analysis, emphasizing as it does Bismarck's own perceptions and motives, does not apply to King Wilhelm and the military, who did simply decide to go for more. However, prior to Sedan the king and many of the generals did not *have* a clear, positive goal. This leads us to another important observation about escalation control in the Franco-Prussian War.

Originally, the only distinct objective of the king and most of the military was the negative one of defending Germany against the attacking French army, and defeating it. It is true that Von Moltke, chief of the general staff, and Von Roon, the minister of war, shared Bismarck's ulterior purpose of founding a Second Reich and had been present when Bismarck altered the Ems telegram. And it was clear enough to the king, and no doubt to others privy to the original telegram, that the chancellor had deliberately "waved a red flag in front of the Gallic bull," to use Bismarck's own phrase for it. In the following weeks this knowledge undoubtedly seeped outward through Prussian military and other governmental circles. Nevertheless, the altered version of the telegram did not actually publish any untruths. The Hohenzollern candidacy in Spain, furthermore, had been withdrawn at the request of the French ambassador. In short, there was nothing that compelled the French to go to war in self-defense.

The salient facts, in the next days and weeks, from the viewpoint of King Wilhelm, of the Prussian military, and indeed of officials throughout all Germany, were that France *had* been the first to mobilize, *had* been the first to declare war, and now was proceeding as rapidly as it possibly could to begin an all-out invasion of the German homeland. Few military officers or civilian officials gave any real thought to what positive objectives Germany might pursue in case of an eventual major victory, because they were too involved with the immediate problem of defense against the invader.

They left possible objectives after victory to Bismarck and, chiefly, to the very hypothetical future. Hence when the generals began demanding Alsace-Lorraine after Sedan, this did not represent going for more—an elevation of positive objectives—as much as a *first* positive objective.

The analytic importance of this is that it underscores, in a very emphatic way, the significance of Bismarck's having provoked the French into initiating the war. Any Franco-Prussian War initiated by Prussia would have immediately raised in the minds not just of all Prussians but of all Germans the question, "What is Prussia fighting for?" (If the answer had seemed to be a Prussian-ruled German Empire, then, as the French hoped, Prussia *would* have been perceived by the South Germans as being an aggressor against them.) In any case, the question of objectives would have become the vital subject of the hour. One of Bismarck's major achievements—analytically a stunning one—in provoking the French to initiate the war was to *submerge that question*. It became "self-evident" to all that the primary objective was self-defense.

With this achievement Bismarck succeeded in pushing well into the future the day when the problem of positive objectives would come to the fore. He could reasonably expect that when that day arrived, circumstances would be in existence that would make it relatively easy to transmute the emotions of military triumph into the foundations of the new Reich. Bismarck's entire strategy depended upon France's initiating the war, and hence upon his ability to act as provocateur.

Terminating the War

The consequences of the German decision to elevate their objectives include the escalations discussed earlier: the seige of Paris, the insurgency and courterinsurgency campaigns, and the more general change in the character of the war. Another major consequence was to prolong substantially a conflict that otherwise could have been a second Prussian Seven Week War. Neither the Germans nor the French at this point could know how much longer the war would last. Paris might surrender soon or in months. A fresh French army from the west or the south might raise the siege. Conceivably the French might fight on even after the fall of Paris. It was primarily the *prolongation of the war*, and not the effect of any of the specific escalations, that provided an opportunity for complications involving outside powers.

The main French hope, indeed, was to buy time—partly to try to train, to equip, and to deploy new armies in the west and the south, but mainly to try to secure some form of intervention by the other great powers. A major diplomatic campaign to this end was launched at the end of September. M. Thiers, an influential Frenchman who had opposed the rise of Napoloen III and the war with Prussia and who was highly respected abroad, was sent on a tour of the major European capitals in an effort to drum up support.[36]

The involvement of outside powers represented a more plausible hope for France than the raising of new military capabilities. Indeed, the latter was justified primarily as a means of prolonging the war so that diplomacy could succeed. Unlike Napoleon, who had held expansionist aims himself, the Government of National Defense could point to its strictly defensive purposes in contrast to Bismarck's intended upheaval in the balance of power, and thereby appeal to the interest of other powers in stability and conservation of the status quo in Europe. Outside involvement might come in two ways. A fresh military ally might appear, or the older intended ally, Austria-Hungary, might be stirred to action. More likely would be a mediation by most or all of the neutral powers acting in concert, which at least could be expected to end the war on less unfavorable terms involving no significant transfer of territory.

In this campaign all other traditional French diplomatic objectives were sacrificed. For instance, where France had been a regular opponent of Russian ambitions in the Near East, Thiers offered the czar carte blanche on that question in return for assistance in the West. But the czar was already preparing a move in the Near East that France could neither aid nor hinder.

The story was similar elsewhere. After Sedan, with almost no army and with its capital under siege, France lacked the power position to manipulate other nations' interests. The French were quite incapable of assisting any other power attain a goal and hence could not offer to do so in return for assistance against Germany. They were also incapable of preventing any other power from attaining a goal and hence could not offer to refrain from doing so in return for aid. The French possessed no *quos* that could purchase the *quids*. And their diplomats found that the regrets and misgivings abroad about Prussia's large territorial demands were sincere, but that no policy-maker would risk his own nation's interests to frustrate these demands.

Bismarck had anticipated this. He was able to embrace the elevated Prussian objective because he recognized that the preponderant German military position in Europe, created by Sedan, would make unlikely any intervention by outside powers. Nevertheless, as the war dragged on he became increasingly worried. He wrote that "the delay in the decision caused me . . . serious disquietude . . . from my anxiety respecting the intervention of neutrals." Bismarck took every conceivable step to reduce foreign sympathy for France. He complained to foreign diplomats about deliveries of arms to France, and he spread reports of the French firing on men sent to negotiate under a white flag and other violations of international law. So sensitive was he to the hazard of some kind of involvement by outside powers that he even did what he could to alienate the United States government from the French cause.[37]

In the end the only significant danger to the chancellor's effort to quarantine his war was posed by the Russians—ironically by mismanaging (from Bismarck's viewpoint) a line of action that he himself had originally inspired them to take up. One of the results of the Crimean War, fifteen years earlier, had been that Russia was forbidden by treaty to build naval vessels on the Black Sea, a restriction imposed mainly by Britain and one that had rankled ever since. At the very outset of the Franco-Prussian War, Bismarck had begun secret diplomacy aimed at arousing St. Petersburg's interest in getting the restriction removed and indicating the possibility of Prussian assistance in doing so in exchange for friendly noninvolvement during the current war.[38] About six weeks after the battle of Sedan the Russians upset Bismarck's plan by unilaterally announcing their intention to abrogate these Black Sea Clauses. The chancellor was furious at the timing, for he feared a violent reaction in England. The Russians simply were making sure, while they still had leverage, that Bismarck would fulfill his end of the bargain. After the war there was no assurance that he might not find it more convenient to remain neutral on the subject.

Public reaction in England was indeed fierce. Most of the newspapers called for immediate war against Russia if the czar carried out his threat. The British ambassador at Prussian headquarters assured Bismarck that the cabinet certainly would go to war in that event, and for a while it seemed that the crisis might ignite the wider war that so far had been avoided. (Here is an example of a device, originally undertaken by Bismarck to try to control escalation, that went astray and threatened to generate escalation.)

Fortunately for Prussia the situation was resolvable. The British government in 1870 was much less interested in the question of Russian ships on the Black Sea than it was in protecting the principle of "no unilateral abrogation of treaties," while the Russians were mainly interested in establishing their right to have ships on the Black Sea and were willing to be cooperative in finding other ways to accomplish it. Bismarck proposed an international conference, which was held in London in January 1871. The British and Russians, eager for the conference to succeed, quietly promised in advance that each would accede to the other's main desire in exchange for the same in return; and they promised Bismarck to limit the conference to these subjects. Despite frantic efforts by French diplomats and despite the fact that Paris was on the edge of starvation, the war going on across the channel was excluded from consideration. With that, French hopes died and the Government of National Defense asked for an armistice.

Actually, the problem of the Black Sea Clauses had turned out to be advantageous to the Prussians. With the Austro-Hungarians now friendly, the only great powers that might have moved toward mediation or some other involvement as the war dragged on were Britain and Russia. The issue of the clauses divided them and kept them distracted, while the Germans tightened the noose around Paris. At the same time, the British-Russian conflict was kept from flaring into fighting, which could hardly have remained separate from the war in France.

Analytic Summary

Like its predecessor in 1866, the Franco-Prussian War did not escalate into a general European war because, in the first instance, the Prussians designed an initial war context specifically aimed at preventing this. The events triggering the war, though, did not represent a "controlled crisis," as in the earlier case, so much as an "exploited crisis." Until the outbreak, Bismarck's policy, carefully planned to take advantage of a certain kind of crisis, required little overt action and in that sense was more subtle. Active measures to reinforce desired behavior by others followed the outbreak. As in the earlier case, the essential precondition making possible this design of a war context was an analytic asymmetry between the Prussians and their intended opponents.

In contrast to Königgrätz, Sedan reduced the danger of immediate intervention by others, but precisely for that reason allowed the

Germans to demand Alsace-Lorraine and accept the longer war entailed by that ultimatum. Until Sedan, German intentions had seemed defensive (to most Germans as well as to outsiders) and the possibility of offensive goals had remained submerged, thanks to Bismarck's stunning success as provocateur. Now Bismarck accepted the objective of Alsace and Lorraine because he shared his generals' estimate of their strategic value and because he wanted to maintain permanent French enmity—and also because he wanted to protect his own primary objective of firing a Second Reich in the kiln of war.

This is unusual logic for a wartime decision to raise the ante. Since for Bismarck the entire war was an instrument that served an ulterior aim, not only defeats but also an unexpected great victory could threaten his real purpose. He needed to espouse the new goal of Alsace-Lorraine to gain time for his domestic political preparations, to protect his enormous influence at headquarters, and, mainly, to preserve and enhance the developing unity and enthusiasm of the German publics, officials, and princes, south as well as north. A latent objective of generations of Germans had been activated when the French army had been crushed.

The demand for Alsace-Lorraine led to several major escalations: the German siege of Paris, the rise of a French insurgency in the German rear and a ruthless German counterinsurgency operation, and a change in the character of the war in which unoccupied France became a nation in arms. None of these, however, posed as much danger of a more comprehensive war as did the simple prolongation of the fighting. The danger was reduced by an absence of moderate military options for potential intervening powers; by sharp constraints (compared to 1866) on the territory embraced by the fighting and on the number of independent capitals at war; and by a tangential diplomatic conflict that sprang up, which divided and distracted two of the three other great European powers.

7

The Crimean War

The first three case studies have examined wars that did *not* escalate uncontrollably despite widespread and well-grounded fears that they might. The remaining two studies will examine wars that *did* escalate, in ways that can reasonably be termed uncontrolled, despite the fact that these escalation sequences were by no means inevitable, as the analyses will attempt to show. The first of these studies will concern the major escalation sequence of the Crimean War.

Historical Overview

From the late 1600s, "for nearly two centuries there had been a war between Russia and Turkey about every twenty years. In October 1853 the ninth of this series began."[1] This time it developed differently. Rather than remaining an isolated and minor conflict on the fringes of the Continent as every previous Russo-Turkish War had, it grew into a war of European proportions and significance. In the last and greatest phase of the war, the Russians found themselves fighting, in the Russian Crimea, the forces not only of Turkey but also of Britain, France, and the kingdom of Piedmont and Sardinia (the nucleus of modern Italy), with Austria and possibly Sweden preparing also to join the Western allies. The war that had begun as another routine Russo-Turkish conflict had somehow grown to become almost a general European war.

The years between the onset of the prewar crisis in 1852 and the conclusion of the conflict in 1856 were a period of intense diplomatic and military activity. An unusually large number of active participants changed their policies repeatedly, and at times they pursued multiple policies simultaneously. The result was an intricate maze in which "the strangest cross-currents confused relatively simple issues."[2] The politico-military events surrounding the Crimean War are the most complicated of any one period in the nineteenth century.[3] A certain amount of the complexity must necessarily be embraced in this case study.

Nevertheless, the underlying cause of the long series of Russo-Turkish conflicts was basically straightforward. The Ottoman Empire, which once had threatened to overrun all Europe, had been undergoing slow decay and a gradual diminution of power since the seventeenth century. The czarist Russian Empire to the north had been enjoying an equally gradual growth in power, and had had the ambition, reaching back almost a millenium, of unconditionally free access to the Mediterranean Sea. Accordingly, Russian power had thrust southward and a series of minor wars with Turkey had ensued, most of which resulted in modest Russian advances. By the 1850s, another was due if the traditional schedule was to be maintained.

The immediate issue, however, in the crisis of 1852 was a competition between Russia and France for influence over the Sublime Porte, as the Ottoman government in Constantinople called itself. The patriarchs of the Orthodox Church, under the protection of the czar, had long controlled the keys to the Holy Places in Palestine—sites such as the church at Bethlehem, considered sacred to Christianity but lying deep within the Ottoman Empire. In 1850 Louis Napoleon had begun a diplomatic effort aimed at bringing these Holy Places under Roman Catholic control. After assuming the imperial crown and becoming Napoleon III, he needed to consolidate his domestic position by winning the active support of French clerics and by demonstrating to audiences at home and abroad that he was a vigorous leader in the Bonapartist tradition. Determined to press the Holy Places issue as a way of accomplishing both objectives simultaneously, he soon obtained partial concessions from the Porte. Nonetheless he sent an impressive new battleship through the Dardanelles and threatened to bombard Tripoli, an Ottoman possession, to back up his insistence on obtaining his full demands. Slowly the Turks gave in—and this was taken as a serious challenge in St. Petersburg, where the czar felt he could not allow the Orthodox patriarchs to be deprived of their traditional rights.

Russian policy-makers had operated for decades on the assumption that Turkey could serve as a buffer state to protect the security of the Black Sea, but they considered that the essential prerequisite was that the Ottomans should be more afraid of Russia than of any other power. Now the Turks were demonstrating that they feared France more. In February 1853, Czar Nicholas I mobilized two army corps on the southern frontier and sent Prince Menshikov to the Porte as a plenipotentiary extraordinary with a series of demands that would extend the czar's influence within the Ottoman Empire.

These vigorous moves were intended primarily to restore the Russian conception of the status quo ante, but they upset the cabinet in London. The English felt that the balance of power in the eastern Mediterranean (conceived to be an essential British interest) was being affected. As the new ambassador to the Porte, the cabinet appointed Stratford Canning, an enormously able man who in an earlier assignment in Constantinople had proved he was a man of initiative, and one who entertained ardent anti-Russian feelings. Meanwhile Menshikov began his mission by demanding that the sultan dismiss his present foreign minister and appoint one who was more of a Russophile; this plus the Russian military preparations led Napoleon to order the French Mediterranean fleet to Salamis in Greece. The Turks, emboldened by these visible signs of support from the Western great powers, refused the more far-reaching of Menshikov's demands and claimed, with Canning's encouragement, that to grant them would turn Turkey into a Russian satellite. The prince departed Constantinople, breaking off relations as he left.

Anticipating that a Russian military stroke was now likely, and unable to obtain assurances from St. Petersburg that Menshikov's demands were really intended to be more limited than the Turks claimed, the cabinet in London turned to stronger measures. Earlier it had refused to send the Royal Navy to the area on the grounds that that would be provocative. Now the cabinet ordered a fleet to Besika Bay, just outside the Dardanelles. At once the French advanced their own fleet to join the British one.

The Russians felt that they had to execute the military threat that had backed Prince Menshikov. In July troops occupied the almost undefended Ottoman principalities of Moldavia and Wallachia (much of what is now Rumania), and it was announced in St. Petersburg that they would remain until the Menshikov demands had been met. There was no significant fighting in the principalities,

Map 4 The Near East in 1854.

and the Porte held off counterattacking with major army units until it could learn the Western reaction. A period of about three months of "phony war" ensued while Britain, France, Austria, and Prussia sent representatives to a conference in Vienna to try to find a peaceful solution. The resulting Vienna note, the sultan declared, did not adequately protect Ottoman sovereignty. After the British and French advanced their fleets through the Dardanelles to Constantinople, and after there had been riots in the city demanding action, the Porte struck at the Russians in October. The ninth Russo-Turkish War got under way in earnest.

In the two principalities the Turks made a surprisingly effective counterattack and, far to the east, they opened a second front in the Caucasus. But in November a Turkish squadron was utterly annihilated by a Russian fleet while anchored at Sinope, a Turkish

Black Sea port. The "Sinope massacre," as it was promptly dubbed in the West, generated extreme public reaction in Britain and in France. The whole of the British press called for war, and in December a cabinet reshuffle brought prowar ministers to the fore. Napoleon declared that the joint Franco-British fleet must sail into the Black Sea. After brief reluctance in London, this was done—in January 1854. Shortly thereafter the czar withdrew his ambassadors from Paris and London. The British and French signed an alliance with the Ottoman Empire, delivered an ultimatum to Russia that demanded a troop withdrawal from the principalities, and when this went unanswered, declared war and began to prepare expeditionary forces for a campaign in the Balkans.

Now there was another phony war period, through the late spring and early summer of 1854, while these preparations went forward. The Western powers made intense diplomatic efforts to bring Austria into the conflict as an ally, and policy-makers in Vienna finally agreed to join in demanding the withdrawal of Russian forces from the principalities. Moldavia and Wallachia bordered on the Austrian Empire, and the Russian forces there had, in fact, been hindering vital Austrian commerce on the Danube. They were also giving signs of intending a long, perhaps permanent, stay —by installing Russian tax collectors, for instance. Decision-makers in St. Petersburg, who recognized that Russia was far more vulnerable to an Austrian attack than to an Anglo-French one, complied with the Austrian demand and withdrew their troops from the principalities over the summer.

The military status quo ante had now returned, and the Western allies were left with no obvious reason to fight. Nonetheless, public opinion in France and Britain demanded a military "victory." For this reason and others it was decided to assault Sebastopol, in the Crimea, the principal Russian naval base on the Black Sea and an important Russian city. So, almost a year after the outbreak of the Russo-Turkish War, the conflict entered a new and greatly enlarged phase, as the Crimean War proper began in September 1854.

On all sides the Crimean segment of the war was badly mismanaged: in strategy, tactics, logistics, and medical and other support services. Typical of a long series of blunders were the British cavalry deployments at the Battle of Balaklava in October. The charge of the heavy brigade was a useful tactic; that of the light brigade, against guns it could not see, was an entirely avoidable catastrophe, in which 500 of the brigade's 700 horsemen were killed or seriously wounded in a few minutes. Throughout the war, casualties were unnecessarily high on both sides, and ever more men were lost to disease.[4]

Largely because of the endemic mismanagement, no military decision could be reached quickly. The combined Anglo-French force repeatedly failed to take Sebastopol, yet the Russians were unable to eject the invaders from the Crimean peninsula. Finally after a year of fighting the Russians were obliged to evacuate the city in September 1855, although the allied force was too weakened to pursue the retreating troops. Still the Russians refused to negotiate. The war threatened to drag on, and Paris and London cast about for more allies. The kingdom of Piedmont and Sardinia had already committed fifteen thousand men. Despite Western efforts, the Prussians persisted in their neutrality: a policy that was to yield dividends in the form of friendly Russian noninterference in the events of 1866 and 1870. Sweden, on the other hand, had concluded a defensive alliance with Britain and France, and the Western powers began a diplomatic effort to extend this to an offensive alliance that would mount a tripartite attack on Russia in the Baltic. As a preliminary, an Anglo-French naval squadron bombarded Riga, a Russian Baltic city.

The most crucial negotiation, though, was with Austria. When the Russians had agreed the previous summer to withdraw from the principalities under Austrian pressure, Vienna had reached an understanding with the Porte that Austrian, not Turkish, troops would occupy them for the duration, a plan that would automatically involve Austria in the war should the Russians reinvade. That autumn the full Austrian army had been mobilized; later it was partially demobilized again. While the war continued, Vienna became the object of intricate diplomacy, as the Western powers sought to gain her active military alliance and Russia sought her fully demobilized neutrality. Discussions with London and Paris yielded a declaration of "Four Points" as war aims, but the interpretation of these became the subject of endless dispute between Austria and the Western powers, and ultimately between France and Britain as well. Yet in 1855 the foreign minister in Vienna judged that Austria, while not actually a belligerent, had committed so many acts hostile to Russian interests that no postwar Austro-

Russian friendship would be possible. Viennese policy drifted toward congruence with the Western position, and finally in December 1855 Emperor Franz Joseph sent the czar an ultimatum: Russia must accept the Four Points or face Austrian military intervention.

The Russians had lost Sebastopol and were now contemplating an enemy alliance made up of most of Europe except Prussia, and attacks on many fronts. The war was also causing mounting internal problems. Even so, the conflict might have gone on much longer if Czar Nicholas had not died in 1855 and been succeeded by the less unbending Alexander II. The Austrian terms were accepted in January 1856. A congress opened in Paris in February to arrive at a peace treaty, but each of the belligerents had its own goals and its own interpretation of the ambiguous Four Points. Russian diplomats were able to exploit the differences among the allies, and in the final treaty signed in March obtained lighter terms than the British, in particular, desired.[5]

The Escalation Dimension of the Conflict

As the above summary suggests, the Crimean War is a rich case for the student of escalation and its control. In addition to the sequence of events by which the Western great powers became embroiled in fighting in the Crimea, the war includes various minor, and at least three other major, escalations: Austria's accession to the Western cause after a lengthy and vacillating effort by policy-makers in Vienna to find a satisfactory role in the conflict; Piedmont-Sardinia's joining the Western camp; and the effort to expand the conflict to the Baltic area, perhaps with Swedish participation. A full treatment of all these features would make for an unwieldy and overlong study; and most of the details of the Austrian, Italian, and Swedish developments largely reflect features of nineteenth-century diplomacy that have little relevance to contemporary escalation control. These aspects of the war therefore will be excluded here.

By contrast, the process by which the great powers became embroiled in a major war is unusually relevant to contemporary escalation control. After the Russian occupation of the principalities, and even after open warfare had begun in the fall of 1853, decision-makers in *none* of the great powers wanted the conflict to escalate into a major war. Even in early 1854 many of them believed the fighting could be limited to the ongoing Russo-Turkish war. Although simultaneously concerned with securing other perceived national interests, policy-makers believed they were acting appropriately to control escalation and to forestall a great-power war. Furthermore, each single step by each nation was entirely under its control, both in the sense that the steps were deliberated upon by policy-makers and in the sense that diplomatic and military institutions implemented the measures policy-makers had decided upon and no others.

Yet the net result of these steps was a long *cyclical-sequence escalation*. The cycle of action by one side and reaction by the other gradually went out of control in the very real sense that it thrust three great powers into just the wider war they had been trying to avoid. Afterward, governments and publics alike wondered what had gone wrong.

The events of the 1850s, indeed, bear a certain haunting familiarity for contemporary Americans. Then, as very recently, a large force of Western troops got bogged down in a seemingly endless war on the edge of Asia. Victory proved strangely elusive for reasons difficult to pin down. In the end, the costs of the war were vastly higher than anyone in the West had guessed beforehand— and vastly higher than could be justified by the original, by then half-forgotten, issues at stake. And no one was very clear just how they had gotten enmeshed in the war.

This classic example of an escalation sequence that got out of control will now be analyzed in moderate detail. Table 4 on pages 156-157 summarizes the major events in the sequence.

The Holy Places Crisis

Napoleon's initiative in 1852 of pressing his demands concerning the Christian Holy Places in Palestine probably would have set off merely one more diplomatic crisis like many others of this period, had it not been that pressure directly on the Ottoman Empire at this time—from almost any source—automatically *activated many latent conflicts* already imbedded in Turkey's international position. This dimension of the situation was vastly underestimated in Paris. At least three separate and important latent conflicts were activated by Napoleon's somewhat hasty policy decision.

In the first place, the "Eastern Question" had been a bone of contention for decades between Russia and Great Britain. In particular, the Treaty of Unkiar Skelessi, signed between Russia and Turkey in

1833 after one of the earlier wars, had seemed to policy-makers in London to permit an extension of Russian naval power into the Mediterranean, and the British Mediterranean fleet had been strengthened in response. The subsequent Straits Convention of 1841 had smoothed relations considerably, but British suspicions were aroused again by various events toward the end of the decade that seemed to indicate a renewed Russian desire for expansionist initiatives in the south. Officials in London recognized that St. Petersburg had an undeniable interest in maintaining a real if informal influence in Turkey, but they were determined to prevent this influence from reaching the level of hegemony and thereby potentially threatening Britain's naval supremacy in the Mediterranean.[6]

The balance between Russian influence and British resistance was a delicate one, and the French upset this balance. They did so by injecting themselves into the Near Eastern situation in pursuit of objectives not previously considered legitimate French interests, employing fast-paced and belligerent tactics, and scoring a highly visible success. In coping with the French challenge, the Russians took actions that were to activate British suspicions. Subsequently the British would find themselves gravitating toward France in search of an ally, and both would assume a gradually more hostile posture toward the Russians as the latter continued to try to regain their pre-1852 influence with the Porte.

The other two latent conflicts that the French initiative activated concerned Russia's bilateral relation to the Ottoman Empire. Two partially competing themes or goals had long been ambivalently traded off against each other by policy-makers in St. Petersburg. One could be tagged "Russia versus Turkey"; the other, "Russia and Turkey versus outside great powers."[7]

On the one hand, there was the long-standing conflict already alluded to between the gradually declining Ottoman and gradually rising Russian empires; this conflict included Russia's ancient desire for free access to the Mediterranean. Added to this was a perception, held generally in many European capitals and especially strongly in St. Petersburg, that the Ottoman Empire was the "sick man of Europe" and might be on the verge of collapse and some form of fragmentation into its component parts. Should that dramatic event occur, St. Petersburg could hope for the best opportunity in many centuries to realize the traditional Russian dream.

At the same time, that event might also pose unprecedented

155

Table 4 Major events in the initial escalation sequence of the Crimean War.

Approximate date	Event
1852: February	Earlier low-key French diplomatic efforts to secure Roman Catholic control of the Holy Places are stepped up to a full campaign; the Porte makes some concessions.
April	The French ambassador returns to Constantinople on the battleship *Charlemagne* with additional demands concerning the Holy Places.
July	Napoleon sends a naval squadron to Tripoli and threatens to bombard the city unless his demands are met.
Late in the year	The Porte gradually complies with the French demands.
1853: January	Austria successfully demands that a Turkish involvement in Montenegro be brought to an end, under threat of Austrian military intervention.
Late February	Russia sends Prince Menshikov to the Porte with demands for Russian protection of the Christians residing within the Ottoman Empire, as well as return of the Holy Places to Greek Orthodox control. Simultaneously two Russian corps are mobilized near the frontier.
Late March	Napoleon sends the French Mediterranean fleet to Salamis in Greece.
April	Stratford Canning, reappointed English ambassador to the Porte, arrives in Constantinople.
Early May	The Porte agrees to restore the Holy Places to the Orthodox but, partly on the advice of Canning, refuses Menshikov's wider demands.
21 May	Menshikov departs. Russia breaks diplomatic relations with Turkey.
Mid-June	British and French naval squadrons arrive in Besika Bay.
Early July	Russian troops cross the border and seize the Ottoman principalities of Moldavia and Wallachia.

1 August	The Vienna Note of Britain, France, Austria, and Prussia proposes a basis for negotiated settlement of the crisis.
Mid-August	The Vienna Note is accepted by Russia but rejected by the Porte.
Mid-September	Policy-makers in Paris and London authorize the naval squadrons to pass through the Dardanelles and sail to Constantinople at the discretion of local commanders, in violation of an international treaty.
4 October	The Sultan declares war on Russia, but takes no immediate military action.
8 October	Paris and London order their squadrons to Constantinople immediately.
23 October	Turkish troops enter the two principalities and open hostilities against the Russians.
End of October	The Ottomans cross the border and attack the Russians in the Caucasus.
30 November	The Russian Black Sea fleet intercepts and completely destroys a Turkish naval squadron in the harbor at Sinope.
1854: 3 January	The French and British fleets enter the Black Sea and protect Turkish vessels.
February	The Russian ambassadors are withdrawn from Paris and London.
March	Britain and France conclude a military alliance with Turkey and demand in an ultimatum that Russia evacuate the principalities; when this is ignored, they declare war on Russia.
3 June	Austria demands that Russia evacuate the principalities. The czar subsequently complies.
August	The Russians conclude their withdrawal from the principalities.
Mid-September	Britian and France open operations in the Crimea with an amphibious landing, aimed at besieging and seizing Sebatopol.

threats to vital Russian security interests. Ambiguously competing with hostility toward the Turks was a Russian policy objective of preserving and protecting the Ottoman Empire as a buffer state that would shield southern Russia and the Black Sea area from the military and politico-diplomatic influences and maneuvers of the outside great powers. The Ottoman Empire also blocked Austrian expansion toward the southeast (which could only lessen Russian security and compete with Russian interests). The precondition for the Ottoman Empire's serving as a satisfactory buffer state, however, was that the Porte be more dependent on, and deferent to, St. Petersburg than any other capital.

The powerful French initiative over the Holy Places had the effect of activating *both* themes in Russian foreign policy. Clearly it threatened Turkey's usefulness as a buffer state to the extent that the Turks began to fear Paris more than St. Petersburg. However, it also activated the ambivalent mixture of hope and anxiety among Russian policy-makers that the politico-diplomatic blows Napoleon was striking, and might continue to strike, could herald the last great crisis of the Ottoman Empire and the beginning of its dissolution.

The extent and depth of the Russian interests being activated by their policies were not appreciated by the French decision-makers, and this was the first of a number of analytic failures we shall observe. The French generally assumed that their competition with the Russians over which set of priests would control the Holy Places was simply that, and not much more. Despite considerable evidence from recent history about Russian interests in the Near East, and despite reasonably full and accurate reports from Castelbajac (the French ambassador in St. Petersburg) about Russian attitudes, Napoleon's impetuous style and his felt need for a quick and dramatic foreign-policy success drove him to insist upon his initiative without a full assessment of his policy's implications. In particular, the French failed to communicate credibly to St. Petersburg what the *limits of their objectives* in this novel initiative were, thereby permitting the Russian policy-makers to conjecture that French designs on the Ottomans might be very extensive indeed.[8]

Many opportunities for defusing the growing crisis would present themselves later, and in no sense did Napoleon's aggressive, undelimited, and somewhat uncomprehending initiative lead him inevitably into the war with Russia. It did lead France into an involvement in Ottoman affairs that was unprecedented, and for which the French foreign ministry, owing to lack of experience, was probably not very well equipped. This impetuosity also included an all-too-effective set of naval demonstrations, the impressive results of which probably encouraged French policy-makers later to resort willingly to further assertive use of the naval arm. And it led directly to the czar's structuring his own counterinitiative in a form that would be generally perceived as highly aggressive.

The Menshikov Mission

If Prince Menshikov's instructions had been confined to regaining for the Orthodox patriarchs their previous privileges, the crisis would probably have come to an end with the conclusion of the competition over the Holy Places. On Stratford Canning's advice, the Porte agreed to restoring Orthodox privileges in May 1853 and the French, lacking British support for their initiative and having confronted an unexpected degree of resistance, had already decided not to pursue that issue further.

However, Menshikov also made much wider demands that amounted to an unprecedented degree of control by the czar over the political status and role of Christians living within the Ottoman domains. (For example, under Menshikov's program Christians involved in some kinds of judicial disputes would be able to appeal their cases to the Russian czar and receive an enforceable ruling.) Thereby the Russians threw the crisis into a second and more severe phase, which ended with the outbreak of a new Russo-Turkish War. The Turks, supported by the West, determined to resist these demands, and later, when the Russians occupied the principalities to enforce them, to resist the occupation too. They did so because they concluded that the Menshikov program represented a powerful Russian offensive move against the Ottoman Empire, designed to create a new and hegemonic Russian relationship over Turkey.[9]

From the Russian viewpoint, this assessment was not clear. The wider demands, in fact, had a substantially defensive motivation and to a large degree were intended only to recreate the Russian conception of what the status quo ante had been.

There was, to be sure, some difference in emphasis on this point between Czar Nicholas on the one hand, and Nesselrode, the foreign minister, and his staff on the other. The sovereign and his principal advisers all recognized both offensive and defensive components in their policy. The czar personally gave considerable weight to offensive motives and privately instructed Prince Menshikov to make the most extreme demands in his package without the knowledge or approval of the foreign ministry. Nesselrode and his staff preferred to emphasize the defensive component of the Menshikov initiative, and later, of the occupation of the principalities.[10]

All the Russian policy-makers agreed, however, that regaining control of the Holy Places did not necessarily restore the status quo ante, for the Turks might yield on this one issue without returning to their previous posture of general deference. In the perception of decision-makers at St. Petersburg, something more fundamental had altered when the keys to the Holy Places had changed hands. The French had wielded new naval capabilities, and the Porte had apparently concluded that "a French fleet would beat a Russian fleet even combined with a Turkish one."[11] Since the Ottomans would favor whomever they feared most, the Russians immediately had a vision of French fleets in the Black Sea. A new device would have to be found to compensate for the new French image, and to restore the traditional Turkish fear of Russia; and it would have to be some *nonnaval* threat, because a sufficient increase in the Russian Black Sea fleet was not possible in the short term. Hence the Menshikov initiative. If successful, it would give the czar a power over the sultan, in the name of protecting the Orthodox, which although different in form would restore approximately the previous relationship of forces. (And unlike other demands that conceivably could have been made, it attached directly to the czar's traditional and well-established role of protector of Orthodox Christianity.)[12]

It was in this fashion that the Menshikov mission followed directly, not just from the French diplomatic initiative regarding the Holy Places, but also from the particular manner in which that initiative had been backed up. If Napoleon had sought, and even obtained, the keys to the Holy Places without putting on an aggressive display of his new naval might, the Russians might have been content simply with regaining the keys for the patriarchs. Conversely if Napoleon in some other situation had wielded his new naval capabilities, but in a way not aimed so aggressively at the Ottoman Empire, the Russians probably would have had little reason to be concerned for their relationship with the Porte. It was the combination of the new French naval capabilities *and* their use in a successful politico-diplomatic assault on the Turks that led the Russians to search for a new device to reassert their primacy in influence over the sultan.

At the same time, the foreign ministry in St. Petersburg as well as the czar appreciated that something like the Menshikov mission, however necessary from a defensive viewpoint, could easily serve offensive objectives, also. It gave the czar a clearer and more direct influence over the Porte than the previous, more generalized fear of Russian military superiority. Furthermore, decision-makers in St. Petersburg assigned a higher probability than did their counterparts in other capitals to the likelihood of a complete breakdown of the Ottoman Empire. They saw in the plan to "protect the Orthodox" a vehicle for securing Russian interests in that contingency that was actually superior to the previous strategy. In the event of an Ottoman collapse, for instance, Russian troops could be dispatched to the major centers of Christian population to "protect them from anarchy."

The Menshikov initiative thus represented an ambiguous mixture of both defensive and offensive motives, with the defensive predominating in the minds of most of the Russian decision-makers (except, perhaps, the czar himself). It was not to appear that way, however, to policy-makers in any other capital, who *evaluated the Menshikov demands against a different framework of perceptions and expectations.* Elsewhere the Russo-Turkish relationship as it existed before the onset of the crisis had not seemed so strongly one of Turkish dependence on Russia as it had seemed in St. Petersburg. Hence where the Russians believed that they were substantially recreating the status quo ante in a different form, to others they seemed to be creating something new instead.

Decision-makers in London, Paris, Vienna, and Constantinople perceived the Menshikov demands against a different framework of perceptions and expectations in other important respects also. They did not have the same expectations as the Russians about the imminence of an Ottoman collapse, and they had reasons to fear, but hardly any to welcome, such an event. With the partial exception of the Austrians, they did not have, as St. Petersburg did, "contingency objectives" for advancing important national interests should that eventuality take place. Therefore they tended to see any Russian move that seemed to be related to the possibility of an Ottoman collapse as more an effort to bring it to pass, and less an effort to hedge against its worst consequences, than the Russians saw it.

This tendency was enhanced by the fact—unfortunate for Russian policy—that all the European capitals shared a detailed knowledge of just what the Russian contingency objectives were. The czar himself had recently discussed his goals in the event of an Ottoman collapse with the British ambassador in St. Petersburg and with Franz Joseph, the Austrian emperor. Other Russian officials had also commented on these aims in diplomatic circles from time to time. The result was that officials of every power in Europe were aware of the Russians' plans for carving up the Ottoman Empire, giving themselves a substantial slice including Constantinople and the straits. It was true that the czar had said that he intended that the carving be done by general European agreement, not unilaterally by Russia, and that Constantinople be occupied by Russian forces as trustee (*en depositaire*) on behalf of Europe, not as owner (*en proprietaire*). But it was also true that officials in every European capital except St. Petersburg felt that the Ottoman Empire could probably be preserved, and that their interests would be better served if this were the case rather than if it were dissolved. Responsible officials everywhere in Europe were made anxious by the prospect of Constantinople in Russian hands, on any basis whatsoever. More than any other single motive, it was their fear that St. Petersburg might be trying to undercut the Ottoman Empire and move toward controlling Constantinople and the straits, that drew the Western powers and especially Britain deeper into the growing Near Eastern crisis during 1853.[13]

When the Menshikov mission was rejected by the Porte, the backup strategy of occupying Moldavia and Wallachia offered the Russians just as much future leverage over Turkey. In any case the occupation was a necessity if Menshikov's mission was not to be a bluff, because of a *power asymmetry*. From the viewpoint of escalation control in the abstract, it would almost certainly have been preferable for the czar to have backed up a (less ambitious) diplomatic effort, and riposted the French naval demonstrations, with his own demonstration of some new *naval* capabilities. A Franco-Russian competition in naval power, while somewhat hazardous, would probably not have posed as great a risk of escalation as the course that was actually followed. But St. Petersburg simply lacked the naval resources at this time to compete with the French in this category. The czar therefore turned to another form of power, the army, where Russia was unquestionably superior in the local theater to any plausible French expeditionary force. In this sense, the power asymmetry between French naval superiority and Russian ground superiority made it "necessary" for any effective Russian counterdemonstration to escalate the competition by breaking into a new category or dimension of power, rather than competing in the original (naval) terms.

Ground demonstrations, however, are inherently less flexible and delicate than naval demonstrations (doubly so in the era before the existence of quick-reaction airlift capabilities and modern communications). When the threat of the mobilization proved inadequate, there was no further gradation available short of actual offensive action; no stronger signal could be sent that was not an overt hostile act. The Russians did take one of the smallest feasible offensive steps they could, and one, furthermore, for which there was a precedent: Russian troops had briefly occupied the same principalities four years before and thereby successfully coerced the Ottomans into granting some significant concessions.

An additional dangerous inflexibility emerged later when it turned out that this time the occupation was not to be brief. Because of climate it was not possible to move the troops in Moldavia and Wallachia in any quantity between late October and March. Hence St. Petersburg knew in July that if the sultan did not bow within four months, the troops would have to remain for most of a year, at a minimum. In this much time, escalatory responses by the Porte or possible allies would be likely, and de-escalatory moves by any participant would be more difficult.

The Russians, remembering the precedent of the successful earlier occupation and feeling the intent of their policies to be legitimate and substantially defensive, did not expect the Menshikov mission or even a temporary seizure of the principalities to lead to a new Russo-Turkish War. Their sanguine expectations derived from several significant analytic failures in their comprehension of the situation.

The putative basis in law and precedent for Menshikov's demands was the Treaty of Kutchuk Kainardji, signed in 1774 at the conclusion of another of the earlier wars. When he dispatched

Menshikov (a tactless military officer with almost no diplomatic experience) on his delicate mission, the czar supposed that this treaty provided grounds for the full scope of the prince's program. In fact, the treaty did not go nearly so far. The czar later confessed that he had not studied the treaty before Menshikov departed and would not have instructed him to make his more far-reaching demands if he had. Nesselrode and most of the foreign ministry staff naturally had not studied the treaty carefully either, because they did not know these more extreme demands were going to be made.[14]

The czar's somewhat hasty decision to dispatch Prince Menshikov was also made with the precedent in mind of a similar action taken by Austria just the previous month. In January Vienna had sent a Count Leiningen to Constantinople with an ultimatum that Turkey stop threatening to invade Montenegro, a non-Ottoman land generally regarded as within the Austrian sphere of influence. Leiningen's mission, like Menshikov's, was bolstered by a mobilization of several army corps near the border. And it was successful. The difference was that Leiningen's mission essentially was a deterrent, not a compellent, one. That is, it did not require the Turks to change the status quo; it did not require them to accept some *new* state of affairs. Compellence usually requires much stronger backing, and other more favorable "requirements," than deterrence does; this was not appreciated in St. Petersburg. Moreover, what the Russians decided in February to try to compel cut to the heart of Ottoman sovereignty. "Austria did not threaten the independent existence of the Ottoman Empire; the Turks could safely give way. The tsar saw only the precedent."[15]

Essentially the identical error was made in July when Moldavia and Wallachia were occupied. When the Russians had carried out the same operation in 1849, the surrounding diplomatic milieu had been quite different. Both France and Britain had been entirely uninvolved, and Austria for various reaons had been unable to oppose the Russian initiative. Again, however, policy-makers in St. Petersburg saw only the successful precedent, without asking what the preconditions for success might have been or how existing conditions might have changed.

These specific errors were part of a more general pattern of failure in Russian policy-making at this time, involving both institutional dysfunctions and analytic errors of comprehension and calculation. The most serious institutional dysfunction was a strong tendency for Russian diplomats abroad to de-emphasize and sometimes even completely suppress, in their reports to St. Petersburg, information that they felt was unpleasant and might be unwelcome. Inevitably, policy-makers in the capital chronically underestimated the degree of hostility their policies were engendering and hence the level of risk they were running. In two important instances in particular, this institutional failure intermeshed with and reinforced what was already a developing and serious analytic failure in Russian perceptions and calculations.

One concerned Anglo-Russian relations, which were an important part of the international landscape for the czar. "Nicholas always had said that he did not care what France thought or did as long as England was in agreement with him."[16] In 1844 the czar had had a series of productive conversations in London with Lord Aberdeen, then foreign minister, and Nicholas felt that friendly personal relations and a mutual understanding of basic national interests had been established. In 1852-1853 the czar drew comfort from the fact that Aberdeen had become prime minister. But he did not fully comprehend the British political system: he correctly believed that Aberdeen would make significant concessions to avoid an Anglo-Russian falling out, but he incorrectly believed that as prime minister Aberdeen had a unilateral final say on policy. Nicholas concluded that his risks were low as far as Britain was concerned. The czar's misplaced confidence was reinforced when, in January and early February 1853, he had a number of long private talks with Seymour, the British ambassador in St. Petersburg, concerning Russian views on the Eastern Question generally and contingency plans should the Ottoman Empire collapse in particular. Nothing specific came of these conversations. Their general effect was to arouse latent hostility in London over Nicholas' continuing dream of carving up the Ottoman Empire. The czar went away from these talks convinced that his understanding with Britain had been confirmed and enhanced, and that London would tacitly sanction his contingency plans regarding a possible Ottoman collapse. Afterward he did not inform the British of Menshikov's instructions, because he believed that their general sense had been covered in the Seymour conversations.[17]

It was true, as the czar understood, that through the winter of 1852-53, the English cabinet assessed the Near Eastern crisis as being the creation of the hyperactive Napoleon. What the czar did not understand was that most policy-makers in London, excluding Lord Aberdeen, believed firmly in the value and viability of the Ottoman Empire and entertained latent and even open suspicions of Russian designs, which the czar's own actions now proceeded to arouse. The Russian embassy did not emphasize this in its reports, but instead reinforced the superficial and more congenial view.

Later, in the spring and early summer, most of the English cabinet grew more and more suspicious of the Menshikov mission; for this reason and others to be discussed later, British policy drifted onto a pro-French tack, to the point that by June there was almost a de facto alliance between the two Western powers. Astonishingly, neither the Russian embassy in London nor the one in Paris reported these developments to St. Petersburg! It was not until autumn, in fact, when Aberdeen was more visibly eclipsed within the cabinet by belligerent ministers and the Western squadrons advanced to Constantinople, that Russian decision-makers finally realized that British policy had changed.[18]

The Menshikov mission and the Russian occupation of the principalities did not create the Crimean War—only the ninth in the series of Russo-Turkish wars (which the Russians had anticipated as a possibility). A number of opportunities for preventing this ninth war from escalating into a great-power conflict would present themselves later, and in no sense did Nicholas' somewhat aggressive and uncomprehending moves lead him inevitably into the wider war. But they did lead directly to the ninth Russo-Turkish War. They convinced the cabinet in London that a significant threat to British interests might be developing, and this had momentous consequences. Furthermore, they created a situation where, from that point on, every nation involved could take actions that appeared only defensive, yet the sum of these actions could be the wider war that none of the great powers wanted.

The Emerging Western Commitment

Contrary to the frequent assumption in the literature of political science, commitments intended to deter a potential opponent from taking action in some gray area often are not made in one clear and explicit decision, but develop gradually over time.[19] It would be hard to find a more eloquent example of this than the development in 1853 of an Anglo-French commitment to the Ottoman Empire.

Almost a full year transpired between the haziest beginnings of this commitment and its appearance in full-fledged form with the entrance of the combined Anglo-French fleet into the Black Sea in January 1854. So gradually did it develop that it is impossible to pick any date or event and say, "Before this there was no Anglo-French commitment; afterward there was." The end of the progression can be specified: in March 1854 the deterrent commitment was converted into a compellent one; communicated to Russia in ultimatum form, it was intended to force an immediate Russian retreat from the principalities. But its beginning cannot be fixed.

One ingredient in the creation of this commitment was the arrival in April 1853 of the aggressive and Russophobic Stratford Canning as English ambassador to the Sublime Porte. While this did not represent a commitment, it did ensure that the commitment, as it developed, would be interpreted to the Turks in the fullest and most far-reaching sense possible.[20]

Another ingredient was the Turkish claim, registered promptly and repeatedly with London and Paris, that Menshikov's demands amounted to establishing a Russian hegemony over the Ottoman Empire. The British, at least, tried to disprove this claim by direct inquiry to St. Petersburg. The lack of a definite denial from the Russian capital, on top of the czar's evident great interest during the recent Seymour conversations in carving up the Ottoman possessions, was disquieting.

An important initiative that would set the stage for developing the commitment was now taken by the French. Napoleon *le petit* dreamed of eventually redrawing the map of Europe, as his uncle Napoleon *le grand* had, but without making what he imagined had been his uncle's great mistake: alienating the English. Indeed, he hoped to achieve his goals with English blessing and even alliance. The prospect was an unlikely one. London's principal concern with the map of Europe was that it might already be weighted too heavily in the direction of Paris, and British opinion of the new Napoleon was not very high. Nevertheless, in 1853 the French launched a diplomatic campaign in the direction of London.

An approach in January for a de facto alliance concerning Near Eastern affairs was rebuffed, because the British cabinet at this time was still feeling that it could trust Czar Nicholas. By the end of the winter the French were concluding that only with British support

167

could reasonable stability and something like the status quo ante be restored to Ottoman affairs, and in March they tried to generate a joint Anglo-French naval demonstration. When the British chargé d'affaires at Constantinople, alarmed by Menshikov's aggressive behavior, sent a request to the Royal Navy base at Malta to bring up a squadron of the fleet, the French chargé sent a similar request to Paris. On the assumption that the British squadron would sail, Napoleon promptly ordered his Toulon fleet to Salamis with orders to cooperate. But the admiral in Malta had referred to London and had been told to remain in port—so that Napoleon was left having committed, as he said later, a faux pas.[21]

Paris took steps at once to recoup. Hostile feeling existed at the time between France and Belgium, whose inviolability Britain considered, as ever, a vital interest. The French now announced that should the czar "ignore his treaty responsibilities" in the east, France would feel free to do so in the west. Threatening signals were sent to Brussels. As expected, these promptly reached London. The obvious implication was that to protect their ally across the channel, the British should cooperate with French efforts to preserve the status quo around the Golden Horn.

If British interests at this point had been on the side of destabilizing the status quo there, it is difficult to know what might have happened next. But they were on the side of preserving it, and the cabinet in London was starting to feel anxious that the Russians might be mounting a challenge. With British interests east and west pointing in the same direction, resistance to the French seduction was not great. "By the first of April England had started on a policy of cooperation with France which led by the end of May to definite concerted action between the maritime powers against Russia in Turkey."[22] Initially the policy of cooperation took the form of instructions to their respective ambassadors in Constantinople to work together (which in practice meant under Stratford Canning's leadership) and to give the Ottoman government general support. The French, however, still wanted a joint naval demonstration.

The deployment of a naval squadron to a trouble spot was a frequent nineteenth-century device, employed especially often by Britain and France, for signaling to a diplomatic opponent seriousness of intent and involvement in some situation. A *joint* demonstration by the two leading naval powers of the world would be particularly impressive. Until May the cabinet in London rejected this step on the grounds that it would be unnecessarily provocative. When the Russians broke diplomatic relations with the Turks that month, the cabinet reversed its view. Either Czar Nicholas had elevated his objectives, the British concluded, or he had been less than candid about them all along. Either way he evidently was overestimating British tolerance of his ambitions, and either way a joint naval demonstration should open his eyes. The cabinet expected that when the czar, who clearly did not want a major war, realized how seriously the British were involved in the situation, he would reestimate the limits of the feasible. More broadly, the British and French expected that the outcome of their signal would be a reopening of Russo-Turkish negotiations, during which the czar would find some reasonable and face-saving way of withdrawing the more extensive Menshikov demands. A Royal Navy squadron was dispatched to Besika Bay, just south of the Dardanelles, where it was joined by the French squadron from Salamis.[23]

While this was being ordered in the Western capitals, a Russian ultimatum was being delivered in Constantinople that gave Turkey eight days to agree to the full Menshikov demands or face Russian military action. By the time the fleets arrived in Besika Bay, the Russian troops were already marching across the border into Moldavia and Wallachia.

From the viewpoint of escalation control, sending the fleets to Besika Bay was an unnecessarily dangerous step in at least two respects. First, it was done precipitously, and on the basis of less complete information about Russian objectives than might have been available. A diplomatic note was sent to St. Petersburg stating that the naval action was taken because of the contrast between Menshikov's behavior and Nicholas' previous assurances. But the British diplomatic and intelligence staffs did not make a major reexamination of the czar's objectives. Inquiry about the perceptions of well-informed neutrals, notably the Austrians and Prussians, might have been helpful. So, in fact, might have been a major direct inquiry to St. Petersburg. The Russians might have offered the explanation that the real intention of the Menshikov mission was to reestablish the same degree of Russian influence within the Ottoman Empire that had existed prior to the crisis over the Holy Places. This rationale would have been only partially plausible to Western diplomats, but it would have established a basis and topic for communication that might have helped prevent escalation later.[24]

Secondly, the Besika Bay step, like the Russian decision to occupy the principalities, had an important built-in rigidity, although of an opposite sort. Where the troops could not *leave* Moldavia and Wallachia between about late October and March, the naval squadrons could not *remain* in Besika Bay during roughly the same period. Winter storms in the bay would make it an unsafe anchorage. If the squadrons were still there in early October, they would be obliged to either advance or retreat.[25]

Both the occupation of the principalities and the Besika Bay deployment are illustrations of the potential escalatory pressures that *inflexibilities* in politico-military policies can exert. The Russian occupation increased Turkish incentives to counterattack fairly promptly, since if the Russian troops were not pushed out of Moldavia and Wallachia by fall, the occupation would continue for the better part of a year. The Besika Bay deployment carried the risk that when the time came for the flotilla to be moved, it would be more palatable for London and Paris to advance it farther than to seem to retreat by pulling it back.

There is no evidence that decision-makers in London and Paris gave much thought to this possible implication before taking their step, apparently because they were thinking of the action almost exclusively as a one-shot signal. The demonstrative value of the step would register immediately, and hence one might assume (almost unconsciously) that the squadrons would not have to remain very long. The difficulty arose with the possibility, evidently hardly considered, that the signal for any reason might not be successful. In that event it might prove desirable to retain the squadrons in the situation for some time, perhaps to use later either for a new signal or for their actual military power. It might then become highly relevant that within a few months the flotilla would be compelled either to advance or to retreat; either move could represent, according to the circumstances, an escalation, a deliberate deescalation, or a sign of weakness. In actuality, the signal was *not* successful, and the necessity of moving the fleet was a contributing factor in the autumn decision to send it on to Constantinople.

From the point of view of escalation control, decision-makers in St. Petersburg now made essentially the same mistake that their

British counterparts had just made. They failed to launch a major diplomatic and intelligence reexamination of their opponent's objectives. On inadequate evidence, the czar and his prinicpal advisers concluded that the Besika Bay deployment was a product of intracabinet and bureaucratic politics within the English government and did not represent a serious expression of true British policy. The Russian embassy in London was continuing to forward to St. Petersburg routine reports of the belligerence of Lord Palmerston and one or two others in the cabinet, and policy-makers in the Russian capital did not doubt that the hated Stratford Canning, and other Russophobes within the foreign ministry and the military departments, were demanding military moves. They explained away the advancement of the Royal Navy from Malta to Besika Bay, then, as a concession by Aberdeen and a majority of the cabinet to hawkish opinion within the government—irritating, but not an expression of any fundamental shift in policy.[26] In the Russian perception, evidently, the French squadron had joined the British because it tended retroactively to justify the earlier deployment to Salamis and because the hotheaded Napoleon usually seized opportunities to do something highly assertive. Thus Russian policy-makers, without a major review of English and French objectives, explained away the Besika Bay deployment *as the product not of policy but of personalities and bureaucratic politics;* so doing, they dismissed the signal that decision-makers in London and Paris had thought so plain.

The Turks, however, did not dismiss it. Although no specific commitment accompanied the fleet movement, this event represented the first *action* the Western powers had taken to support them, as opposed to mere verbal support from Canning and the French ambassador, de la Cour. What the Turks now did was to have a subtle, far-reaching, and very favorable effect on their cause, although whether they consciously anticipated its full possibilities is difficult to ascertain.[27] The Turks did *not* attack the Russian troops occupying their principalities. They also did *not* communicate a more cooperative attitude toward the Russians' demands. They simply did nothing at all.

This may have reflected, in part at least, someone's realization that this was the moment for inaction, not action. Or it may have been entirely fortuitous. The politics of the Turkish capital were as byzantine as ever, and the vector sum of the many-sided tug of war was frequently zero. The effect was the same in either case: it kept the initiative in the hands of the great powers and implicitly encouraged them to retain and even heighten their sense of being responsible for events.

If the Turks had launched the rather effective attack on the Russians in June that they actually launched in October, it would have strongly tended to define the situation as the ninth in the series of Russo-Turkish wars *before* the two Western powers had gotten very involved. Britain and France, however, were starting to involve themselves. By not launching the war at this time, and thus, analytically, by holding partially open the *definition of the situation*, the Ottomans—deliberately or not—gave the Western powers an extended opportunity to get more deeply involved on the Turkish side before the fluid situation crystallized.

There were some preconditions for the Turks' inaction. It depended upon their ability to tolerate for some time a Russian occupation of Moldavia and Wallachia without suffering too greatly in political, economic, or other ways, and without lessening too seriously their chance of launching a successful counterattack on the Russian forces later. It also depended upon domestic opinion and the Turkish military not insisting uncontrollably upon immediate war. If the Ottoman inaction was deliberate, it may have depended in part upon a realization that the Western powers within a few months would have to make at least one more positive decision—to advance or withdraw their squadrons from Besika Bay—and that circumstances might well develop in such a way that a decision to advance would seem easier than one to withdraw. Deliberate inaction may also have depended in part upon the Turks having some understanding of cultural biases: West Europeans (and Americans) characteristically feel that to decide on an action in a certain situation is "doing something" about it, but that to deliberately and consciously decide on *a policy of inaction* is not "doing something" about it.

In any event, the French and British did do something about it. They organized the conference in Vienna, with Austria and Prussia, to try to find a peaceful solution. And when the results of that conference came to nought in a way that enhanced French and British suspicions and anxieties, they advanced their fleets much farther.

172

The Western Commitment Develops

The Vienna Note was designed by the French and British—and Austrians[28]—to end the phony war before the Turks counterattacked in the principalities. Calling for a Russian troop withdrawal, the note attempted to grant some claims of the czar to protection of the Christians within the Ottoman Empire without subverting the basic sovereignty of the sultan. To this end the document was deliberately vague, and in fact it was open to multiple interpretations. Czar Nicholas pronounced himself willing to agree to it, but in mid-August the sultan, with Canning's encouragement, demanded amendments to the key clauses concerning the czar's powers within Ottoman territory. In reply, policy-makers in Vienna, Paris, and London agreed to insist upon the original, vague wording of the note and to add to it a multilateral guarantee of the sultan's sovereignty (which might or might not mean much in practice later). This strategy was pursued well into September.

Meanwhile popular demands in Turkey for liberation of the principalities were growing more and more vociferous and culminated in riots in Constantinople in September. (In actuality, the riots were secretly instigated by a prowar faction within the Ottoman government, in an effort to provoke and pressure the sultan and his more cautious advisers into beginning serious warfare against Russia.) The sultan now appealed to the French and British to advance their fleets to the harbor at Constantinople. To do so, he said, would show that the two great powers of the West stood behind his regime and its policy of having avoided active warfare; and it would calm the populace. His ability to restrain his troops would otherwise soon be in question, and he hinted at the danger of outright revolution. Furthermore, there might be danger from the rioting to European residents of the city.[29]

De la Cour, the French ambassador, was alarmed by all this and wanted to bring up the squadrons at once. The more experienced Canning demurred. Since the end of May, Canning had had the authority to move the squadrons on his own initiative in an emergency. But he perceived that in fact there was little immediate danger to the sultan or to the European residents. Canning also pointed out that to bring the fleet through the Dardanelles would be a violation of the Straits Convention of 1841, which all the great powers had signed. He agreed, though, to the extent of ordering a few small ships to come to Constantinople—on the excuse of carrying mail.

On September 23rd, Paris relayed to London de la Cour's somewhat exaggerated reports about the rioting and its significance, coupled with a declaration that advancing the joint fleet to Constantinople was now (in the words of the French ambassador in London) "indispensably necessary."[30] With much of the English cabinet away on holiday and without waiting for the *English* ambassador's reports of events in the Turkish capital, Prime Minister Aberdeen and Foreign Minister Clarendon on their own authority dispatched an order to Canning to bring up the squadrons.

The extent to which policy-makers in London were in command of the prerequisites for sound decision-making may be judged, aside from the haste and the questionable authority with which this critical step was taken, by the fact that the two men had opposite reasons for taking it. Aberdeen favored it because he thought it would calm the Turks and extend the time during which a peaceful resolution might be found. Clarendon favored it because he wanted to make a strong move against the Russians, even at the risk of war.[31]

The order that Aberdeen and Clarendon sent did leave open, however, the *time* at which Canning must call up the fleet; and in Constantinople the ambassador took advantage of this by postponing his execution of the order. But on October 4th the sultan declared war on Russia. He was less and less able to resist the prowar faction within his government, and in addition, the Ottomans had learned a few days earlier that Czar Nicholas had positively refused to agree to their proposed amendments to the Vienna Note. However, Canning extracted a promise from the sultan that for some time the declaration of war would remain pro forma and that Turkey would not actually open hostilities against the Russians. Such tactics had been employed on other occasions, and outright fighting avoided.

The situation, therefore, still had not changed decisively, although some new indication of a promising development in the negotiations would have to arrive soon or both Canning and the sultan would be obliged to carry out their respective, so far postponed, actions. Ironically, this kind of indication *would* shortly be available. But on October 8th, the first full cabinet meeting in some weeks was held in London, and the outcome was a peremptory order to Canning to bring the Royal Navy squadron to Constantinople immediately. The squadron entered the Dardanelles on the 22nd, followed shortly by the companion French squadron.

On the 23rd, Turkish armed forces advanced into Wallachia and engaged the enemy. The phony war was over and the ninth Russo-Turkish War had begun in earnest.[32]

There are several strands to the explanation of the cabinet's crucial decision in ordering the immediate advance of the fleet. An important one was the leak and publication in mid-September of an internal policy memorandum of the Russian foreign ministry, which demonstrated conclusively that the government in St. Petersburg had interpreted the ambiguous Vienna Note as sanctioning the full reach of the Menshikov demands. This had been an important reason for Clarendon's action, jointly with Aberdeen, in bringing up the fleet and now had a major influence on the cabinet as a whole.[33] Here is another of the several examples in this book of a *chance event* activating an escalatory development. Here, as elsewhere, the particular circumstances of the chance event mattered greatly. The publication of a similar memorandum about Russian objectives a few months earlier, for instance, probably would have intensified the diplomatic crisis, without having the same effect on British military decisions that this publication had in the particular atmosphere that followed the Constantinople rioting and the failure of the Vienna conference.

Another major factor in the cabinet's decision was the impact of a personal meeting held between Czar Nicholas and Austrian Emperor Franz Joseph at Olmütz at the end of September. Such meetings were relatively common in this era, but this one was looked upon suspiciously in the West as a collusion between the two eastern empires. The reaction to this perception differed, however, in Paris and in London. Napoleon and his advisers felt that if Vienna was starting to align itself with St. Petersburg, the time had come to moderate the conflict. The announced outcome of the meeting had been agreement that a fresh interpretation of the Vienna Note, more protective of the sultan, would be drafted to which the czar would agree. Napoleon felt that this was potentially a new and promising development in the negotiations that should be pursued.

A majority of the cabinet in London, on the other hand, concluded that the two eastern emperors had really been conspiring to divide up the Ottoman Empire, and decided that a new and stronger assertion of Britain's interest in preventing this was required. Napoleon, unwilling to alienate himself from his valued alliance with Britain—and reminded that he himself had urged the same action earlier—was obliged to go along with redeployment of the fleet.

The British were correctly informed that the two emperors had discussed partitioning the Ottoman Empire, but were uninformed of, or misinterpreted, the significance of this. The czar had raised this topic mainly to quiet the Austrians' anxieties about what overall Russian objectives were, by offering them what he believed to be a generous portion of Turkish territory in the event the Ottoman Empire collapsed for any of numerous possible reasons. Austria and Russia, being the two powers contiguous to Turkish territory, had by far the greatest stake in its possible disposition, and Nicholas was eager to reach a full understanding with Franz Joseph and his advisers, in order to head off any possible conflict later.[34] Here we see again the potentially pernicious effect of contingency objectives. The British, on somewhat scanty information, interpreted what was actually the czar's effort to forestall the contingency of an intense European crisis over an Ottoman collapse as, in effect, a conspiracy to create one.

The essence of the problem was that St. Petersburg *began from an expectation of probable future reality* that was different from that of the other major capitals. For a variety of reasons Nicholas in particular was convinced that revolution, temporary near-anarchy, and a splitting up of the sprawling, multinational, and multilingual Ottoman realm was only a few years, perhaps only months, away. Recognizing that such an event could challenge the most vital interests of several great powers and pose the greatest danger in decades of a major European war, the czar—from a sincere desire for peace —wanted an understanding in advance among the principal capitals about how that situation would be managed. Policy-makers in the other capitals began from the expectation that a complete Ottoman collapse was *not* imminent, although certainly possible. From an equally sincere desire for peace, they wanted to avoid making a collapse more probable by planning for it, and perhaps by taking actions as a result of the planning, to get ready for it. To do so would be too likely, for instance, to be taken as a signal to act by several subject populations within the empire who had long been dreaming of revolt. This *fundamental difference in expectations* was one of the underlying causes of the escalation sequence that culminated in the Crimean War.

Two additional factors must be included in an explanation of the quick decision by the English cabinet to advance the Royal Navy squadron to Constantinople. One was the excited state of domestic public opinion. In response to the publication of the internal Russian memorandum proving St. Petersburg's "aggressive" designs on the Turks, nearly all the major English newspapers were calling strenuously for powerful measures. Public reaction in France, if not quite so extreme, was also strong.

In different ways the highest-level policy-makers in both Paris and London were sensitive to that opinion. The regime of Napoleon III, like that of his uncle, rested ultimately upon popular enthusiasm for the glory that the emperor could give to France. But enthusiasm for the nephew, unlike that for the uncle most of the time, was shallow and volatile. It was always politically difficult, therefore, for Napoleon III to pull back from a foreign military adventure even on the rare occasions when he wanted to. In the English democracy, of course, a government could be unseated at any time by losing any major vote of confidence in a parliament that, to a considerable degree, reflected the popular mood. In 1854 this was less of a danger than usual because Aberdeen's cabinet was a coalition one. The coalition, however, could continue only at the price of endemic compromise, a process that tended over time to favor the ministers with the strongest policy convictions and the strongest public support. Now and on subsequent occasions, this meant a strengthening of the hand of those ministers like Palmerston, Russell, and—increasingly—Clarendon, who were advocating a more belligerent Near East policy, and a weakening of the position of moderating influences like Aberdeen.[35]

The other factor was "alliance politics." In part, the English decision was aimed at demonstrating to the French that Great Britain could be a strong and reliable ally—ironically, since Napoleon for once was not advocating more forceful action. Indeed, alliance politics were at work throughout. A few months later, it would be Napoleon who would threaten to break up the alliance unless London went along with his insistence that their joint fleet sail into the Black Sea. Still later, it would be each ally's desire not to seem craven to the other that would prevent both from suggesting that they abandon plans for the Crimean landing. As A. J. P. Taylor, the English diplomatic historian, has put it, "The maritime Powers were drawn along from first to last by the need to prove to each other their mutual good faith."[36]

This is a powerful illustration of the likely effects of alliance politics, under conditions where escalation is tempting, when the original raison d'être of the alliance is not *defined and delimited* explicitly and carefully. Each side is likely to advocate, or at least accede to, steps that it might not take on their own merits, to demonstrate its commitment to the alliance and its "good faith."

The British decision to advance the squadron to Constantinople is understandable as an expression of these factors. From an analytic point of view, however, it was insupportable. The ambassador on the spot, who hardly lacked for aggressiveness, had been given full authority to take this step himself. He possessed far more information than London did, yet had not made the move. The misperception that the Olmütz conference had planned a partition of the Ottoman Empire could have been checked and corrected using both Austrian and Russian sources—and also Prussian, as the Prussians at this time were in very close touch with policy-making of the other two nations.[37] This coordination was not done because it would have taken time. There was no military need for such a move; for even in the unlikely event of a Russian strike toward Constantinople the city was well defended, and there was a Turkish army in the Russians' path. Besika Bay was less than a full day's voyage away in any case. The Turks' request for an appearance by the Royal Navy to quiet public opinion was disingenuous, to say the least: it was more likely that it would greatly excite public opinion. This is what had happened the previous month, when the arrival of a less powerful and symbolically less significant Egyptian fleet had enormously heightened the Turkish war fever. To advance British warships through the Dardanelles was a direct violation of international law. And finally, the Russian ambassador in London had specifically warned against this very action, pointing out that it would complicate the situation and raise the risk of a wider war.[38]

If the decision had been made under strong pressure of time, it would be somewhat more understandable that these analytic factors could have been overlooked. As Ole Holsti has demonstrated, the number of considerations that decision-makers can give attention to drops sharply under the stress of time pressure. The striking thing about the cabinet's decision of October 8th, however, is that the same order had already been given, in less peremptory form, by Aberdeen and Clarendon on September 23rd. Cabinet ministers, and supporting military and civilian staff, had had some two weeks to consider the implications of the order that had already gone out, and to contemplate the possibility of amending it to make its execution less imperative and urgent, rather than more so.

Having committed themselves to this step, the British, followed by their French allies, now compounded the error by *failing to couple to their action several important concomitant actions to control its escalatory impact*. At a minimum, certain declaratory actions should have been taken to mitigate possible ill effects on public opinion, both domestic and foreign. Emphasis should have been publicly laid only on the intention to protect the city of Constantinople and its European residents. The intent to grant any blanket protection of the Turkish navy, or any general commitment to the defense of Turkey, should have been explicitly denied. Such a declaration *in advance* would have gone far toward minimizing public reaction to any Russian countermoves—a reaction that ex post facto might not be controllable (as the Sinope "massacre" was to prove amply a month later).

This policy should also have been supplemented with a signal to the Porte, making the naval action *contingent* upon good behavior. Constantinople could have been told that the naval advance was only defensive and would be withdrawn if Turkey unilaterally opened hostilities. Making this signal public would have forestalled the later public pressure for the Western powers to stand by their "ally" Turkey. It would also have persuasively communicated the contingent character of the action to St. Petersburg and thereby greatly lessened the Russian reaction.

At the absolute minimum, the naval action should have been made contingent upon Turkey taking hostile action only to regain her principalities. Constantinople should have been made to understand clearly that the West did not desire to back any general Turkish revanche and would not sanction any attacks along additional fronts. Such a message would probably have forestalled the opening of the Caucasus front and would have relieved Britain and France of much of their "obligation" to respond to Sinope.

None of this occurred. Instead, the worst of all possible kinds of "commitments" was created by the new fleet deployment—a commitment *felt* to be real by both the deterring and the proxy nations, but completely nonspecific, inexplicit, and, as it were, "psychological." London and Paris still had made no explicit commitment to the Turks to defend them in the event of any particular identified contingency. They had merely sent a fleet that was more powerful than any possible foe or combination of foes, to the harbor of the Turks' capital, as general support to the Turkish position!

In effect, decision-makers in London and Paris did not know whether they were attempting a policy of deterrence or of compellence. If compellence, they had done too little; if deterrence, far too much. If the effort was to compel a Russian withdrawal from the principalities, the deployment of a naval squadron, even all the way into the Black Sea, was insufficient, as the Western powers were to learn in a few months. The application of naval power could not dislodge the Russian corps dug into the principalities, who could be supplied overland. A compellent (or deterrent) threat, to be fully credible, must be backed by military capabilities that can execute the specific threat made, not by one's general military power.[39] Conversely, if the effort was to deter a Russian descent into Turkey proper, or into the well-defended European approaches to Constantinople, then the deployment of so powerful a fleet was redundant. Merely placing the French and British navies on alert in their own Mediterranean harbors would have been sufficient, combined with an appropriate declaratory policy, for the Russians lacked the capability to assault the Ottoman citadel with any speed.

The Anglo-French action did not, of itself, create a wider war in the following year. Several more opportunities for preventing the Russo-Turkish war from escalating into a great-power conflict would still arise, and one cannot say confidently that this hasty and apparently almost unanalyzed decision led inevitably to the Crimean War. But it did lead to the Ottoman attack on the Russian troops in the principalities. And it created a *set of preconditions* whereby the next major occurrence would make the larger war exceedingly difficult to prevent.

The Culmination of the Western Commitment

Policy-makers in London and Paris were surprised by the Ottoman attack, but they did not expect that the outbreak of open fighting would lead to war among the great powers. They had several reasons for this opinion. They knew that the czar did not want a major war and would try to avoid one. Secondly, St. Petersburg announced shortly after the Turkish declaration of war that Russia would remain on the defensive in the principalities and would not extend the war to any other region. Thirdly, at most only six weeks of fighting weather remained before the Russian and Turkish armies would have to dig into static positions until the end of March. London and Paris, therefore, expected a few weeks of hostilities—not enough to change the situation drastically—followed by many months during which diplomacy could work toward a negotiated agreement, or at least an indefinite military armistice, while bargaining continued. Expectations in St. Petersburg and Vienna were much the same. Policy-makers in none of the major capitals expected a wider war.[40]

For their part, the Ottomans now looked upon the conflict not as an effort merely to regain the immediate status quo ante—the recapture of the principalities—but as an opportunity to regain ground lost to Russia over a long period, and to stimulate British and French assistance in doing so. Thus the Turks did not limit themselves to action in the principalities, but launched an attack along the Russo-Turkish frontier in the Transcaucasus region, far to the east between the Black and Caspian seas. Early in November a major Russian fort in this region fell to the Ottomans.[41] Here was a distinct expansion in the limits of the conflict, on a new front with no direct connection to the issue of the principalities. This step was one none of the great powers had expected, but it was one that London and Paris had, in a sense, tacitly abetted. The British and French had failed to anticipate the extent to which moving their fleet to Constantinople had encouraged the Turks to believe that a generalized Western commitment to them now existed—or could now be activated by taking an appropriate step up the escalation ladder. And Western policy-makers had failed to make their naval action contingent upon the Turks *not* escalating the conflict. In this sense they had, without intending to, encouraged the Ottomans to escalate a war that involved, after all, far greater stakes for Turkey than it could for Britain or France.

Thus by November 1853 St. Petersburg found itself faced with a discouraging Turkish escalation in the east, as well as an unexpectedly serious advance by the Turks into the principalities. Russian objectives seemed to be receding. The Black Sea fleet was therefore ordered into action. On 30 November the fleet attacked a Turkish flotilla of warships and transport vessels in Sinope harbor on the way to the eastern front. Employing their new armor-piercing Paixhans shells, the Russians completely annihilated the Turkish squadron.

There is evidence indicating that policy-makers in Constantinople had deliberately sought a *losing* sea engagement with the Russians, although presumably not such a disastrous one. By this sophisticated device, they may have hoped to activate a greater commitment from the Western naval powers, who might well take a defeat at sea as a challenge to themselves.[42]

In any case the Russians considered the Sinope attack only a slight expansion of the war. While this was the first use of the Black Sea fleet in this conflict, several factors suggested that the move was a very moderate one. From the standpoint of international law, the operation was a strictly legal one: one belligerent had intercepted another belligerent's military resupply mission to a declared war front. The action was over 500 kilometers from Constantinople and hence should not represent any threat to that city or to its protective Western naval squadrons. Furthermore, the destroyed Turkish fleet had been on its way to the Caucasus, not the Balkan, front. Therefore, the Russian assault represented an effort to counter the Porte's unprovoked escalation, not the more legitimate effort to recapture Turkey's own principalities.

Finally, the czar had taken positive steps to control any escalatory effect of his action. The British had previously informed him through diplomatic channels that the Royal Navy would take no action as long as the Russians did not attack any Turkish Black Sea *port*. The czar, therefore, had ordered that Turkish ships be attacked only at sea. However, by the time his instructions had filtered down through the chain of command to the admiral commanding the Russian squadron, the restriction had been interpreted in as loose a sense as possible, and the admiral had felt free to attack Turkish ships at anchor in Sinope bay.[43]

This is an unusually clear example of the kind of effect that "normal" *bureaucratic and institutional processes and incentives* can have on well-meant efforts by high-level policy-makers to control escalation. A necessary part of the value system of the military of all nations is aggressiveness in engaging the enemy; restraints upon the scope of action within which the military may be aggressive are normally generated outside the military departments and imposed upon them. In this case the czar did not include with his order an explanation of the reasons behind his restriction on Black Sea naval actions; nor did he take the steps required to ensure that its meaning remained as he had originally intended. Hence the natural military value system began to have its impact as the order filtered through successive layers, and the literal reading was interpreted in as aggressive a spirit as possible.

Even so, when the czar learned of the Sinope attack he did not expect it to inspire the kind of reaction in the West that it did. Again, policy-makers abroad *perceived events against a different background of expectations*. The British and French perceived Sinope as a striking escalation of the conflict. It took them utterly by surprise, it seemed to violate the ground rule the British had laid down, and it was an attack on the Turkish navy, which implicitly was under some degree of protection from the Anglo-French squadrons at Constantinople. The vital point was that previously all hostilities had been on land; now the opponent had extended them to sea with a major, in fact overwhelming, naval victory. In this era France to some extent, and Britain almost entirely, based their international position and strength on their naval power. Having made some degree of naval commitment to Turkey and dispatched fleets to the Goldon Horn, they interpreted Sinope as a direct slap at themselves.

The seeming challenge to their world role appeared all the more acute because of the complete one-sidedness of the battle. The easy and almost costless annihilation of an enemy flotilla was an action typical of a distinctly superior naval power. Russia had never been such a power, and in fact the real effectiveness of the Russian navy, compared to the British and/or French navies, did not significantly change because of Sinope. But the *appearance* of Russia as a major naval power was being created or might be created—in the eyes of the Russians themselves, and in the eyes of many others in Europe and elsewhere. Russia might now begin to act more like a major naval power, and might be permitted to do so by other nations. It was the *expectation of a basic change* in the interplay of forces in the international system that generated the intense response, both within the governments and among the public, that now occurred —not any direct implication of the Sinope victory for, say, the British or French admiralty "threat estimates."

The public reaction in Britain especially was extreme. In the era before electrical communications or public polling, newspaper editorials were the main gauge of public opinion; after Sinope every major newspaper in Britain vehemently demanded a decisive counterstroke that would reestablish Britain's image as the preeminent naval power of the world. As one historian has summarized the impact of Sinope, "Few governments have ever been subjected to pressure so sudden and so severe, and few ministers would have dared to resist it. In fact, most of them did not want to."[44]

To advance the Anglo-French naval squadron at Constantinople into the Black Sea was the obvious counterstroke, but Prime Minister Aberdeen and others initially balked at this for fear that it might lead directly to war with Russia. The French, however, insisted on this step. Napoleon had already proposed it back in September when the Vienna Note had failed. Now he informed London that, should Britain not accede to his desire for a joint Black Sea operation, he would either carry it out unilaterally or withdraw his entire Mediterranean squadron all the way to Toulon.

It was a potent message, even though it was actually a bluff. The cabinet calculated that if the French withdrew, Britain would be left holding the Near Eastern bag—including whatever was the ongoing risk of major war, some degree of commitment to the Porte, and a public that would not stand for any similar withdrawal. If the French acted unilaterally, the cabinet would be faced with trying to explain to an inflamed public why France could respond vigorously to the challenge of Sinope, but the greatest naval power in the world, with a more direct Turkish tie, could not. In fact, Napoleon could not execute either one of his threats. London guessed as much, but the cabinet had no way to be sure. In any case what the French demanded might be in the British interest. Many argued it was.

These matters were mooted at a series of cabinet meetings in December, from which Palmerston, the "strong man," temporarily withdrew in order to return riding a wave of popular support for himself and for vigorous action. Aberdeen and several waverers were brought along when a device was hit upon that seemed to promise a possible outcome other than war. The French had been laggard in pressing upon Constantinople the latest in a long series of possible peace plans. So London could propose a quid pro quo:

Napoleon's support of the new peace proposal in exchange for the British fleet joining the French on the Black Sea. This was agreed upon in Paris.

The Turks, currently winning and with every expectation of receiving active support from the Anglo-French squadrons, did not pay much attention to the peace proposal and it soon died. The Western fleets entered the Black Sea in the first days of 1854, accompanied by a diplomatic demand that the Russian navy take no further action against Turkey. To Stratford Canning the cabinet admitted that "Her Majesty's Government do not disguise from themselves that it may at no distant period involve England and France in war with Russia." Yet they still hoped for the reopening of negotiations, based on the Russians at last having become persuaded that Britain and France were determined to preserve approximately the status quo in the Ottoman Empire.[45]

Sinope and the Anglo-French reaction of injecting their fleet into the Black Sea are an example of reciprocal escalation—tit for tat. What is analytically most significant about this pair of actions is the way in which the reciprocation followed so easily from previous events. Sending the squadrons into the Black Sea was the next step in the steady process of advancing them, and it was the only significant naval maneuver left to the Western powers short of opening hostilities. By advancing their flotilla earlier, French and British policy-makers had unconsciously encouraged themselves, and their publics, to think of the diplomatic competition in the Near East in naval terms; hence they subtly had made more probable both the extreme public reaction to Sinope, and the choice of the Black Sea movement as the next step.

What may be most significant of all is that sufficient information was available, in principle, for British and French decision-makers to understand in October that by advancing their squadrons to Constantinople in the unconditional way they did, they themselves had *established all the preconditions for the subsequent reciprocal escalation.* They not only had placed their squadrons physically, and themselves and their publics psychologically, in position to go on into the Black Sea; they had made Sinope, or something like it, possible. It was the proximity of the Western squadrons that had made Sinope such a challenge. The Russian attack on the Turkish task force would have had incomparably less effect had the British and French Mediterranean fleets been at their bases or in their normal cruising areas in the western and central Mediterranean. London and Paris had also made Sinope possible by failing to tell the Turks that the Anglo-French fleet would remain at Constantinople only on condition that Turkey take no military action beyond a straightforward effort to regain the principalities. There was no lack of information to prevent the French and British from grasping analytically that by sending their fleet to Constantinople unconditionally they had set up the situation for the next stage in the escalation process. They did not understand this, however, and when the reciprocal escalation arrived, it threatened to launch a great-power war at once.

However, the war did not come immediately. The czar comprehended that British policy had completely reversed itself from the previous spring and decided to attempt to control any further escalation and avoid a wider war. This decision was not an easy one, for in the meantime the Russian population, in reaction to Sinope and to the outbreak of fighting in the Caucasus and the principalities, had worked itself into a frenzy for war. Nonetheless, the government at St. Petersburg made no immediate military, or even hostile diplomatic, response to the entry of the Western fleets into the Black Sea. Rather, the Russians confined themselves at first to inquiring whether the Western admirals would bar the Turkish navy from using the Black Sea, as they now were barring the Russian navy.[46]

Such were not their orders, but they could have been. In January 1854 the British and French lost another opportunity to control the escalation sequence that was driving them toward a major war, through a *failure to analyze the full possibilities inherent in the action they were taking.* The superiority of the combined Anglo-French squadron over either or both the Turkish and Russian fleets was so complete that their deployment could have been used to delimit the conflict by barring *both* belligerents from use of the Black Sea. Alternatively, the British and French could have made the deployment contingent upon Turkish behavior. They could have told the Ottomans that the squadrons would promptly return to Constantinople unless the Turks halted operations on the Caucasus front and took the new peace plan seriously. Doing either of these things, and informing St. Petersburg, might have laid the basis for serious negotiations. Yet the British and French consistently failed to employ the leverage that their fleet movements potentially gave them.[47]

Indeed, the point can be generalized. From the failure of the Vienna Note on, British and French policy-makers *identified their national interests more and more with one side* in the developing conflict, the Turkish. Therefore they continually bypassed opportunities to extract from their escalating deployment of the fleet the fullest possible benefit, in terms of restraining Ottoman policy.

When Czar Nicholas discovered that the Western squadron would continue to let the Turkish navy use the Black Sea, he recalled the Russian ambassadors in London and Paris. To avoid incidents, the Russian navy was kept in port. It was clear that the squadron could not remain in the Black Sea forever, and Russian troops in the principalities could be supplied overland.[48]

Since their navies could not eject the Russians from Moldavia and Wallachia, the French and British now began preparing a joint army expedition to do so. The preparations would take months, and meantime French and some English policy-makers hoped to reopen negotiations. Napoleon sent the czar a new peace message at the end of January.[49]

A temporary and not very stable politico-military plateau thus was established. A significant period of time might have been available for negotiating before the Western expedition to the Balkans matured, if the delicate balance had not been upset by the Austrians. In Vienna policy-makers were finding the Russian interference with traffic on the Danube increasingly burdensome and were nervously anticipating the renewal of major fighting as winter lifted from the principalities. Expecting that the czar would yield to united pressure, the Austrians hinted to the French and British that, should they present Nicholas with an ultimatum demanding evacuation of the principalities, Vienna would support it. London and Paris acted promptly on the suggestion, and a partial troop mobilization in the Austrian Empire was ordered. The czar refused the ultimatum (on 19 March), and the French and British had little choice but to declare war. Quickly they discovered that Austrian support was only diplomatic. For the moment, Vienna could go no farther without support from Prussia, which was not forthcoming. The czar had foreseen this, hence his refusal of the ultimatum.

Almost two months passed, during which the great powers were formally at war, but fighting took place only between Russians and

Turks. It was widely expected that there would be a test of strength between the Russian army and the Anglo-French expeditionary force, soon to be landing in the Balkans, and this expectation helped to stultify any effort toward reopening negotiations. Major new bargaining waited upon the outcome of the test of strength. By May, though, Vienna's politico-military position had been improved through an increase in her ready forces, and, more importantly, by a new treaty with Prussia signed in late April. Under its terms the Prussians were partially committed to support an Austrian effort to free the Danube, so now the Austrians sent St. Petersburg a unilateral ultimatum demanding evacuation of the principalities. Faced with a diplomatic combination of the two great powers on which the Russian Empire bordered, the Russians withdrew—at first only partway and then, after St. Petersburg tried and failed to get Prussia to reverse Austrian policy, entirely. By agreement with Constantinople, Austrian forces occupied the principalities to remove them from the fighting.[50]

The temporary occupation of Moldavia and Wallachia by a non-belligerent represented, in some respects, a sophisticated escalation-control measure, for it effectively prevented contact between Russian and Turkish (or Western) troops on that front. Furthermore, the Russians had not been as humiliated by the withdrawal demand from "neutralist" Austria as they would have been by forceful ejection by the British and French. And there was no fighting between the departing Russian and arriving Austrian troops. Finally, the Russian withdrawal recreated the military status quo ante. The stage was set, therefore, for a general armistice and the reopening of negotiations on the broader issues.

Czar Nicholas was now ready to be moderate in his demands, for he had been unpleasantly surprised by the Austrian ultimatum. Throughout the sequence of events to this point, in fact, he had been presuming that the Austrians would not oppose him seriously. Only a few years earlier, in 1849, Nicholas had probably saved the Hapsburg regime by lending Franz Joseph troops to put down revolts, and earlier there had been a Holy Alliance between the two eastern empires to defend Christianity and the traditional social order against the "red revolution" symbolized by France.[51] The czar's presumption of at least passive acquiescence from Vienna in this period would probably have been valid, had the subject not been the Balkans (or Galicia). There the Austrian interests were too deeply engaged: the potential threat to the sprawling Hapsburg empire from any of a number of possible upsets of the status quo was too great. But this was not fully appreciated in St. Petersburg. Russian policy-makers had been mildly surprised when Austrian diplomats had signed the Vienna Note and were much more surprised by the Austrian ultimata, multilateral and then unilateral, of the spring of 1854. This continuing analytic failure, somewhat comparable to the earlier, long-standing Russian misperception of the British, had been a contributing factor all along in the czar's somewhat aggressive behavior. Probably neither the more far-reaching portion of the Menshikov demands, nor the occupation of the principalities, nor some intransigent Russian responses to various diplomatic inquiries subsequently, would have been risked had the Russians realized that Austria might be ranged among their active enemies. The Russian Empire was far more vulnerable to military attack from Austria than from Britain or France, and when the unilateral ultimatum arrived in May, Nicholas complied and reassessed downward his position and expectations in the event of new negotiations. [52]

It is not often that history is generous enough to provide policy-makers with a final opportunity to pull back from the brink of a wider war. In this case there was an excellent opportunity. The original Ottoman objective, the regaining of the principalities, had been accomplished. The British and French had little strategic reason to involve themselves further. They might have assisted at this point in launching negotiations between the Russians and Turks, who presently were engaged only on the Caucasus front; or at worst they might simply have allowed the ninth Russo-Turkish war to continue, as fighting proceeded on that front. They could have made a useful contribution to limiting the war by employing their Mediterranean squadrons to prevent both belligerents' navies from operating on the Black Sea, as the Russians had suggested months before.

None of this occurred. Instead, the British and French missed their opportunity and went ahead with plans for an amphibious landing in the Crimea. Military staffs had already begun preparations for an assault from the landward side upon Sebastopol, the major Russian military and naval base in the Black Sea area; these preparations went forward.

Again there are several strands to the explanation for this outcome, which from a detached viewpoint seems so curious. One relatively minor element was the sheer bureaucratic and institutional momentum of the policy, launched as it was in mid-June *before* the success of the Austrian ultimatum. Another element was alliance politics. The French had tentatively concurred in this plan for some time and it was officially decided upon at an Allied War Council in mid-July, after the Austrian ultimatum had been delivered but before it was clear that it would remove all the Russians from the principalities without bringing Austria into the fighting. Through the spring the Anglo-French alliance had been strained and, once this policy had been agreed upon, the British were not eager to reopen the question and perhaps make it possible for the French to move in directions distasteful to Britain.[53]

More important than these factors was an interlocking effect that now emerged between a gross analytical error in the military planning, and domestic political and psychological factors. After the Anglo-French declarations of war Lord Aberdeen had begun to withdraw from the intracabinet debate, and the Palmerston wing more and more had determined British policy. This group, having long thought that the basic Russian objective was control of Constantinople, had conceived the previous autumn the goal of near-complete destruction of Russian military power in the Black Sea area through an assualt on Sebastapol. This objective, not the liberation of the principalities, served what the Palmerston wing regarded as the basic British interest (as opposed to the immediate Ottoman interest) in the Near East in this period: reduction of the perceived Russian threat. Throughout the preceding months this goal had been pursued in various ways. As Palmerston and his friends gained increasing influence over policy, Sebastopol became the principal military objective.[54]

In turn, the ascendancy of this wing of policy opinion, paralleled to a lesser degree in the French government, was partially the result of trends in public opinion in Britain and France. The frenzied emotions created by the Sinope "massacre" had been somewhat satisfied by the entrance of the Anglo-French flotilla into the Black Sea in January. After the declaration of war and the dispatch of an expeditionary force to the Near East, the public mood had grown even more belligerent and demanded a military victory.

In essence, this was a phenomenon of mass psychology. The

policy purpose of both the war declaration and the dispatch of the expeditionary force was to compel a Russian retreat from the principalities. But the *psychological effect* of these two steps upon the British and French publics was to create an expectation of military victory. When Austrian diplomacy removed the Russian troops from the principalities, the policy purpose was satisfied but the psychological expectation was not. Thus in some respects Austria's removal of the principalities from the conflict was not a successful escalation-control measure. The mass emotions aroused by Sinope, then further aroused by the war declaration and by the labors and excitements of launching an expeditionary force, could not be satisfied by the mere removal of the principalities from the conflict. By midsummer the expeditionary force had not yet "done" anything. Mass opinion demanded some kind of action by the force—if not in the principalities, then elsewhere. The advocacy of Sebastopol by the Palmerston wing of the government provided a plausible target for popular emotion to seize upon.

Meanwhile, the Allied War Council decision to strike at Sebastopol was adopted in the expectation that the operation could be accomplished easily, cheaply, and quickly. The Crimean peninsula is attached to the Russian mainland by only a very narrow neck of land, about five miles wide at the narrowest point, with the roads not in the center but somewhat toward the sea. It seemed evident that, with their total command of the sea, French and British squadrons deployed on both sides of this neck could sweep it with their guns and effectively choke off the peninsula, which at this point was only lightly garrisoned with Russian forces. The joint army expedition, landed amphibiously on the peninsula, could then readily approach Sebastopol, at this time almost undefended from the landward side. The British and French commanders fully expected to capture the city and the Russian Black Sea fleet harbored there in just a few weeks—certainly before the early Russian winter arrived.

Only after this operation was actually begun, in August, did the allied commanders discover that the water on either side of the narrow Crimean neck was shallow. The warships could not get close enough to the shore to interdict the roads supplying the peninsula. The Russians therefore could send reinforcements and supplies down the peninsula to their forces in the Sebastopol area. The joint army expedition, by this time in the process of being landed, would not be able to defeat the greatly reinforced Russian detachments, if they could defeat them at all, before the Sebastopol garrison had time to erect major defensive works on the landward approaches to the city. And the expedition could not be taken off the peninsula again without risking heavy losses on the beach, and of course, not without the entire operation representing a major Anglo-French defeat![55]

For our purposes the most important thing to note about this stunning analytic error in the Anglo-French military planning is the way in which it *interacted* with bellicose public opinion. On the one hand, the public enthusiasm for war had become translated into pressure from the capitals on the in-theater commanders to generate and execute a plan promising a dramatic and quick military victory. The public enthusiasm was also vigorously represented within the military ranks themselves. The infectious mood of overconfidence and belligerence among the higher English and French army and navy officials in theater, combined with the pressure from home for prompt action, provided one of the least supportive psychological atmospheres imaginable for cautious and careful intelligence-gathering, planning, and analysis.

At the same time, the confident expectations of the military commanders for a quick Crimean victory made it unnecessary for the high-level policy-makers at home to try to resist, or to change, public opinion. One can almost excuse a popularly based government's escalating a war to win the military victory the public is loudly demanding, when this victory is expected to be extremely cheap and to take only a few weeks.

Could British and French domestic opinion have been satisfied in some way if the analytic planning error had been discovered in time? One cannot be confident of an answer at the distance of more than a hundred years, but it would seem possible. The harbor and military districts of Sebastopol could have been shelled from the sea, as later they were. The harbor at Odessa, another major Russian city on the Black Sea, could have been shelled by a major task force, instead of by the minor one that subsequently did shell it. The same kind of attack, combined perhaps with brief amphibious raids to give the expeditionary forces a role, could have been made on the harbors of other, lesser coastal cities and towns and on other targets near the coast.[56] The English and French publics could then have been told, with appropriate fanfare and exaggerations, that the joint Anglo-French fleet had destroyed the whole of Russian shipping and dock areas in every significant harbor on the Black Sea. This might have reasonably satisfied the public demand for a victory. While still an escalation, this action would have been dicontinuous and one time only. And because of the Russians' inability to strike at Britain or France, or even at their fleets, a lasting great-power war would not have been a likely result.

In any case, the reality was that the psychological-political atmosphere greatly discouraged the kind of careful planning and analysis that might have caught the error. The Western troops were landed and became bogged down in a land war on the edge of Asia, which turned out to last far longer and to be far more costly than anyone in the West had anticipated.

Analytic Summary

The Crimean War was the product of a lengthy cyclical-sequence escalation, the principal events of which are summarized in Table 4. Through most of this sequence, policy-makers in none of the major nations wanted events to develop into a major European war, but they lost full control of the cycle of action and reaction.

Two steps in the sequence were initiatives undertaken offensively to change the status quo in some respects. Napoleon's original policy of coercive diplomacy toward the Turks activated conflicts latent in the Near Eastern situation in ways the French did not fully comprehend and was unaccompanied by communication to St. Petersburg of the limits of French intentions. The mission of Prince Menshikov, intended only somewhat offensively, was generally perceived by decision-makers abroad as much more so, because they evaluated it against a different universe of perceptions and expectations from that of St. Petersburg.

After these two early steps, all others were motivated defensively. The cycle proceeded through a combination of causes: numerous analytic failures by the Russians, French, and British in assessing one another's objectives and expectations; interlocking institutional failure on the part of the Russians especially; deliberate effort by the Turks through their own inaction to draw the Western powers deeper into the situation; and an asymmetry between Western naval power and local Russian predominance on the ground. Other contributing factors included public opinion in the West, which at several crucial junctures influenced policy toward more escalation, and the sheer complexity of the interactions among the five powers deeply involved.

Perhaps the most crucial element in the sequence, and the one that might have been most readily reversible, was a continuing failure by the British and French to comprehend and exploit the potential of their progressive fleet advancement to fulfill an escalation-control function as well as a deterrent function. The squadron was not used to prevent *both* sides from using the Black Sea, and at no time was its deployment made contingent upon Turkish behavior. Neither did the British and French realize, in the weeks preceding the Sinope massacre, that they themselves had set up nearly all the *preconditions* for some event like Sinope that would propel the escalation sequence to the very edge of war.

8

The Seven Years War

Almost exactly a hundred years before the escalation sequence that culminated in the Crimean War, there was another sequence that had still greater consequences. Britain secured a vast empire in the Seven Years War of 1756-1763, generally known in the United States as the French and Indian War. (Paradoxically, by making that empire's most valuable component, the American colonies, safe for the first time on their own continent, the war also set the stage for the revolution of these colonies two decades later.) Neither Britain nor her opponent, France, had intended to fight. The war grew, against all efforts to contain it, out of a long cycle of escalations.

Historical Overview

In October 1747 the War of the Austrian Succession had come to an end, a conflict in which Britain and France had found themselves on opposite sides, as usual in the eighteenth century. Whatever its merits, the resulting Treaty of Aix-la-Chapelle papered over and evaded grave questions still at issue between the British and French colonial empires. Neither a decisive victory in the fighting nor a clear decision in the bargaining emerged to settle the conflict where these empires met at four strategic locations. In India, the English and French competed for control of the Deccan and the Carnatic, regions that were keys to mastery of the subcontinent. In the West Indies, they disputed ownership of certain islands which if added to either empire promised control of the Caribbean. Along the west coast of Africa, they clashed over access to slaves, the main source of manpower for the labor-intensive Caribbean economies. And in North America, the expanding English colonies along the eastern seaboard and the expanding colony of New France (Canada) disputed control of the key areas along their mutual border and in the continent's interior.

The failure of Aix-la-Chapelle to settle any of these conflicts led in the following years to what has been called a "cold war" between the two empires.[1] In the West Indies, the French and British maneuvered furiously for de facto dominance of the strategic islands because, according to the mercantilist theory of the day, control of the Caribbean was crucial to the homeland's economy. Along the African and Indian coasts, open battles sometimes accompanied the competition for strategic footholds. By midcentury, "local and desultory clashes . . . in the four quarters of the globe had become the normal accompaniment of the . . . rivalry."[2] A joint Anglo-French Delimitation Commission proved unable to settle the issues by negotiation.

In North America the rivalry at first was somewhat less acute. But during the early 1750s gradually more serious incidents occurred between the English colonials and the French troops and their Indian allies. Appeals from both sides for help from the homeland found willing ears in London and Paris. Strong measures were taken, which to each side's dismay received even stronger replies. By early 1755 war seemed possible; before the end of the year, certain.

Its outbreak was deferred while the principals searched for allies. For decades, Austria had been allied to Britain and Prussia to France. The Diplomatic Revolution of 1756, however, reshuffled the balance of power under the design of Count Kaunitz, the master realpolitik minister in Vienna. In the ensuing Seven Years War, Prussia under Frederick the Great fought a coalition of Austria, Russia, Saxony, and Sweden, partly supported by France. King George II of England, who was also monarch of Hanover, aided Frederick with the resources of that German state, and with British money and some troops. In a simultaneous but mostly separate war, France and Great Britain and their respective empires battled each other around the globe. Subsequently Spain allied herself to France and Portugal to Britain. As one historian has described it, "Fighting took place in the Philippines, India, the Mediterranean, Spain, Portugal, and West Africa; in Germany, Austria and on the coast of France; in North America, the Caribbean, and Cuba; by sea and on land. All the great powers were involved . . . This wide geographical spread; this involvement of the major powers; this

loss of life and outpouring of treasure; marked the greatest upheaval the world had yet seen. The Seven Years War may well
claim to be the First World War."[3]

The ultimate causes of the war were many, the reigning European balance of power being delicate, adrift, and buffeted by many
hostilities. But the immediate cause was the outbreak of violence in
North America and the sequence of escalations that followed. Vol-
taire later wrote that "such was the complication of political interests that a cannon shot fired in America could give the signal that
set Europe in a blaze."[4]

The Escalation Sequence

Through most of this sequence policy-makers in London and
Paris wanted no major war—neither a war between their two
worldwide empires nor a general European war. They were determined, in fact, that the conflict between their representatives in
North America remain strictly limited if indeed it could not be resolved completely. In both capitals decision-makers were willing
to make what they regarded as major sacrifices to ensure that the
conflict not expand. Nevertheless, the escalation continued and
mounted all the way to general war. This chapter will look into
how this occurred.[5]

There were somewhat different perceptions in Paris and London
of how the conflict in America had started.[6] To the French it
seemed that the English colonists were beginning to trespass on an
area that had long been under French influence. La Salle had explored the Ohio River valley and claimed it for France as early as
1679. The river was the obvious and easy link between the established settlements of New France along the St. Lawrence and the
small French colony along the lower Mississippi, in "Louisiana."
Only two short portages were required along this route: between
Lake Erie and the headwaters of the Ohio; and even shorter,
around Niagara Falls. Otherwise the entire journey from the mouth
of the St. Lawrence to New Orleans could be made by water. Although there were few established French forts or posts along this
route before 1750, the route itself was traveled with some frequency. Development of New France and Louisiana seemed to depend upon this link being maintained.

Yet in the 1730s and 1740s, a trickle of Englishmen has started to
enter the region south of the Great Lakes, and by 1750 some three

hundred of them were crossing the Appalachians every year to explore, to trade with Indians previously contacted almost exclusively by Frenchmen, and to begin to establish posts. As the English colonies along the coast were much more populous than the French colony along the St. Lawrence, this incursion would be likely to increase. Clearly action was required with some urgency if the vital connection between New France and Louisiana was to be protected. Starting in 1753, a new governor of New France, Duquesne, began to establish a defensive chain of forts in the Ohio Valley to protect this lifeline and to keep France's colonies in North America from being split in two. And he ejected—by force when necessary, to be sure—the Englishmen who crossed the mountains.

There were other conflicting claims in North America between the two great European colonial powers. The French considered the British fort at Oswego on lower Lake Ontario (in what is now western New York State) to be on French territory. The border between the two areas was poorly defined, too, in the (upper New York State) region of Lake Champlain and Lake George. Finally, conflict had been rife for many years in the Nova Scotia area, where the two empires' claims overlapped seriously. But these conflicts were not urgent and had not, in the period following Aix-la-Chapelle, broken into open fighting (with the exception of Nova Scotia, where occasional raids were limited to a very small area). It was the accelerating English penetration of the Ohio River valley that seemed to the French to be the most serious threat to their interests.

To the British, Duquesne's action of fortifying the Ohio territory was a highly aggressive seizure of land "notoriously known to be the property of the Crown of Great Britain."[7] The original charters held by the English colonies clearly specified British claims of North American territory between two latitudes "from sea to sea." While there might be a conflict between Virginia's charter and Pennsylvania's (both of which seemed to include the Ohio territory), there was no doubt that it was English land. French colonists were not living in the Ohio area, but the English colonists, who felt they were becoming somewhat crowded, wanted to begin to live there. The traditional principle had been that steady occupation, not mere occasional passing through, gave possession. The British found it absurd that New France and Louisiana, sparsely settled even in their own territories and with comparatively poor and slow-grow-

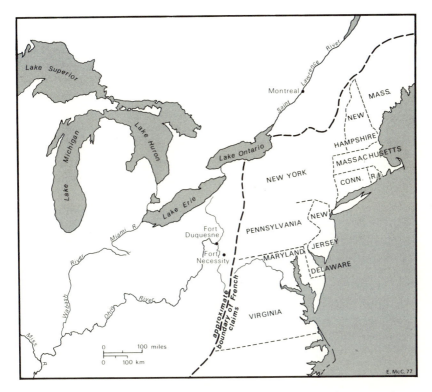

Map 5 North America in the 1750s: the Anglo-French conflict over the
Ohio area.

ing economies, should try to deny the Ohio region to the energetic,
richer, more ambitious, and vastly more numerous English colonists. In any case, the French claim, if allowed to stand, would have
the long-range effect of penning the English colonists into a narrow
coastal strip along the Atlantic seaboard, and clearly this was intolerable. Accordingly, in August 1753 the English secretary of
state, the Duke of Holdernesse, ordered Virginia—and secondarily Pennsylvania—to "require any intruders" in the Ohio area to
withdraw. He sent cannon to Virginia with instructions that two
forts were to be built in the Ohio region.

Hence both the French and the English tended to see themselves
as acting *defensively*, as the conflict warmed up in the early 1750s.
In June 1752 the French attacked and destroyed a British trading

post on the Miami River, a tributary of the Ohio, and in the spring of the following year Duquesne began his forts—one on the southern shore of Lake Erie (Presque Isle) and one halfway between it and the forks of the Ohio (Fort LeBoeuf). Late that autumn the Virginians, in obedience to Holdernesse's instructions, sent a mission to Fort Le Boeuf requesting the French to leave. The message was passed on to Montreal but received no answer. Accordingly, the following February (1754) a Virginia detachment began to construct a fort at the forks of the Ohio (the site of present-day Pittsburgh) to serve as a base for English clearing operations in the area. In April, before it could be completed, a much stronger force of some five hundred French troops with light cannon besieged it, and the English were obliged to surrender and withdraw. Completed and strengthened by the French, it was named Fort Duquesne.

The governor of Virginia, an appointee of the king, considered that the forcible ejection of his men under threat of artillery bombardment was an act of war. He ordered all immediately available forces—about three hundred men—to gather and establish themselves on the western slope of the Appalachians (in what is now southwestern Pennsylvania). One detachment, commanded by Major George Washington, discovered it was being stalked by a group of French and Indians and attacked, killing a French officer and nine men. These were the first casualties in any engagement where an officer of either king commanded.

When the news reached Montreal, reinforcements were sent to Fort Duquesne with orders to eject all Englishmen from the Ohio area immediately. Shortly a powerful detachment commanded by a brother of the slain officer found Washington and his Virginians camped in a place called the Great Meadows, behind hastily erected defensive works named Fort Necessity. After a day-long battle on July 3rd, the British-Americans were obliged to surrender, conditional on their safe-conduct home. By the fourth of July, "not an English flag . . . waved beyond the Alleghenies."[8]

Since transatlantic communication at the time was by sailing ship, it was early September 1754 by the time Paris and London received word of the killing of French soldiers and an officer by Washington's troops, and of Washington's subsequent defeat at Fort Necessity. In France, officials were angered that a British officer and unit should have attacked Frenchmen on—as Paris saw it—French territory. Still, no immediate action beyond a protest seemed required. The French hoped to maintain the peace, and the Fort Necessity victory had repelled the incursion. French forces were in full possession of the Ohio area.[9]

In Britain, policy-makers were equally angered at the French attack upon Fort Necessity and the ejection of the British forces from—as London saw it—British territory. From this point forward there was a division of opinion within the Whig government. Prime Minister Newcastle and most of his cabinet believed for many months that a negotiated solution to the North American problem might be found, or at worst that a military conflict could be held limited to that continent. "It was . . . held that hostilities . . . might proceed some lengths in America without leading to a general European war . . . The conflict in America would thus be isolated . . . This was the idea of the limited war and it was the one upon which Newcastle and his inner cabinet worked."[10] A few influential figures, however, interpreted the French attack as an indication that Louis XV intended to pursue maximum objectives not only in North America but all around the world, with the implication that he was ready to risk a major war. Therefore they were skeptical about the possibility or desirability of trying to keep the war limited. This group included the Duke of Cumberland, then commander of the British army; Henry Fox, undersecretary at the War Office; George Anson, First Lord of the Admiralty, and William Pitt, a Member of Parliament who was later to become prime minister.

In late July Governor Dinwiddie in Virginia had sent to his superiors a request for two regiments of British troops; this was received in London hard upon the news that all English forces had been compelled to retreat from the trans-Appalachian region. With the French firmly in possession of the disputed territory, it was felt that some positive response must be given to Dinwiddie. At first, Newcastle proposed that Virginia be sent only a sum of money with which to raise and equip colonial troops, and officers to command operations and give advice and training to the colonials. Although the proposal was considerably less than what Dinwiddie had requested, the king initially supported Newcastle's preference not to commit British forces. By the end of September, however, he had reversed his opinion. The Duke of Cumberland—the king's son— after repeated efforts had succeeded in persuading George II that regular troops would be required to cope with the French forces in

America. The Newcastle cabinet agreed, if the mission remained a secret as long as possible. Although tactical surprise in America was hardly to be hoped for, French discovery of the mission only after it had landed in America might be too late for them to take effective countermeasures. Seizure of the Ohio would then confront Paris with the difficult problem London had just faced—the need to take positive action because the opponent was in possession of the objective—with the additional disadvantages that the British forces would have a much greater logistical and manpower base to draw on than Duquesne in Montreal did, and that the Royal Navy could take control of the sea at any time.

However, the prime minister did not achieve his fait accompli. In October, while the British force was being outfitted, the fact of the mission was deliberately leaked to the London press by the "war party" within the government. This group thought that Britain was better prepared for a major war than France; since they believed that war was inevitable in any case, they felt it would be better to precipitate it quickly while Britain held the advantage.

The distress in Versailles was limited by prompt action on Newcastle's part. He quickly ordered the English ambassador, Albemarle, to assure the French that the intent of the mission was peaceable and that orders given the English commander, General Braddock, were strictly defensive. In the first days of 1755, however, French intelligence obtained what was believed to be an actual copy of Braddock's orders and learned that the intent was certainly not defensive only. The orders included recapture of the entire Ohio region (which might be considered defensive in London, but not in Paris), plus the capture and destruction of the long-standing French forts at Niagara and Crown Point and a French fort in eastern Canada that guarded the overland approach to the St. Lawrence from Nova Scotia.

Louis XV and his advisers decided on a double response: to send Mirepoix, the ambassador to England currently home on leave, back to London to make a new effort to negotiate the North American issues; and to reinforce New France. Orders were sent to the seaport city of Brest to prepare for a counterexpedition to America. "The force scheduled was out of all proportion to that of Braddock's two poor battalions . . . Six of the finest regular battalions in the French service were to go . . . three thousand men in all, with a squadron of eighteen sail to carry and escort them."[11]

As soon as the English cabinet learned of the French preparations, it resolved that the counterexpedition should not reach its destination. The Royal Navy was put on a war footing, Brest was guarded with frigates to bring word the instant the French flotilla should sail, and in April Admiral Boscawen was sent with a still more powerful squadron to cruise off Newfoundland and intercept the French flotilla.[12]

In ordering the interception performed in North American waters rather than near Brest (which would have been much easier), English policy-makers deliberately were signalling the French that they hoped to keep the conflict limited to the Western Hemisphere. Boscawen's mission essentially failed. The French flotilla sailed from Brest on 3 May, and in the heavy fogs off Newfoundland, all but two ships slipped past the English squadron. On 10 June Boscawen did succeed in capturing the *Alcide* and the *Lys*, vessels carrying only a few troops.[13]

The news of Boscawen's seizure of two of the eighteen ships in the French expedition reached Europe in mid-July. Yet the French did not immediately declare war; they only recalled Mirepoix and broke relations with Great Britain. Shortly the news arrived that Braddock's force had been decimated by a French and Indian detachment in western Pennsylvania and Braddock himself had been killed. Later the French flotilla, which Admiral Boscawen had been blockading inside the mouth of the St. Lawrence, used a little-known channel to break out into the North Atlantic; with considerable good luck it reached Brest without being intercepted by Royal Navy detachments.[14]

Thus the situation of the late summer and early autumn of 1755 came to resemble that of the previous late fall and winter. The French were still in unchallenged control of the Ohio region; the British retained control of the seas and had won a victory in Nova Scotia during the summer. Both sides had suffered losses, but not yet major ones.

This state of affairs might have permitted a renewal of efforts to negotiate the issues, and each side, having been blooded to little profit, might have had an incentive to pull back from the brink. But negotiating efforts had collapsed late in the spring, and relations had since been broken. All the major policy-makers in London and Paris were now convinced that a major war was inevitable, necessary, and, some felt, even desirable.[15]

The Continental balance of power was so constructed at this point that either nation would be disadvantaged by being the first to declare war or commit large-scale aggression. (For instance, most of the major treaties in force could be activated only for defensive action; hence the state taking the offense risked losing its own allies while activating its enemy's.) The result was a period of about ten months of phony war, while the French and British engaged in furious diplomatic activity aimed at rejuggling the complicated system in a way that would permit launching a war under advantageous circumstances. This activity intersected and became part of Count Kaunitz's schemes for a Diplomatic Revolution. In January 1756 an alliance was formed between Britain and Prussia, previously traditional enemies, and this was followed by a "reversal of alliances" and an unprecedented agreement among Louis XV, Empress Maria Theresa of Austria, and the Czarina Elizabeth of Russia. Meanwhile the French had seized Minorca, at that time part of the British Empire. In London the cabinet declared war on France, and the Franco-British portion of the Seven Years War began in earnest, on 18 May 1756.[16]

The Pattern of Escalation

The sequence of escalations leading to the Seven Years War is summarized in Table 5. In this chapter we shall not dissect the intricate diplomatic maneuvers in search of allies of the English and French before war was declared, for this process involved complicated eighteenth-century practices of little relevance to the contemporary era. The lengthy sequence of steps up to the mutual decision for general war, however, has many features of interest and importance.

The pattern that emerges is a classic instance of what we have called *cyclical-sequence escalation:* an open-ended action-reaction cycle, wherein each step by one side triggers a reply by the other, and so on "inexorably" up the scale of violence. The beginning of the sequence in this case is difficult to specify, so gradually did the conflict start; the end of it was a worldwide war.

It is partly because this chain of events seems to be a textbook case of cyclical-sequence escalation that I have been willing to include in this study a war from as long ago as the mid-eighteenth century. It seems relevant for other reasons as well: the conflict was a *bipolar* one during its main escalation sequence; it began as a *proxy war* in a geographically remote theater, in which the principals were determined to limit their involvement; and it had its origins in what has been called a cold war between the principals around much of the world—one that had been continuing for a considerable time. All these features lend it a certain familiarity for the late twentieth-century politico-military analyst.

Undoubtedly a great many things were very different in the eighteenth century, one of the most significant being the long time lag in communication between the principals and the proxies. This factor lends a slow-motion quality to the escalation sequence by contemporary standards. A passage of three years between the first important hostilities and the decision for general war between the principals (and almost another year before its actual outbreak) would hardly be accepted among analysts today as a hypothetical scenario of escalation going out of control! Three weeks or three days, conceivably three hours, would be more realistic.

Yet the striking aspect of the slow-motion process in this case is that *despite* it, a seemingly inexorable escalation cycle took place anyway. Neither in London nor in Paris did decision-makers want an escalation sequence or a major war (except, later, a minority of officials in London), and indeed they tried hard to prevent it. Furthermore, none of the significant steps up the ladder taken by either side was decided upon in haste, with a sense of crisis urgency, or under an overwhelming flood of communications. *Still* the escalation process cycled back and forth, seemingly inexorably and out of control, all the way to general war.

This is powerful evidence that however important such factors as haste, fatigue, information overload, or a felt sense of crisis urgency may be in narrowing policy-makers' perceptions and encouraging "irrational" decisions—and undoubtedly these factors are extremely important in many situations—they do not by themselves fully explain how escalation processess go out of control. There are other important elements, which exacerbate and are exacerbated by these factors, but which also exist and operate independently. It is these that we shall try to identify and assess as they operated in this particular instance of uncontrolled escalation. To facilitate the analysis, this case study is organized according to logical categories, not chronologically. First, policy-makers' objectives.

Table 5   The main escalation sequence of the Seven Years War.

Approximate Date	Event
Before about 1750	Scattered English and French explorers, predominantly French, enter the area south of the Great Lakes and west of the Appalachian Mountains. The French and Indians establish trade and some simple alliances.
About 1750 and thereafter	Frenchmen and their Indian allies begin to warn Englishmen not to enter the Ohio region. The warnings are ignored, and the number of English explorers and traders in the trans-Appalachian area steadily increases.
1752: June	French attack and destroy a British trading post on the Miami River.
1753: Spring and summer	Duquesne, governor of New France, begins to have forts erected in the Ohio region.
August	English secretary of state, Lord Holdernesse, orders Virginia and Pennsylvania to defend British interests in the Ohio region.
December	Governor Dinwiddie of Virginia requests the French to leave the Ohio area, asserting that it belongs to England. Montreal gives no reply.
1754: February	Virginians begin construction of a fort at the fork where two tributaries join to form the Ohio River (now Pittsburgh).
April	French forces eject the Virginians from the half-finished fort and continue to construct it under their own flag, renaming it Fort Duquesne.
Late June	A group of Virginians under the command of Major Washington approaches Fort Duquesne and finds that it is being stalked by Frenchmen and Indians. Opening fire, the Englishmen kill ten Frenchmen, including an officer. When Montreal learns of this attack, reinforcements are immediately sent to Fort Duquesne.

3 July	A strong sortie from Fort Duquesne besieges Washington's force at Fort Necessity, and after a day-long battle compels its surrender and retreat across the mountains.
Late July	Governor Dinwiddie requests assistance, including two regiments of regulars, from Great Britain.
1755: Winter	The regiments, about a thousand men in all, are dispatched under General Braddock.
May	French send reinforcements to Canada that number three times Braddock's force.
10 June	Admiral Boscawen and a squadron of the Royal Navy attempt to intercept the French convoy off Newfoundland, but capture only two vessels.
9 July	Braddock's expeditionary force is ambushed and badly defeated before reaching Fort Duquesne, its first target. Braddock himself is killed.
Summer (through spring 1756)	Britain and France engage in complex diplomatic maneuvers in search of allies among the other great and middle-range powers of Europe.
1756: 18 May	Britain declares war on France.

The Pattern of Objectives

The previous chapter noted that near the beginning of the Crimean War escalation sequence there was one action that clearly represented an offensive step deliberately intended to alter the status quo, and another action that more ambiguously was so intended. The sequence of events leading to the Seven Years War represents a different, perhaps more common, version of cyclical-sequence escalation: the version where *none* of the steps—including the first one, if a first one can be identified—seem to the respective actors to be offensive. From the very beginning of the conflict, both the proxies and the principals on both sides saw themselves as acting chiefly from defensive motives.

It seems possible that where motives are consistently defensive, escalation might be more difficult to control than in cases where at least one party admits to offensive motivations. The essential preconditions establishing such situations seem to be two: a standing disagreement that has been in existence for some time; and, more essential, *differing perceptions of the status quo*. It was primarily because the British and French both saw themselves as protecting interests that were really already theirs that they could both believe that they were acting defensively. It then followed logically that the other party must be acting offensively.

This instance also provides a striking illustration of just how far the defensive justification can be taken. Let us consider some observations of the famous English military historian and strategist, Julian Corbett, which are worth quoting at some length.

> At first sight [Braddock's orders] will appear as a complete plan of attack upon Canada, but it must be observed that there was one line of operation left out of the programme, and this was the most important of all—the one which finally succeeded [later in the war]. No provision was made for a direct attack upon Louisbourg to open the way up the St. Lawrence to Quebec. It is obvious that such an operation would have differed entirely from all the others. All those operations that lay within the four corners of Braddock's instructions were directed against points that were actually in dispute between the two countries, and had been actually *sub judice* before the Delimitation Commission. Louisbourg was in a different category. It was a recognised French possession, to which we ad-

vanced no claim whatever, and any attack upon it must be a measure of conquest, an open act of war, which would fix us beyond dispute with a fatal act of aggression. Thus we may see how cleverly Newcastle's action was adjusted to the difficult situation. Nothing was to be done to which the French could take exception without condemning their own previous action. "You will try," wrote Newcastle to Albemarle, "to give such a turn to these defensive measures as may make the French Ministers ashamed to complain of them." Thus we were able, without taking a step that could be called first aggression, to commence a widespread strategical defensive.[17]

The logic is impeccable, on its own terms. What Corbett fails to note is that precisely the same reasoning had lain behind France's "own previous action." From the French point of view, all *their* activities along the Ohio were also a "strategical defensive," and not even a particularly "widespread" one!

The French failure to "demarcate the limit of their intentions," as Thomas Schelling terms it, had contributed somewhat to the fears of the British and hence to their motives for these actions. Neither in Virginia nor in London were officials in 1754 certain how far the French objectives extended. In actuality, the intent of the French was defensive. The chain of forts along the Ohio River, indeed, represented a far less vigorous strategical defensive than did the Braddock operation, since it involved no attacks upon any established British fort or position, whereas Braddock was ordered to seize many established French forts. To apply Corbett's reasoning, Duquesne could have gone much farther; for instance, he could have attacked the British fort on Lake Ontario (Fort Oswego) and British installations in Nova Scotia, all of which were within French-claimed territory. Such attacks presumably would have called forth a much more severe British counterreaction than did erecting a chain of forts along the Ohio; yet they would have been just as defensive as Newcastle believed the Braddock mission to be.

Thus not only did decision-makers in both capitals take no steps that they considered offensive, but in only one of the two capitals did they even interpret generously the scope of what defense might allow. (In the other capital they interpreted defense cautiously.) Yet the action-reaction phenomenon *still* operated.

What made this possible, more than anything else, was the large physical area where the two powers' claims overlapped; too many possibilities for clashes could arise. Had the area of overlapping claims been much smaller and had policy-makers of at least one capital still interpreted defense cautiously, the conflict might have been held to North America and escalation controlled. The action-reaction process was also made possible by the fact that the immediate conflict took place against a backgound of more general conflict in North America (and around the world). Additional feasible objectives for Braddock's mission—the French forts at Niagara, Lake George, and on the Nova Scotian peninsula—were therefore "connected," albeit loosely, to the battle over the Ohio and thus could be added to his orders with some plausibility.

This matter of the scope of the two empires' overlapping claims and interests is not the same as the observation most commonly made about defensive justifications in escalation. As noted in Chapter 2, there is a frequently employed image of escalation in which a belligerent takes additional steps in order to defend forces deployed or commitments made in earlier steps, and then must take more steps to defend these, and so on. The stakes rise, in short. But a defensive justification can also apply, as here, to the *first* steps each belligerent takes, to protect the original stakes.

The more familiar version of stakes-raising is also illustrated in the Seven Years War escalation sequence at a later stage. During 1753 and the first half of 1754, Prime Minister Newcastle's main objective was to improve British control of the Ohio territory by erecting a fort at the forks of the Ohio.[18] When the colonials (apparently) proved themselves unable to do this without help, Braddock's mission was launched with this as his highest-priority objective. Then, to protect Braddock's chances of accomplishing this, Boscawen had to be sent out to intercept the French reinforcements to Canada. It was the same on the other side. It was only because it was (apparently) necessary to protect the Ohio forts from Braddock that Louis XV dispatched six battalions. At these points and perhaps others in the escalation sequence, the threat that the opponent's actions seemed to pose to one's original objective "compelled" one to raise the stakes by committing more and more forces to the struggle.

This is one form or version of stakes-raising. Another is what might be more precisely termed a progressive *rise in motivation.* The sequence of escalation in the Seven Years War provides a particuarly rich illustration. Early in the competition, policymakers on both sides were uncertain of their motivation for involvement in the affairs of North America. In London, decision-makers perceived the British colonists as insolent, uncooperative, and in many ways determined not to play their proper mercantilist role. In Paris, high officials perceived Canada and Louisiana as liabilities, not assets, to the French mercantile and imperial system, because both cost more to maintain and develop than they yielded in economic returns to France.[19] In each capital, then, policy-makers had reason to detach their primary mercantilist and imperial interests from the interests of their American colonists. Had this ambivalence continued, a negotiated compromise might have been worked out, or at worst a war limited to the proxies might have ensued. However, as escalatory steps were taken on each side, for several reasons officials in London and Paris *increasingly identified their major national interests with those of their proxies, and their motivation hardened.* This important process is worth discussing in a little detail.

As actual fighting occurred and after each side had suffered casualties from the other's military attacks—the English at Fort Necessity and the French immediately before—the competition seemed to engage the honor of each nation (as it was called then; today it might be called their credibility).[20] The same argument was heard in London and Paris in the 1750s that was to become so familiar in Washington, D. C., in the 1960s and 1970s: if we do not stand by our proxy, our commitment to all our alliances will be called into question. However convincing this was or was not in the 1960s and 1970s, it was much more convincing in the 1750s, for the colonists in America were citizens of England and France, who flew the flag of the homeland. The linkage between principal and proxy was much tighter than in nearly any of the cases that contemporary analysts are familiar with.[21]

There was also a subtler and more complicated, but at least equally important, set of reasons why motivations hardened in London and Paris as escalation proceeded in the early 1750s. They concern the relations between each side's minimum and maximum objectives.

In the first place, policy-makers in both capitals gradually came to believe that there was an irreconcilable conflict between what might be called the *immediate minimum* objectives of each side.

Following the attack on Fort Necessity, all members of the Whig government perceived the minimum French objective in America to be control of the Ohio region. This appeared to conflict (actually it did not) with the minimum British objective of providing the English colonists room in which to expand westward. In addition, the war party within the cabinet came to see the French as pursuing a maximum objective of pushing back English influence throughout North America and around the world.[22]

Decision-makers at Versailles suspected that the minimum British objective was possession of the Ohio territory. This appeared to conflict (actually it did not) with the minimum French objective of maintaining communications between New France and Louisiana. In addition, after Braddock's orders were penetrated, the French saw their opponents as pursuing a maximum objective of pushing back French control throughout North America.[23]

Thus some policy-makers in each capital came more and more to suspect the other of pursuing maximum objectives; in any case they all came to perceive the opponent's immediate minimum objective to be irreconcilably in conflict with their own. At one level this may be said to have been a major source of the escalation sequence that resulted, finally, in general war. But behind the problem of immediate minimum objectives lay a far graver problem of what might be termed *long-range minimum* or *absolute minimum* objectives. To illuminate this, a little background is required.

For decades the French and British had been building worldwide colonial and mercantile empires that, in a general way, competed with each other. Under the reigning mercantilist doctrine, the purpose of these empires was economic enrichment of the mother country, and comparative profitability was one medium in which the Anglo-French competition was conducted. However, this goal was increasingly being supplemented (and in the minds of some policy-makers superseded) by more general "imperial" goals such as overall political strength, total military resources, aggregate population, control of geopolitically strategic areas, and the like. The expectation in London and Paris was that this general or background competition between them—this "cold war"—would continue for a long time to come.[24]

For economic and other reasons, certain areas seemed to both sides to offer particular advantages: various locations in North

America, the West Indies, locations on the western coast of Africa, and the Deccan and Carnatic districts of India. For these the competition was more direct and more violent. An advantageous position in most or all of them would give the advantaged power superior economic resources that would allow it subsequently to pull ahead in the more general competition for world empire. At the same time, the advantage offered by a *moderate* gain for one side or the other in most of these locations was not so large or so immediate as to warrant a major war. And from time to time, various opportunities arose, some of which had been seized upon and usefully employed, to divide the spoils, postpone some issues, and otherwise defuse actual or potential crises.

Much more vital in the long run than the positive, but only slowly achievable, objective of gaining the superior world empire, was the negative objective of denying the opponent any really decisive advantage that might foreordain the results of the general competition. Here North America, and particularly the central area of the continent, was far more important than any of the other disputed areas, even though it was of much less short-term or even medium-term economic significance. For the North American continent, temperate and very similar to Europe, promised eventually to be the home of a populous and powerful political entity or entities. Beyond the hope of policy-makers in London and Paris that this foreseeable entity might belong to their own empire, more important was their fear that it might belong to the other. Versailles had long recognized that New France and Louisiana would not pay their own way for many years to come. But to give most or all of the North American continent to Great Britain could be extremely dangerous in the long run to France herself, for an England backed by the wealth and manpower of a continent would be overwhelmingly preponderant in Europe. Just the reverse calculation was made by the British, who feared that their colonies—if not eventually driven into the sea by a French America—might be forever shut in to a narrow coastal strip, while France controlled the vast interior and North America as a whole, and went on to become overwhelmingly dominant in Europe and the world.[25]

In both London and Paris, therefore, policy-makers held it as an absolute minimum objective not to allow a situation to develop whereby the colonists of the opposing empire could seize such a preponderant position in America that it would be virtually impossible to dislodge them, and from which they could then go on subsequently to colonize and control the great bulk of the continent. This absolute minimum objective had been recognized for some time. It was not new in 1753. What *was* new was the interpretation that now became accepted in London and Paris of what this meant operationally. Policy-makers in both capitals came to the conclusion, for somewhat different reasons, that the Ohio territory was the key to the American continent.

Officials in France believed (erroneously) that the Ohio River was the only major water route between the St. Lawrence and the Mississippi. They thought that to allow the English to control the Ohio River would be to lose ready access to the lands farther west, in the center of the continent, and to the Indian tribes living there who so far had been contacted almost exclusively by Frenchmen. The waterway represented by the Ohio River appeared to the French to be critical to the American interior.[26]

The British were not primarily interested in the Ohio River; what they were interested in was the surrounding land. In the late 1740s and early 1750s, the expansion-minded citizens of Virginia concluded that desirable new land, land that could readily be cleared and farmed, lay not to the southwest or due west, but to the northwest. Explorers reported that the land was mountainous in the other directions, but to the northwest only a few mountains (the Alleghenies) needed to be crossed before broad fertile plains began, extending indefinitely westward. The Virginians in turn reported to London that the Ohio area represented the only real opening westward for the English colonists in America.[27] With benefit of hindsight, we know that perceptions in the two European capitals were exaggerated, and in some respects false. Yet in the early 1750s the expectation in Paris was that to lose control of the Ohio River was probably to lose access to the American interior, and the expectation in London was that to lose possession of the Ohio territory was to give up the door to the west from the eastern seaboard.

What is analytically important here is that these perceptions *activated* the long-standing absolute minimum objective of each side. Previously this goal had seemed somewhat abstract and generalized, however vital in principle—a possible problem for the future. The events of the early 1750s crystalized this diffuse objective on each side. They brought a possible, future, and nonoperational problem down to a real, immediate, and operational one; they made concrete what had been abstract. Policy-makers in London and Paris came to perceive their respective colonists' scrap over a couple of small forts as actually being the opening engagement in "the battle for North America."[28] It was this *crystalization of long-standing but previously diffuse objectives* that was one of the most important reasons why attitudes on both sides now hardened rapidly, motivation rose to gain the goal even at a high price, and decision-makers proceeded to fling more and more powerful forces into the fray.

The Transformation of Perceptions and the Narrowing of Expectations

Both French and British had been wearied by the War of the Austrian Succession, and in the years after the Treaty of Aix-la-Chapelle they included in their foreign policies explicit efforts to maintain the peace between the two nations if at all possible. As one historian has noted of the French during this period, "A general war with Great Britain was not part of the design of the French government. For the sake of peace it had sacrificed . . . [important gains] in India, and . . . it was prepared to suffer the most humiliating indignities to avoid a general war."[29] A similar generalization could be made about the British government at this time.

To a degree both capitals recognized that they shared the objective of maintaining the peace. In addition to a symmetrical perception that the two world empires were competing, there was also a roughly symmetrical perception that their competition, however serious over the long run, would be restrained at any one time. The term *limited adversary*, which has been used to characterize Soviet-American relations since the end of the acute Cold War, describes perfectly relations between the French and English empires in the late 1740s and early 1750s, as perceived in both capitals. Despite the serious long-term conflict, the perception on both sides was that the opponent was *not* seeking specific short-term objectives around the world that would give it decisive advantage in the world competition. (And the absolute minimum objective on each side of not allowing the other to obtain hegemony in North America had not yet crystalized.)

Decision-makers in both countries therefore entertained a wide range of expectations about plausible future developments and anticipated being able to employ a substantial range of policy instruments, with direct military action included only rarely. They expected that various political, economic, and diplomatic maneuvers would gain them modest advantages from time to time. They may have expected to employ military, but not too violent, demonstrations for deterrent and compellent purposes. And they certainly expected to employ diplomatic negotiations for resolving, compromising, or at least freezing, serious disputes.[30]

As events unfolded, all these things changed. On both sides *the perception of the opponent was gradually transformed*, until policy-makers were perceiving the opponent as striving rapidly for a decisively superior competitive position. Their *range of expectations about the plausible future* narrowed steadily, until acute competiton—and very possibly war—seemed the only realistic expectation. The *range of policy instruments that could be expected to be useful* also narrowed, until only major military action still seemed to offer a reasonable expectation of securing fundamental objectives.

The important part played in this process by crystallization of the absolute minimum objectives has already been indicated. Let us look next at changes in the range of apparently useful policy instruments, and in the related range of expectations about plausible futures. First, the matter of negotiations.

Recognizing the potential seriousness of their disputes in the West Indies, in the western and northern parts of the English colony of New York, and in Nova Scotia, the French and British in 1750 created a joint Delimitation Commission to negotiate all territorial disputes in the Western Hemisphere. (The Ohio was hardly yet an issue.) The meetings of the commission were infrequent, however, and almost completely nonproductive. The commissioners discovered fairly early that the fundamental conflict between Britain and France in North America was too basic to be resolved by the limited authority they had been given by their governments. Paradoxically, though, none of the disputes seemed to be pressing enough to demand energetic bargaining. The combination of little reason for speed on immediate issues, and an expectation of inevitable failure on the central questions, meant that the commissioners had the least possible incentive to proceed with vigor. There were also technical impediments, such as differences in the English and French maps of North America. And despite the ample time available, individuals with expert knowledge of the disputed areas in North America were not called in to assist the commission. Finally, after four fruitless years, it was dissolved.[31]

As the Delimitation Commission's activities ground to a halt, a perception grew among policy-makers on both sides of the channel that many extensive efforts to negotiate an understanding in North America had all ended in failure. In actuality, inspection of the commission's deliberations suggests that by no means had all avenues been tried, and some that had been tried had not been explored very thoroughly.[32] To high-level decision-makers at the time this was less clear. What was more visible was the evident fact of an attempt to negotiate for years, and failure. The expected value of negotiations now declined considerably.

Motivation to negotiate in other ways fell victim to the growing suspicion on both sides. The British, reacting against the slow pace of the commission, had repeatedly proposed direct negotiations at the ambassadorial level. Until 1754 these were rejected by the French as a possible British effort to evade the semijudicial commission and gain a more advantageous outcome through diplomatic maneuver. The French rejection, in turn, was interpreted in London as suggesting that Louis XV's real goal was to keep the commission going in a desultory and inconclusive fashion while his agents maneuvered in the colonies. The British constantly saw the French as evasive about their overall intentions in North America and elsewhere, and once caught the French foreign minister lying (at least in the British perception) about French activities in the West Indies. Subsequently, Versailles discovered that Prime Minister Newcastle had lied (at least in the French perception) when he gave assurance that General Braddock's orders were strictly defensive. Another factor that deepened the mutual distrust was a growing suspicion in each capital that the other side was stalling for time. The English observed a steady effort, alarmingly successful, to build up the French navy. The French perceived a steadily rising threat to the Ohio area from the English colonists in America and growing English influence on the Continent, including in capitals such as Madrid that traditionally had been friendly to Paris.[33]

Negotiations were discouraged, then, by mounting suspicions on each side about the opponent's real objectives, and by the important happenstance that policy-makers in each capital calculated that *their opponents stood to gain more from the passage of time*

217

than they did themselves. Seeming evidence that their opponents might be delaying and obstructing real progress in the bargaining became translated into *changing perceptions about the opponent's probable objectives* and *changing expectations about what the future was likely to bring.*

After military action had begun in North America, policy-makers in France and England, anxious to terminate the conflict or at least to limit the scope of the war, had a new and more urgent motive to negotiate. Bargaining now began at the ambassadorial level. But Albermarle, the British ambassador to His Most Catholic Majesty, died in December 1754 and was not immediately replaced. The French ambassador to the Court of St. James's, Mirepoix, did not return to London from leave until mid-January and was ignorant of North American affairs. Several rounds of bargaining proposals were made, but the French accompanied theirs with the demand for an end to all military action *prior to* the resumption of full negotiations on the issues. For the British to have agreed to this would have meant that they could not prevent the French from reinforcing Canada with the six battalions, which potentially could do tremendous damage. So the French demand was refused. For this reason and others to be mentioned shortly, this round of bargaining ended in deadlock like its predecessors. By May 1755 policy-makers on both sides became convinced that the opponent's objectives were intolerable and that further negotiations offered little expectation of agreement.[34]

As the negotiating instrument came to seem useless, so eventually did the instrument of military demonstrations for deterrent and compellent purposes. The effects of earlier attempts by both sides to use this instrument, though, were extremely significant.

Almost every step early in the escalation sequence was taken primarily for its politico-military effect (deterrence or compellence), and only subordinately to accomplish some specific military end. Governor Dinwiddie's original message to Montreal, and subsequent dispatch of a few hundred armed men to an area where they could expect to meet many more Frenchmen and hostile Indians, was intended mainly to demonstrate to the French Great Britain's "official" legal and military interest in the area. Earlier, Duquesne in Montreal had been aware that his line of forts could be conquered by the English colonies, but by constructing them he hoped to show that New France was resolved to hold the Ohio, and could and would impose a high cost on any attempt to take it. A similar demonstration of resolve was one ingredient in the decision in Paris to dispatch six of its finest battalions to the New World. Similarly, Prime Minister Newcastle in London agreed to the Braddock mission quite explicitly on the grounds that it would indicate to the French how seriously Britain intended to defend its ownership of the Ohio; whereupon Louis XV, he hoped, would disavow Duquesne's "aggression."[35]

Almost any of these steps might have been successful if the opponent had perceived it as the *deterrent* measure it was intended to be; in each case the opponent perceived it instead as a *compellent* action. As we have had occasion to note before, compellence is much harder to accomplish than deterrence, and every one of these steps failed in its primary purpose of coercing the opponent to withdraw from the competition. Again we observe a consequence of each side's belief that it was basically the defending power and that the opponent was acting offensively: it was this belief that allowed each of these actions to be intended as deterrent while simultaneously being perceived as compellent.

Because of this continuing illusion on both sides, policy-makers in London and Paris gradually found that, contrary to expectation, their efforts to demonstrate their resolve were not succeeding. Hence the demonstrative line of policy, too, came to offer less and less expectation of achieving fundamental objectives. With the (apparent) failure of negotiation as a promising line of policy at about the same time, the only major line of policy left was overt military action to achieve objectives by force. The range of plausible futures, which had always included major war as a possibility, now was narrowing to the point where major war appeared to be the main probability.

Unlike the British and French effort to negotiate the issues, which could have succeeded, this decline in the expected usefulness of "demonstrations of motivation" was the inevitable consequence of policy-makers on both sides having entered the problem *failing to comprehend the fundamental perspective and assumptions of the opponent.* In effect, although not in intent, the escalating sequence of demonstrations of resolve became a process of mutual discovery of the opponent's profound motivation not to give away the Ohio. By the time this was ascertained, however, the sequence had proceeded to the point where the direct military consequences of each step back and forth (as opposed to the symbolic politico-military effects) were so great that each step by the opponent absolutely demanded a counterescalation if the absolute minimum objective in North America was not to be abandoned.

This is the essence of how a process that began as a relatively controlled series of escalatory steps gradually went out of control. The earlier steps in the sequence were intended primarily for their value as politico-military demonstrations, and only very secondarily for their concrete military benefits. But the demonstrations back and forth were based on inadequate and uncomprehending ideas, entertained on both sides, about the opponent's basic assumptions and perceptions of the situation. Therefore the demonstrations did not achieve their demonstrative intent. Collectively they merely succeeded in revealing to policy-makers in both capitals how deeply committed their opponents were to the objective of retaining the Ohio. By the time this had been accomplished, however, the ratio of demonstrative value to direct, military consequences of each step had shifted. Each step was distinctly tilting the advantage in-theater one way or the other. The concrete military implications of each step were becoming so great that from then on neither group of decision-makers could afford to allow the opponent to enjoy the military consequences of his deed, unless they were prepared to abandon their absolute minimum objective in North America. That objective was assessed on both sides as so vital that it could not be abandoned even at the risk of general war; the competition, which by now was largely military, proceeded to full-scale conflict.

When one remembers that in addition, the early steps in the sequence had the effect of crystallizing the absolute minimum objectives on both sides, the two themes in combination provide much of the answer to why the escalation process was so inexorable, even though it stretched over years.

Even after this crystallization and after the demonstrations, there still were opportunities to decouple the two sides' absolute minimum objectives from the developing situation, by negotiating a compromise solution for the immediate conflicts and pushing into the future the long-range problem of hegemony in North America. The most important opportunity of this kind was a proposal made by the English on 20 February 1755. They suggested that the Ohio territory be made a neutral zone, in which English Americans would have some limited trading rights with the Indians, but which they would not settle or colonize. The French would not use the upper Ohio River to communicate between Canada and Louisiana; instead they would use a route along the Wabash River (which flows into western Lake Erie from the southwest) and the Miami River (which flows southward into the lower Ohio in what is now Illinois). This was a route the French had already used occasionally and along which they had a couple of small forts; it was at least as direct as the route via the upper Ohio and required an almost equally short portage. The question of the ultimate ownership of the Ohio area was to be deferred indefinitely.[36]

Even though it failed, this proposal is a striking one for London to have made, for in effect it would have protected French interests in North America somewhat more thoroughly than British. It is notable evidence of the extent to which Newcastle and most of his colleagues still sought to avoid general war, and also of the extent to which they were willing to sacrifice the interests of their American colonists in trying to do so.

A proposal of this sort could have been used—and to some extent may have actually been used—by the British as a means of *testing the opponent's objectives.* Acceptance by the French would not just have indicated their ability and willingness to decouple their absolute minimum objective from the immediate issues. It would also have thoroughly scotched the argument of the war party in London that Louis XV had decided to go for maximum objectives in North America and worldwide. In fact he had not. As it was, the failure of this proposal (and more generally, the evident failure of the bargaining in this period to get anywhere) underlined the war party's perception of French objectives and helped to transform the perceptions held by other, less suspicious British policy-makers.

The French initially rejected the British plan of 20 February because they could not accept several of its secondary features, such as a demand for English trading privileges along the shores of the Great Lakes and another concerning Nova Scotia. In the course of the next two months the English were to express willingness, at one time or another, to greatly soften all of these demands, although there was no one time when the gaps between the shifting English and French positions on all these complex issues narrowed enough *simultaneously* so that actual agreement seemed within reach.

The underlying problems were that policy-makers on both sides had now grown skeptical about the value of a serious negotiating effort and about their opponents' real intentions and goals; and, equally important, that time was running out. The English were unsure when the flotilla carrying the reinforcements to Canada would sail from Brest; they estimated that it could leave anytime from the end of March on. The decision to send Admiral Boscawen out to intercept it was made at a meeting of the "inner cabinet" on March 18th. That decision could hardly be postponed, and presuming (as the cabinet did) that Boscawen would be successful, the action could very well lead to war.[37] In short, the negotiating process by this point had gotten enmeshed in the cogs of the relentless clock set by military actions and preparations on both sides.

In fact, the British may have purposely delivered a mortal wound to the negotiations in March by putting forward a new demand (for land adjoining the St. Lawrence River) they may have realized the French could not possibly accept. While definite evidence is lacking, it seems likely that the cabinet, with little time left before the Royal Navy would have to be ordered out to intercept the French fleet, was trying to provoke Louis XV and his ministers into declaring war first and thereby allow the British to invoke their defensive alliances in Europe.[38]

Expectations by this point had narrowed sharply on both sides. Negotiations had been tried and apparently had failed. Military demonstrations of resolve by each side had not convinced the opponent; they had only inspired him to similar demonstrations, which had brought the situation to the point where the feasible next steps would have a tremendous impact on the military situation in North America and would sharply heighten the risk of general war. Where previously several alternative lines of policy had offered reasonable expectation of protecting basic objectives in North America, increasingly only strong military action seemed to. Where previously a number of futures had been plausible, now only acute crisis, and very possibly a major war, seemed plausible.

That the range of acceptable options and plausible futures had narrowed so sharply and so rapidly was partly the product of what might be called technical aspects of the politico-military situation. These deserve attention next.

Asymmetries and Disproportionalities

Central to the cyclical escalation sequence of the Seven Years War was a set of asymmetries in the capabilities of the various actors. Similar to these in their structure and in their effect, and potentially more controllable by decision-makers in the short run, were several "disproportionate" actions they took. Let us look at each of these categories in turn. First, the asymmetries.

(1) The desire and efforts of all parties during much of the sequence to limit the conflict to North America failed in part because of a strong asymmetry, in favor of the French, in the capabilities of the two proxies on that continent. Unlike the thirteen English colonies (fourteen, if we count Nova Scotia), New France was a single unitary state, controlled for all practical purposes by one all-powerful governor. In military power, New France was much more than a match for any one of the British colonies acting alone—as Virginia, the most powerful colony, discovered. The English colonies, if they could act together, were potentially far stronger than New France. But, as the French knew, they were highly particularistic and mutually uncooperative; so far they had proved totally incapable of banding together for any political purpose whatsoever. Dinwiddie in Williamsburg had made repeated efforts to get assistance from the other colonies in dealing with the French, but with a couple of minor exceptions had failed to receive any effective aid at all. (Pennsylvania, which along with Virginia had perhaps the most direct interest in the Ohio, was governed at this time by a majority of pacifist Quakers who refused to involve the colony in military action.) Subsequently, Benjamin Franklin and others called an intercolonial congress at Albany in 1754 to discuss the French and Indian situation; the congress' scheme for united action was subsequently ignored by most of the colonies.[39]

It was partly for this reason that Duquesne and his associates in Montreal believed that their policy of fortifying the Ohio territory could be successful. They had long held the expectation with considerable confidence that, as long as the Old World was not called in to redress the balance of the New, their cause would prevail. Any single English colony could not oust them from the Ohio, and all the colonies together clearly would not.[40]

It was on the basis of this expectation that the Virginians felt compelled to appeal for help to the mother country; and it was on the same basis that London felt compelled to respond. If the English colonies in America, or even most of them, had been able to act in concert, Duquesne might have been deterred from fortifying the Ohio. Even if they had waited until after this action and then been able to act in a fairly unified way, the subsequent contest would probably have been recognized in both London and Paris as a proxy war, which both capitals would have urgently desired to limit to such. It was the total inability of the individualistic (and in some cases pacifistic) Englishmen to unite for action even after frontier fighting had broken out, that "compelled" the involvement of Great Britain herself.[41]

(2) New France and the English American colonies were also asymmetrical with respect to the *kind* of forces they maintained. The English colonies were self-sustaining, with no British forces regularly stationed there. New France, on the other hand, was much more a military creature of Versailles; regular French troops were routinely stationed there in significant number and routinely rotated back and forth to France. For the French this represented a kind of counterweight to the greater population of the English colonies. Still, the English colonials in any action against Canada were facing regular French forces, while themselves not maintaining regular British troops. Dinwiddie's request to London for two regiments of regulars therefore seemed highly reasonable, and the English cabinet could say that with the Braddock mission it was only beginning to do what Louis XV had been doing all along. Yet from the French point of view, the Braddock mission was an unprecedented act that broke the previous limits of the conflict and established new ground rules.[42]

In this way, the previously existing asymmetry in *kinds of forces* in the Western Hemisphere became translated into an asymmetry in *perceptions* in the Eastern Hemisphere. What could be seen in London as merely an equalizing action that corrected an asymmetry, was seen in Paris as an unprecedented escalation that threw out of line a previous rough balance between the French soldiers and the far more populous British civilians in America.

(3) The next asymmetry was introduced by the fact that Britain was a sea power and France primarily a land power. Despite French efforts to catch up, the Royal Navy in 1755 was over twice as large as the French navy, the nearest competitor, and promised complete control of the sea to Britain in any war. France's army, though, with over a hundred battalions, was the largest in Europe and far larger than Britain's. Accordingly, the French could send to Canada

two or three soldiers for every one sent to America by Britain, whereas the two regiments sent with Braddock represented a significant fraction of the entire ready British army.

It was for this reason that when Versailles replied to the Braddock mission by sending 3,000 men to Canada, the Whig government could not easily respond by sending an additional army detachment to reinforce Braddock. Had the two powers had even roughly symmetrical capabilities in ground forces, a pattern of responding to each troop deployment with a troop deployment of one's own might have gone on for some time. Although still an escalation, it would have been an escalation within the North American limits of the conflict. Also, additional time would have been made available for the principals to engage in the negotiations both sought, and part of the time were pursuing. The conflict would not have so readily and so rapidly escalated to general war.

The limited number of British ground forces available made this impossible. London's options were reduced to two: to allow Braddock to be confronted by superior forces and defeated, or to prevent the French reinforcements from arriving in America. British naval supremacy seemed to promise the latter with high confidence of success. So rather than throw Braddock's force away with no gain, London opted for halting the French reinforcements.

(4) The Whig government attempted to stay within the North American limits of the conflict by having its navy perform the interception in North American waters (although it would have been easier and surer in European waters). This effort to control escalation was unsuccessful because in its turn it confronted the French with a severe asymmetry in capabilities.

It was recognized in Paris that the reinforcement mission to Montreal had gotten past the British fleet by luck. The French were compelled to agree with the calculation the British cabinet had made—that in general the Royal Navy could intercept and capture reinforcements sent to Canada. Policy-makers in both capitals expected that under such ground rules New France could be cordoned off from aid, while the British could assist their colonies at their leisure. Had the French possessed a naval capability comparable to the British, this conclusion could not have been drawn. The French could have attempted naval missions to Canada and the result might have been a series of naval engagements in the North Atlantic. Like the repeated reinforcements of ground forces that also did not occur, this series of naval engagements might have offered the principals some additional time and incentive to find the negotiated settlement they both desired.

However, the possibility of a serious naval challenge to Britain was lacking. Paris was confronted with the identical two options that London had just chosen between: to allow the opponent to reinforce his proxy at will without reinforcing one's own proxy (a sure recipe for defeat in theater), or *to apply one's asymmetrical advantages* to halt the opponent's reinforcements.

The French possessed the latter option in an army (and potentially, a set of allies) that could draw off the opponent's troops into European battles, or even keep them at home under threat of invasion. (Twice during the Seven Years War the French made preparations for an invasion of the British Isles.) Versailles therefore chose just as London had—to escalate, rather than to abandon the proxy. By threatening Hanover, by threatening an invasion of England, and by finding allies who could help him do both, Louis XV brought George II's attention back from the Ohio valley to the defense of his most immediate and vital possessions and ensured that no major reinforcements of the American colonies would be made.

In effect, the French chose to protect their proxy by raising the stakes. Just as King George had decided to expand the conflict from the North American continent to include the North Atlantic Ocean, where his comparative advantage lay, so Louis XV decided to expand it to include the European continent, where *his* comparative advantage lay. Each relieved the pressure of a disadvantageous asymmetry by throwing a new part of the world into the cauldron.

To sum up: from a technical point of view, escalation proceeded from the banks of the Ohio River to the Seven Years War up a ladder of four situationally generated asymmetries in the players' capabilities. The absence of any of them might have at least slowed the process, and perhaps halted it.

Similar to asymmetries in logic and effect are steps that actors take during an escalation sequence which represent disproportionate responses to preceding steps. Two stand out in the escalation sequence leading to the Seven Years War.

Newcastle's original plan for responding to Dinwiddie's appeal

226

for assistance was to send advisers, equipment, and financial support, but no troops. This would have been much less likely to trigger a serious French response than his actual dispatch of two regiments of regulars. A sufficient financial commitment on Newcastle's part would certainly have raised volunteer colonial troops in the numbers required to regain the Ohio. Contrary to the Duke of Cumberland's belief, colonials would have had a higher probability of success than British regulars, since the English Americans were experienced in fighting Frenchmen and Indians in the backwoods.[43] The Braddock mission was a disproportionate response, because a lesser response would have served the objective at least equally well and would have been much less likely to trigger an escalatory response by the opponent.

Similarly, the French reply to this mission was, in Corbett's words, "out of proportion to Braddock's two poor battalions." For Louis XV to send six elite battalions to New France suggested strongly to decision-makers in London that he might have additional, offensive objectives in North America beyond the defeat of Braddock. The French action further helped to transform British officials' perceptions and expectations, and provided them with a partial basis for their belief that Boscawen's interception mission was defensive.[44]

The French shared the great British overestimation of the effectiveness in the American forests of Braddock's two battalions of regulars. Even granting this, the French might have better controlled escalation and better served their own immediate goals in the New World by sending reinforcements to Duquesne that roughly matched Braddock's force—some two battalions only. It is entirely possible that this would still have motivated English decision-makers to send out Boscawen's naval squadron. But French policy would not have seemed to the British to be such convincing evidence that Louis XV was willing to accept general war in pursuit of greatly elevated objectives, and would not have discouraged the British as strongly from pursuing negotiations.

Both of these disproportionate steps were meant, in part, to be demonstrations of policy-makers' resolve and of the seriousness with which they viewed the developing situation. Disproportionate moves are sometimes made because decision-makers wish to signal their resolve and seriousness to their opponents and feel that a proportionate action, being too obvious and natural from a purely practical viewpoint, might not get the message across as clearly. This is an understandable, and on its own terms reasonable, motive; from this viewpoint a disproportionate action could even serve as an escalation control device by warning the opponent to back off from the situation before it is too late.

The assumption, sometimes unspoken, that underlies this viewpoint is "policy-makers on the other side are less motivated than we are." If they really are equally or even more motivated, the disproportionate action will not cause them to back off, nor will it control escalation. As suggested earlier, it will merely narrow the range of expectations and harden motivations on both sides; simultaneously it will shift the conflict to a higher level of violence, where the purely military aspect of actions is relatively more important than their politico-military, signalling aspect.

Furthermore, it is often hard to separate the signal of serious motives from the signal of elevated objectives. A disproportionate action and even many proportionate escalations usually are just as likely to suggest the latter as the former (if not more so). The principal exception to this generalization is the case of a skillfully constructed dual policy, where the action intended to signal serious motivation is coupled with another action that credibly communicates the limit of one's objectives. Most often this second action will be a serious negotiating proposal, one that offers to settle the dispute on terms that meet one's less extensive goals.

Because the escalatory action is likely to speak more loudly to the opponent than the conciliatory words, policy-makers must try to surround the negotiating proposal with as many indications of its seriousness as they can. (Often, regrettably, they do not, and it is the escalatory action that gets most of the attention in, for instance, declaratory policy.) If the British had coupled the rather generous plan that in fact they developed on 20 February 1755 with the revelation of Braddock's mission the previous fall, and if they had communicated to the French that Braddock's mission would be called off in the event of successful negotiations, subsequent events might have been quite different. As is so often the case, though, the British moved first to secure their objective by military means, and only afterward tried to control the escalatory effect of what they had done by means of negotiations. But meanwhile the military means had damaged the opponent's expectations about the usefulness and meaningfulness of negotiations.

Analytic Failures

Another aspect of the escalation sequence of the Seven Years War is a series, on both side, of analytic failures, as they are being termed here. It is, of course, easier to identify these in retrospect. Even so, almost every step in the sequence betrays some instance of policy-makers failing (in ways that hardly seem inevitable) to analyze their information fully and calculate their steps carefully, or to seek important additional information that could have been obtained.

(1) In the first place, the fundamental objective of the French was impossible. In the long run and probably even in the medium run, the French colonists in America could not hope to keep penned in against the ocean a population twenty times the size of New France and even disproportionately richer. Quite apart from any action by Britain, the French economy could not possibly have afforded to sustain an expeditionary force in America remotely adequate to make up the difference.

The chain of defeats inflicted upon Virginia by New France encouraged Versailles in its misestimate and contributed importantly to the dispatch of the 3,000 elite troops. Decision-makers in Paris did not clearly comprehend that it had taken a significant fraction of Canada's total military power to defeat English Americans whose numbers were utterly trivial compared to the potential mobilizable manpower resources of the English colonies. Had the French made a more accurate estimate of the cost involved in any sustained and systematic defense of the Ohio—even presuming the Royal Navy did not interfere—they would have discovered it to be prohibitive. Even before the original French effort to fortify the Ohio was begun, it should have been clear that the French hope of seizing the continent was doomed. But appropriate negotiation *then* could have secured a large French Canada and probably guaranteed its communication with the small settlement in Louisiana.[45]

(2) As the French failed to analyze their capabilities, the English failed to analyze the threat. In reality, no action by Great Britain was required. The asymmetry between the *potential* power of the English and French colonies in America was evident enough, as was the inability of France to make up the difference. That the *actual*

power of New France was relatively so great, compared to any one English colony, was the best argument for the partial and pragmatic union of the colonies that British policy-makers were seeking anyway. Had they not intervened dramatically in America, British policy-makers would not have permanently lost the Ohio to France, since the English Americans in any case could take it whenever they were determined to do so. And by not intervening, the British would have maintained the colonists' dependence upon the homeland. By conquering Canada, as they did in the subsequent war, England removed the last threat to the American colonies and set the stage for their rebellion—as a few farsighted observers perceived at the time.[46]

(3) No British action being required, the Duke of Holdernesse's orders to the colonies to resist French encroachments were superfluous. Significant encroachments would have been resisted in any case. His orders, however, made Virginia's later request for troops—to carry out the orders—appropriate, plausible, and difficult to refuse. The orders tended to create in both colonial and English minds the fallacious assumption that Britain had a direct interest in a military defense of trans-Appalachia and hence could be expected to assist therein. Without the full realization of English policy-makers, they created a potentially hazardous commitment for the future.[47]

(4) If one allows for the above miscalculations, the sequence of events then follows reasonably to the point where Virginia requested troops from Britain. But London's acquiescence was a serious error. The belief of the war party in London that British regulars were needed to cope with the French forces in Canada was wrong. Indeed Braddock's troops were subsequently decimated because their tactics were utterly unsuitable for the kind of fighting they were required to do.[48]

Far more appropriate than the decision to send Braddock was Newcastle's original plan: to respond to Virginia's request with moral support, money to pay colonial volunteers, officers to help plan and lead a campaign and give some military training to colonial troops, and perhaps a few specialists in artillery and engineering to provide needed technical skills. Such a response could have secured the Ohio with colonial forces and would have been less likely to draw any severe French reaction.[49]

230

Had the French not responded to the Braddock mission as they did, triggering Boscawen's naval effort and so on up the ladder, English policy-makers would have discovered through Braddock's defeat that a British expeditionary force was inappropriate for his mission. Options for merely assisting the colonies to fight their own battle would probably then have been reexamined, and the conflict perhaps de-escalated.

(5) The French did not need to reinforce Canada as they did, since the forces already available to Duquesne were ample to deal with Braddock. By sending a force so overwhelming, the French encouraged officials in London to fear that the French troops might have not only defensive orders to defeat Braddock, but also offensive orders to attack British forts in New York and Nova Scotia.

Further than this, Versailles presented British policy-makers with an enormous temptation. The French wanted their expeditionary force to arrive in Canada as quickly as possible to meet Braddock and did not think the British would risk war to halt it at sea. So the French decided not to send the force in slow troopships, but to strip their fastest and largest warships of most of their guns and carry the troops in them. (A handful of fully armed warships went along as escort.) The flotilla of eighteen ships, therefore, *both* made up of the pride of the French navy *and* was unable effectively to defend itself against Boscawen's squadron.[50] If the French had been trying to present the British with the greatest possible temptation to escalate the conflict by means of a naval action, it is hard to imagine how they could have better done so. To destroy or capture the French flotilla whole, as British officials expected Boscawen to do, at one blow would have prevented the French reinforcements from arriving in Canada, would have captured or destroyed six of the finest battalions in the French army, and would have captured or destroyed approximately one-third—the highest-quality third— of the major fighting vessels in the French navy. Versailles so crippled could hardly contemplate a major war with Great Britain, and it was partly for this reason that the English expected that Boscawen's mission might not actually lead to war.[51]

(6) However, British policy-makers failed to think through the full implications of the admiral's mission. Here the cabinet displayed a strange mixture of perspicacity and easily avoidable

miscalculation. To order Boscawen to perform the interception in North American waters rather than in European waters demonstrated a sophisticated awareness of the requirements of escalation control. So it is mystifying why this appreciation fled while his exact objectives were being penned. Boscawen's orders should have specified clearly that hostilities were to be opened only if the tactical situation offered the capture or destruction of *all*, or at any rate most, of the French flotilla. Such a coup would have virtually won the war it might have caused. But English decision-makers contented themselves with *expecting* this outcome, and neglected to *order* Boscawen to risk beginning a war only if he could victoriously engage the entire flotilla. That the capture of a few French ships was too much or too little was realized in London only afterward.[52]

Intragovernmental Factors

In addition to the factors that have been discussed so far, institutional and other factors played a role in the escalation sequence leading to the Seven Years War.

Policy-makers both in London and in Paris were excessively dependent upon very few channels of information. The French colonial system heavily emphasized the role of the military. Duquesne and his predecessors as governors of New France in the period from the late 1740s on were all military officers, as were most of his staff. It appears that almost all the reports that Versailles had from Canada originated from or passed through the hands of these men. In London, decision-makers had a slightly wider range of information sources, but the bulk of their information came from the several governors of the American colonies who were most involved with the problems of the western frontier. As noted earlier, neither in Paris nor in London did policy-makers make an effort to bring lower-ranking individuals familiar with the Ohio region back to the capital for consultation.

The significance of the few information channels on both sides was enhanced by the fact that governors Dinwiddie and Duquesne both had a stake in securing the Ohio. Dinwiddie was a major stockholder in the Ohio Company, the group of Virginians most anxious to expand their land holdings into that region. He therefore had a direct personal interest in obtaining Great Britain's military protection of the territory where the Ohio Company was beginning to stake out its claim. Furthermore, much of his information (and the basis of his reports) came from other members of the company. Although the evidence is less clear, it appears that Duquesne in Montreal may have been involved with the Grande Société, a group of French businessmen anxious to expand their trade with the Indians in the Ohio area. On both sides, then, the real importance of the Ohio region and the significance of events therein were undoubtedly exaggerated in the reports on which higher-level policy-makers partially based their decisions.[53]

An example of the problems created by policy-makers' limited sources of information is a report sent to London by Governor William Shirley of the colony of Massachusetts. In the spring of 1754 Shirley, a firebrand imperialist who was convinced that the British should take over Canada at the first opportunity, reported on slender information that the French had begun a settlement on what was unquestionably Massachusetts territory, in an area that had not previously been under dispute. It later turned out that this information was completely false, but Shirley did not send a second report canceling the first until August. Meanwhile the news of Washington's defeat at Fort Necessity had reached London. Shirley's report provided a germ for the developing perception among British decision-makers that the French had elevated their objectives and were shifting over to a general offensive, and it helped create the climate of opinion in which Braddock's mission could be ordered.[54]

Decision-making in both capitals was further handicapped by the sudden deaths in 1754 of key figures—in London of Pelham, who had been a cornerstone of the long-standing Whig government; in Paris of St. Contest, the foreign minister. Partly for this reason, during 1754 policy-makers in both capitals saw the opposing regime as being disorganized and more than usually engulfed in intragovernmental politics. The British, not inaccurately, perceived the new French foreign minister, Rouillé, as peripheral to the center of decision-making, and suspected that the king's favorite, Madame de Pompadour, enjoyed heavy and somewhat unpredictable influence. The French, not inaccurately, perceived the Whig government as torn by infighting among Newcastle, Pitt, Fox, and a number of others and suspected that the cabinet was heavily influenced by "capitalistes" in London.

Thus on both sides there was a suspicion during 1754 and early

1755 that the initial tendency of policy-makers in the opposing capital to back up their proxies in North America was a product not of high policy but of high-level politics. Correctly believing that on the whole the upper echelons of the opposing government did not want a major war, decision-makers on both sides concluded that the opponent's escalations to date had been caused by overeager subordinates in North America and by hawkish, but minority, elements at the capital. As one historian remarks, "The question of ministerial unity . . . conditioned the intransigence of both governments, since each thought the other to be fundamentally divided and vacillating. It also enabled the warmongers on both sides of the channel to deprecate the usefulness of negotiation and to question the authenticity of the other nation's peaceful intents."[55]

Part of the motive for the politico-military demonstrations that ensued on both sides was an effort to awaken the whole of the opposing government to the potential gravity of the situation—after which, it was assumed, previous deeds would be disavowed and serious negotiations could begin.[56] In fact, these demonstrations did succeed in forcing the issue to the center of attention of both governments, but thereby only narrowed expectations, crystallized previously diffuse objectives, and heightened and unified motivation to achieve them.

Until well into 1755 there were no ardent advocates of war with Great Britain in the highest policy-making circles in France, with the exception of the Abbé de la Ville, an adviser to Rouillé. French decision-making in this period, however, was a maze of intrigue, in which secret Continental diplomacy by some officials, unknown to others, was also involved. The effect was to complicate and cloud all issues. With no first-rate statesman in French councils at this time, it is not surprising that the labyrinthine decision-making process lumbered into an escalation sequence abroad, and subsequently into the designs of the Austrian Count Kaunitz in Europe.[57]

Although decision-making in London was more rationalized, there was a war party that had a powerful and direct effect on policy. This group's deliberate leak of the secret of Braddock's expedition failed to ignite immediate war, as was intended. Earlier, though, the Duke of Cumberland had successfully persuaded his father that Virginia should be sent regular troops, not just advisers, money, and other support, and thereby had caused the reversal of a cabinet decision that might well have halted the escalatory process. The war party was also successful, during early 1755, in so denigrating the prospect of any further negotiations with the French that they were dropped and were not resumed late that summer when the approximate status quo of a year earlier had reoccurred.

In these efforts and in their continuing general influence in favor of war, this group was more determined, and more definite about what British objectives should be, than Newcastle and other policy-makers. Cumberland, Anson, Fox, and Pitt were all able and aggressive men, with informal influence far beyond their formal authority; they were positive that the war policy they promoted was right, necessary, and even urgent. By contrast, Newcastle, although prime minister, was weak-willed, unintelligent, ignorant of the details of both Continental and North American issues, and extraordinarily vacillating and uncertain in his policy goals. He was much more anxious to maximize and perpetuate his own personal influence and his political power than to pursue *any* particular policy, and in coping with issues he took the initiative as little as possible. Inevitably he was much swayed by the war party (although never to the point of promptly taking some extremely vigorous actions the war party urged, which if well-timed might have finished the war almost as quickly as they began it).[58]

Like the dog in the Sherlock Holmes story that does not bark in the night, what is probably most significant about the intragovernmental politics in London in this period is the group that was not present at all. English policy-making circles at this time did not include *any* ranking individuals who were as motivated to explore all options for controlling the conflict as the war party was to activate all options for escalating it. Such an element, had it existed, might or might not have been able to balance the opposing group in influence. But it almost certainly could have demanded, and helped to create, a more analytic policy debate, and perhaps could have succeeded in uncovering and correcting some of the analytic failures as they developed.

Analytic Summary

The escalation sequence leading to the Seven Years War has been summarized in Table 5. Until its last stage the conflict was a bipolar one; the respective proxies were backed by stronger and stronger moves of their principals, which thereby generated a classic instance of cyclical-sequence escalation.

The competition mounted up a chain of asymmetries imbedded in the situation and a couple of disproportionate actions, the absence of nearly any of which would have slowed and perhaps halted the sequence and given the concurrent negotiations more time to succeed. Some half-dozen failures of analysis, the result in part of intragovernmental factors, permitted the progression to continue.

Unlike many escalation sequences, this one witnessed no offensive steps by any player at any time. The different perceptions held in London and Paris of the long-standing disagreement in North America made it possible for every action by both sides to be undertaken defensively. Indeed, on one side the scope of what defense might allow was interpreted cautiously.

Nonetheless, each side perceived the other's moves as offensive and compellent, because each failed to comprehend the other's fundamental perspective and assumptions. The result was that the actions each side took to demonstrate its own resolve did not have a demonstrative effect. Instead they progressively narrowed the other side's expectations about likely futures and transformed its perception of a limited adversary into an implacable enemy. And they crystallized each side's absolute minimum objective of avoiding the final loss of North American hegemony. By this time the direct military consequences of each step were outweighing the symbolic meaning and tilting the in-theater advantage so decisively that thereafter policy-makers could not afford to hold back their responses unless they were ready to abandon their absolute minimum objective.

Part Three
Toward the Control of Escalation

9

On the Assessment of Conflicts

Among the five wars we have considered there is great variation in the ways in which escalation did and did not occur. In the final part of this study we shall draw together many of the analytic observations made along the way and try to derive some conclusions about the task of keeping escalation from going out of control.*

Conclusions from the Cases

From many points of view the diversity of the five wars is an advantage, not a disadvantage. Their diversity brings to light a larger number of significant aspects of escalation than a more homogeneous grouping might. And it demonstrates the many kinds of complexity that can arise. Indeed, one very general and elementary conclusion we can draw from the totality of these case studies is precisely that escalation is a very diverse and very complicated matter. It reminds us, if any reminder is needed, that there are no simple rules for controlling escalation that can be applied mechanically to all or even most war situations.

Still, there are interesting and suggestive similarities among these wars, and between them and the more familiar conflicts of our own day. Let us take a moment to glance at some of these similarities. The Spanish Civil War is the case chronologically closest to our own era and the one that in many respects most closely resembles recent proxy wars. Then, as recently, a conflict that otherwise

---

*The reader is reminded that phrases like "escalation going out of control" and "uncontrolled escalation" are not to be taken overliterally. Such phrases are a grammatical and stylistic convenience, and name processes that this study attempts to analyze. As discussed in Chapter 2, I do not accept the validity of a pure phenomenal model of escalation. Decisions are always made by someone, even if it be a computer (or, more exactly, its programmers).

would have remained at a moderate level of violence was escalated by the involvement of outside great powers, acting substantially (but not exclusively) on ideological motives. A major difference between the Spanish case and more contemporary ones, though, was the presence then on the international scene of neutral great powers, equal or superior in capabilities to the ideological powers involved in Spain and determined to control escalation. A vital feature of the Civil War was its tripolar rather than bipolar context.

The Austro-Prussian and Franco-Prussian wars are both cases in which a short but sharp duel was fought in an area where close and very powerful neighbors had a profound interest in the outcome. In both instances escalation was controlled at first by the careful prewar design of an initial war context. In both conflicts unexpected events rapidly exploded these contexts; but in one the initiating power was able to terminate the fighting quickly, and in the other the international constellation fell into a pattern that permitted continued fighting without escalation. As examples of how conflicts can be isolated from outside involvement even where, at first glance, this seems most improbable, Bismarck's two major wars could hardly be surpassed.

The Crimean War resembles the Spanish Civil War in the large number of nations actively involved, and in that there was one major power—in the 1850s, Austria—where policy-makers were primarily interested in limiting the conflict. In the Crimean and Spanish wars, as in so many recent ones, the essential escalation problem lay in preventing a local conflict on the periphery of the international system from expanding into a "big" war involving the great powers. In the Crimean case, decision-makers failed to control escalation and the conflict did expand this way. Still, it was not quite a proxy war. The Russo-Turkish War, which was its trigger, was a conflict between two sizable and important states, the weaker of which sought and found outside assistance. The seeming inability of the French and British to reconcile their conflict-control objectives with their goal of preserving the desired balance of power in the region helped to generate a long cyclical escalation sequence.

A similar sequence led to the Seven Years War. Here again, the essential problem lay in preventing a local conflict on the periphery of the system from expanding. Until the last stage, though, this *was* a proxy war, a bipolar conflict with its roots in a cold war in which the local clients of two world powers requested and obtained mounting assistance from the principals. That the resulting sequence progressed very slowly by contemporary standards, but nevertheless culminated in the general war that neither side had wanted and both had tried to avoid, makes this a classic instance of escalation going out of control.

As noted in Chapter 3, it is possible to compare these cases not only for their similarities, but also for their differences—where the reasons can be identified why a pattern developed one way in one set of circumstances and another way in another. In the final part of this book, both similarities and differences will be tapped in developing general conclusions about controlling escalation.

Because there are no simple rules for controlling escalation, general conclusions cannot take the form of isolated principles or automatic formulas. Instead, conclusions of two other kinds will be presented.

First, these final chapters will explore several broad themes that emerge from the case studies. Although all the themes apply to escalation generally, they will apply in different measure in different cases. Research findings will be grouped under the headings of these themes. I shall discuss only themes directly applicable to *contemporary* international affairs.

Second, Appendix A contains several dozen questions that decision-makers and their staffs may find useful in coping with present-day escalation problems. The questions suggest issues, derived from all parts of this study, which arise in wartime and which it may be helpful to identify and deal with in particular situations.

Let us now lay the groundwork for the first of the general themes to emerge from this investigation.

Two Dimensions of Escalation

Both the limits that constrain wars, and the escalations that create new and wider limits, have at least two intricately related aspects or dimensions. One is their bargaining and demonstrative aspect. As discussed in Chapter 2, Thomas Schelling (followed by many others) has shown that both the process of fixing stable limits and the process of executing controlled escalations are, in a very important way, bargaining processes. Limits that last for any time represent a tacit agreement by the belligerents on the rules of the game. Similarly a controlled escalation (to less than all-out war)

241

represents a tacit proposal by one belligerent for new ground rules. Often a controlled escalation also represents a demonstration of will, commitment, or motivation, which is part of the bargaining and which may heighten the risk for everyone involved.

Much of the evidence collected here reconfirms this well-established view. In the escalations of the Spanish Civil War, the Crimean War, and the Seven Years War, there is ample evidence of decision-makers bargaining tacitly with their opponents to find advantageous ground rules, yet constrain the fighting and forestall the much bigger wars that all recognized as possible and few desired. Many of these escalations were also executed as demonstrations of will and commitment.

Besides their bargaining aspect, limits and escalations clearly have a direct or intrinsic significance also. This includes the vital matter of the immediate military implications for each side of a particular limit or escalation. But it is by no means limited to these implications. As this chapter will try to show, often much of the nonbargaining significance of limits and escalations lies in various deep-seated features of the context or situation within which limits are formed or escalation occurs. Lacking a more adequate term, I shall refer to these features collectively as the *framework* of conflicts.[1]

The direct or instrinsic aspect of limits and escalations and the bargaining aspect are very intimately related. For instance, much of the demonstrative impact of an escalation is carried by its direct consequences: the higher level of violence, the greater casualties and other costs, the greater risk of more escalation, and so on. Despite their close connection, however, it is important to distinguish between these two dimensions.

One reason for doing so concerns the relative scope of the bargaining dimension. Schelling suggests in introducing his bargaining theory that the scope of its applicability to nations' real behavior in different circumstances needs to be established by empirical research.[2] Scholars and analysts have hardly taken this hint, as evidenced by the dearth of escalation studies noted earlier.

The evidence gathered here suggests that, indeed, the *applicability of bargaining is a variable, not a constant*. It hardly ever vanishes entirely as long as there is some potential for an action-reaction cycle. However, it may be greatly reduced in importance, and become partly or wholly unconscious in decision-makers, if for

242

any reason good or bad they minimize the danger of a prompt counteraction by the opponent. To put it formally: the applicability of tacit bargaining varies greatly according to circumstances—if by tacit bargaining one means a conscious strategy that policy-makers employ deliberately.[3]

The early months of the Spanish Civil War, for instance, witnessed some gifts of aircraft and materiel to the Spanish belligerents from several outside nations, followed by a reciprocal escalation that involved much larger (but mostly secret) assistance, including air and tank specialists, from the Soviets and the fascist powers. All these steps were taken essentially for their practical effect on the immediate military balance in Spain, and with only minimal attention to their tacit bargaining significance. The initial French, Italian, and German assistance was provided, more or less simultaneously, in the belief that it would lead to a prompt end to the war. The reciprocal escalation a little later by the Soviets, followed by the Germans and Italians, was executed in the assumption that the secrecy of the operations much reduced their riskiness, and that in any case the military urgency of the situation in Spain demanded immediate action no matter what (within limits) the opponent's counteraction might be.

Later in the same war, however, the bargaining aspect became more important. Mussolini gradually escalated the Italian involvement in the Civil War, not only for the direct military value of the steps taken, but also for their value as demonstrations of Italian motivation and commitment. Furthermore, being willing to accept somewhat higher risks than the French and British, Mussolini was able to engage in what could accurately be labeled a *competition in risk-taking*—one that he expected (correctly) to win. The demonstration of Italian motivation and willingness to run risks was further enhanced by Mussolini's decision in 1937 to begin publicizing Italian actions in Spain.

In the two Prussian wars the dimension of tacit bargaining was almost entirely absent. The belligerents fought all out, and the limits that prevented the war from widening were created, not by tacit bargaining through military moves, but by explicit diplomacy before the fighting began. The important escalations that did occur during the Franco-Prussian War also involved little in the way of tacit bargaining. The siege of Paris, the insurgency/counterinsurgency campaigns, and the more general change in the character of the war were not steps taken as tactics in a strategy of demonstrating commitment or manipulating risk, but were consequences that followed necessarily, by the nature of the context or framework of events, from the German demand for Alsace-Lorraine and the French refusal. The change in the character of the war and the insurgency did, indeed, show a new and greater French motivation and will—but one that was automatically aroused in the French public by the German demand, not one that was calculated by French decision-makers as part of their strategy.[4]

By contrast, bargaining was strikingly important in the escalation sequences leading to the Crimean War and the Seven Years War, although in somewhat different ways. Both the advance of the Anglo-French fleet in 1853, and the sequence of steps the British and French took against each other in the early 1750s in North America, were actions motivated as much by an intent to demonstrate resolve and commitment as by a calculation of immediate miliatry consequences. However, only in the Crimean sequence did policy-makers also take their steps with the additional motive of heightening the risk, shared by all parties, of general war. In that sequence the British and French advanced their squadrons with the explicit motive of creating a greater shared risk of a big war than they believed the czar would accept. Simultaneously Czar Nicholas kept his troops in the principalities and rejected various diplomatic initiatives, even after the Russo-Turkish War had begun, probably in part to preserve and even enhance a risk of general war which he believed the Aberdeen government in London would not, in the end, accept.

Through most of the escalation sequence a century earlier, policy-makers in London and Paris acted only marginally, or not at all, on the motive of heightening a mutual risk of general war. They did not underestimate how grave the consequences of a general war might be, but until late in that sequence they assessed the *probability* of that contingency as fairly low. An important variation on the idea of risk manipulation does emerge, however. In both capitals policy-makers assessed the opposing government as fragmented and insufficiently alert to the possibility of a grave general war (however low its estimated probability). They therefore took demonstrative actions to awaken the whole of the opposing capital to this possibility, thereby—far from heightening the shared risk—*lowering* it, by providing the opposing capital with a motivation to begin serious negotiations.

In sum: only sometimes is the conscious exploitation of shared risk for its bargaining value a central part of escalation decisions; indeed, only sometimes are bargaining strategies of any kind central. And the relevance of all kinds of bargaining may change in the course of a conflict (as in the Spanish Civil War).

Not only is the relevance of bargaining in escalation a variable, but for policy-makers to *discover* the applicability of bargaining tactics in any given case depends upon their assessment of the situation specifically from this point of view. In this sense, the framework, or context, is the first aspect to be considered when policy-makers turn to the problem of escalation. It precedes—and provides the basis for—questions about tacit bargaining, demonstrations of will, manipulation of risk, and the like.

The first general theme I want to strike, then, is the high importance in controlling escalation of the framework of conflicts. There has probably been a tendency among many analysts to assume that the well-known bargaining aspect will play a dominant role in escalation processes. By comparison, the framework aspect may have faded somewhat into the background. To be more exact, this aspect has tended to be reduced to an obvious and simple truth: the immediate military implications of any escalation really matter. Certainly they do. No matter how important the signal being communicated by some move, its tangible effect in changing the immediate military situation is vital also. The significance of non-bargaining considerations in controlling escalation, however, goes far beyond the matter of immediate military consequences of moves.

This is a theme which, depending on how exhaustive we wish to be, could be applied to many aspects of international conflict and could be explored at length and from many points of view. Here I shall confine it to those matters that seem to be most significant operationally in controlling escalation. Let us begin with something that is found rather often in the framework of conflicts, something that can be dangerous.

Latencies

One of the ways in which escalation gets out of control—one that is not always apparent—is a seemingly careful step that activates some nation's previously latent motive or interest. A classic example is the Russian attack on the Turkish naval flotilla in Sinope Bay. Although this attack may have been within a very technical reading of what the British had previously communicated they would tolerate, the overwhelming margin of the victory was not within its spirit. By annihilating the Turkish squadron so easily and completely, the Russians activated an extremely important British security interest: general naval supremacy. This interest previously had been entirely latent. It had not been challenged or engaged by events up to that point, and neither the British nor anyone else expected it to be challenged. Their complete surprise, almost as much as their estimate of the significance of the challenge itself, accounted for the vehemence of their reaction. This is a particularly vivid example, because the interest activated here was the kind Ernest May calls *axiomatic* rather than *calculated*—that is, an interest so fundamental that it is part of the bedrock of foreign policy, not a quantity handled, and perhaps shifted up or down in value, in the day-by-day and month-by-month calculations of policy-makers.[5]

Less sudden but equally profound was the process in the early 1750s by which the latent goals of the British and French not to allow each other hegemony over the North American continent were gradually activated by the conflict over the Ohio territory. In its latent form the motive here was somewhat abstract and diffuse. But the mounting conflict in that region focused the attention of policy-makers in London and Paris on the Ohio and, with the assistance of somewhat biased information from the supporting bureaucracies, led to the crystallization of the latent concerns on both sides.

Another example is the French activation in 1870 of the latent security fears of the South Germans. Although the South Germans' policies and other behavior in the preceding period suggested that their primary, overt security anxieties concerned a possible Prussian threat, they also had latent anxieties about a possible French threat. The French, who did not appreciate this or analyze what circumstances might arouse these latent motives, thereby permitted those circumstances to emerge by default.

One of the paradoxes of escalation, which makes its control more difficult, is that latent interests and objectives may be activated not only by challenges and defeats but also by victories. This may be especially likely where the victories are unexpectedly great. Such was the case, for instance, with both of the one-sided battlefield victories in the Prussian wars. Both Königgrätz in 1866 and

Sedan in 1870 activated and brought to the fore latent Prussian objectives. They did so in the sense that objectives previously not considered attainable suddenly came to seem feasible; more important, objectives became central that policy-makers and the Prussian public had not previously been thinking about, or aware of, *at all*. In 1866, the final destruction of Austrian influence in Germany and far-reaching territorial gains had not even been part of the Prussian conception of the possibilities before Königgrätz. Afterward they were rejected as war objectives only after tremendous exertions by Bismarck. In 1870, Alsace-Lorraine as a possible offensive objective had not been part of the defense concerns of the Prussians and other Germans as the French began to attack. After Sedan, Alsace-Lorraine became a war objective so firm that soon there was no longer any discussion in German circles of ending the conflict without winning it, despite the longer and more costly war this implied.

Victories do not need to be as sudden and complete as Königgrätz and Sedan were, in order to activate latent objectives. The success of General MacArthur's Inchon landing in South Korea in September 1950 and the accelerating collapse of the North Korean army during succeeding weeks had a similar effect. Policymakers in Washington rode the momentum of enthusiasm that this victory generated and lacked the equivalent of a Bismarck to insist forcefully that a neighboring great power was likely to intervene if the enemy were not offered moderate terms. They permitted a latent U. S. objective, the liberation of a nation from communism, to be activated. The neighboring great power did intervene, and the result was two more years of costly war, war that ended on terms probably less satisfactory than might have been obtained in the fall of 1950.[6]

Nor do victories need to occur on the battlefield, as Königgrätz, Sedan, and Inchon did, in order for latent objectives to be activated. In the early 1850s the Turks held the latent objective of regaining territories lost over the decades in previous Russo-Turkish wars, if opportunities to do so presented themselves. This objective was not activated by the eruption of a major Russo-Turkish crisis in 1853 or by the Russians' seizure of the Ottoman principalities. It *was* activated by the slowly deepening commitment the British and French made to the Ottoman Empire and the prospect that events could be manipulated to deepen it further. In this case, the latent objective was activated by the Turkish "victory" in drawing the West into the conflict. The opening of a second front in the Caucasus followed (and so, perhaps, did the Turks' ploy of setting up the Russians as naval challengers to the West, by way of a Russian victory at sea).

Thus latent objectives, which may be axiomatic, unconscious, or simply not yet operationalized, may have decisive effects on the prospects of escalation when they are activated. There can be other reasons, not exactly involving latencies, why objectives may not come into play, or may come into play indirectly, until activated by events. And these can also have very significant effects. In the Spanish Civil War, the *negative objective* held by the Soviets, and to some extent the French, that the Spanish republic not be defeated was the source of a new burst of intervention in the spring of 1938—intervention that included a potentially dangerous opening of the French border. Here the course of events activated an objective which, although not exactly latent, had not come heavily into play since 1936. In the early 1850s, Czar Nicholas held *contingency objectives* concerning the supposedly imminent collapse of the Ottoman Empire; these influenced his decisions and, being known, also aroused French, British, and Austrian security interests.

As in so many conflicts, policy-makers' objectives here were plural in number and graduated in importance and immediacy. The goals of these officials included relatively far-reaching gains for which they would incur only modest costs and risks, smaller-scale objectives worth very great costs and risks, and a spectrum in between. Indeed, in none of the escalation problems analyzed in this book can one reasonably speak of "the" single war objective pursued by policy-makers.[7] Many things can activate some objective other than the one(s) being pursued at a given moment, and this change may lead to escalation.

A final kind of latency that may be activated by an escalation and may lead to a wider war is a set of *latent conflicts* external to the immediate hostilities. Napoleon's belligerent coercion of the Turks in the early 1850s, for instance, aroused latent conflicts between Turkey and Russia, and between Russia and Great Britain. External and partly latent conflicts were aroused when the Anglo-French duel of the 1750s spread to rivalries on the Continent. And several latent conflicts were almost aroused by the two Prussian wars.

More Framework Elements

Latencies, then, come in various forms. Lying imbedded within the framework that surrounds a conflict, they can be activated by some nation's escalation and promote further escalation. Another element found in the framework of some conflicts that can trigger escalation are asymmetries in belligerents' capabilities.

On occasion these may be as simple as basic asymmetries in their military forces. In the Seven Years War escalation sequence, for instance, there were four major asymmetries in military forces, each of which, as it was activated in turn by the developing conflict, led policy-makers to escalate further. The absence of any of them might well have halted or slowed the process long enough to promote success of the ongoing diplomatic efforts to resolve the conflict. In the Crimean War, the asymmetry between the naval power that the British and French could deploy into the theater, and the ground forces that the Russians could deploy, allowed both sides to escalate the conflict substantially without much fear of an immediate, dangerous military clash. However, the same disparity allowed a passage of time during which there were no great-power clashes, and during which various measures to control escalation might have been (but were not) implemented. In the Spanish Civil War, it may have only been the inability of the republic and its Soviet ally to defend their shipping from Italian attacks that prevented the conflict from escalating into an air-sea war in the Mediterranean, and gave the British and French time to work out the Nyon solution.

Besides simple asymmetries in forces available, there may be less obvious asymmetries in the available options that belligerents or potential belligerents are capable of executing. In the Spanish Civil War, the French in many respects were at a disadvantage compared to the Italians, because France borders on Spain. Basic French and Italian military capabilities were comparable in this period, but the French had fewer moderate-risk options for intervening in Spain because of the greater difficulty in keeping such actions disconnected from French territory. In the two Prussian wars, although neighboring great powers resembled belligerents in their basic military capabilities, the situation was such that they lacked options for effective *low-level* military interventions. Indeed, one of the major attributes of the initial war contexts that Bis-

marck constructed was that these contexts presented potential interveners with a gap between feasible but ineffectual options of
purely diplomatic actions, and military options that would effectively influence events but only with a sizable risk of general war.
In the Crimean War sequence, the Anglo-French naval deployment
and Russian troop deployment imposed limitations on the flexibility
of these powers' politico-military tactics. The Russian occupation of
the principalities was a somewhat blunt coercive instrument to begin with, but was the only conceivably effective one the Russians
had. Then, a few months later, the troops could not be withdrawn
for a lengthy period because of weather. For the same reason the
Western squadron moored in Besika Bay had to be moved, either
forward or back, after a few months. In all these instances,
asymmetries in the number, kind, or quality of the practical
options available, not just in basic military forces, played a role in
encouraging or discouraging escalation.

Somewhat similar to asymmetries in capabilities are what might
be termed asymmetries in motivation and interest. Such asymmetries can be important and quite real, although motivation and
even "national interests" usually can, within limits, be reevaluated
and deliberately adjusted.[8] In the Spanish Civil War, the French for
geographic reasons had a greater interest in the outcome in Spain
than any of the intervening great powers, and it was partly the
recognition of this fact that inhibited Hitler and Mussolini from
greater involvement early in the war.

However, as long as the British were restraining the French from
acting, this asymmetry did not come directly into play. In its
absence, a different asymmetry did. Mussolini and his advisers were
operating under fewer inhibitions and gradually demonstrated that
they perceived a greater national interest in Spain than did, for example, policy-makers in Nazi Germany or the Soviet Union.
Indeed it is probable, although difficult to demonstrate, that the
extent of the Italian motivation in Spain was somewhat underestimated by decision-makers of some or all the other great powers.
Certainly the extent of the Italian escalations, even within the first
year, far exceeded those of the other powers; equally certainly,
some deterrent steps that might have been taken by the French and
British were not. In this case the asymmetry of interest in favor of
the Italians was the source of most of the escalations that did occur;
while the one in favor of the French would have posed the greatest

danger of uncontrolled escalation, had the French been allowed to act on it.

Other elements in the framework of conflict can be crucial in triggering escalation, or in controlling it. One is the extent to which the situation provides means for the reinforcement of limits. During most of the Spanish Civil War, for instance, the French deliberately reinforced the salience of the border by closing it to military commerce. Bismarck found many ways to reinforce the limits he wanted on the wars of 1866 and 1870. During the events leading to the Crimean War, the British and French had several opportunities (which they passed up) for reinforcing the geographic limits on what was originally a quite confined Russo-Turkish war.

The opposite side of the coin is the problem of hostilities spreading out of their arena to nearby combustible material, or along lines of connection to homelands. In the early 1750s, smouldering conflicts between the English and French in the north and west of the colony of New York and in the Nova Scotia area were readily ignited by the nearby conflict in the Ohio region. But during the Spanish Civil War there were no points of direct contact between the fascist and communist powers anywhere other than Spain. There were, however, lines of connection between the arena and all the intervening great powers. The most dramatic escalation of the war, the submarine campaign, was an attempt to sever the republic's connections with the outside world and above all with the USSR. Significantly, all other lines of connection from that arena had already been cut, or escalation along them blocked, in other ways. In the early 1750s, the extreme vulnerability of France's maritime connection with Canada to attack by the superior British navy provided a major stepingstone in the escalation sequence.

In sum, we may say that adjacent combustible material, lines of connection, means for reinforcing limits, latencies, and asymmetries in capabilities, motivation, and interests are all features that may be present or absent in the framework of a particular conflict, and that may have a triggering or dampening effect on escalation. Analytically speaking, all these features, and others that may be significant in some cases,[9] represent *irregularities* in the pattern of a conflict's potential escalation. The smooth and uniform escalation "ladder," picturing hierarchically ordered levels of violence, is an abstraction developed by theorists, not a description of reality.

To be sure, in some theoretical applications this abstraction has utility. Omitting the contextual richness of real-world interactions has made it easier for analysts to focus on tacit bargaining, potentially a useful tool in efforts to control escalation. In most real conflict situations, however, the "ladder" is neither uniform nor orderly. It is full of irregularities and distortions. And it is full of elements important not only because they are positioned at some level hierarchically, but even more because they have qualities of their own that may influence events profoundly. In most real conflicts the potential escalation sequence is more like a ladder that has been bent and twisted out of shape, with all sorts of extras and odd protuberances added on, which vitally affect how the conflict does or does not climb it. There are different ladders for every conflict, and they bear only a loose resemblance to one another. Controlling escalation in any particular conflict will often depend crucially on identifying the particular twists and protuberances of *that* conflict's misshapen ladder.

On the Assessment of Conflict Frameworks

As the cases here demonstrate, policy-makers can be largely or wholly unaware of these framework features. Every example of a failure to restrain escalation mentioned in the last few pages passed unappreciated by decision-makers of at least one nation involved. The implication is too obvious to need much elaboration: the quality of the situational analysis being performed by policy-makers and their staffs often contributes heavily to success or failure in controlling escalation.

Yet assessment of these features, however vital, is not enough. Many analytic staffs understand, at least in a general way, that the quality of a situational assessment depends in part on recognition of the sorts of things just discussed. Beyond this level of assessment lies another range of issues that may be even more fundamental to controlling escalation. The notion of conflict frameworks must be deepened to include them.

A striking aspect of the five studies presented here is the number of times it was necessary to identify *failures of analysis*, as they were termed, on the part of policy-makers and their staffs. Some were failures to identify the kind of factors just discussed. But a number of them represent more fundamental failures to comprehend how the world looked to others. More formally, they con-

252

sisted in inattentiveness to, or outright unawareness of, the basic assumptions and presuppositions of decision-makers in other capitals and their overall perspectives on the situation; their underlying goals (as opposed to immediate objectives); and their full range of options as these appeared in the context of *their* presuppositions, perspectives, and goals. Such lapses can be regarded as failures of imagination, failures of empathy, or failures of conceptualization and analysis. Since what is needed can, to a large extent, be obtained through high-quality analysis, I shall call them *conceptual failures*, a term that may have been used first in this sense by George Kennan.[10]

All of our cases include such conceptual failures, and they play a dominating role in those where escalation got out of control. During the sequence leading to the Seven Years War, for instance, the French apparently did not appreciate what their preparations for a massive reinforcement of Canada would suggest to the English about the possible extent of French objectives. In the two wars of German unification, laspes of this kind by the Austrians and French played an essential role in their permitting, by default, the initial war contexts desired by the Prussians to emerge. During the Spanish Civil War, it was a failure of this kind that led officials in London and Paris to overlook available strategic warning—of not one but several kinds—of the most dramatic escalation, the Italian submarine campaign.

A full listing of the conceptual failures occurring in the five cases appears in Table 6. The table includes an additional category: failures to *reassess* opponents' presuppositions, perspectives, and the like in the wake of an event that may have changed them.

In all these instances, the deficiency did not lie in intelligence failures in the ordinary sense: failures by working-level officers to uncover vital information, or report it upward high enough for its significance to be assessed by officials aware of "the big picture."[11] Nor did the deficiency lie in the inevitable limitation on what governments can find out in times of crisis and war. All or nearly all the necessary information could have been available to policy-makers—or could have been made available if lower-ranking officials had been appropriately queried and directed. The deficiency lay at the policy-making level itself, in inadequate conceptualization of the information at hand and in the absence of accessible information which, also because of inadequate conceptualization, was not

Table 6 Conceptual ingredients used in assessing conflicts, and examples of failures to consider them adequately.

Ingredient	Example where ingredient was missing or deficient among policy-makers	
	Policy-makers	Missing or deficient ingredient
Basic assumptions and presuppositions of policy-makers in other nations, and their overall perspectives	British and French	Italian presuppositions and perceptions of potential extent and value of Italian leverage on outcome of Spanish Civil War
	Russian	Austrian assumptions about Austrian interests in Balkans and Ottoman Empire in early 1850s
	British and French	Russian assumptions of imminence of collapse of Ottoman Empire
	Russian	British and French assumptions of imminence of collapse of Ottoman Empire
	Russian	British assumptions of significance of a Russian naval victory of the magnitude of Sinope victory of November 1853
	British	French presuppositions of significance of Ohio region in North America
	French	British presuppositions of significance of Ohio region in North America
Underlying goals (as opposed to immediate objectives) of policy-makers abroad	Austrian	Bismarck's underlying goals in Central Europe in 1866
	French	Bismarck's underlying goals in Central Europe in 1870
	Russian	Before 1854, both British and Austrian goals vis-à-vis Ottoman Empire

Full range of plausible opponents' options in context of opponents' presuppositions and perspectives	French and British	In 1937, possibility that Italians might escalate Spanish Civil War at sea
	Austrian	Before 1866, possibility that under certain circumstances Prussians might find a war attractive
	French	Before 1870, possibility that under certain circumstances Prussians might find a war attractive
	French	In 1754, possibility that British might perceive Canadian reinforcement as evidence of maximal French objectives and might expect to intercept entire French flotilla in North American waters
Reassessment of above ingredients in altered circumstances	French and British (probably)	In 1937, alteration in Italian assumptions created by Anglo-Italian Gentlemen's Agreement
	French and British	In 1853-1854, effect on Russian perceptions of Besika Bay deployment, and again of entrance of squadrons into Black Sea
	Russian	In 1853, significance of Anglo-French Besika Bay deployment, and again of Constantinople deployment
	British	In 1853, significance of Olmütz conference for Russian assumptions and goals

255

sought out. To put it colloquially, at the highest levels the big picture wasn't big enough.

The evidence of the cases studied here is plentiful and consistent. One must conclude that *conceptual failures in this sense contribute substantially to many instances of escalation getting out of control.* Events can begin to get out of hand when one side does not adequately comprehend the other's basic *frame of reference* (as these conceptual ingredients may be termed for brevity).

And conversely, one must conclude that high attentiveness to other capitals' basic frames of reference contributes substantially to controlling escalation. The outstanding examples among the cases studied here are the Prussian performances of 1866 and 1870. The next general theme to be struck, then, is that in controlling escalation, attentiveness to others' basic frames of reference really matters.

Not surprisingly, a number of scholars have come to similar conclusions in studying foreign policy disasters of various sorts.[12] Many officials experienced in foreign and national-security decision-making also appreciate the importance of this kind of attentiveness. It is usually taken as axiomatic at the working level of state departments and foreign ministries, where officials have responsibility for just this sort of effort. At high policy-making levels, too, the need to "appreciate the other side's point of view" is an idea that usually commands decision-makers' assent.

Assenting to the idea, however, is not the same thing as initiating a conscious, active effort to bring to light the basic frames of reference of their counterparts in other capitals. The attention that decision-makers nearly always pay to their counterparts' *immediate objectives* does not substitute for this deeper conceptual understanding. And often they may not be aware of the extent of the conceptual deficiency. Partly this is because the deficiency is somewhat circular: one must be at least slightly aware of what is not known about the other side's frame of reference in order to be aware that one's understanding may be lacking. Partly it is because of some very real hindrances in the decision process. These hindrances are important enough for us to examine.

Impediments to Assessment

Nothing said here is meant to imply that obtaining an adequate conceptual understanding of others' frames of reference is easy. It is not. Many things can conspire to hinder the thoughtfulness, imagination, and empathy needed to achieve it. For one thing, policy-makers and their staffs must be allowed a good deal of time to make a decision. And time is a luxury that is not always available in the fast-paced escalation sequences of the contemporary era. (However, it is interesting that with a couple of marginal exceptions,[13] lack of time was not a factor in any of the analytic failures noted in this study.)

Many hindrances can arise from ordinary, human limitations on rationality, and from the distortions that often creep in when policy evolves through interactions among individuals and in group sessions. These psychological and social-psychological impediments have been systematically reviewed elsewhere, and that review will not be repeated here.[14] Finally, major hindrances can arise from bureaucratic politics and from the distortions that the standard operating procedures of large organizations sometimes produce in implementing policy-makers' decisions.

The importance of bureaucratic politics and organizational processes is now being widely emphasized by political scientists and other specialists. Often such factors are heavily responsible for well-intentioned decisions leading in practice to unwanted final outcomes—including uncontrolled escalation. The inevitable corollary, for instance, of the Prussian analytic superiority in the wars of German unification was Prussian superiority in the efficiency and effectiveness of policy-making processes: definite superiority over the French counterparts before July 1870, and very dramatic superiority over the Austrian counterparts in the mid-1860s. Similarly, a variety of procedural and organizational lapses among the various parties to the Crimean and Seven Years War escalation sequences played an important role in letting events get out of control. These instances will not be reexamined here, for the details have largely a historical significance. Governmental processes and institutions, unlike some of the factors involved in relations among nations, vary enormously from one time and place to another. The impediments and malfunctions to be found in the contemporary world, and ways to cope with them, are best studied with contemporary data.

Let me make two general observations, however. First, the evidence of the cases suggest that at least when it comes to controlling escalation, the importance of minimizing these impediments should not be allowed to obscure the equally significant conceptual dimension of the task. Contrary to a suggestion sometimes encountered in oversimplified discussions of bureaucratic politics, analytic failures cannot be accurately seen as merely a result of these politics and distortions in standard procedures (nor, of course, vice versa). The relationship between the two is not one of simple cause and effect in either direction. It is a more complicated one that involves *reciprocal* cause and effect, where the influences flow both ways.

Of the various indications of this point in available information about the wars studied here, the most obvious appears in the Austro-Prussian conflict. Procedural and bureaucratic hindrances to effective decision-making were particularly severe in Vienna before June 1866; in the same period there was a diffuse but serious conceptual failure in Austrian policy-making circles. It is true and important that the pathological state of the decision-making processes contributed heavily to the analytic failure. But it is also true, and equally important, that the ongoing conceptual failure in policy-making circles contributed to the continuing seriousness of the poor processes. Because of the ongoing conceptual failure, for instance, suspicions were not aroused among policy-makers that otherwise might have been aroused, about the real adequacy of their information or the real flexibility of their options. Therefore they did not take steps they might have to begin to recheck information, to expand the categories of information, and to create new options. For a second instance, suspicions were not aroused among policy-makers concerning the full range of the possible options and goals of other nations—suspicions which, had they existed, might have generated instructions to seek additional information that could have proved crucial. For a third instance, the conceptual failure and resulting lack of suspicion meant that corrective reforms of the institutions and decision procedures were not undertaken that could have been undertaken (and in future years were).

In short, the conceptual failure meant that the full extent of the malevolent consequences of these decision-making processes would not be comprehended until they had materialized.[15]

The second general observation again concerns the complex interrelationship between procedural/institutional considerations and conceptual ones. To some extent, policy-makers who do comprehend the scope of their conceptual needs can take steps to turn the perennial competition among different officials, groups, and agencies into a positive advantage. The possibility that they will do so is becoming increasingly familiar among specialists, and the cases studied here tend to support it. A striking negative illustration is provided, for instance, in the English decision-making of the early 1750s. Prime Minister Newcastle did *not* bring into the policy-making process, formally or informally, any individuals who could have served as countervailing influences to the war party. Such individuals might have challenged the inadequate and somewhat distorted information about the North American conflict that reached the cabinet in London, and made the case for a more pacific policy. The tension between these two groups, in turn, might have produced a more analytic approach to the policy problems posed by the mounting escalation sequence.

Other decision-makers at other times have exploited intra-governmental diversity, however, and with profit. In recent American history this approach was particularly favored by Franklin Roosevelt, who deliberately created countervailing tensions among his advisers as a way of forcing alternative perspectives and a wide range of information to his desk. President Kennedy drew on his own sad experience in the Bay of Pigs crisis of 1961, where a diversity of viewpoints was almost totally absent among those privy to the planning, to introduce a more competitive approach to decision-making in the Cuban missile crisis.[16]

Strategies for exploiting intragovernmental diversity in a controlled way are deservedly becoming a subject of study for specialists. Graham Allison, Morton Halperin, and others have included it in their research on bureaucratic politics; Alexander George has proposed a procedure of "multiple advocacy," in essence a more sophisticated version of the well-known devil's advocate;[17] and Irving Janis, in his book *Victims of Groupthink*, dissects some triumphs and fiascoes in American foreign policy and shows how the presence or absence of diversity in perspectives among U. S. decision-makers goes a long way toward accounting for success or failure. These and other efforts are intended, more than most work by researchers, eventually to have a tangible impact on how policy-makers go about their business. But all such efforts require that the community of decision-makers accept a somewhat higher level of internal disagreement, with its potential for unpleasant tension, than is necessary if a closed, hierarchical system is chosen. If the benefits are to be acheived, therefore, decision-makers themselves must conceptually grasp that the cost of accepting this disagreement is far outweighed, in the long run, by the sounder policy that results.

Two Cognitive Desiderata for Assessment

Reducing the impediments to decision-making and turning them, where possible, to positive advantage may be particularly vital in the context of escalation control. Assessment of the conflict's framework and of the frames of reference of other capitals, so important to controlling escalation, depends heavily upon the effectiveness of the policy-making process. At the same time, warfare often creates a peculiarly nonsupportive environment for effective decision-making. This is true in several important ways that will be discussed in the next chapter. It is also true in that warfare makes it harder for decision-makers and their staffs to achieve two very desirable conditions for high-quality assessments, conditions that are psychological in nature.

Psychologists call the management of information within a person's mind *cognition* or *cognitive processing*. The feelings aroused by crisis or war can generate an emotional atmosphere that makes sound cognitive processing more difficult. A simple but vivid illustration was mentioned in the discussion of the Crimean War escalation sequence. In mid-1856 British and French policy-makers and commanding officers were so caught up in the popular enthusiasm for a victory that they were careless in checking their information. Their plans for a brief raid on Sebastopol were wrecked when the water around the Crimean peninsula proved to be much shallower than they had believed.

Usually the effects of feelings created by crisis or war are more subtle and complicated than they were in this case (and the account here has been somewhat oversimplified). Naturally, such feelings may have positive effects also. But on the whole, a wartime atmosphere is likely not to support the particular modes of cognitive processing that are most helpful in controlling escalation. Two such modes stand out. One is that decision-makers need to be able to envision, at least roughly, possible *sequences of events* as they stretch over time, not just the present situation and its likely immediate development. Too often, wartime discussions of escalation possibilities focus heavily on two-step, reciprocal escalation.

Decision-makers ask themselves, "If the other side does x, what will we do in response?," or "If we do y, what will the other side do to counter it?" Less attention is given to questions like, "If we do x, he may enter on a whole series of moves," or "If he does x, our counter of y may encourage him to do z next," or even, "If he does x, we ourselves may be tempted to enter on a whole series of moves." To be sure, imagining sequences of events is hard. But it is often through cyclical progressions that escalation goes out of control, not in any one moment or through any single decision. (One helpful tool for visualizing sequences will be mentioned shortly.)

In other contexts and using other terms, specialists have already observed decision-makers' need to use sequences of events, not just single events, as a unit of analysis. John Steinbruner has noted how frequently decision-making focuses on single situations, has suggested the term _cybernetic processing_ to describe this, and has analyzed it in depth using formal psychological theory.[18] The term does not refer to computers, but to the original Greek word meaning _steersman_. In ancient times the steersman of a ship knew his destination but did not know exactly when or by what route he would get there. So he steered in response to the winds and currents he encountered, keeping his goal in mind. Similarly, contemporary decision-makers frequently deal with each new situation that arises during a crisis or war in its own terms, keeping their policy goals in mind.

Charles Lindblom has called this the _incremental_ approach to decision-making and has pointed out that in many cases, particularly in domestic politics, it is a more effective mode of making decisions than drawing up a plan and trying to stick to it.[19] Where there are many voices and forces at work, and situations can move in many directions, responding flexibly to developments is more useful than hewing rigidly to a plan. (Some officials refer to this as "pragmatism" in decision-making.)

But as Steinbruner, Robert Coulam,[20] and others have shown, policy-makers who take this approach run the risk of losing control of events in those circumstances where the situation tends to shift over time in one general direction. Where there are underlying forces at work, unknown to decision-makers and tending one way, assessment of each new situation by itself and strictly on its own terms will never uncover them. This kind of "pragmatism" is not pragmatic.

Whether situation-by-situation decision-making is flexibly incre-

261

mental or shortsightedly cybernetic, then, depends on the pattern of the underlying forces, including in particular the *unrecognized* underlying forces. If they are pulling in many directions, thereby mostly canceling one another out, a creative pragmatism that assesses each new situation afresh may be most effective. If they are tending more or less in unison in a single general direction, decision-makers using this approach may come to feel they are losing control of events without quite knowing why.

In warfare the tendencies are very largely escalatory—in the direction of a higher level of violence—for many reasons known and perhaps some unknown. Decision-making that takes each new situation by itself cannot be counted on to control these tendencies. The alternative is not following a rigid plan. The valid alternative is, indeed, to assess each situation afresh but to supplement this assessment with an awareness of the sequential nature of what is occurring. Any new situation (for instance, one resulting from a move by the opponent) not only must be analyzed in itself; it also provides new information by which the unfolding sequence can be assessed, and alternative paths along which it may develop in the future can be envisioned and considered.

The second cognitive desideratum applies to space approximately the same concept that has just been applied to time; and it may be more obvious. Just as decision-makers need to take sequences as a unit of analysis if they are to have the best chance of controlling escalation, so they need to take as a unit of analysis the *interactive pattern of relationships* in any one situation, and not just the situation's meaning or impact for their own objectives.

Escalation processes, perhaps more than any other processes in international affairs, are interactive in nature. They come about through a complicated intersection of the interests, goals, and presuppositions of at least two nations, sometimes more. Hence they cannot be fully grasped by decision-makers who adopt too exclusively a perspective in which "the" meaning of an event or situation is its meaning for their own immediate national interests. Such a perspective will tend to divert attention from the other side's frame of reference. Even more damaging, perhaps, it will overlook meanings and possibilities in situations that involve interactions between the two sides' frames of reference, interactions that are not fully explainable in terms of either alone.

An example appears in the events leading to the Seven Years

War, in which the English-versus-French escalation process was driven in part by an interaction between each side's perception of itself as the side that was acting defensively. Or, to put it differently, the escalation was driven in part by an interaction between each side's perception of its own actions as the deterrent ones and of the other side's actions as compellent and offensively motivated. Through most or all of the sequence neither side appreciated this, because each was evaluating events from the viewpoint of its own immediate national interests and its own frame of reference. Each was also trying to avoid an unwanted, uncontrolled escalation sequence; but each failed to translate this motive adequately into a perspective that recognized the interactive pattern of relationships at work.

What is needed, then, if policy-makers are to have the best chance of controlling escalation, is a version of what computer and managerial experts, and others, call *systems thinking.*[21] The comprehensive situation as it exists at any particular time needs to be addressed as a "whole system," in which the framework of the conflict and the participants' frames of reference, as well as the tangible elements more obvious to all, are recognized as mutually interacting subsystems. What will be most important for controlling escalation will be the major possibilities inherent in the pattern of subsystems and the relationships among them, taken as a whole —not just the possibilities the situation suggests for a single subsystem, a single nation such as one's own.

To perceive and comprehend situations in this way is a very demanding task for a decision-making body to attempt, especially amid the stresses of wartime, and achieving the ideal is hardly to be hoped for. In fact, both of these cognitive desiderata are highly exacting even under the best of circumstances. For harassed policy-makers and their staffs in time of crisis or war, they can only serve as ideals, to be entertained with realistic expectations about the probable shortfall.

In particular, sequence cognition and systems cognition require a high degree of detachment, both psychologically and organizationally. Psychologically, one must disengage oneself from the emotions and immediacies of the current situation. Some personalities find this easier to do than others. Organizationally, the analytic tasks involved probably require some form of separation from other responsibilities. These tasks seem likely to conflict too greatly,

263

for instance, with the role and demands imposed on military officers who have responsibility for pursuing immediate national interests. What seems desirable is a separate group of civilian or military officers, preferably both, who can assess the developing conflict from a detached vantage point that permits them to focus on its sequential and system aspects.

The difficulties that individuals with this assignment would face in the ongoing bureaucratic politics and the hurly-burly of decision-making should not be underestimated. A "whole systems" assessment could seem wrongheaded and even questionably patriotic by other officials who are more deeply involved in the excitements of the moment, the national dangers presented by the conflict, and its opportunities for victories. Lyndon Johnson, for example, took dissenting analyses of his Southeast Asian strategy not merely as dubiously patriotic, but even as disloyal to himself personally. In this sense, the wisdom, humility, and self-restraint of staffs and policy-makers may be challenged as much by the task of controlling escalation as by any other they face.

On Preconditional Analysis

Before this chapter is brought to a close, one technique should be mentioned that can make the difficult conceptual and cognitive suggestions given here slightly easier. It is a technique long known to intelligence analysts, and can readily be extended to conflict assessments more generally.

Intelligence analysts commonly begin from the known present information about a situation and reason forward to adduce a spectrum of probable ways the situation could develop; or less desirably, their single "best guess" about its future. In addition, there is a special kind of forecasting sometimes attempted, variously called *analytical forecasting* or *conditional predicting*, which is different. Here analysts begin from a single, hypothetical image of a possible future situation and reason backward to adduce what hypothetical conditions in the present might lead to the actual occurrence of that future situation. Then they search through available information to see if those conditions are being met, or seem about to be met. Sometimes they begin from a future situation which at first blush seems very unlikely, but on examining its preconditions they discover that these are closer to being met than they would have initially believed.

An example of such a case, where this technique apparently was *not* employed in time, is the Cuban missile crisis of 1962. During the preceding months responsible American officials considered the possibility that the Soviets might be tempted to put offensive missiles in Cuba with a range great enough to strike many U. S. targets. They dismissed the possibility as unlikely because both Bolshevik doctrine and established Soviet practice rejected high-risk ventures. To the Americans it was clear that an offensive missile deployment in Cuba would be a high-risk venture for the Soviets. What neither American policy-makers nor American intelligence officers apparently examined was the possibility that the *Soviets* might regard this as a comparatively moderate risk option *if certain preconditions could be fulfilled.*

Although we still do not know all the sources of the Soviet decision, we can identify some of the preconditions the Soviets may have had, and seen fulfilled, during the months prior to October 1962. First, Soviet medium- and intermediate-range ballistic missiles were becoming available in quantity at that time. Second, a rapid deployment in Cuba seemed possible, so that the missiles might become operational before they were discovered by the Americans. (This expectation almost came to pass; the missiles nearly did become operational before being discovered.) Third, in the event that the missiles were discovered while still being deployed, there seemed to be a good chance that the U. S. policy-making machinery would be too sluggish to take decisive action before some of the missiles, at least, were ready. It had proved somewhat sluggish in other recent crises; in addition, President Kennedy might be young and inexperienced enough to be incapable of taking strong action promptly. (Such apparently was Khrushchev's assessment of Kennedy at their 1961 summit meeting in Vienna.) Fourth, if worst came to worst, the American government could probably be trusted to take diplomatic, not military, action first. (This expectation proved quite correct.) Perhaps there were additional preconditions that seemed to be fulfilled in 1962, so that the Soviets could assess a Cuban missile deployment as a moderate-risk option. American analysts, however, evidently did not approach the problem from the direction of examining Soviet preconditions for such an option.[22]

This technique of reasoning backward from a specific hypothetical future situation to determine its present preconditions does not need to be confined to relatively exotic intelligence problems. In principle the method can readily be extended to the broader assessment of conflicts, in which case it might be termed analysis by preconditions, or simply *preconditional analysis.* Applied to the problem of controlling escalation, preconditional analysis could be a very useful tool. In essence, one would try to identify the preconditions that might encourage a major specific escalation by the opponent *or by oneself,* and then do whatever was feasible and consistent with other policy to prevent the emergence of those preconditions.

A particularly vivid example of a major escalation that might have been forestalled had this approach been tried—but in its absence was not—occurred during the Crimean War. The Sinope massacre was interpreted in the West as a major Russian escalation of the conflict, and it led directly to a major Western counter-escalation in reply. The attack on the Turkish flotilla at Sinope might have been avoided, however, if the British and French had used the leverage provided by advancing their fleets to Constantinople to restrain Turkish initiatives. The Ottomans could resupply their army in the principalities overland, and with a navy weaker than the Russian fleet, they had no reason to deploy it except to resupply the Caucasus front to the east.

The British and French did not prevent the Turks from deploying their ships in this way, nor from opening the Caucasus front in the first place, when they advanced the Anglo-French squadron to Constantinople. They did implicitly place the Turkish navy somewhat under their protection, though. The Turks certainly realized this, and so did the Russians and British. (There was a diplomatic exchange, for example, in which the Russians inquired what naval action against the Turkish fleet the Anglo-French squadron would tolerate.)

By advancing their squadrons almost to the mouth of the Black Sea, by implicitly extending a protective umbrella over the Turkish navy, and by not restraining the Turks from deploying ships to a fresh front, the British and French established all the preconditions for an event like the Sinope massacre, and for the popular and governmental reaction that followed in Britain and France.

Establishment of the preconditions for something like Sinope might have been observable at the time. The British and French could have attempted a preconditional analysis, perhaps taking "an event activating major concerns about naval security" as the hypothetical future occurrence. Reasoning backward, they might have identified a great Russian victory over a Turkish navy under Anglo-French protection as such an event. In turn, the French and British might have identified conditions similar to those just listed as plausible preconditions for occurrence of such an event. In this fashion, the possible significance of the conditions actually being created in October 1853 might have been highlighted for policy-makers. In the interest of controlling escalation, British and French decision-makers might then have acted to alter those conditions.

Preconditional analysis is rarely an easy method, and the results are not always convincing to policy-makers. It is helpful all the same. Simply making an effort of this sort tends to lead analysts in the direction of sequence cognition and systems cognition, and may make both somewhat easier. The effort also tends automatically to lead analysts toward an improved awareness of the frames of reference in other capitals, and toward attentiveness to the frameworks of conflicts. Even without a fully successful identification of a particular set of preconditions, therefore, it can make a useful contribution to controlling escalation.

10

The Heart of Escalation Dynamics

The preceding chapter has explored how conflicts may be assessed by policy-makers and their staffs for the optimum chance of controlling escalation. This chapter approaches the problem of escalation and its control on a different level. It addresses the internal dynamics of escalation processes in broader, more general terms, and thereby tries to shed additional light on the task of controlling these processes.

Some of the forces that drive escalation were touched upon in Chapter 2. Policy-makers want to win the conflict. At worst, they want not to lose it. They have a personal and political stake in a successful outcome. The battlefield presents many tactical demands for steps to avert a defeat or win a victory. As the stakes rise, so does the motivation policy-makers feel. An action by one side inspires a reaction by the other, which in turn inspires a new action by the first; the action-reaction effect keeps producing new situations that cannot be entirely anticipated and that usually place still higher stakes in jeopardy.

Of these, the rising stakes and the action-reaction effect are the most fundamental, particularly in escalation sequences of any length. The mechanisms by which they work, however, have not been adequately described by anything said here so far. In this chapter I shall argue that these mechanisms are simultaneously politico-military and psychological: that is, they concern both the actions of nations in war, and the mental features of decision-making by responsible officials. The interplay between the objective and subjective aspects lies at the heart of escalation dynamics.

The Centrality of Expectation

To lay the groundwork for this analysis it should not be necessary to dwell on the fact that there is a highly subjective component

268

in the cognitive processing done by policy-makers, and hence in their decisions. As Robert Jervis, Joseph de Rivera, and other specialists with a psychological perspective on international politics have emphasized, policy decisions are made on the basis of *perceptions* about international reality. There are many reasons why such perceptions may sometimes be less than accurate and complete. There are definite limits to available information, and distortions and gaps may develop as a result of procedural and organizational biases. Even if these limitations were somehow to be removed, officials would still be making their decisions on the basis of an image or model or construct of reality. Such constructs may misrepresent reality for a variety of reasons having to do with the personalities of individuals, and with more basic limitations on human rationality and cognitive processing.[1]

Examining policy-makers' contructs of reality is a productive analytic approach to assessing and improving their decision-making. In major policy-making during war, one element of this construct seems to be important in a particular way that is interesting to us here. Officials evidently make major decisions not only on the basis of perceptions of present events and their immediate consequences, but also on the basis of more general *expectations* about the future progress and outcome of the war. (Expectations may be regarded as a special kind of perceptions—perceptions about the probable future.)

To illustrate this simple idea let us take as an example an event that was extraordinarily dramatic, and that in many ways made for unusually clear perceptions: the atomic bombing of August 1945. Even in this case expectations, not just immediate perceptions, played a crucial role. The Japanese policy-makers' decision to surrender shortly after the bombing was based not primarily upon their perception and assessment of the sudden, complete loss of one or even two cities. It was based primarily upon their expectation that the United States would be able promptly to destroy every Japanese city in the same fashion. (In fact, the United States at the time did not have nearly enough fissionable material in hand to do this, a closely guarded secret which, if penetrated by the Japanese, might well have led to a different decision.)

Even in a case where perceptions of immediate events were remarkably unambiguous, then, plausible (though erroneous) expectations played a crucial role in the major policy decision that followed. The construct of reality, future as well as present, that the

269

Japanese policy-makers were obliged to employ inescapably contained a subjective element: subjective not in the sense that it was arbitrary, whimsical, or utterly groundless, but in the sense that it had to be supplied by the policy-makers themselves and could not be confirmed or tested.

Now, to some degree, nearly all the perceptions of international reality with which decision-makers work are subjective in this sense. Complete information and total confirmation are rarely available. Generally speaking, though, the plausibility of most perceptions about *present* international reality can be checked to a considerable extent. The plausibility of expectations about the future is far less confirmable; these expectations cannot really be checked until the future arrives.[2]

The first theme I want to strike, then, and to explore in this chapter, is that officials making major wartime decisions do so not only on the basis of perceptions of present reality, but also to a large extent on the basis of expectations about future reality. These expectations are derived in sundry direct and indirect ways from perceptions of the present, but they are more subjective because they involve "reasonable"—but not confirmable and not always accurate—presumptions and extrapolations provided by decision-makers themselves.

The Field of Expectation

The Hiroshima-Nagasaki example is a case of a highly specific expectation that arose suddenly and had a decisive impact on policy. Usually decision-makers' expectations are more diffuse and tentative than this. Expectations may also contain a number of different ingredients, of varying degrees of specificity and explicitness. At any given time during a war, policy-makers normally have some notion of the approximate *costs and risks* their nation is likely to have to bear during the remainder of the war, assuming it remains approximately within its current bounds. They usually have an image in mind of the outlines of the *pattern of the war's development;* or at most two or three alternative images of how, broadly, the war is likely to develop. They usually will have some rough expectations about what the *consequences* to the belligerents are likely to be when the war is eventually ended—the terms of victory or of some negotiated settlement. In many cases they have expectations, as Fred C. Iklé has pointed out,[3] about the approximate

270

length of *time* the war is likely to continue, an estimate that has much to do with expectations about its costs and risks and its likely pattern of development. Decision-makers may hold some images about their *nation's place and role*, and perhaps that of other nations, in the world as it will be after the war; and about changes (if any) in *general world politics.* (Together these are sometimes called systems effects.) And they may well have some expectation about their own *personal position and role* in their nation, and perhaps in the world, following the war; and expectations or intentions about how history will judge them.

Usually policy-makers recognize that there are great uncertainties attached to their expectations and that it is unrealistic to place high confidence in expectations that are too specific. Nevertheless, expectations and images about the future course of the conflict and its outcome play an important and inescapable role in their decisions. A decision for or against escalation, for instance, cannot be made except with reference to ideas or images about how the war will develop if the level of violence is raised and if it is not. Expectations about the future function as part of the logical foundation upon which decision-makers erect the more familiar contents of policy—their strategies, options, and so on.

Partially or wholly unarticulated expectations also become incorporated in the personal judgments that high-level policy-makers bring to bear in making their decisions. They do not rely entirely upon reports and analyses flowing upward to them from bureaucracies and staffs. From personal and vicarious experience they often feel that the conclusions of "analysis" do not capture everything that is important in a situation, and they temper those conclusions with their intuitive judgment. This feeling for the meaning and pattern of events is highly subjective (as many frankly acknowledge), and it incorporates their implicit presuppositions and hazy images about the future course of events.

But the role of expectations goes well beyond the necessity that projections of some sort must be employed in planning. Once used in planning, these ideas tend to influence decision-makers' beliefs about how the war itself will evolve. In other words, projections tend to become incorporated into their images of future *reality*. The emotional impact of surprise depends upon this. One cannot be surprised without *some* previous notion of what future reality will be.

271

Furthermore, it is not possible psychologically for policy-makers to take responsibility for their decisions without believing to some extent in whatever expectations are involved. The personal commitment they must make to their decisions creates a need for them to believe that the future they have explicitly, *or implicitly*, assumed in making them can actually be realized. In other words, because of having made specific decisions, policy-makers tend to believe in the images of the future that undergird these decisions; the same is true of "decisions" made by default not to change ongoing policy.

The role of expectations in decisions about escalation, then, is a pervasive one because they function in ways that are not completely logical, analytic, or conscious. This is the more true because some of the basic expectations at work may be shared so completely among the ranking officials within a government that they remain tacit. For instance, some background images about the likely pattern of the war's development or the main lines of the final outcome may be stated rarely or never.

By no means can decision-makers tap all this simply by asking themselves what expectations underlie a decision presently being made. Some of the ingredients are far too diffuse and too unconscious. The new field of forecasting is developing in part for this reason, as specialists labor to devise techniques for reliably uncovering what peoples' expectations actually are. Certain forecasting techniques may be useful in controlling escalation, not merely because they can raise new possibilities concerning the future development of a war, but perhaps more important, because they can help reveal the present expectations of decision-makers, which in turn may bring dubious or risky assumptions to light.[4]

This theme may be summarized by observing that decisions for or against escalation are made in part on the basis of a diffuse constellation of images and ideas about the future course and likely outcome of the war. Collectively these may be termed a policy-maker's *field of expectation*. The politico-military facts and analyses of the conflict are the source of material, but the field itself is mental and subjective, and it functions in important ways that are not totally analytical or conscious. The significance of this for our purposes is best explored by examining how these fields of expectation change. We shall cut into this twice, from two different angles.

272

Changes in Expectations (First Cut)

The expectations of policy-makers may change during wartime for any of several reasons. At least two need not concern us much here. In wars of attrition and other trials of strength between evenly matched opponents, expectations about costs, terms, duration, and the like may change gradually.[5] This was the case in much of World War I. In any war, there is the further possibility that expectations may change very rapidly as a result of a dramatic battlefield victory. After the battles of Königgrätz and Sedan in 1866 and 1870, for instance, expectations among decision-makers in all the involved and onlooking nations changed sharply.

Expectations also change rapidly as a result of an escalation (or de-escalation) by one of the belligerents. This is the case that interests us here. With a few rare exceptions, the main significance of an escalation does not lie in its direct, tangible consequences that impact almost immediately. *The main significance of an escalation lies in its effect on the expectations of policy-makers in all the nations concerned.* Escalations quickly shift the policy-makers' field of expectation about the course and outcome of the war, and this will generally be more sigificant in subsequent decision-making than the action's direct, physical results.

This is not invariably the case. Exceptions are actions recognized by decision-makers everywhere as definitely one-shot actions. For instance, if the United States for technical reasons had not been able to produce another atomic weapon after the Nagasaki bomb for, say, several years, and if the Japanese had known this confidently, the effect of the first two bombs on the course of the war would have been largely confined to their direct, tangible consequences: the destruction of two important cities. Cases like this are rare in warfare, since most actions that can be performed once can be performed twice or more. Almost an example was the Doolittle raid on Tokyo in 1942, which could not have been repeated for some time. Even this is somewhat ambiguous, since it was intended partly as a warning to the Japanese of things to come eventually. Another type of one-shot action is the action that policy-makers can credibly show to have been accidental or unauthorized such as, perhaps, a "hot pursuit." Still, if the operation was not a clear failure, it may be hard to communicate credibly that it will not be repeated. In short, the instances are few and rare where the direct, tangible consequences of an escalation are its most significant effects. Normally, the most significant impact is on policy-makers' expectations about the future course and likely outcome of the war.[6]

This observation has implications for a general understanding of escalation in warfare, of the kind discussed in Chapter 2. Schelling's identification of limits in wars as saliencies, and of escalation as the crossing of saliencies,[7] may be refined by adding to it this theme of changes in expectations. In most war situations, geographic and political boundaries and various legal and political conventions will provide not just a few, but a great many, possible saliencies. All of them may be crossed at one point or another, but not all of them matter. From the viewpoint of escalation dynamics, the ones that count when they are crossed are the ones where policy-makers' expectations are altered in the crossing.

These are not necessarily the "bigger" or more obvious saliencies. Early in the Spanish Civil War, for instance, the narrow straits between Spain and Spanish Morocco were crossed by aircraft and ships carrying the Spanish foreign legion and its equipment to Nationalist territory in Spain. Late in the war, the much greater distance between Spain and the island of Minorca, held for a long time by the republic, was almost crossed by aircraft and ships carrying Nationalist troops. It would have been, had the island not surrendered when invasion became imminent. The two saliencies involved are comparable in kind, and the geographic separation to be crossed in the later instance was much the greater of the two. However, no one regarded the threat of Minorca's invasion, or would have regarded an actual invasion, as an escalation. It came at a time when the Nationalists were already advancing rapidly on many fronts, and there was nothing about Minorca that would have given the Nationalists much advantage in the remainder of the fighting. Hence the event changed no one's expectations about the course and outcome of the conflict. But earlier, the foreign legion's crossing of the lesser gap of the straits changed expectations everywhere and represented a significant escalation of the conflict. The legion was the only hardened Spanish force available to either side, and its presence on the mainland changed all policy-makers' fields of expectation considerably.[8]

An action will be generally perceived and treated as an escalation, then, when it involves *both* the crossing of a saliency *and* the

alteration of policy-makers' expectations about the course and outcome of the war. Let me suggest the term *expectation levers* for
this. Expectation levers are saliencies that, if crossed, have leverage
on policy-makers' fields of expectation. They are the saliencies that
count.

More on Expectation Levers

The principle of expectation leverage applies to other aspects of
escalation dynamics. Consider, for instance, the fact that an elevation of objectives by one side in a war often functions as an escalation. So often does it function this way, in fact, that some analysts
simply lump it together with escalation of operations and refer to
an elevation in objectives as "escalation" also. Under some circumstances, one side's announcement of new and grander *objectives*
might even call forth an immediate escalation in the other side's
military *operations*, as a counter.

An elevation in objectives may be seen as having its effect
through its impact on the other side's expectations. The new objectives change opposing policy-makers' expectations of the consequences that seem likely to come with the end of the war, and may
also change their expectations about the costs, risks, or duration of
the fighting. It is because of this change in expectations that the
higher objectives have their escalatory impact.

Note that an elevation in objectives has little or no escalatory
effect when it comes from a side that is clearly losing the war and
has no immediate means of implementing the new objectives. It has
so little effect precisely because in this case the new objectives,
however loudly announced, do not change the winning side's expectations.[9]

Consider also *gradualism*, another somewhat ambiguous topic in
contemporary thinking about escalation. As discussed earlier,
decision-makers may employ a gradualist strategy to try to
smudge, or avoid as much as possible, the discreteness and
obviousness of saliencies they are crossing. For example, American
policy-makers did this in 1965 and 1966, carrying out a very slow
advance in their targeting of air attacks on North Vietnam.[10] Italian
policy-makers did it in 1936 and 1937, with their slow deployment
of troops to Spain.

In gradualist escalation of this kind, usually what counts most is
not the saliencies being crossed (which some analysts might be able

275

to identify after all) but the leverage that the gradual progression has on expectations. The escalatory impact comes when expectations shift, and this may or may not have much to do with any saliencies present. One or more segments of a progression, for example, may make little sense except as a prelude to further segments. In Spain a handful of planes or tanks were of value in themselves; therefore the Italian gift of a few to the Nationalists did not necessarily mean that more were following. But a handful of Italian troops made sense only as the advance guard of a sizable body. It was principally for this reason that their discovery by the republic registered as a worrisome Italian escalation.

Or, for a second instance, expectations may shift during a gradualist progression because of the size or pattern of the opponent's capabilities. For technical reasons having to do with the way the Italian troops were deployed, the difference between, say, two Italian divisions in Spain and the four that eventually arrived made relatively little difference in republican expectations about their effectiveness, and hence in republican expectations about the course and outcome of the war. The difference between zero divisions and two, though, had made a difference in the winter of 1936-1937, and several additional divisions later would have too.

The Shifting Expectations of Others

From the viewpoint of controlling escalation, clearly the most important leverage an escalation has is on the expectations of the other side. For it is the opposing policy-makers, obviously, who will decide whether to counterescalate; if they do, a developing action-reaction sequence could result.

At first glance one might think that this fact should make little difference. Shouldn't there be an approximate similarity between expectations of the adversaries and those of decision-makers on the first side? But recall that fields of expectation are subjective. Several of the manifestations of this subjectivity have been discussed already. Another aspect is the different points of view that officials in different capitals have. Often the fields of expectation on different sides are *not* similar; or a rough resemblance may mask important variations in particulars. For example, near the beginning of the Spanish Civil War, French policy-makers on the one hand and German and Italian ones on the other, each expected that their own de facto ally in Spain would win the civil war. In fact, both sides expected that their own ally would win it quickly!

276

This leads to a general remark. The evidence of the cases studied here suggests that policy-makers tend to underestimate this dissimilarity in wartime expectations from one capital to another. They appreciate that, naturally, their opponents' objectives are radically different from their own. But the evidence suggests that policy-makers tend to underestimate how much *their opponents' expectations also differ from their own.*

In the Crimean conflict, for instance, British and Russian decision-makers much more clearly understood that each other's objectives vis-à-vis the Ottoman Empire were divergent and partially competing, than they understood how much each other's expectations about the future of that empire differed. And is was crucially on the basis of these different expectations, not just their divergent objectives, that each side made decisions. In the wars of 1866 and 1870, the Austrians and French had an inadequate understanding of Prussian objectives, but they had if anything an even more inadequate understanding of Prussian expectations—expectations into which they could have inquired, but mostly did not. In the escalation sequence leading to the Seven Years War, British and French policy-makers each understood the other side's objective of controlling the Ohio region relatively early. Only much later did each understand the other's expectation that historical trends in America would "naturally" assure this control unless the opponent took violent initiatives. Only then—too late—was each able to comprehend that the other had been acting defensively all along.[11]

It is crucial in controlling escalation that policy-makers realize that in other capitals the expectations, not just the objectives, may be radically different from ther own. This can be a difference that really matters, because others are making their decisions on the basis of their own expectations. Hence the conceptual attentiveness to the frames of reference of policy-makers abroad, discussed in the previous chapter, needs to include prominent attention to their expectations. Examining others' expectations, indeed, will lead one automatically toward attending to their underlying presuppositions, their basic perspectives, and other ingredients in their frame of reference.

There is no simple formula for controlling escalation. Yet if just one "quick-and-dirty" idea were to be demanded from this study, one simple rule of thumb that in practice would lead one to many of the points being made, it should probably be this: pay attention to others' expectations, not just their objectives.

Action-Reaction Cycles

Decision-makers may tend to underestimate how much their opponents' expectations differ from their own in part because those expectations are not as visible as, for example, the opponents' objectives. The two sets of objectives obviously are in conflict. Often the opponents have openly defined their objectives, a definition that normally bears at least a substantial relation to their true objectives. And one can more readily infer objectives than expectations from the opponents' behavior. For instance, an escalation by the opponents naturally raises the question, "What are they aiming at?," and nearly always provides some evidence from which one can make plausible inferences. Usually it provides less reliable evidence about their expectations. For all these reasons, decision-makers in one capital are likely to find the expectations of decision-makers in another capital less obvious than their objectives. The expectations are, as it were, at a further remove.

This fact with the resulting tendency to underestimate how different expectations are, combined with the idea of expectation leverage, suggest an observation about how action-reaction cycles work in escalation sequences. As action and reaction cycle back and forth, officials make each escalation decision partly on the basis of their subjective field of expectation about the future course and outcome of the war. The escalation by one side that results from such a decision, though, has its most significant impact on the expectations of decision-makers on the other side. Their field of expectation is likely to be significantly different, and this difference is likely to be not too visible to policy-makers on the first side, and therefore underestimated by them. The opponents, then, may do the same thing. On the basis of their *own* field of expectation they may escalate, which action has its most significant impact on expectations on the first side. In action-reaction sequences, then, each escalation is undertaken on the basis of expectations likely to be not entirely known by those on whom the escalation is inflicted, and has its most important impact on expectations likely to be not entirely known by those who undertook it. Each side's field of expectation shifts with the leverage of every escalation, and each side's is partially hidden from the sight of the other.

If this observation is generally correct, it means that the critical interactions in escalation are not between each side's relatively tangible deeds. These deeds provide the vehicle, as it were, for the

278

process to go forward. But the most critical interactions are between the two fields of expectation, which are subjective and intangible.

From a theoretical point of view there is another, in some ways simpler, model of the action-reaction effect in escalation—one that is implicit in many discussions of the subject. In this model each action has its impact not on the opponents' expectations, but what is subtly different, on their estimates of the probability of achieving their objectives. Their reaction simply follows from their assessment that the probability of achieving their objectives has fallen unacceptably low in the wake of the first side's escalation. (Or that escalation may activate a new objective of the opponents).[12]

model #2

This is valid and important, and part of the analysis on the preceding pages could be rewritten in terms of the shifting of "estimated probabilities of achieving objectives" rather than the shifting of "fields of expectation." But this view of the action-reaction effect does not seem to me to catch fully its intricacy or its psychological aspect. Nor does it seem to catch one of the sources of the anxiety that escalation can get out of control.

Taken by itself, this second model can be interpreted as implying that both sides have similar images of *what is likely to occur* as the conflict proceeds, and differ mainly in what they *want* to occur. That is, they differ mainly in their objectives. Most of the time, though, policy-makers know their opponents' objectives to a considerable degree. And policy-makers can calculate rather closely what the impact of their projected escalation on the opponent's objectives ought to be. By focusing on objectives, therefore, this model may carry an implication of escalation being more calculable than it really is.

How the opponents *actually* perceive the impact of the escalation on their objectives depends in part on what *their* expectations were previously about the progress and pattern of the war, and what those expectations are now. In their field of expectation, the implications of the event for their objectives may be greater than, less than, or simply different from, the implications the first side imputed to them. This occurred several times, for instance, during the Crimean War escalation, when both the Russians and the British, confident that they knew each other's objectives in the Near East pretty well, took actions whose implications for each other's objectives they believed they had calculated. They were wrong, however; while they did indeed know each other's objectives pretty well, they did *not* know each other's broader expectations about what might occur in the Near East, nor comprehend how different those expectations were.

Knowledge of the opponents' objectives, even rather accurate knowledge, is not sufficient by itself for one to calculate what the impact on them of a proposed escalation will be. For this one also needs to know the opponents' images of how the pattern of events is likely to develop and what is likely to occur in the presence or absence of specific contingencies. For the sake of clarity, let me put the point in an extreme form. For decision-makers to plug the opponents' objectives into their *own* model and images of the probable pattern of events, and then calculate from this the opponents' likely estimates about the impact of an escalation, is to invite seriously erroneous predictions of the opponents' behavior.

More generally, this second model emphasizes the one element in wartime policy-making—objectives—that decision-makers everywhere are most conscious of. They are very aware of their own objectives; and usually more aware of their opponents' objectives than of anything else about the opponents, except perhaps basic military capabilities.[13] (In addition, the idea of "probabilities" can imply a highly conscious estimating process.) This emphasis on what everyone is already most conscious of is a subtle limitation to this approach. Unintentionally, such an emphasis tends to promote the idea that escalation dynamics are more calculable and more controllable than they are.

In actuality, expectations in opposing capitals are not something that decision-makers seem to be highly conscious of; yet these expectations form a major part of the substratum from which opposing capitals draw their probability estimates about achieving objectives. And this, I think, is one source of the anxiety that escalation may go out of control. People sense that it is the leverage of one side's escalation on the opposing side's expectations that may trigger an unanticipated counterescalation and, perhaps, an uncontrolled sequence thereafter.

Certainly it seems to be mostly this factor that accounts for one of the most important kinds of so-called inadvertent escalation. The unauthorized action by one side's forces, which policy-makers did not suppose would occur, is not the only kind of inadvertent action that can escalate a war. Policy-makers themselves may commit an inadvertent escalation by ordering an action that does not much change their own expectations about the future of the war, but does change the opponents'. (Such an action might be ordered for many reasons: to gain what seems to be only a minor tactical advantage, or even for bureaucratic reasons.) The leverage the action has on the opponents' expectations makes it into a real escalation, to which they may respond with a counterescalation. Policy-makers may even have thought of the possibility of a countermove by the opponents and dismissed the possibility by erroneously assuming—consciously *or unconsciously*—that the opponents' expectations were basically similar to their own.

Always it is the shift that may occur in the other side's expectations, not one's own, which determines whether or not an action will trigger a response, and perhaps the beginning of a whole sequence of steps back and forth. From the point of view of whether such a sequence will be triggered, only the leverage on the opponents' field of expectation counts. In fact, strictly speaking it is the leverage on the opponents' expectations that defines *whether or not an escalation has taken place.*

Changes in Expectations (Second Cut)

Let us now proceed with our second approach to the theme of this chapter: the central role played in escalation dynamics by changes in policy-makers' fields of expectation. Up to this point, we have discussed shifts in expectations that occur promptly in the wake of escalations. Such shifts may be termed *discontinuous* in the sense that after they occur fields of expectation again stabilize, to a large extent, in their new pattern until another escalation occurs or until they are altered for some other reason.

There is another process at work too, in escalation, which also involves change in policy-makers' fields of expectation but which may be termed *continuous* because it involves slower and more gradual, also more steady, change over time. Briefly mentioned earlier during the discussion of the Seven Years War escalation sequence, this process consists in the progressive narrowing of the range of future possibilities decision-makers find plausible, and of the range of policy decision-makers find feasible and worth pursuing.

This is not a process necessarily found in all cases of escalation. It does not appear much, for instance, in the Spanish Civil War, where there were opportunistic escalations and a reciprocal escalation, but not a long cyclical sequence. Nor does it appear in the few escalations of the Franco-Prussian War. It is likely to occur as the cumulative effect of a *sequence*. And it may be especially characteristic of sequences which, however high a level of violence they eventually reach, begin at a low level. Let us briefly review the two cases in this book where escalation (beginning, in both instances, at a low level) proceeded through a long sequence. The narrowing effect appears in both.

The escalation sequence that culminated in the Seven Years War was an almost perfectly bipolar action-reaction cycle. Before and at the beginning of the cycle, the French and the British perceived themselves to be in a limited-adversary relationship. They recognized a possibility that their global cold war might become acute at some point and perhaps lead to a general war between them. But policy-makers on both sides had no reason to assess this possibility as an especially likely one. A variety of low-level conflicts, situations of tension, minor crises, and occasions for negotiations seemed to be equally likely future possibilities.

Accompanying this image of a broad range of plausible futures was an expectation on both sides of employing a considerable range of policy instruments. Decision-makers expected to proceed indefinitely by shifting back and forth among sundry political, economic, diplomatic, and occasionally military devices and demonstrations, including only rarely direct military action simply to seize objectives. They also expected to employ serious negotiations for resolving or at least muting significant conflicts.

As the escalation sequence subsequently proceeded, the range of expectations steadily narrowed. The number and variety of plausible futures decreased and the expected value of policy instruments short of direct military action declined. Plausible images of the near future became fewer, until extremely acute crisis and very possibly war seemed to be the only realistic expectations. Negotiations, signals, and outright military demonstrations all came to seem less and less promising ways to secure objectives; only military action seemed feasible. (The objectives were not elevated, basically, on either side.) For instance, negotiations were not pursued at all during the final weeks of 1753 and early weeks of 1754, a time when they might have been most valuable. When they were resumed in February 1754, it was for only a brief time and (the evidence suggests) without a serious expectation on either side that they might succeed. That summer, when the status quo of the previous year had almost entirely returned and considerable time was available for another effort, negotiations were not resumed at all.

The same effect may be observed in the escalation cycle culminating in the Crimean War. Here it is, if anything, more striking, because actual fighting between the military forces of the eventual great-power opponents did not occur until the end of the sequence. Military action between the Russians and Turks began with the Russian occupation of the Ottoman principalities in July 1853; however, not until the beginning of the following year did the French and British use physical coercion against the Russians, by barring the Russian navy's use of the Black Sea, and not until August 1854 did fighting break out between them, with the Crimean landing.

Even so, the same narrowing of the range of plausible futures and the range of apparently promising lines of policy set in during 1853 with the advancing sequence of Western military demonstrations. During most of 1853 the Russians and the Anglo-French alliance actively pursued diplomatic negotiations, but as time passed and escalation mounted, negotiations were reduced; by early 1854 they were abandoned, although diplomacy was not yet impossible and war was not yet close to starting. Again, when the British entered the crisis in the late spring of 1853, their image of the future included war with Russia as a possibility. But it did not seem a likely one. By the spring of 1854, however, even Prime Minister Aberdeen, who had worked throughout for a resolution, felt that war was highly likely and ceased to try seriously to avoid it. Czar Nicholas' expectations narrowed in the same way and he reacted in the same way. In reality this was almost certainly premature. With hindsight one can observe that war between the great powers probably did not become unavoidable until the summer of 1854.

There is evidently something at work here that goes beyond what one would anticipate from "rational" calculations of the probabilities of alternative futures and "rational" calculations of the probable usefulness of alternative lines of policy. Such calculations, done at various points, would have indicated that the future was not yet as closed as it seemed. They would have indicated that general war was not becoming inevitable as rapidly as it seemed and that alternative lines of policy were still worth pursuing. Instead, policy-makers apparently found the range of plausible futures closing faster than it "really" was. Why?

The Psychological Root of Narrowing Expectations

The causes behind this tendency for fields of expectation to narrow prematurely during escalation are somewhat complicated. They are worth exploring, because the phenomenon is an important part of how escalation may go out of control. The core of the explanation appears to lie in the need for *cognitive consistency*, as specialists term it.

Psychologists have shown that the mind tends to avoid disharmony in attitudes, beliefs, and views of the world. This disharmony, called *cognitive dissonance*, is uncomfortable and at times may create real anxiety. Therefore the mind tends to avoid fully recognizing any information which conflicts with the construct of reality that has already been accepted. Such information is required, in effect, to meet higher standards of validity before it is seriously recognized and considered than information which implicitly confirms what reality already appears to be.[14]

Most of the time this need for cognitive consistency is balanced against the normal ability to recognize and accept significant new information. Information conflicting with the construct of reality is normally required to meet only moderately higher standards of validity, then an appropriate modification is made in the image of reality to integrate this information. However, this does not always occur. Some personalities protect their construct of reality more strongly and require in effect that inconsistent information or ideas achieve an extraordinary (perhaps impossible) degree of proof.

Researchers have found too that *all* individuals tend to protect cognitive consistency more when they are in difficult and threatening situations. The stress accompanying such situations imposes a need for a simpler kind of consistency. Tolerance of ambiguities and complications drops markedly. Under high stress individuals simplify their perceptions of reality; they fail to observe features that in more relaxed states they would readily notice and recognize as important.[15]

Many political scientists have pointed out that this reality-simplifying process comes into play during intense international crises—which are usually experienced by policy-makers, even more than by ordinary citizens, as threatening. Such crises often include an element of surprise, and surprise itself is a source of additional stress. Still more stress is generated by anxiety and by sheer physical fatigue as officials try to cope with the emergency, often by working long and irregular hours.

One carefully studied crisis, for example, is the one that resulted in the outbreak of World War I. Ole Holsti has shown that the stress on policy-makers resulting from an overload of communications and strong time pressure, as well as anxiety, threat, and fatigue, tended to reduce sharply the number of alternatives that could be seriously considered. He also found that under these conditions policy-makers tended to single out *threats* from the avalanche of incoming communications from other nations, and paid less attention to offers of negotiations, conciliatory messages, and the like. Both these tendencies became stronger as the stress on policy-makers increased.[16]

In short, during intense international crises policy-makers everywhere must work under the pressures of time urgency, information overload, surprise, anxiety, and fatigue. Under these conditions they begin to lose sight of some of the complications in the situation and the full range of its possibilities. Reality becomes simplified.[17]

Some wartime escalation decisions are made in this atmosphere of intense crisis. In such cases the reality-simplifying effect of crisis stress undoubtedly works in the same way. Policy-makers' perceptions of the conflict, and their images of how it could plausibly develop, may narrow down to focus almost exclusively on escalation options. Other possibilities, and other lines of policy to pursue instead *or in addition*, which in calmer moments might be taken seriously, are quickly dismissed or not noticed at all. Here, then, is one reason why in some escalation situations, decision-makers' expectations and perceptions may narrow more than a "rational" calculation would indicate they should.

By no means, however are all escalation decisions made under conditions of intense crisis stress. It appears that few if any were, for instance, during the U. S. escalation in Vietnam. Certainly none or almost none were during the escalation sequences leading to the Crimean War and the Seven Years War. There were no unmanageable floods of communications during either of these escalation sequences, and each was stretched over a long time. Indeed, the Seven Years War sequence was by twentieth-century standards downright leisurely. Cognitive consistency was clearly not simplified by crisis stress in these cases. Yet during both these sequences there was a noticeable narrowing, beyond what a rational assessment would have indicated, of policy-makers' expectations about plausible and feasible ways the situation could develop and lines of policy worth pursuing.

Evidently the reality-simplifying effect can be activated during escalation sequences for reasons other than crisis stress. There seem to be several reasons, mutually reinforcing one another, why *escalation sequences cumulatively activate cognitive consistency and thereby narrow policy-makers' fields of expectation.* Let us look at these with a little care.

The Raising of the Stakes

One reason for this occurrence involves the progressive increase of what is at stake. As escalation proceeds, the price for the mounting operations (in casualties, economic costs, and opportunities foregone) rises steadily, and policy-makers become more anxious to have their increasingly costly policy succeed. (U. S. policy-makers felt this way, for instance, during the Vietnam escalation.) In addition, as the stakes rise still higher, the costs that a defeat might inflict (in losses in military capabilities, reduction of general national power in world politics, and the like) become even graver and more intolerable. Policy-makers find themselves with a greater and greater need to protect their investment: to justify their costly policy with success, or to stave off a really serious defeat.

British policy-makers in 1757, for example, sent General Braddock and his regiments to protect English claims in North America. Then, when the French sent reinforcements to Canada in response, the British felt they *had* to take the admittedly risky step of intercepting those reinforcements on the high seas because they could not afford the loss of Braddock's regiments. This kind of rise in the stakes, "compelling" additional action, is not uncommon in escalation. It is characteristic of escalation sequences in fact, that the steps decision-makers take to protect their investment tend to have the effect of increasing the investment, and thereby increasing the necessity of protecting it further.

This widely recognized motor driving the escalation process would be serious enough by itself. Its consequences are worsened, however, through the psychological effect it has on decision-makers. For as the stakes rise to put great values at risk, decision-

286

makers' anxiety and their sense of being threatened rise too. Previously, when the stakes were low, less serious values were being risked and, if the worst had come to the worst, the price to be paid might not have been too terribly high. As more and more is at stake, the price to be paid if the worst happens becomes increasingly intolerable. Under these conditions policy-makers may well start to feel real anxiety and a sense of deep threat. These feelings in their turn are likely to arouse the reality-simplifying effect. It becomes more difficult to think of the other side as anything other than a hostile enemy, and more difficult to visualize plausible ways the situation could develop other than more acute conflict.[18]

Let us be clear about this. It is not simply that, in the bureaucratic politics within a government, some decision-makers develop a personal stake in pursuing an escalation policy—perhaps because of having committed themselves earlier to a recommendation of this policy, or perhaps because they represent an agency or department that favors it for its own organizational reasons. This common observation about escalation is true and important. And as the sequence proceeds and the opponent, rather than backing down, counters each move with one of his own, decision-makers who had invested a personal stake in the escalation policy might become anxious about whether their recommendation was turning out successfully.

The psychological effect of an escalation sequence, however, goes beyond the perennial struggle within a government over policy. As the stakes at risk become more and more important for the whole nation, a sense of threat and anxiety may develop among all high-ranking officials. The extent to which the reality-simplifying effect is invoked may or may not depend on where in the government an official is located or on his policy biases. In 1853 Lord Aberdeen, the prime minister and long an advocate of concessions to the Russians, was apparently affected by reality-simplifying about as much as the cabinet hawks like Lord Palmerston were. (Possibly more, although hawk opinion also simplified as the escalation sequence proceeded.)

This psychological effect of rising stakes is significant, partly because there is a tendency in the literature about escalation and limited war for analysts to discuss "the rising stakes" as an analytically clear and calculable process. There is an implicit suggestion that as escalation reaches a higher rung, the costs and risks being incurred are higher, naturally, but the way in which costs and risks are weighed and evaluated has not changed. To put it in the language of decision theory, although some of the numbers in the payoff matrices have gone up and are still going up, one continues to perform the probability calculations in the same way.

This is true mainly in the abstract, hypothetical world of strategic analysis. In the concrete world of actual policy-making, the progressive rise in stakes may well generate a progressive rise in feelings of threat and anxiety among decision-makers. In this state of mind they cannot really contemplate all possibilities in an identical neutral spirit, as is implicitly required in formal strategic analysis. They may, as Bernard Brodie has pointed out, "yield to emotions like rage or fear."[19] Even if they do not simply yield to their emotions, an unconscious cognitive dissonance is created whenever they turn to options such as making a new and generous negotiating offer to the other side. The dissonance makes it more difficult to explore and weigh such possibilities carefully and creatively.

In a state of great anxiety and with a deep sense of threat, in fact, *a truly imaginative and creative approach* to the question, "What generous new offers can we make to the other side in a renewed negotiating effort?," could be so dissonant as to be psychologically almost impossible. Yet a renewed negotiating effort, and some generosity on at least some issues, might be the only thing that could control the further escalation of the conflict.

If policy-makers feel deeply threatened and anxious, these feelings are likely also to invoke the cognitive consistency need for a higher standard of validation for information inconsistent with present perceptions. For example, information suggesting that the opponents—without abandoning their basic objectives—might be able to put together a negotiating offer at least interesting enough to begin discussions, would be likely to have to meet a higher level of validation than information suggesting that they were preparing to escalate the conflict further. It might have to appear highly authoritative, and the positive features of their exploratory effort might have to be specific and definite. Yet a specific and definite new positive offer, part of an authoritative new negotiating effort, is just what policy-makers on the other side will find most difficult to make! A creative departure of this sort will be the hardest thing for the other side's decision-makers to achieve, because of their own cognitive dissonance resulting from their own mounting anxiety and sense of threat.

As escalation proceeds, then, a double gap is likely to open up between the two sides. Each finds it cognitively more dissonant to make a significant new offer, and cognitively more difficult to "hear" any hints of a new offer from the other—which the other is also finding it cognitively more difficult to make. As the escalation sequence goes on, this double gap will widen. As time passes and events become more threatening, each side may, so to speak, gradually retreat into its own universe.

Reinforcement

The psycological effect of rising stakes is not the only reason why a sequence of escalation cumulatively narrows policy-makers' subjective fields of expectation. Another reason involves the well-known psychological process called *reinforcement*. Many researchers have pointed to a feedback process between hostile behavior and perceptions of hostility. It occurs in relations between individuals and groups as well as between nations.[20] Hostile behavior by one party tends to reinforce others' perception of that party as hostilely motivated, and this arouses hostility in the others. How does this work in escalation?

Consider, for the sake of clarity, an action-reaction escalation cycle beginning at a low level of violence and perhaps also involving military demonstrations and signals short of violence. At this point policy-makers on both sides still are entertaining a relatively wide range of images about plausible futures and expectations about potentially useful lines of policy.

Now one side escalates. Particularly if this escalation is not accompanied by a very visible negotiating effort, it tends to shift the perceptions of policy-makers on the other side: their image of the opponent as potentially reasonable has *not* been reinforced; their image of the opponent as potentially hostile and aggressive *has* been reinforced.

If, then, the other side counterescalates in its turn, the perceptions of decision-makers on the first side tend to be shifted in the same way. Particularly if the counterescalation is not accompanied by a negotiating initiative, their perceptions too are reinforced in the direction of seeing the other side as more hostile and aggressive.

As the sequence of action and reaction proceeds, this cross-rein-forcement continues. The effect does not have to be great at any one step for the cumulative effect over a sequence of steps to be quite significant. More and more, each side sees the other as an enemy and the conflict as an acute one.

For that matter, escalation does not need to proceed in an action-reaction cycle for reinforcement to come into play. There is also a *self-reinforcement* effect when a policy departure in one direction is not balanced by a policy departure in the contrary direction.

The escalation process that led to the Crimean War provides an excellent example. As conflict between the Turks and the Russians deepened during 1853, the French and British found themselves identifying more and more with the Ottoman side. Although their primary goal at this point was preservation of the status quo (and they had a definite interest in preventing the Turks, as well as the Russians, from upsetting it), they undertook an escalating series of military demonstrations intended to force a Russian withdrawal without restraining the Turks in any significant way. At each step in the advancement of their fleets toward and into the Black Sea, there were options available—at the later steps, important ones—for exploiting these escalations for their potential value as leverage on Turkish policy, and/or for their potential value in circumscrib-ing and delimiting what was now a Russo-Turkish War. At no step did the British and French take advantage of these possibilities.

The consequences were disastrous in an immediate operational sense, such as by permitting the Turks to expand the war into the Caucasus. They were equally or more disastrous in an indirect, psychological way by cumulatively reinforcing French and British perceptions of the situation, in the direction of their perceiving the Russians as enemies and the Turks as de facto allies and friends. Toward the beginning of this sequence, the Westerners were still making modest but significant efforts to use their general diplo-matic influence to hold Turkish policy in check. By the end of the sequence, when the Western navies entered the Black Sea, British and French decision-makers did not apparently even give serious consideration to acting as a third force, as they could have, to bar *both* belligerents from the use of that sea. Through step-by-step self-reinforcement they had by that time unconsciously narrowed their perceptions of the situation, and their images of its range of possibilities, to the point that only a purely escalatory, one-sided policy seemed reasonable.

290

On Expectations and Decision

This description has not explicitly included the diplomatic commitment that the Westerners gradually made to the Turks. Some might argue that the decision to make this commitment provides the main explanation for the Anglo-French policy of acting almost exclusively in the Turkish favor, and that because this decision was made, their policy was a logical one, however regrettable the consequences. I believe, however, that this is an inadequate way of approaching the problem—inadequate particularly from the viewpoint of controlling escalation.

It is certainly true that whenever a commitment is made through a deliberate, specific, highly conscious decision, self-reinforcement plays a much smaller role and the commitment should be analyzed primarily in terms of the logic that supported it at the time it was made. If the consequences of this commitment turn out to be not what policy-makers anticipated or wanted, analysts or the policy-makers themselves are justified in reexamining the policy mainly in terms of errors of fact and/or logic in the calculation of the commitment decision. The same is true when a series of several deliberate and highly conscious decisions are made to increase the commitment in stages.

Nevertheless, many of the important commitments that nations actually make, including many made during escalation sequences, arise gradually over time.[21] Like the Anglo-French commitment in 1853, these commitments may not come about through deliberate and consciously thought-through decisions; like this commitment, it may not be so much that they are "made" as that they simply "grow." In such instances a retrospective analysis in terms of errors of fact and/or logic in the calculation is an analysis of an artifact. While not utterly pointless, such an analysis must be secondary from the viewpoint of explaining what occurred and why. In such cases the primary explanation is on another level or levels.

What seems to matter a great deal in such cases is the gradual transformation of policy-makers' basic expectations and perceptions, not their conscious superstructure of calculations. Conscious calculations may be made at certain scattered times, but they are re-erected each time on the foundation of the gradually transforming expectations and perceptions. These expectations and perceptions change—shift, transform, widen, or narrow—for many reasons. Specific discrete, identifiable changes in international reality

291

are one, but not the only, reason. During escalation sequences, for example, expectations and perceptions can narrow faster than a "rational" calculation of the changes in international reality would indicate. As we have seen, one reason for this *constriction of the foundations of calculation* is cross-reinforcement that results from the action-reaction process; another is self-reinforcement that results from repetitively taking policy departures in one direction that are not balanced by policy departures in the contrary direction.

In the case of the Anglo-French escalation in 1853, then, a commitment certainly did develop, but it grew gradually, hand in hand with the narrowing of the Westerners' perceptions and expectations. The British and French policy-makers self-reinforced their perceptions and expectations in one direction by repetitively taking "unbalanced" policy departures. Their images of what the significance of the situation was, and what its possibilities were, narrowed as time passed, and these in turn became the basis of the developing commitment. Indeed, one could go slightly farther. Since the Western decision-makers apparently did not recognize that they were creating a major commitment until they were well on the way to doing so, one could accurately say that up to that point, the developing commitment *was* the narrowing universe of perceptions and expectations.

In this case, the triangular relationship of the Western allies, the Turks, and the Russians reveals with special clarity the self-reinforcement by the Westerners. Acting very differently along one side of the triangle than along the second, the British and French progressively collapsed their perception of a tripolar relationship into a bipolar one. The Russians, previously perceived to be in an ambiguous relationship with the West, gradually came to be perceived in an unambiguous, hostile role.

In a situation like the Seven Years War escalation sequence, which was bipolar from the beginning, there is no possibility of collapsing a tripolar relationship this way. Even so, the process of cross-reinforcement of each side's perceptions by the other side's escalations still operates. Each side's image of the other becomes progressively transformed, from an originally ambiguous and complex role as a limited adversary, in the direction of becoming an entirely hostile enemy.

One tactic for trying to control a developing escalation sequence, then, might be to make conciliatory efforts for the sake of holding perceptions in balance, even where there do not appear to be other reasons for doing so. But this is a difficult suggestion for policy-makers to carry out, precisely for the reasons this analysis has suggested. Making a new conciliatory effort always has a cost, both tangibly in the sense that the other side must be offered something, and intangibly in the sense that undertaking any new departure requires a degree of struggle in the bureaucratic and policy-making process. In almost any specific case, decision-makers' narrowing expectations about what the near future will bring may make the effort seem pointless.

The Closing Future

The foregoing analysis suggests several reasons why escalation sequences result in a cumulative narrowing of decision-makers' fields of expectation. There is self-reinforcement that results from a series of unbalanced policy departures. There is cross-reinforcement that results from a hostile action-reaction cycle. And there is reality-simplifying that results from deepening feelings of anxiety and threat.

As a practical matter, it is impossible to assess how much of the narrowing that occurs during any particular sequence (including the Crimean and Seven Years War sequences) should be attributed to each of these causes. Evidently all of these processes are at work, to one degree or another, simultaneously and for the most part unconsciously. Operationally it makes little difference, since they all lead to the same practical result.

In any case, because of these processes and perhaps others as well, policy-makers' subjective perceptions of a situation and their expectations about plausible ways it could develop do narrow as escalation proceeds. The stage is then set for cognitive consistency to make a further contribution to escalation dynamics; for cognitive consistency becomes involved in the relation between officials' expectations and perceptions and their own policy-making.

Governments typically do not pursue just one line of policy at a time vis-à-vis a situation of major importance, but a number of policies. A spectrum may be pursued, including negotiations (and explorations of the possibility of negotiations), conciliatory gestures of various kinds, signals of intentions and attitudes, demonstrations of resolve and commitment, and, during escalation, outright military measures to seize or secure objectives. As the range of decision-makers' perceptions and expectations narrows, the range of their policies narrows also. It becomes cognitively dissonant to couple policies to control escalation with policies for unilaterally pursuing national interests. And since the range of perceptions and expectations narrows faster than a "rational" analysis of the situation might indicate, so in turn does the range of policies.

The overall role of cognitive consistency in escalation dynamics is thus a complicated one. Two cognitive processes should be distinguished clearly. The *reality-simplifying effect* is created by mounting anxiety and mounting feelings of being threatened. This contributes to the narrowing of perceptions and expectations beyond what a "rational" analysis might indicate. Self-reinforcement, and the cross-reinforcement resulting from action-reaction cycles, also contribute to this premature narrowing of perceptions and expectations. The *need to avoid cognitive dissonance* then ensures that decision-makers will unconsciously tend to narrow the range of their policies in tandem with the narrower perceptions and expectations.

One might summarize this complex process by saying that a *hostile shift* occurs in the spectrum of policies being pursued, in order for the range of policies to remain psychologically consistent with narrowing expectations. This hostile shift in policy is then perceived by officials on the other side. Through the same sort of psychological process, a similar hostile shift occurs in their own range of policies. By means of the familiar action-reaction effect, this impacts upon decision-makers on the first side, and so on.

At each step, a rational analysis of the opponents' escalations might also result, of course, in a change in probability estimates in the direction of more acute conflict seeming more probable: that is the purely strategic or analytic effect of action-reaction cycles, which is serious enough all by itself. But the hostile shifts, resulting from premature narrowing of expectations and the consequent premature narrowing of policy, go beyond what a rational analysis would indicate.

As escalation continues, decision-makers' subjective universes of perceptions and images become steadily narrower. The range of expectations tightens: fewer and fewer possibilities seem plausible. Policy-makers begin to feel that the future is closing in on them. This sense of a closing future—the sense that the worst possibilities

294

are the only ones to expect—then becomes its own additional source of anxiety. Policy-makers, unaware of the cognitive effects being created by the sequence of events, attribute their sense of the future closing in to the enemy's actions and to his intolerable objectives—simultaneously wondering, perhaps, why the future seems to be closing in so fast. The subjective future closes in faster than one anticipates it should because it is closing in for psychological, not just objective, reasons. And as the cycle feeds on itself, the closing future is confirmed and made real by the policy decisions that are made.

One could say that the narrowing expectations are self-confirming and self-fulfilling. This is not quite the same as the usual sort of self-fulfilling prophecies, though. Generally that phrase refers to one or more specific predictions or ideas—ideas which, though their self-fulfilling quality may not be obvious, are themselves reasonably clear and definite. What seems to be at work in escalation is more diffuse, more global, and more subjective than this. Policy-makers hold vague images, semi-consciously and even unconsciously, about the way things may develop, as well as certain specific predictions and expectations quite consciously. *All* these images and expectations together make up the range of subjective impressions about the future, which decision-makers draw on in making policy. As this range narrows during the escalation process, not only are certain specific ideas or possibilities confirmed and others consciously abandoned, but the complete subjective experience of what the future might be closes in.

Thus the secret of the closing future evidently is not the expectations that are confirmed or fulfilled, but the many images that gradually become missing, eliminated from the subjective universe by cognitive dissonance. One cannot quite say, then, that expectations function as they do in escalation dynamics because they function as self-fulfilling prophecies. One would have to say, if catch phrases for such a complicated process are required, that escalation proceeds through hostile shifts in the range of policies officials pursue, which in turn are created by, if you will, "self-narrowing cognitive cycles."

Initial Stability

If the analysis presented here is correct, it may clarify why escalation sequences can be hard to control. Policy-makers working under intense crisis stress are often aware that the quality of their decision-making has declined and that not all possibilities are receiving adequate attention. But when there is no atmosphere of intense crisis surrounding the decision process, it may be more difficult for them to be aware that potential paths toward freezing a conflict at its present level of violence, or de-escalating it, or resolving part or all of it, are probably being underestimated or overlooked. Officials will not be aware that cognitive consistency needs are being activated, even while hostile shifts are occurring in their range of policies. They may simply attribute their stronger measures to a rational assessment of the enemy's intolerable behavior. During the escalation sequences leading to the Crimean War and the Seven Years War, for instance, policy-makers evidently were not aware that they were prematurely downgrading, and later prematurely dismissing, possible lines of policy other than further escalation.

One way in which the cycle of narrowing expectations may be interrupted or forestalled is suggested by the three wars studied in this book in which escalation did *not* get out of control. In both wars of German unification and in the Spanish Civil War there was an initial period of stability during which the early limits of the wars were not crossed. In the Austro-Prussian War, this period lasted throughout the seven weeks' duration of the conflict. In the Franco-Prussian War, it lasted about the same length of time, before the elevation in German objectives raised the level of violence. In Spain, the initial limits created during the fortnight following the putsch remained stable for a period of over two months.

Although a number of the initial limits of these three conflicts were later crossed, in all three cases they lasted long enough for expectations to develop among policy-makers in all the potentially involved countries that the war might well remain a reasonably controlled one. The stability of the initial limits created an image among decision-makers of a potentially nonescalating conflict. These expectations by no means entirely dissipated in the cases where some of the initial limits were subsequently crossed. In the Spanish Civil War, for instance, policy-makers clearly continued to believe in the possibility of the war remaining under control even after major escalations had occurred. The possibility remained a vivid one (as well as a desirable one) for them, and they continued to act in ways consistent with its being realized. In this conflict and the two others, therefore, the temporary stability of the initial limits of the wars became translated into a more lasting stability in expectations about the future of the wars.

Again we see an intimate relationship between policy-makers' expectations and their policy decisions. (Here the relationship is indeed one of self-fulfilling expectations.) In these three cases an image of stability was the first general image of the war to be created among policy-makers, and it evidently tended to become the central image. Subsequent escalations, even major ones, apparently were perceived as modifications to a basic pattern that had been established, not as a new basic pattern. The image of overall stability remained.

These three are also cases where the transition from peace to war was relatively clear and distinct. It appears that the period of time immediately following the sharp "outbreak" of war may be important to ultimate success or failure in controlling escalation, because an image of stability is, or is not, created during that time. Where policy-makers have tried to design an initial war context for a planned war, as in the two German wars, they will be successful in creating an image of stability if the essential features of that context last for a reasonable interval. Where fighting has broken out spontaneously, as in the Spanish Civil War, the definitional phase of the conflict extending over the following days and weeks is evidently a time when great caution is required among policy-makers in all the involved nations if an image of stability is to develop.[22]

Some period of stability in the initial limits of a new war also seems to contribute to controlling escalation in another way, which is closely related. The outbreak of a new war, particularly if the transition from peace is sudden and sharp, is among the most dramatic events known to mankind, and until some limitations are placed upon its likely consequences, among the most dangerous. The days and weeks just following such an outbreak are usually ones of extreme uncertainty for policy-makers among all the nations that could become involved. Some stability in the initial limits functions to lower the uncertainty. Indeed, the expectation of continuing stability may derive some of its strength from the psychological relief from unbearable uncertainty that an initial period of stable limits provides.

Epilogue

The era during which the term *escalation* was coined and came into general usage (in its military sense) has tended, not surprisingly, to shape perspectives on what is important in controlling the escalation process. Those perspectives may not be adequate, however, for the rather different world of the late 1970s, 1980s, and 1990s. In this epilogue let me elaborate very briefly on this idea.

The Cold War years were in many respects a period during which international politics was simplified, compared to preceding eras and also compared to the post-Cold War era we now are in. The East-West conflict was, or appeared to be, a sharply bipolar one, in which most of the world's nations either lined up on one side or the other, or else seemed to be potential targets for the efforts of one side or the other to expand its influence. The nuclear balance was utterly bipolar. (British forces appeared to most observers essentially as an adjunct to the American strategic arsenal.)

Under these circumstances it was plausible to regard most conflicts that occurred, or seemed likely to occur, essentially as successive acts in the East-West drama. The outcome of any particular war or crisis seemed significant, at least from the viewpoint of the superpowers, mainly in its implications for the overall balance between them. In the Korean War and most of the more dangerous crises, furthermore, the superpowers determined or heavily influenced the decisions made by proxies where they were not acting themselves. Controlling escalation under such conditions is likely to be a more straightforward problem conceptually, though not necessarily an easier one in all respects, than when there are multiple centers of decision with each pursuing its own interests independently.

However, the condition of multiple decision centers exists now and seems likely to exist for some time to come. It has become a cliché that the post-Cold War world is a multipolar one, indeed increasingly so. Rather than a single dominant cleavage, there is now a variety of tensions and hostilities around the globe. Conflicts that erupt are not necessarily, in fact are not usually, traceable back to the interests and maneuvers of two great powers. They arise mainly from local and regional motives, although at some point they often become involved in a multidimensional web of global political interests (of which the traditional Soviet-American rivalry, now somewhat muted, is only one). Controlling escalation under such conditions seems likely to involve more numerous considerations, of more different kinds, than analysts in the last several decades have tended to regard as important.

Demonstrations of will or commitment, and competitions in risk-taking, for example, have been widely stressed as being of central importance in escalation. Such elements are significant in many kinds of escalation situations, but especially under certain circumstances: where the opponents each possess a relatively extensive and flexible set of options to employ against one another, and where the significance of local interests in and around the conflict is relatively minor compared to the much broader interests of the opponents tangibly or symbolically engaged. Under these conditions the opponents may well have a deep incentive to, and be able to, engage in demonstrations of will and risk-taking, with the competition comparatively unimpeded by local details. Exactly these were usually the conditions of the Cold War. But such conditions are not typical of crises and local conflicts in the post-Cold War world, and where these conditions do not exist, the bargaining and demonstrative approach to controlling escalation is likely to be only one, and not necessarily the foremost, approach to the task.

The same theme applies to the grim prospect of conflict involving nuclear weapons. Analysts now find that they need to consider a more diverse range of possibilities than previously. In recent decades the two commanding images of war with nuclear weapons, for analysts and officials alike, have been the overwhelming first strike (the "bolt from the blue") and a battle in Central Europe that erupts into full-scale nuclear war. These important possibilities have now been joined by others. The increasingly widespread deployment of Soviet as well as American nuclear weapons, combined with the great variety and by now enormous number of these weapons, make possible many kinds of nuclear confrontations between the superpowers, and in many parts of the globe other than Europe.

In addition, if the grave warnings about proliferation being issued by many concerned experts come true, there will be more and more nuclear arsenals, of varying sizes and capabilities. Under those circumstances the probability of actual use of atomic weapons may grow alarmingly high within the next couple of decades. If they are used, the current attitude that utilization of such weapons is "unthinkable" almost surely would dissolve, and *all* the nuclear weapons in the world's arsenals would immediately become much more usable. Furthermore, the number, wide deployment, and great flexibility of the superpowers' weapons would give leaders of these nations many options for intervening in a local nuclear war—the first that may occur, and subsequent ones.

In short, a great range of possibilities may be opening up for initially low-level nuclear conflicts in many parts of the world. The danger they pose of nuclear escalation, including "catalysis" of a superpower confrontation, may be serious. Comparatively little analytic attention has been devoted to these possibilities by strategic specialists, however, perhaps in part because many of the most critical questions concern not strategy per se, but conceptual, informational, psychological, and other aspects of decision-making.

To summarize: the circumstances of international conflict in the late twentieth century involve a wider range of more complicated possibilities than did the actual and hypothetical conflicts of the Cold War era. Broadly speaking, the variety of considerations that might be important to controlling escalation is becoming proportionately greater. Demonstrations of will and commitment, and competitions in risk-taking, are only one strand—often a subordinate one—in the larger fabric.

If this argument is correct, then decision-makers need a new and richer kind of assistance from analysts and researchers. Controlling escalation cannot be left until crisis or war erupts. The speed of contemporary communication and transportation has enormously shortened the time that decision-makers may have available, after the eruption, to find ways of preventing or halting the conflict's intensification. And short decision time, as discussed earlier, not only prevents extensive analysis on the spot, but also creates stress that reduces the range of decision-makers' perceptions.

Attempts to forecast specific scenarios for the future, or to "pre-program" military options to meet those scenarios, are not likely to be very useful and can even be dangerous. Yet some forms of analysis and planning might well be able to come to the aid of decision-makers. Preconditional analysis can sometimes identify ways of heading off some of the most dangerous possibilities. At a minimum, *factors* likely to be important in various alternative sets of situations can often be identified in advance. To the extent possible, means must also be found for improving the decision-making process in times of crisis.

Research on the eras prior to the Cold War, which in some respects resemble the world of the coming decades more than the Cold War period does, helps indicate the range of assistance decision-makers may need. But this kind of research is only one of many potential approaches to a fateful problem. Every promising avenue must be explored, if decision-makers coping with the complexities of the late twentieth century are to be given the best possible chance of controlling escalation.

Appendixes
Notes and Bibliographies
Index

Appendix A

Operational Questions for Decision-Makers

The following list of questions is intended to be helpful to decision-makers seeking to control escalation in a particular situation. By no means will every question apply in every situation, but some may prove suggestive. Many of these questions can also be used as starting points for what is referred to in the text as preconditional analysis.

The questions are grouped into six somewhat arbitrary categories (with some overlap among the categories and, to some extent, within individual categories):

    The decision-making process
    Expectations and perceptions
    Objectives
    Options for escalation and its control
    The framework of conflicts
    The initial limits of war.

This is a different and somewhat broader set of categories than the list of conceptual ingredients presented in the text (pp. 252-255). Those ingredients are distributed through these questions in various ways, however.

Key words are italicized where feasible. Page numbers in parentheses refer to locations in the text where discussions or examples of that issue appear.

The Decision-making Process

(a) In analyzing escalation situations, it is often useful not only to reason forward to future possibilities that may result from present events, but also to reason backward to the *preconditions* that perhaps are being established in the present, preconditions that might make certain events likely to occur (for instance: major esca-

305

lations or major opportunities to control escalation). Has such pre-conditional analysis been attempted? (264-267)

What present conditions or combinations of conditions—that might change in the future—are preventing one side from under-taking a particular escalation? (73, 124) What specific events, presently unexpected, could greatly increase the momentum of events, or raise new security concerns for nations presently in-volved or uninvolved, or activate latent objectives of any nation, or create a dangerously fluid situation, or otherwise raise the risk of uncontrolled escalation? (108-109)

(b) To what degree do *bureaucratic politics* and the normal oper-ating behavior of departments and agencies impede policies to con-trol escalation in the specific case at hand? How can significant in-formation relevent to questions like the ones posed here be tapped from working levels? Can military directives and operational in-structions for agencies, intended to control escalation, be followed up to ensure that their intent is not unwittingly dissipated at lower levels? (182-183)

(c) What *assumptions* about the situation, and about the wider framework of the conflict, may have been inadequately examined? What assumptions are being made which, if they turn out to be wrong, would be likely to mean unexpected escalation by the other side, or unexpected pressure on our side to escalate? What other assumptions are being made about the conflict that would be par-ticularly risky if they turn out to be wrong? (165-166, 188-189)

(d) There is a tendency for the *range of policies being pursued to narrow* over time for nonrational reasons. How aware have we been of this narrowing as time has passed? Have we tended to ex-plain it as the result of the other side's behavior when in fact it may be partly the result of psychological mechanisms operating on both sides? What can be done to compensate for this tendency? For in-stance, can an extra weight be assigned to the value of continuing seemingly unproductive negotiations? (293-295)

(e) Policy departures in one direction that are not *balanced* by policy departures in an opposing direction tend gradually to alter, in ways we may not mean them to, the way the opponent sees us.

They also tend to alter the way we ourselves interpret the meaning of the situation. How aware have we been of these changes over time? Have we tended to believe that our own changing interpretations have been entirely the result of the other side's behavior, when in fact there may be psychological mechanisms operating on both sides? Can efforts be made to better balance policy departures against one another? (290-293)

(*f*) To be most probably successful, policies aimed at controlling escalation need to be *integrated* into a coherent foreign policy. Only then are they not likely to be contradicted, and their effect lost, by other policies simultaneously pursued by other parts of the government. Has this integration been accomplished in the specific case at hand? Does an adequately coherent foreign policy exist, including a systematic and reasonably stable assessment of the risks facing, and opportunities open to, the state and the costs of meeting them? (98-99, 133)

(*g*) Has every effort been made to slow down the pace of events, so that adequate *time* will be available for assessment of the situation? Can our own policies be adjusted to help slow things down? Can efforts to slow the pace of events be a subject for informal discussion with the other side, even if negotiations have failed on the substantive issues? (41, 205)

(*h*) It often appears that the case in favor of an *escalation control* strategy seems more *tenuous and hypothetical* than the case in favor of an escalation or a continuation of the present level of violence. This is because the case for escalation control often depends upon estimates of abstract future possibilities. What can be done to compensate for this disadvantage by, at a minimum, making all the relevant decision-makers aware of it? (113)

(*i*) Are policy discussions and documents employing the verb *escalate* almost entirely in the transitive form? Or the intransitive form? (And hence are they biasing conclusions in favor of the actor image? Or the phenomenal image of escalation?) Are policy-makers implicitly presuming that one escalation will be followed at worst by one counterescalation (here called *reciprocal escalation*), when

307

in fact a series of steps back and forth could be triggered (here called *cyclical-sequence escalation*)? (21-23)

Expectations and Perceptions

(*a*) Decision-makers in all nations involved in a conflict act partially on the basis of a *subjective field* of expectations and images about the future course and likely outcome of the conflict. Since these expectations and images are sometimes held semi-consciously and even unconsciously as well as consciously, it is useful to examine our own expectations. What images and expectations about the future of the conflict and its likely outcome do we really hold? (270-272)

(*b*) Since the field of images and expectations is heavily sub-jective, it is difficult to discern fully the expectations of policy-makers in other nations. Coping with this question to the extent possible can be valuable, however, both for its own sake and as a way of shedding light on the more general assumptions, perspectives, and perceptions held by decision-makers abroad. What are the *expectations of the opponents* about the future course and likely outcome of the conflict? What are the expectations of deci-sion-makers among our allies and important neutrals? (276-277) May decision-makers of another nation be evaluating the signifi-cance of events that occur against a fundamentally different frame of reference—a fundamentally different set of assumptions, per-spectives, and perceptions—than we have tended to impute to them? (252-255) What can be learned of information from which some of their perceptions and expectations are derived? (169, 258) How may their universe of expectations and perceptions be tested, so that additional expectations are revealed? (175-176, 331)

(*c*) Policy-makers on the other side will counterescalate following an escalation our side undertakes, if they do, because *their* expecta-tions about the future course and final outcome of the war have been significantly altered. How may their *expectations be shifted* by our contemplated escalation? (280-281)

(*d*) What other diplomatic, political, or military actions, not directly part of this conflict, may we or our allies be taking that may alter others' expectations in ways important to their policies toward the conflict? (69-70)

(*e*) Expectations and perceptions narrow as the result of a sequence of escalations, for reasons involving psychological mechanisms as well as "rational" calculations. How may we try to cope with this process by, at a minimum, being particularly aware of the shifts that occur in our own expectations and perceptions? (293-295) Can a period of stability be created in the *initial limits* of a new conflict, which might tend to halt or forestall this narrowing and lead to expectations being generated among policy-makers in all the involved nations of possible lasting stability in the conflict? (295-297)

(*f*) Might major preparations for new military action in the future create expectations and a psychological atmosphere that would tend to stultify efforts toward controlling the conflict? Can this tendency be combated by a deliberate effort to pursue strategies for controlling escalations? (192, 227-228)

(*g*) Under certain circumstances policy-makers' perceptions of an escalation situation can be deliberately manipulated through the action—or calculated inaction—of another nation. Such action or inaction may, for example, work to hold open policy-makers' definitions of the meaning of the situation, and thereby hold open possibilities for escalation. It may also work to create perceptions that the initiative is in our hands, when it might not have to be. Are manipulations of perceptions of this sort occurring in the situation at hand? (171-172)

(*h*) Do different sides have different perceptions of the status quo, which could lead to each side's escalating in the belief that it is acting defensively? (208-210)

(*i*) Has critical information on which an escalation decision will be based been checked, to the extent feasible, through more than one communications channel? (96, 232)

(*j*) May policy suggestions or minor assistance to a proxy or weak ally involved in a low-level conflict create expectations among both donors and recipients of additional, perhaps more significant, assistance later? (171, 230)

(*k*) What important differences exist among policy-makers within another government in their perspectives, assumptions, or values in the conflict? (159, 234-235)

Objectives

(*a*) Policy-makers normally pursue a *range of objectives*, including small-scale objectives that are highly valued, far-reaching objectives that are rarely assessed as worth major risks, and a spectrum in between. What is the opponent's range of objectives in the present situation? Can escalation be controlled through postponement or avoidance of direct conflict over immediate objectives, even though longer-run objectives certainly clash? (66, 220)

May some escalation of ours suggest to the other side that we are going for maximum objectives, even though we actually are not (or not yet)? (161, 231) Does one side or more hold a strong negative objective—an objective that some event not occur—in addition to weaker positive objectives? (64)

If policy-makers in one nation do hold a negative objective, what is their perception of the status quo? What are their expectations about how closely the status quo is approaching, or in the future is likely to approach, a threatening of their objective? (212-215)

(*b*) What changes in the general foreign policy objectives of policy-makers of another nation might lead to an increase (or decrease) in their motivation to escalate? (136-137) What domestic political changes in that nation might have this effect? (139-140) What domestic political or economic interests might be energized, as the conflict develops, to try to shift that nation's policy? (58-59)

(*c*) What *latent objectives* of some nation might be activated as escalation proceeds, and lead perhaps to strong counterescalations? (245-248) Might an "axiomatic" objective, previously not relevant or even considered, be activated? (183-184) Might a generalized, diffuse objective crystallize into a very sharp and firm one as escalation proceeds? (213-215) May objectives of these kinds be kept from being activated through a credible initial communication of the limits of our own intentions? (158-159)

(*d*) What strategies may be available for *testing* the extent of the opponent's objectives? Can action be taken that has the effect of revealing objectives, without itself being perceived as an escalation of the conflict? Can a negotiating offer be made that holds out the promise of the opponent's achieving his absolute minimum objectives at far less cost than by pursuing or escalating the conflict (thus suggesting, if it is declined, that more than minimum objectives are being pursued)? (70, 221, 331, 335)

(*e*) What *other foreign policy interests* or objectives do we have, besides those that are directly part of the conflict, which may be competing with the objective of controlling escalation? What others may foreign nations have? (69-70) Do policy-makers here or abroad have objectives of their own, domestic or foreign, with prospects for eventual achievement which must be protected by pursuing and perhaps escalating the war? (139-141)

(*f*) Where we are involved in an alliance, may *alliance politics* and the objective of maintaining the alliance compete with the goal of controlling escalation? How may this competition be reduced or eliminated through a more careful definition of the purpose and goals of the alliance? Would a special communications channel among the allies, devoted to considerations of escalation control only, be a useful device? (177-178)

Options for Escalation and Its Control

(*a*) What changes in the pattern or process of the war might make feasible for another nation escalation options that so far have not been feasible? Can an analysis of the *preconditions* for specific escalation options help in being receptive to strategic warning that escalation is about to occur? (330-331)

(*b*) What escalation options of the opponent may be perceived as unusually legitimate or unusually illegitimate? What options may be unusually visible, perhaps even provocative, and what options comparatively invisible? Can the opponent carry out certain options in real secrecy, and if so is the secrecy likely to be temporary or lasting? May the opponent be tempted to escalate in the expectation, correct or incorrect, that the option carried out will prove unusually legitimate, invisible, or secret? (53, 77, 123)

(c) Is the opponent likely to take a *disproportionate* step? May we be considering a disproportionate step (or one that could be perceived as disproportionate) as a way of signaling motivation or commitment? In this case, may the action be misread as an indication, not of increased commitment, but that we have elevated our objective? Is this likely to call forth a major counterescalation by the other side? (227-228)

(d) Might the opponent rightly or wrongly perceive us as making ourselves temptingly *vulnerable* by some action? (182, 231)

(e) Ambiguity in public declarations and private communications to other nations about the circumstances under which we might escalate (response thresholds) could help deter escalation on their part because of uncertainty, or could invite a testing strategy of gradualist escalation, or some of both. Clarity about response thresholds, on the other hand, deters some escalations by the opponent while definitely inviting others. Is a mixed strategy feasible, which incorporates elements of both ambiguity and clarity? If the other side does begin a testing strategy, can escalation options of our own be found that will halt the opponent's progression without triggering a major counterescalation? (71-72)

(f) What options are available for *coupling* policies for controlling escalation to policies we may feel compelled to undertake for pursuing objectives by unilateral, military means? Can our unilateral, military options be adjusted to render these policies more easily coupled to escalation control policies? (179)

(g) What escalation options might we undertake, or the other side undertake, that could introduce *inflexibilities* into one or both sides' future range of options? (163, 170)

(h) If one or both sides are engaged in *gradualist* escalation, at what point is the progression likely to significantly change expectations on the other side about the future course and likely outcome of the conflict? (275-276)

The Framework of Conflicts

(*a*) *Bargaining strategies* are more useful under some circumstances than others. That is, it is not always useful to take steps as demonstrations of commitment or will, or to deliberately heighten the shared risk of a much bigger war. Do present circumstances favor this kind of strategy? (242-245) May the opponent be escalating as part of a bargaining strategy? If we escalate to demonstrate commitment or will, may the other side interpret this, rather, as an indication that we have elevated our objectives? (228)

(*b*) Sometimes in escalation, not only are previously known possibilities made real by someone's escalation, but the general character of the war may change in a way that widens the *scope of the possibilities* themselves. Might this occur here? (123-124)

(*c*) Might some escalation, or some elevation in objectives, lead to a *prolongation* of the conflict, which could provide additional opportunities for uncontrolled escalation? (142)

(*d*) May policy-makers abroad perceive us as more likely to gain by the passage of time than they are, and therefore be suspicious of anything we do that could be perceived as delaying events? (217-218)

(*e*) Might a nation threatening to involve itself in a conflict be distracted by our invoking some of its other foreign-policy interests? (144-145)

(*f*) What *chance events* could occur that would significantly change the framework of the conflict? (108, 116, 175)

(*g*) What *asymmetries* in capabilities exist among the different nations involved, which could provide motives to escalate to avoid a disadvantageous asymmetry at a particular level of violence? Might an asymmetry in capabilities become translated into a potentially dangerous asymmetry in perceptions about one another's objectives? (224-227) What asymmetries in motives or in-

313

terests, not easily changed in the short run, could lead to decisions to escalate? (249-250)

(*h*) What *latent conflicts* may be imbedded in the situation, which may be activated if escalation proceeds? (248)

(*i*) May some action that was successful in the past be likely to fail if repeated, because the *preconditions* for its success have changed? (164)

(*j*) Under what circumstances might the situation become highly *fluid*? (108)

(*k*) What wider changes in world politics may increase the motivation of one belligerent to escalate? (73)

(*l*) How may the arena of the war be sharply delimited? How may the geographic limits be reinforced? (179, 186) Between the arena and the major powers involved in the conflict, what lines of connection exist that may provide pathways for escalation? How may new firebreaks be created along these pathways, and existing firebreaks be reinforced? (73-76) May the war spread to nearby combustible material? What firebreaks exist and may be reinforced, or may be created, to prevent this? (251-252)

(*m*) Is there a significant gap between the ongoing level of violence, and the next higher level that is widely perceived as being likely to prove reasonably stable? Can this gap be exploited in controlling escalation, for example by reinforcing the perceptions of all parties that the gap is a sizable one? (134, 135-136)

The Initial Limits of War

(*a*) A period of initial stability in the limits of the conflict, after war has begun, seems necessary to establish expectations that the conflict may continue relatively stable and not escalate out of control. Can we be especially cautious in preserving the initial limits, and can we encourage others to be cautious also, during the *definitional phase* of a new conflict? (295-297)

(*b*) During the definitional phase of a new conflict, are policymakers in different nations making it publicly and privately clear to one another that they are centrally concerned with controlling escalation? What *highly visible policies* can we undertake to empha-size our concern? What provocative actions must be especially avoided? (70, 76-77, 228)

(*c*) Prior to the outbreak of a fresh conflict, policy-makers abroad may be trying to create an *initial war context* for a war they plan or expect. What indications may be available that an initial war con-text is in preparation? If there is a diplomatic crisis, do policy-makers in one nation appear to be trying to control the basic frame-work of the crisis? For instance, are they attempting to reinforce desired behavior by others, hedging carefully against certain un-desired developments, creating or exploiting misperceptions among others, or using special communications channels to influence be-havior? (86-92) Are circumstances developing where a crisis could be exploited, with little visible action, to define an initial war context? (124-128)

(*d*) May the process of defining the initial war context include an effort to *provoke* some party (ourselves?) into being the first ones to take offensive action? (142, 222)

(*e*) What foreign policy objectives of decision-makers in another nation might motivate an attempt to define an initial war context, only when certain preconditions were fulfilled? What might those preconditions be? (85-86, 125, 131)

(*f*) Since no initial war context can be expected to be perfectly escalation proof, or to last a long time, policy-makers may be ex-pecting to move the situation to an entirely new stage in a fairly short time. What might this new stage be, and how might the tran-sition occur? (135)

Appendix B

The Research Methodology:
Presuppositions and Rationale

In order that the discussion of escalation remain sharply focused, the research method of this study was mentioned only briefly in Chapter 3, and almost nothing was said about its wider intellectual premises. This appendix offers additional remarks on these subjects. Having discussed elsewhere and in some depth the most technical issues of methodology and theory involved,[1] I shall adopt a somewhat broader view here, intended to be useful not only to scholars but also to policy analysts and others.

Approaches to International Relations

If we set aside the personal stories contained in biographies and memoirs of government officials, we can identify three general approaches to the subject of relations among nations, including war. There is a detached, scientific approach, which attempts to create a body of knowledge and theory about the nature of international relations at all times and in all places—or at least, all times and places in the modern world. There is a moral approach, which attempts to show how international relations *ought* to proceed, how the world system should be changed, and perhaps how we should go about accomplishing these ends. And there is an operational approach, which attempts to find ways of helping officials make decisions that are truly consistent with their values and goals, and carry out policy that will have the results it is intended to have.

Hardly anyone is interested in only one of these approaches to the total exclusion of the other two. Nor, from the abstract point of view, can they be pursued in complete independence from one another. For instance, a convincing proposal for moral betterment of the system must draw heavily on an objective understanding of how the system works at the present time. Or again, operational

316

suggestions for the rationalization of policy-making must draw heavily on whatever systematic knowledge is available concerning the decision process, and what the actual consequences—indirect as well as direct—of a particular policy are likely to be.

Nevertheless, these three approaches are quite distinguishable, as Walter Lippmann, Stanley Hoffmann, and many others have pointed out.[2] Associated with each one there is, or could be, a body of theorization: a literature exploring abstract ideas relevant to the approach.

The body of theorization associated with the detached, scientific approach is relatively large. Academic specialists have not confined themselves to assembling histories, chronologies, and data banks that contain much of mankind's knowledge about present and past international affairs. They have also gone on, in the last two generations or so, to create an extensive body of theories and hypotheses about how the world system functions and how relations among nations proceed—and also about research techniques appropriate to the subject. It is probably fair to say that this work absorbs the bulk of the research time of most academicians specializing in international relations. *Empirical theory* is the name Stanley Hoffmann gives to this intellectual universe of hypotheses, theories, paradigms, research techniques, and so forth. (It could be called "scientific theory" except that this label might imply that the others are "unscientific." The primary motive for it, though, is definitely that of the scientist.)[3]

The body of theorization associated with the moral approach is astonishingly small. On the whole, individuals interested in international affairs have accepted their own values as a starting point for defining the policy objectives they would urge on decision-makers, without developing them to create, over time, a universe of ethical and political ideas that could give coherence to a systematic vision of world betterment. So totally is this universe lacking, in fact, that it is difficult for us to visualize what exactly it is that does not exist. Works such as Immanuel Kant's *Perpetual Peace* and, more recently, the Clark and Sohn volume on *World Peace Through World Law* are only a few candles set on a vast dark landscape. The idea of "peace," at least, is clearly a central element in any inspiring and reasonable vision of a superior world order, and it may be that some of the products of the so-called peace research movement represent a beginning in the direction of what

317

Hoffmann and others call *normative theory*. We may catch a glimpse of what could become another strand of normative theory in the international debate that is developing, as the 1970s proceed, on the future of the world economic order. For the rest, however, we lack even the beginnings of what could become an inspiring, yet reasonable, vision of the future of the world system.[4]

Except for a handful of specialized topic areas, the body of theorization associated with the operational approach is also fairly small; it is growing, however. Of course, some attention has always been paid to how the decision process should be managed and how policies should be constructed to have their intended effect. Much of this has traditionally been passed along from senior to junior officials, as the latter advance in experience and position. There has also been a small amount of literature of the "how to" variety, such as Harold Nicolson's classic work, *Diplomacy*. In addition, efforts have been made in recent decades, perhaps first in the United States and subsequently among its allies, to tap the developing field of management science to improve the organizational structure of governmental institutions and the procedures through which policy is made.

Theorization oriented systematically and specifically to improving the operation of foreign policy is relatively recent, however; the bulk of it has come in the last two decades. It appears to have its roots in two fields or areas of study. One is national security affairs, where specialists created a variety of operational theories for military policy during the Cold War and afterward. It became apparent during the 1950s that the unprecedented security problems created by a starkly bipolar political universe and rapidly advancing military technologies could not be adequately coped with by employing only traditional military experience and doctrine and simple modifications thereof. Analysts were called upon, therefore, to develop new ideas and theories on such topics as strategic deterrence, limited war, and arms control. Tested and refined by experience, these concepts have been incorporated into major portions of national security policy, perhaps particularly in the United States. In the same period, analysts have also attempted to extend this approach to wider aspects of foreign policy, by considering problems of deterrence more generally, as well as the coercive use of force and threats of force, and similar policy "instruments," as they might be called.

The other area fundamental to operational theorization is the study of foreign and military policy-making processes. Economists and operations researchers developed systems analysis and PPBS (Programming-Planning-Budgeting Systems) as contributions to solving the difficult challenge of managing an immense national security establishment. Political scientists and other social scientists, in exploring crisis management, have developed simulation and gaming techniques for assisting decision-makers to gather experience in dealing with crises. This group of researchers has also made suggestions and contributions toward improving additional aspects of the foreign and military policy-making process, as mentioned in Chapter 9.

A body of theorization has been developing, therefore, both about some foreign policy instruments and about ways officials can make effective decisions regarding the use of their instruments. These are two major components of what Stanley Hoffmann calls *policy theory*. (A third component, which has been less studied, concerns the images and models officials possess of the basic significance of events and of other states' basic goals.) Accenting different aspects of this sort of theory, others have referred to it as "design theory," the problem of "undertakings," "engineering analytical frameworks," "policy science," and other such terms.[5]

On Policy Relevance and Operational Applicability

There can be abstract *empirical theory* in international relations which has negligible operational significance, and which contains no normative elements beyond the values influencing (perhaps implicitly) the choice and definition of the subject matter and the principal variables. Such theory is motivated strictly by scientific concerns. With this partial exception, however, ideas and theories about international relations do not fall exclusively into any one of the three categories and are better visualized as located inside a triangle whose points represent the three "ideal types" of theorization.

For example, much of the literature relevant to operational aspects of foreign policy has been intended simultaneously as a contribution to empirical theory on the same subject. Since there is hardly any aspect of policy that cannot become a subtopic within empirical theory as well as an operational issue, writers having academic and scholarly interests (as most writers do) have usually addressed instruments and processes with a varying mixture of both points of view.

To take, for instance, the policy instrument probably most written about to date, the literature on deterrence has been motivated both by a desire to assist in the creation of strategy for use by Western decision-makers coping with communist military threats, and also by a desire to contribute to the abstract theory of deterrence—theory about the deterrent relationship between any two nations armed with nuclear weapons, and about deterrence in international relations in general. Something similar applies to policy-making. Most of the work done in this area has been intended, in varying proportions, both as research on the sources of foreign policy for its own sake as part of comprehensive scientific knowledge about all aspects of international relations, and also as a contribution toward making the policy-making process more effective, efficient, and "rational."

Partly because of this dual motivation of the majority of researchers, much of the theorization that takes some operational interest in foreign policy has proved to be not really applicable by government officials in their actual decision-making and policy choices. Indeed, some of it is not intended to be applicable. Though it may be "policy relevant," in today's jargon, most of this theorization is intended to some extent to meet *empirical* criteria of interest and admissibility which, depending upon their interpretation, often have the effect of reducing the operational applicability of results. In short, the policy relevance of theorization about foreign policy is a variable, not a quality that is either present or absent. In particular, some degree of policy relevance does not necessarily translate into the same degree of operational applicability. (The catch phrase, "policy relevance," can, in fact, mean a number of things.)[6]

However, theorization about foreign policy that is not itself directly applicable at the operational level may sometimes be suitable for adaptation to that level (or "implementation"). Here it is useful to distinguish sharply between theorization about the decision-making process and theorization about other aspects of foreign policy, for ideas about the process seem to be inherently more suitable for adaptation to operational application. (A reason for this will be suggested shortly.) Research on bureaucratic politics, for example, has generated not only an explanatory paradigm of interest mainly to analysts and scholars, but also a number of specific suggestions of ways decision-makers could improve their policy processes.[7] Even such a comparatively abstract treatment of the policy process as John Steinbruner's book, *The Cybernetic*

Theory of Decision, suggests implications that can be operationalized.[8] The continuum is evidently unbroken between theorization like this and, toward the opposite pole, works like Irving Janis' *Victims of Groupthink*, which are intended to be applicable by decision-makers directly. In the case of research on the policy process, then, there is an essentially continuous spectrum: theorization which itself may not be directly applicable in its original form can usually be "stepped down" through one or more stages of adaptation to have at least some potential applicability at the operational level.

Research on policy instruments and other aspects of foreign policy, however, is not always so adaptable to operational application. For instance, much of the literature on the deterrence of threats less than strategic war has taken a somewhat abstract and deductivistic approach to the problem. Though deterrence research has generally been intended to be policy relevant, the fruits of this approach have been only modestly applicable at best to decision-makers' actual planning of deterrent strategies. Thus the theorist attempting to design research on a foreign policy instrument must give some thought to what kinds of conclusions could actually prove applicable at the operational level (if that is his goal), or could prove suitable for subsequent adaptation to become applicable.[9]

Operational Applicability of Research on Policy Instruments

Consider two illustrative examples of research on policy instruments, one of which is considerably more applicable operationally than the other. Somewhat fortuitously, considering the dearth of studies on the subject, two examples are available that concern escalation and its control. First, the work whose operational applicability is low (but not zero).

Quincy Wright's study, "The Escalation of International Conflicts," is an analysis of estimated numerical data about forty-five conflicts that occurred between 1920 and 1965, of which nine did not result in war. The paper has several purposes, but a major one is to identify factors that promote escalation. Wright's conclusions about this (page 441) are as follows:

The study suggests that the factors promoting escalation in international conflicts are perceptions of vital national interests by both parties, relative equality of forces immediately

321

available, and belief by each party that superior forces will eventually be available to it from its own efforts or from allies, rendering its opponent more vulnerable to unacceptable losses and costs.[10]

The identification of these factors has some modest value from the operational viewpoint, apart from their empirical value (which will not be assessed here). Although each of the three factors is one that policy-makers or others might well anticipate, nonetheless there is a value in having each confirmed as present in most of the cases Wright scores as occasions of escalation.

The sharp limits on the operational applicability of these results are created mainly by the fact that Wright makes no effort to identify the *conditions* under which any factor was present, or influential. In some cases, escalation occurred where one or more of these factors was absent. In other cases, one or more of these factors was present and yet escalation did not occur. There is no analysis of the surrounding circumstances or conditions that account for these variations. Policy-makers would need such an analysis in order to be able to assess the relevance or importance of each of these factors in a particular problem.

Compare, now, Richard Barringer's study, *War: Patterns of Conflict.* This is an analysis of a more extensive set of data, both known and estimated, about eighteen conflicts that occurred between 1935 and 1968, of which all involved hostilities at least at a low level. The book has several purposes, but a major one is to identify situations in which escalation is likely to occur.

Barringer's conclusions are too extensive to be briefly repeated. He identifies four frequent patterns, or what he terms types, of escalation: escalation in a local war on the presumption of immunity from involvement by outside powers; escalation as a reaction to unacceptable losses; and two varieties of escalation when the war outcome is becoming clear—by the winning side to accelerate the emerging outcome, and by the losing side to try to forestall it.[11]

As before, the results taken by themselves have only modest value from an operational viewpoint, being patterns that policy-makers or others might well anticipate. Where this study differs from the previous one is in Barringer's identification of a variety of conditions that, he finds, usually accompany each pattern. With each of the four types of escalation he provides a listing of the circumstances in which the particular type is likely to occur. By doing so, he substantially raises the operational utility of his results because decision-makers and their staffs could, in principle, search for the presence or absence of these conditions in a given new problem. They would receive some guidance in estimating the hazard of escalation in the specific case at hand and, perhaps even more important, be assisted in identifying factors in the situation which, if changed, might reduce the hazard.

One reason I have employed these particular examples is to demonstrate that, contrary to what is sometimes suggested, the identification of conditions having operational significance is *not* necessarily part of the long-standing argument over "quantitative methods." Both the Wright and Barringer studies employ quantitative methods, yet the latter is much more interesting from the operational viewpoint than the former. The methods employed by Barringer are, in fact, quite elaborate and mathematically sophisticated. Probably most members of the policy-making community would not have the interest or time required to trace his derivation of all his conclusions. They would not have to, however, in order to appreciate the value of the conditions he identifies in each type of escalation situation, or to be able to apply this information if and when a similar situation arose.

(Incidentally, the debate that has raged in academic circles over the use of quantitative or qualitative methods is a debate that exists within, and applies mainly to, the universe of empirical theory. It arises far less in the universe of theory intended for policy application, in part because other tests of plausibility and usability are available there.[12])

Research about policy instruments like controlling escalation is apt to have greater prospects of operational applicability, then, if it aims—by whatever methods—for conclusions that specify the conditions likely to create, or lead to, or "activate" a particular development in which policy-makers are directly interested. Such an approach can duplicate, in a potentially more systematic fashion, a portion of the logic that policy-makers themselves, and governmental analysts and researchers, apply to many of their foreign policy problems.

Simplifying and idealizing their approach, policy-makers often proceed by trying to identify the plausible alternative paths along which the present situation might develop. They then try to identify the most important decision points, their own and their counterparts' abroad, that will principally determine which path the situation takes, and the conditions and circumstances that are likely to heavily influence those choices. From this an estimate of the most likely line of development may be attempted. Experienced decision-makers and analysts often go on to ask themselves what the effects would be of changes in the perceived circumstances: of present information proving inadequate, of a new and seemingly improbable condition arising, of one or more present conditions being removed, and so on. Might such changes lead the situation onto another path? If time and information permit, the conditions and circumstances that could lead to *those* changes occurring may then be explored, and so on, sometimes to several levels of contingency.

This approach cannot be duplicated in toto by the researcher interested in operationally usable ideas about, say, controlling escalation. With extremely few if any exceptions, theory cannot reliably predict the emergence of a new conflict situation nor the paths along which it might develop. What the researcher can do, however, is try to identify the crucial conditions which, in specified kinds of circumstances, could heavily influence the progression of, say, escalation. Policy-makers and government analysts faced with similar circumstances in a fresh problem, then, might be able to draw on that list of conditions (probably making some adaptations) to expand and refine their own analysis of what ultimately must be a unique situation.

It is characteristic of the way the study of international affairs has been dominated by the concerns and interests of *empirical* theorists that there is no quick and simple term for this way of going about a research task. It is not quite disaggregation, as statisticians use the term, because most analyses can potentially be disaggregated in a number of different ways. To reach toward operational applicability, a particular kind of disaggregation is needed: in one way or another the theorist must search out variables whose variation has, as it were, policy leverage. The variables must represent conditions—present, absent, or changing—that are readily identifiable by decision-makers and that, singly or in combination, can significantly shift decision-makers' calculations and policy.

In other words, some form of cause-and-effect linkage must be shown among the following: variance in conditions, decision-makers' calculations about the meaning of the situation, their calculations of their own strategy, and hence their actions. Merely showing a probability or frequency correlation (as, for instance, Quincy Wright does) between certain factors and a general outcome fashions a weak link, at best, to decision-makers' calculations and actions. For research results to have real operational applicability, policy-makers and their staffs must be able to see in them some causal relation between specified changes in the conditions and circumstances of the situation confronting them, and specified changes in what their own ultimate actions are or should be.[13] (Incidentally, this is one main reason why research on policy-making *processes* is more readily adaptable to operational application: the conclusions, being already about decision-makers' actions or behavior, are more readily linked to what their actions or behavior should be.)

On the Comparison of Case Studies

There are a number of techniques potentially usable in a search for results involving policy-leverage variables in this sense. The choice among them is guided by a number of considerations, including, for example, the present state of development of a given topic area, other goals for the same research, and the investigator's desire to approach the topic broadly or to concentrate on a particular aspect of it.

One technique that is particularly advantageous for exploratory research on an underdeveloped topic like escalation is the comparison of case studies. The case study technique permits the investigator to be flexible in his exploration of the factors that in each instance appear to have contributed to the success or failure of efforts to control escalation. Each analysis can generate a relatively large number of variables, and the case study method is a useful one for tracing chains of cause and effect.

A *series* of case studies can yield even more variables, of course, but the greater value lies in making comparisons among them. It is then possible to identify some of the possible consequences of variation in a variable from one case to another. Where surrounding circumstances are similar—or different in specifiable ways—a shift in any one variable may have traceable consequences in the differing development, from that point on, of the two or more cases being compared. A comparison of case studies, therefore, is a particularly useful method for identifying the variations that have policy leverage in the conditions of, say, escalation situations.

Where a large number of possible cases is available, furthermore, exploratory research is markedly aided by the potential for *selection* of some number of cases to be compared. Having a wide field and more than one selection to make, the analyst is in a position to be able to choose cases that appear particularly rich in the dimensions he wishes to explore. (Some preliminary investigation can indicate, with moderate confidence, which cases these are.) This is especially advantageous for a study emphasizing operational applicability in results, because it permits the selection of cases where the policies undertaken were particularly successful or particularly unsuccessful, and hence permits the identification of conditions that contributed to making them so.

The comparison of case studies has the significant disadvantage that, except in a few special cases not relevant to this study, it does not permit estimates of the frequency with which any particular combination of variables may appear. This disadvantage is of secondary interest, however, in any study emphasizing operational applicability. As long as a particular combination is not overwhelmingly probable or exceedingly improbable, policy-makers and their staffs are less interested in its frequency than in being able to identify the circumstances that generate it. They mainly want to know how to recognize it, not whether it comes up, on average, every five or every twenty years![14]

In recent years a number of scholars interested in operational applicability for their research and theorization have employed variations on the comparative case study method, for the reasons stated here, among others. These include: Lincoln P. Bloomfield and Amelia C. Leiss, *Controlling Small Wars;* Glenn Paige, "Comparative Case Analysis of Crisis Decisions: Korea and Cuba"; Ole R. Holsti, *Crisis Escalation War;* Alexander L. George, David K. Hall, and William E. Simons, *The Limits of Coercive Diplomacy;* and Alexander L. George and Richard Smoke, *Deterrence in American Foreign Policy: Theory and Practice.* Because the technique does not compare the cases in all respects, but focuses on a limited set of aspects or attributes common to each one, it is sometimes referred to as focused comparison.

Appendix C

The Italian Submarine Campaign
in the Spanish Civil War

In August of 1937 the Italians launched a campaign of torpedoing merchant ships all around the Mediterranean. The unacknowledged "pirate" submarines, which eventually also attacked the British destroyer *Havock*, purported to be Spanish Nationalist, but it was known everywhere that they were actually Italian—like the surface warships and aircraft that also made several attacks on Mediterranean merchant shipping. The campaign was so effective that a few weeks later when Mussolini was about to call it off, Franco begged him to keep it up because "just one more month" of the attacks would bring him complete victory in Spain.

Of the many escalations of the Spanish Civil War, this was the only one that transcended the territorial limits of the conflict. It engaged the vital interests of the great European nations as no purely Spanish event could have, and in retrospect it clearly is the most interesting escalation of the war. Table 7 summarizes the military events of the submarine campaign.[1]

The last time a naval power had attempted general submarine warfare, it had brought the United States in, to decide the outcome of World War I. Furthermore, the London Naval Treaty, which Italian representatives had helped to write only seven years earlier, specifically outlawed the sinking of merchantmen by submarines without their surfacing, giving warning, and attempting to rescue the crew. It was for these reasons, as well as the obvious riskiness from the escalation viewpoint, that policy-makers in Britain and France were surprised by the Italian step. They apparently had not thought much about having to deal with an escalation to general submarine warfare, even geographically confined to one sea. They might have, for there had been no fewer than three indications in

Table 7 Major events in the general submarine campaign of 1937.

ITALIAN ATTACKS, SUBMARINE AND OTHER

Date	Nationality of ship(s) attacked	General location	Mode of attack
6 August	Three ships: British, Italian, French	Near Algiers	Aircraft
7	Greek	Near Algiers	Aircraft
11	Spanish republic	Near Tunisia	Submarine
12	Danish	Off Barcelona	Aircraft
13	Spanish republic	Near Spain	Submarine
13	French	Near Tunisia	Submarine
14	British	Near Tunisia	Surface warship
14	Spanish republic	Dardanelles	Submarine
18	Spanish republic	Dardanelles	Submarine
23	British	Near Barcelona	Submarine
26	British	Near Barcelona	Aircraft
29	Spanish republic	Near Marseille	Submarine
29	French	Dardanelles	Submarine
30	USSR	Near Tunisia	Submarine
31	British (destroyer)	Near Spain	Submarine
1 September	USSR	Near Greek island of Skyros	Submarine
2	British	Near Spain	Submarine

RESPONSES

Date	Response
Mid-August	Britain sends a destroyer group to the Mediterranean; France provides air cover for French ships traveling between Marseille and French North Africa.
25 August	Britain and France begin mutual consultation on joint measures.
2 September	Britain dispatches a second destroyer group to the Mediterranean.
6	Invitations to the Nyon conference are sent out.
10-14	The Nyon conference is held.

the immediately preceding period of the possibility of this or some similar action—a *strategic warning* that had gone unappreciated.[2]

The least significant of the indications was the evident fact that the Italians for many months had carried on a sequence of unilateral escalations within Spain and its environs. As detailed in Table 1 in Chapter 4, nothing had been done to discourage this progression; indeed, if anything, British policy implicitly encouraged it. There was no reason to assume that Mussolini would halt the sequence by himself, unless and until his steps were effectively countered and/or his fear of uncontrolled escalation was activated more than it evidently was. Yet his expectations and future options seem not to have been assessed from this point of view.

That some of his major options lay at sea was suggested by the gradual augmentation over many months of the Spanish Nationalists' search and sometimes diversion of neutral ships on the high seas, and Nationalist and Italian air attacks on neutral shipping. This increasingly activist marine policy through the winter and spring drew protests and diplomatic activity, but no sanctions from either the USSR or the Western democratic sea powers—and, more important, no threat of any.

An indicator that should have warned the democracies of likely Italian naval escalation specifically, was the rapidly approaching fall to the Nationalists of the previously Loyalist Basque provinces. Beginning in the spring, Franco had concentrated his offensive there, and it was clear by about May that it was only a matter of time (and not much time) until they fell and he controlled the entire northern and northwestern coasts. (Santander, the last significant northern city, fell in late August. See map page 53.) With the northern coast in the army's hands, all the Spanish Nationalist and committed Italian naval forces could be concentrated along the east and southeast coasts of the remainder of republican Spain. In March the British had declared the Spanish Nationalist blockade to be "paper" because merchant vessels were getting through it unchallenged: the blockading naval units were stretched too thin. A true blockade of only about half as much coastline might have been much more feasible, and combined with greater Italian naval effort might have hoped to cut the flow of goods to the Loyalists almost entirely. (Besides her constant need for war materiel, the republic was far from self-sufficient in food and could be almost crippled by a near-stoppage of her external commerce.) The timing consideration suggested by the impending collapse of the Basque provinces, expectations of the Nationalists and Italians for the resulting situation, and their likely high motivation to exploit new opportunities, could have been readily grasped in London and Paris, and Italian naval escalation options accordingly scrutinized.

The third element of strategic warning was the most clear-cut of all. During June and July nine merchant ships flying the flag of the Spanish republic were attacked by submarines, and four of them sunk, all in the general vicinity of Spain. There had been a very few such events during the previous year of warfare, and submarine attacks at the rate of about one a week represented a sharp upsurge. It is difficult to escape the conclusion that this prelude to the general submarine campaign, besides being a significant escalation in its own right, was employed by the Italians as part of their *testing strategy*, to see what response the Western naval powers or others might make.[3] There was *no* response—in action or in declaratory policy. On the contrary, July witnessed a letter from Chamberlain to Mussolini that again expressed his hope for harmonious relations.

If we presume that the inference is correct and that the June-July submarine actions served, in effect, as a test, the failure of policymakers in London and Paris to appreciate their strategic warning is especially significant because it suggests that a modest deterrent effort might well have succeeded. This conclusion is reinforced by the prompt and meek Italian retreat later, when the Nyon policy began. Simple communications in July to Rome and to the Nationalists that Britain and France as great mercantile nations naturally would not tolerate any extension of the submarine attacks beyond the vicinity of Spain might plausibly have deterred the general Mediterranean campaign and would have been extremely "inexpensive," even in the context of Britain's policy of wooing Italy. (If the British felt too great a tension between this and their ongoing Italian policies, the message could have been delivered by the French alone and still have enjoyed a high probability of being effective.)

The caution with which the Italians initiated their Mediterranean campaign substantially reinforces these inferences. Gradualism and a testing approach were also employed deliberately as *tactics* in executing the escalatory step. Table 7, which presents information beginning August 6th, follows the historian's usual dates demarcating the opening and closing of the submarine campaign. But we notice that in fact the first four ships were attacked by aircraft, and that the first two ships attacked by submarines belonged to the Spanish republic. These actions only slightly extended activities already established: air attacks (usually nearer Spain, and gradually more frequent over the previous months) and regular torpedoing of the republic's ships (for the preceding two months, also nearer Spain). A sharp break in the previous limits of the war actually came only on the 13th, with the attack on the French merchantman. Then there was not another submarine attack on a non-Spanish ship for ten days—again, time to observe what reaction might be forthcoming. When there was no serious reaction to a single incident, another non-Spanish ship, this one British, was attacked. Then came another waiting period of three days. Only then did submarine attacks on non-Spanish ships become general. They halted again on September 2nd, after the British had increased the Royal Navy destroyer force in the Mediterranean for the second time, and it was clear that they and the French were consulting on a joint response. Attacks were not resumed before that response became known; then, since it was an effective one, they were not resumed at all.

The success of the Italian testing approach in the preliminary phase of the operation may have served as a precondition for the decision to begin more general maritime operations. In addition, the option of a (predominantly) submarine campaign had several advantages, enumerated below.

(a) Torpedoing by a submerged submarine was an anonymous attack, as no identification of the attacker was possible. The immediate and direct connection to the responsible nation in this sense was broken, and the probability of a response directly against Italy reduced.

(b) The submarine campaign would not encourage escalation by launching new battles. With the single exception of the attack on the British destroyer *Havock* (which may have been made in error), all the ships torpedoed were merchantmen, which could not defend themselves. Even in the event a nearby warship was called to the scene (or, as in the *Havock* case, a warship was attacked either deliberately or in error), the probable worst outcome would be destruction of the attacking submarine. Inasmuch as the submersible operated as a lone craft in the high seas, it did not carry the built-in connection to other military forces of many other escalatory options.

(c) Additional disconnection between the submarine campaign and Italy resulted from mounting the submarine attacks principally from the Italian naval base on the Spanish island of Majorca. Decision-makers in Rome could therefore hope that, should the Western naval powers decide upon military retaliation against the "source" of the submarines, they would strike Majorca and not any naval base within Italy proper. (Still, they made such a response somewhat more likely, for in the West too, people could calculate that an attack on Majorca would be relatively safe, whereas an attack on an Italian harbor would be a much graver step.)

(d) The submarine campaign could enjoy a high degree of connection to the Nationalist cause and to ongoing Nationalist activities. Franco was known to have three submarines in his service. The attacking Italian submarines carried Spanish flags and insignia, visible if they had to surface, and were painted to resemble the Spanish submarines. This, plus the heated denials of responsibility that emerged from Rome during August, made it at least possible that the attacks were being conducted by Nationalist forces.

In addition to these special attributes of a submarine campaign, there were several other preconditions, mutually interrelated, which it was necessary or at least desirable be met if *any* major naval escalation by Italy was not to pose serious risk of touching off a rapid escalation sequence.

(e) The French and British had a wide range of options for moderate response not necessarily military in nature. Many of these, if executed, would leave the Nationalist-Italian cause worse off than if no submarine campaign had been tried; but at the same time, this lengthy menu of moderate responses made it implausible that the Western powers would resort to any drastic counterescalation.

(f) This expectation of a controlled reaction was enhanced by the fact that the only two powers whose capabilities were such that they could make a really unacceptable response to the submarine campaign were nations already deeply committed to doctrines and policies that emphasized a minimum use of force. The USSR lacked effective military power deployable against Italy. Britain and France, as upholders of the Nonintervention Committee, the League of Nations, and international law generally, could be counted upon to find a legal or at least semilegal response. The expected probability of, say, a surprise attack by the Royal Navy upon the major naval bases in Italy could safely be taken as negligible. Of Western options involving little force, the most obvious retaliatory counterescalation would be for the French to reopen their Spanish frontier to Soviet Comintern and black-market arms traffic, and perhaps send the republic materiel of their own. The British, however, were likely to be as opposed to such action in August 1937 as they had been in August 1936, and the French were just as dependent on their British alliance. In Rome planners therefore could expect that either the democracies would wink at the submarine campaign, as so far they had winked at all the other fascist escalations (including previous attacks on merchant shipping nearer Spain); or else they would try to find ways of bringing pressure to bear on the submarine campaign directly, such as some kind of convoying or patrolling scheme, rather than counterescalating somewhere else in the Spanish theater. Other counterescalations would not help these mercantile nations with their shipping problem in the Mediterranean.

(g) It was still more plausible that the democracies would try to find means for dealing directly with the submarine threat because of Italy's relative naval *inferiority*. This imbalance could be turned to Rome's advantage. For it meant that the democracies would not have to make some particularly violent response to react at all in the Mediterranean. A lesser fleet might have had no choice but to execute reprisals against, say, Majorca, or even naval bases in Italy. British and French naval power was so ample that a milder and more defensive option—such as escorting convoys or instituting a patrol—was perfectly feasible.

(h) A patrol was an especially salient option, because it required only an extension of an already ongoing activity. Britain and France already had a naval patrol in place around Spain—the patrol of the coastline that was part of the Nonintervention Committee's control plan. An expansion to antisubmarine duty would be an obvious possibility.

In actuality, the Western naval powers did react to the submarine campaign, and very much along these lines. When their initial modest responses were not effective, they determined to call a conference at Nyon of all nations fronting on the Black Sea and the Mediterranean (including Italy), plus Germany, to determine collective sanctions against the "pirates." They declined to name the culprit on the grounds that nothing would be gained and a possible diplomatic opportunity lost; but the Spanish republic, backed by the USSR, officially accused Italy—whereupon Rome, followed by Berlin, declined the invitation. The Italian and German foreign ministries hoped that the conference would fail without their participation and proposed the submarine pirates as an appropriate topic for the Nonintervention Committee. But leaders of the Western maritime democracies were unwilling to subject their Mediterranean shipping to the deliberately desultory mechanics of the committee. The vital national interests of the British and French were now engaged, and they were motivated to cope with this escalation as they had not been with any previous one. They proceeded with the conference.

In four days the Nyon participants agreed on a collective policy. The Mediterranean was divided into patrol zones, the major portion going to Britain and France. Within their zones naval units of the patrol were to attack any submarine detected in the process of sinking a non-Spanish merchant vessel, or any in the vicinity of one that had been sunk. None of the signatory powers' submarines were themselves to sail the Mediterranean except as preannounced, and then on the surface and escorted by surface ships. Merchantmen sailing the Mediterranean were asked to keep within predesignated routes. The expectation at Nyon that these measures would provide an effective deterrent proved correct: the "pirate" attacks did not resume.

It is significant that the successful Nyon program was not itself a counterescalation to the submarine campaign. It was not an increase in any activity that would necessarily impose positive costs upon the opponent. The Nyon step was a negative one in the sense that if the "pirates" stopped their activity, nothing would happen. If no merchantmen were sunk, no submarines would be. The only cost to the Italians as a result of Nyon was the negative or opportunity cost of not being able to pursue a line of activity they wanted to pursue.

Nyon then was a highly successful exercise in a particular kind of denial. It controlled escalation not by threatening to match the escalator's activity or by actually doing so and thereby forcing both players to proceed at higher cost; nor by threatening some other kind of reprisal; nor by getting him explicitly to agree not to escalate as an arms-control or conflict-control bargain. It controlled escala-

335

tion by posing a threat that could only be activated by the escalator's action—coupled with a promise that if he did not take the action, nothing would happen and he would not suffer. It was an exercise in virtually pure deterrence. As such, it offered an enormous advantage: it was entirely nonprovocative.

In addition, the Nyon action had a number of other analytically important attributes. Some of these represented "requirements" for it to succeed; some were advantages that made its success more rapid and more certain.

(a) The threat had to be credible. The formal conference, the international backing and naval support, the French and British naval deployment in the Mediterranean, the moderation of the proposed action, and its limitation to the specific perpetrator of the crime all helped make it so.

(b) The threat had to be effective. The number of patrolling warships (sixty-three in the critical French and British zones), and the additional measure of herding merchantmen into designated route lines, raised to a substantial level the probability that an attacking submarine would still be in the vicinity of a sinking merchantman when a warship arrived, summoned by radio.

Nonetheless, the effectiveness of the Nyon policy depended not upon the *general* capabilities of Britain and France in the Mediterranean area, but upon the *specifics* of the capabilities they actually *committed*. This is indicated by the resumption of the Italian submarine campaign in January 1938 when the patrol was reduced—that is, when the probability that a submarine would be attacked fell below the Italians' "critical risk."

(c) The threat had to impose a marginal expected cost greater than the marginal expected value of continuing the proscribed activity. This requirement could be readily attained because the nation commanding and owning the submarines was not the same as the nation to whose principal advantage they were acting. Although the Nationalists valued tremendously the tightening of the blockade accomplished by the submarine campaign, the Italians counted the loss of even one submarine as worse than the destruction of many ships headed for the Spanish republic—especially as the submarines were only enhancing an already moderately effective blockade to hasten an already probable victory.

(d) There could not be an effective military response that might nullify the threat. A military reply by Italy to the Nyon action was simply not feasible. A submarine attack on a destroyer would be risky for the submarine; and any larger attack, as with air or surface units, would have amounted to a major naval engagement with the principal naval powers of the era.

(e) Though perhaps not essential, it was helpful that neither was there open to Italy an effective nonmilitary response to the Nyon deterrent action. The Nyon arrangement was based explicitly on the London Naval Treaty of 1930 and other international law, and clearly represented the enforcement of peaceable maritime commerce. The action was collective, enjoying the support of all the riparian states except Italy and her Albanian satellite. These features made it not merely a prudential act by the maritime democracies, but a visibly moral and generally sanctioned one. A nonmilitary reply—diplomatic, political, economic, or other—would therefore be potentially as unrewarding as a military one.

(f) It was helpful that the Nyon deterrent action presented the Italians with a carrot as well as a stick. The opportunity was carefully left open for them to join the Nyon agreement and patrol and thereby place themselves on the side of international law and against the "pirates." An additional carrot emerged later when Italy was allowed to join the patrol on the basis of parity with France in forces committed, a traditional Italian diplomatic objective in maritime affairs.

(g) The Nyon action had the additional advantage that, unlike many actions intended to compel the halting of an escalation and the restoration of the previous limits of a conflict, it did not require a physical withdrawal of forces. Ground forces that have crossed some saliency and taken possession of a new piece of territory, for instance, must, if the previous limits are to be restored, either be withdrawn by their government or else they must be physically compelled to retreat by counterattack (both nearly impossible to do without imposing some degree of humiliation). Either of these hypothetical actions poses greater difficulties for the states hoping to reestablish some previous set of limits than were actually faced by the Nyon policy. For Nyon required only that a particular *activity* by submarines be halted. Italian submarines could still cruise the Mediterranean submerged; they merely would no longer receive orders to attack merchantmen. The leaders and institutions of the Italian government did not have to pull back any of their forces or witness any of their forces thrown back. In theoretical terms the Nyon policy was not a compellent one.[5]

The Nyon action thus managed to perform the following re-

337

markable feat: it halted an ongoing activity and coerced the escalator to pull back his *level of escalation* one notch, restoring the previous set of limits to the conflict; yet it did so while remaining only a deterrent, *not a compellent*, action. This singular combination was only possible because of the special feature of naval, as distinct from ground, warfare—that it roams territory without possessing or holding it.[6]

(*h*) Finally, there was one more precondition or requirement, possibly essential, for this deterrent escalation-control measure to work. The threat was vastly improved by not originating from any of Italy's opponents in the Spanish conflict.

If the Spanish republic had announced a policy comparable to the Nyon policy in every respect, except that republican warships would carry it out, the situation would have been very different. And likewise if the USSR had done so. (Assume for a moment that these powers had the requisite naval capabilities, which as it happened they did not.) Much of the weight of international law and sanction would have been lost, even if, implausibly, the riparian nations had appointed the republic or the USSR their agents. More importantly, much of the deterrent effect would also have been lost, for two reasons. First, such a development would not clearly have included the implicit threat that two great powers, Britain and France, might enter the conflict against Italy. Second, the move would have been a military reply by one belligerent to an escalation by another belligerent. The Italians, faced with riposte by their opponents in war, would have had a much higher incentive to continue the submarine campaign and add republican and/or Soviet patrol ships to the target list. As a matter of "honor" (to which Mussolini, and others among the fascist leaders in Rome, were highly sensitive), it would have been harder to accept being stymied in the submarine campaign by the enemy than by neutrals. And the opponent's warships would have been an additional inviting target, another avenue along which to strike and weaken him. A running battle in the Mediterranean among warships, submarines, and merchantmen could then have been expected to become part of the Spanish Civil War.

This final requirement for the success of the Nyon patrol is neither academic nor trivial. Had the leaders of the republic and/or the Soviet Union happened to possess, separately or jointly, the requisite naval capabilities, it is by no means improbable that they would immediately have countered the submarine campaign this way themselves. Theirs were, after all, seven of the eleven merchantmen attacked by submarines. Such a naval "patrol" by a belligerent and its ally might have been difficult for neutral nations to join. From the standpoint of escalation control, therefore, it may have been fortunate that both the republic and the USSR lacked the necessary capabilities.

In sum, the Italian submarine campaign during the Spanish Civil War possessed a number of unusual features. The British and French overlooked three kinds of strategic warning and failed to try to deter the campaign, although a deterrence effort would have been easy and probably successful. Italy edged into the campaign with a testing approach and took advantage of several special aspects of submarine activity and of the overall naval context of the time, which served as preconditions for the campaign's being only moderately hazardous despite its drama. The collective response of the riparian powers at Nyon also had a number of special advantages, many of them not easy to reproduce in other contexts. Peculiarly, the response was a deterrent, not a compellent, action, although it coerced Italy to contract the scope of the war.

Notes and Bibliographies

Notes to Chapter 1 - Introduction

1. I have not been able to discover when the term was coined in its military sense, or where, or by whom. It was commonplace in the American literature on national security affairs by 1960, but does not appear in the literature through most of the latter part of the 1950s. The *Supplement to the Oxford English Dictionary* gives the first citations in the contemporary military sense in 1959. Since that time the Soviets have expropriated the term without compensation and contrived a Russian neologism, *eskalatsiya*.

Although this book confines itself for the most part to actual warfare, the concept of escalation is certainly relevant to other kinds of conflict also. It has long been employed in economic contexts as well, for instance "escalation clauses" in contracts.

2. For example, this was an issue in the debate within the U. S. government in 1964 and 1965 over escalation of air attacks in Indochina. The Joint Chiefs of Staff favored a "fast, full squeeze," while most civilian officials favored a "slow squeeze" of North Vietnam; the latter was subsequently performed. See *Pentagon Papers*, vol. 4, chap. 6, esp. pp. 312-314, 323-331, and 355.

3. Iklé, "When the Fighting Has to Stop," p. 692.

4. A partial exception to these generalizations are arguments that arise during wartime or crisis and advocate a particular escalation or de-escalation as policy. But these are not research.

5. Other instances of a hypothetical, modeling approach to escalation include Jones, "Framework for Exploring Escalation Control"; and Wharton School, *Escalation and De-escalation of Conflict*. Singer discusses some of the ingredients of a general systems model in "Escalation and Control in International Conflict"; his essay is pitched at a more general level, where escalation refers to any sort of intensification of international conflicts of all kinds. George's paper, "Some Thoughts on Graduated Escalation," raises a theoretical issue that will be discussed in Chapters 2 and 10 here.

6. Brown has written a useful essay on the construction of scenarios relevant to escalation and other policies: "Scenarios in Systems Analysis."

7. After publication in earlier forms (see bibliography), Ellsberg's analysis of escalation dynamics in Vietnam was substantially revised and incorporated into his book, *Papers on the War*. Fairbanks' article, "War Limiting," is an investigation of the factors that were at work to escalate, as well as to limit, the 1911-1912 war between Italy and Turkey.

Since the term *escalation* is so recent, the number of other articles that may be identified as assessing individual historical cases for their *escalation dynamics* depends on how broadly or narrowly one interprets the term. Under a moderate-to-broad interpretation, a great many case studies are relevant. Very few single out escalation dynamics for theoretical treatment, however. Two works that investigate the Korean War explicitly and fairly narrowly from this viewpoint are Halperin's *Limited War in the Nuclear Age* and Osgood's *Limited War*.

For more on the problem of cumulating theoretical results from case studies, see Rosenau's *In Search of Gobal Patterns*.

8. The Bloomfield-Leiss study, which yielded a number of results not discussed here, later evolved into the CASCON computerized information system, designed to alert policy-makers to similarities between a developing new crisis and one or more crises of the past. The Barringer study is a complicated one, both methodologically and substantively, and to summarize here his four types of escalation situations would not do justice to their meaning. A statistical approach to escalation has been taken by Wright in his paper, "Escalation of International Conflicts," discussed in Appendix B.

9. An exhaustive listing of this sizable literature is not feasible; a valuable annotated bibliography to that which appeared prior to 1963 is given in Halperin's *Limited War in the Nuclear Age*, itself an important contribution. Any listing of the most influential works (prior to the contributions of Thomas Schelling, which we will take up momentarily) would certainly include the following: Brodie, "Unlimited Weapons and Limited War," "More About Limited War," and *Strategy in the Missile Age*, chap. 9; Kaufmann, "Limited Warfare" and "Crisis in Military Affairs"; and Osgood, *Limited War*.

10. Osgood's "Reappraisal of Limited War" is an assessment of the strengths and weaknesses of contemporary understanding of this topic. Although his paper was published in 1969, the literature on limited war has developed so little since that time that it is almost equally relevant today.

11. The American viewpoint has been argued at the theoretical level in different variants by, for example, Kahn, Brodie, and Schelling. See respectively, *On Escalation*, *Strategy in the Missile Age*, and *Arms and Influence*. On the European side, the French general Gallois has made an articulate statement of an opposing theoretical position in "U. S. Strategy

and the Defense of Europe" and *Balance of Terror*. I am indebted to Uwe Nerlich for emphasizing to me the significance of the dominant European perspectives on this question.

On Russian strategy see, for instance, Wolfe, *Soviet Strategy*. In recent years Soviet and East European doctrine has shifted slightly. Its viewpoint now is that low-level clashes could be kept limited even in Europe, but major hostilities probably could not, particularly if they involved the use of nuclear weapons.

12. Massive Retaliation was announced on January 12, 1954, in a speech, "The Evolution of Foreign Policy," by Secretary of State John Foster Dulles. The so-called New Look in U. S. military force structure and planning had already been decided upon. History and analysis of these events from different points of view are provided by, for example, Huntington in *Common Defense*, Quester in *Nuclear Diplomacy*, and Kahan in *Strategic Arms Policy*.

13. Since Flexible Response is a collection of ideas and an approach as much or more than it is a specific doctrine, there is no completely authoritative theoretical statement of it. In style and tone as well as in substance, Brodie's *Strategy in the Missile Age* is probably as representative of Flexible Response as any single book. Kaufmann, who was one of the developers and advocates of Flexible Response, imputes it to Robert McNamara and describes it as part of the *McNamara Strategy*.

14. That both sides in World War I entered the conflict with quite modest goals, which expanded later as the costs soared, has long been the established opinion. Fischer, however, in *Germany's Aims in the First World War* (translated into English in 1967), argues that the kaiser's objectives were substantial from the first.

15. For more on the dynamic relationship of ends and means, see Kaufmann's "Crisis in Military Affairs." This review article of Kissinger's *Nuclear Weapons and Foreign Policy* was the first widely influential statement to point out that limited objectives need *not* correlate with limited means or scope in war. Kissinger's book, asserting that limited objectives were the basic means of restraining escalation, repeated in this respect the conventional wisdom of the period, to be found in many other treatments of limited war during the 1950s. Kissinger's 1960 sequel, *Necessity for Choice*, reflected development of the theory to include the recognition that this is not true.

16. Schelling, *Arms and Influence*, p. 137; *Strategy of Conflict*, p. 262. Max Singer has coined the phrase "an agreed battle" to describe limited warfare.

17. Schelling, *Strategy of Conflict*, p. 87; *Arms and Influence*, p. 137.

18. Schelling, *Arms and Influence*, p. 138. Note that Schelling's best-known "games" illustrating his views all concern this problem: the two commanders parachuted into territory roughly divided by a river, at-

tempting to avoid contact with each other; the two incommunicado players told that if they can independently name the same sum of money they can have it; and so forth. (See *Strategy of Conflict*, chap. 3.)

19. Schelling, *Strategy of Conflict*, p. 104. Something very similar to this was actually done by the United States in its air war against North Vietnam. Until May of 1967 no air strikes were made further north than the latitude of Hanoi, but then CINCPAC and the Navy and Air Force theater commanders were allowed to strike targets in the northern part of the country, up to but not over the Chinese border. To avoid any possibility that this line of demarcation might be violated even accidentally, a ten-mile strip of North Vietnamese territory just south of the border was held off limits.

20. Schelling, *Strategy of Conflict*, pp. 190-191, 193, and chap. 8; *Arms and Influence*, p. 166.

21. Schelling, *Strategy of Conflict*, p. 75.

Bibliography for Chapter 1 - Introduction

Barringer, Richard E. *War: Patterns of Conflict.* Cambridge, Mass.: MIT Press, 1972.

Bloomfield, Lincoln P., and Amelia C. Leiss. *Controlling Small Wars: A Strategy for the Seventies.* New York: Alfred A. Knopf, 1969.

Brodie, Bernard, "Unlimited Weapons and Limited War." *Reporter*, 18 November 1954, 16-21.

————— "More About Limited War." *World Politics* 10 (1957):112-122.

————— *Strategy in the Missile Age.* Princeton, N. J.: Princeton University Press, 1959.

————— *Escalation and the Nuclear Option.* Princeton, N. J.: Princeton University Press, 1966.

Brown, Seyom. "Scenarios in Systems Analysis." In E. S. Quade and W. I. Boucher, eds., *Systems Analysis and Policy Planning: Applications in Defense.* New York: American Elsevier Publishing Co., 1968.

Ellsberg, Daniel. "Escalating in a Quagmire." Paper presented at the 1970 convention of the American Political Science Association. Abridged version published as "The Quagmire Myth and the Stalemate Machine" in *Public Policy* 19 (1971):217-274.

————— *Papers on the War.* New York: Simon and Schuster, 1972.

Fairbanks, Charles. "War Limiting—A Historical Analysis." In Klaus Knorr, ed., *Historical Dimensions of National Security Problems.* Princeton, N. J.: Princeton University Press, 1976.

Fischer, Fritz. *Germany's Aims in the First World War.* New York: W. W. Norton & Co., 1967.

Gallois, Pierre M. *The Balance of Terror: Strategy for the Nuclear Age.* Boston: Houghton Mifflin Co., 1961.

———— "U. S. Strategy and the Defense of Europe." *Orbis* 7 (1963):226-249.

George, Alexander L. "Some Thoughts on Graduated Escalation." RAND P-3169. Santa Monica, Calif.: RAND Corp., May 1965.

Halperin, Morton H. *Limited War in the Nuclear Age.* New York: John Wiley & Sons, 1963.

Holsti, Ole R. *Crisis Escalation War.* Montreal: McGill-Queens University Press, 1972.

Huntington, Samuel P. *The Common Defense.* New York: Columbia University Press, 1961.

Iklé, Fred C. "When the Fighting Has to Stop: The Arguments about Escalation." *World Politics* 19 (1967):692-707.

Jones, W. M. "A Framework for Exploring Escalation Control." RAND R-1536-RC. Santa Monica, Calif.: RAND Corp., June 1974.

Kahan, Jerome. *Strategic Arms Policy.* Washington, D. C.: Brookings Institution, 1975.

Kahn, Herman. *On Escalation: Metaphors and Scenarios.* Rev. ed. Baltimore, Md.: Penguin Books, 1968.

Kaufmann, William W. "Limited Warfare." In William W. Kaufmann, ed., *Military Policy and National Security.* Princeton, N. J.: Princeton University Press, 1956.

———— "The Crisis in Military Affairs." *World Politics* 10 (1958):579-603.

———— *The McNamara Strategy.* New York: Harper & Row, 1964.

Kissinger, Henry A. *Nuclear Weapons and Foreign Policy.* New York: Harper and Bros., 1957.

———— *The Necessity for Choice.* New York: Harper and Bros., 1960.

Osgood, Robert E. *Limited War.* Chicago: University of Chicago Press, 1957.

———— "The Reappraisal of Limited War." In *Problems of Modern Strategy,* pt. 1. Adelphi Paper No. 54, pp. 41-54. London: International Institute of Strategic Studies, 1969.

The Pentagon Papers. Senator Gravel ed. Boston: Beacon Press, n.d.

Quester, George. *Deterrence Before Hiroshima.* New York: John Wiley & Sons, 1966.

———— *Nuclear Diplomacy: The First Twenty-five Years.* Rev. ed. New York: Dunnellen Publishing Co., 1973.

Rosenau, James N. *In Search of Global Patterns.* New York: Free Press, 1977.

Sallagar, Frederick M. *The Road to Total War.* New York: Van Nostrand Reinhold, 1975. First published as *The Road to Total War: Escalation in World War II.* RAND R-465-PR. Santa Monica, Calif.: RAND Corp., 1969.

Schelling, Thomas C. *The Strategy of Conflict.* Cambridge, Mass.: Harvard University Press, 1960.

——— *Arms and Influence.* New Haven, Conn.: Yale University Press, 1966.

Singer, J. David. "Escalation and Control in International Conflict: A Simple Feedback Model." *General Systems Yearbook* 15 (1970):163-173.

Wharton School of Business, University of Pennsylvania. *The Escalation and De-escalation of Conflict.* Report prepared for the U. S. Arms Control and Disarmament Agency (ACDA-ST-149). Philadelphia: University of Pennsylvania, 1969.

Wolfe, Thomas W. *Soviet Strategy at the Crossroads.* Cambridge, Mass.: Harvard University Press, 1964.

Wright, Quincy. "The Escalation of International Conflicts." *Journal of Conflict Resolution* 9 (1965):434-439.

Notes to Chapter 2 - The Many Meanings of Escalation

1. Both *expand* and *spiral* seem to imply homogeneous, quantitative growth rather than discrete steps. The spiralling image has also been associated with a particular group of theorists who have emphasized the danger of processes "going out of control"—not only escalation in warfare, but also deterrence policies in peacetime, arms races, and so forth. Jervis discusses this school at some length in *Perception and Misperception,* chap. 4. Representative works of the "spiral theorists" include Boulding, "Toward a Pure Theory of Threat Systems"; Etzioni, *Hard Way to Peace;* Milburn, "Concept of Deterrence"; Osgood, *Alternative to War or Surrender;* Rapoport, *Strategy and Conscience;* and Singer, "Threat Perception," and *Deterrence, Arms Control, and Disarmament.*

2. Formally, the criteria for selection among alternative images are as follows. An image must be (*a*) at least as plausible as any of its competitors, (*b*) mutually consistent with other images selected, and (*c*) apparently of greater significance than any of its competitors for the problem of controlling escalation.

Each of the selected images will be, in effect, a hypothesis that we shall adopt with respect to some substantive issue. At the end of the process of reviewing images and selecting among them, a consistent set of hypotheses about escalation will emerge. These will be combined into a single working definition of escalation, which may be regarded as "the hypothesis" of this study.

Although (*a*) and (*b*) are not entirely objective criteria and cannot be fully operationalized, I believe that for the particular images to be assessed in this chapter, the two criteria will not prove problematical. Much of what is meant by "significance for controlling escalation" is intrinsic to our discussion in this chapter and will become clear as we proceed.

There is only one major alternative to this approach: to test all the important alternative images explicitly and formally against some body of empirical data for their significance vis-à-vis escalation control. I have rejected this approach for a number of reasons. First, since the total number of images is rather large, as a practical matter one would have to winnow down the list, employing the same sort of partially subjective and a priori judgments used in this chapter. Second, the omnipresence of escalation phenomena in war would make it difficult to obtain a representative sample for one's data base. Third, it would be extremely difficult to generate objective and operationalizable criteria by which to measure any particular image against the data base—precisely because of the lack of even preliminary or heuristic escalation control theory. Finally and pragmatically, such an approach would absorb the full scope and resources of this study to derive a usable working definition of escalation.

3. On the distinction between continuous and discontinuous models, see Siegler and Osmond, *Models of Madness, Models of Medicine.*

4. A fairly extreme example is Ferguson's "Tactics in a Local Crisis," which implicitly adopts an almost pure actor model. Kahn's *On Escalation* also tends strongly toward the actor model. However, Kahn makes reference to the possibility of escalation going out of control, and mentions upward pressures at various points in the book.

There is a tendency for the two images of escalation to develop in opposition to each other, and typically for each to impute to the other an extreme version. The extreme version of automaticity, for example, is opposed by someone's arguing that a particular escalatory step need not lead to an infinite spiral—but the tendency is to say "will not" rather than "need not." The other side then argues that it "could"—but tends to use the word "will." Because the images are likely to be developed and used in policy argument, in the process of advocacy and opposition, there is a tendency for the polarized views to be the ones articulated. (I am indebted to Thomas Schelling for these observations, in a private communication.)

5. A reasonably consistent use of escalation in, say, the transitive verb form will tend to lead the writer or speaker toward substantive conclusions consistent with the actor model. Or, to put it the other way, it is enormously easier and more persuasive to see escalation as potentially going out of control if one is accustomed to using *escalate* as an intransitive, rather than a transitive, verb.

It is interesting to observe the behavior of the competitors of *escalation* in this respect. *Expansion* is an even looser term and likewise possesses both verb forms. It is possible, but rare, to use *intensification* transitively: normally it is the conflict, not the decision-maker, that intensifies. It is possible, but rare, to use *elevation* intransitively: normally it is the decision-maker who elevates the level of the conflict.

Eruption and *spiralling* may be the most interesting cases. They are intransitive terms only. The conflict spirals upward or erupts, but policy-makers do not spiral up or erupt the conflict. I argue that it would be necessary to observe nothing more than this to guess, with fair confidence, the substantive positions that spiral theorists (see note 1) or writers stressing the possibility of eruption, would come to.

6. From an abstract viewpoint there is nothing odd about both these aspects being true at the same time. The social sciences (and also biology and ecology) are full of phenomena that in one sense are traceable entirely to specific decisions by specific individuals or groups, yet in another sense, because of interactive effects, are much more than the sum of these parts. It may be somewhat harder than usual to keep both sides in mind in the case of escalation because the interactive effects can be so rapid and so extreme.

7. For example, consult Jones, "Framework for Exploring Escalation Control"; Ferguson, "Tactics in a Local Crisis"; and, to a substantial degree, Wharton School, *Escalation and De-escalation of Conflict.*

8. "Limited Warfare," p. 112. I am indebted to Kaufmann for personal communications that have suggested many of the points in this section of the chapter.

9. Sallagar, *Road to Total War,* especially chaps. 5 and 7; and Quester, *Deterrence Before Hiroshima,* pp. 142-145. As noted earlier, some historians argue that the Central Powers' initial objectives in World War I were not modest.

10. "Crisis in Military Affairs," p. 595. World War I is the classic instance.

Purer than poker as an analogy for escalation is a heuristic device called the dollar game. A single one-dollar bill is to be auctioned off: two players bid for it in turn; bids must be raised by at least ten cents over any preceding bid; highest bid takes the dollar bill, but *both* players must pay their highest offer at the termination of the betting. A few trials will convince the reader that there is no reason for the game to stop at $.90, $1.00, $1.90, $2.00, or in fact at any particular point. One vital difference between this game and escalation is that in the game there is no penalty for refusing to play.

11. These illustrations derive respectively from the U. S. conflict in Vietnam, the Korean War, a German decision in World War I, and an American problem in the Pacific theater in World War II. The first and third were escalation options accepted; the second and fourth, denied. The fourth is an interesting instance of refusing the escalation option. Local U. S. commanders during the latter stages of the war several times relayed up the chain of command a request to use gas against Japanese troops dug deeply into the caves of Okinawa and other islands. Going in after them resulted in many casualties, but the decision was always to forgo gas for fear it would trigger general use of it by both sides.

12. A more recent example is U. S. policy in Southeast Asia in 1970 and early 1971. In the Cambodian and Laotian campaigns certainly, and debatably elsewhere as well, the United States performed a series of escalations

without a clear escalatory reply coming from Hanoi, at least in the short run. This type of escalation situation is one that Barringer has identified (*War*, pp. 116-118).

In general, a series of escalations that passes unanswered by the opponent is feasible only when the opponent either (*a*) lacks the capability to respond, or (*b*) is far less motivated than the escalating nation. Some of the early escalations by the Viet Cong, in the late fifties and early sixties, against a lethargic Saigon regime may be a partial example, at least, of the latter. If one extends the discussion to crisis diplomacy, then another example may be the U. S. escalations during the Cuban missile crisis.

13. Like all the images of escalation in this chapter, this one may be used or assumed without the implications or the alternatives being spelled out. Here, for instance, is an excerpt from a discussion of escalation by Halperin:

> In considering the possible improvement of the tactical military situation by the expansion of a local war, the possibility of *an* enemy response needs to be taken into consideration. There is no reason to assume that every expansion of a local war will lead to *a* counterexpansion. However . . . each side must at least consider the possibility of *an* enemy response. The enemy's reaction to a particular expansion may be to take the same action; however, if this option is not available, the opponent might expand the war in *a* different way . . . Since counterexpansion is possible and in some situations perhaps likely, the decision-maker must analyze the situation with *two* changes, that is, the initial expansion by one side and *the reaction* by the other.

(*Limited War in the Nuclear Age*, p. 29; emphasis supplied.) I do not mean to imply that Halperin, even at the time he wrote this in the early 1960s, was limiting himself to the reciprocal image of escalation; indeed, in a following passage he makes it clear that he is not. I do mean to say that it is neccessary for analysts and for those occupied with making policy to be explicitly aware of the number of different images of escalation available, and the fact that choice of one's image will strongly influence (even govern, when employed consistently) the kind of conclusions—policy conclusions as well as theoretical conclusions—one will come to.

14. The reciprocal-escalation image contains a notion of symmetry. The symmetry may be of several kinds, however. It may be symbolic. Some move, which either cannot or need not be countered on narrow military grounds, may nevertheless receive some kind of militarily unimportant reply, to demonstrate seriousness of intent, motivation, or a spirit of "not letting the other fellow get away with something."

Another and more general version of symmetry is "response in kind." Schelling has discussed this possibility in *Arms and Influence* (p. 155): "In a war in which both the United States and the Soviet Union participated, the introduction, say, of nuclear weapons by one could be 'matched' by their use on the other side. ('Matching' would not mean that the equivalent nuclear firepower is introduced or that consequences cancel out, only that there is a response in the same currency.)" It seems likely, though, that further escalations would follow if the consequences did not roughly cancel out, and perhaps even if they did.

There is a third version of reciprocal escalation where it is assumed that the consequences do cancel out and the escalation process halts. If both players have strong incentives to avoid launching a perhaps indefinitely long chain reaction, the responder may tailor his reply to rebalance the situation, and the originally escalating player may expect that this response (if any) is the likely one. It is not necessarily the case that in this situation the original player would have no reason to escalate in the first place. He may believe that his relative position will be marginally improved after the reciprocation, or that the new situation will be more stable than the previous one. Or he may believe that he can sustain the higher costs implicit in a higher level of operations better than the opponent can. Or he may want to demonstrate resolution, motivation, or spirit to his home populace, his allies, his opponents, or his own troops and officers in the field.

A somewhat related notion of symmetry in limited war has been explored briefly by Nitze in "Symmetry and Intensity of Great Power Involvement."

15. Schelling, *Strategy of Conflict*, p. 194. A more extreme version of this same image, often encountered in hypothetical discussions of nuclear warfare, suggests that as the situation becomes less and less stable, a chain reaction sets in, and escalation erupts or explodes. This is a purer version of the phenomenal model of escalation. One might contrast this divergent form of cyclical-sequence escalation with a convergent form, wherein the repeated escalations gradually clamp down and the steps become smaller and less consequential. The process tapers off as the escalations converge on some firebreak, as may or may not have been anticipated by the belligerents.

16. It would be erroneous to conclude that such cases are analytically uninteresting because the weaker power cannot react at all to the increased great-power commitment, hence no action-reaction phenomenon is possible. Such may not be the case. There may be a highly predictable reaction consistent with a closed-ended projection. The weaker power may be able to call up its last reserves or take other extreme measures to meet the greater power's escalation for a while. This can even proceed in several steps, as repeated great-power escalations are met (very temporarily) by increasingly desperate measures on the part of the small power. The important point is that the greater power *knows* what remaining steps are available to its opponent and includes them in its calculations. Even though a simple case

of action and reaction may exist, the great power can see down the action-reaction chain to its end. In this hypothetical and extremely rare case, uncertainty and risk are at a minimum.

17. This is not the same as embracing the phenomenal aspect of escalation to the exclusion of the actor aspect. As the case histories that make up the bulk of this book will try to demonstrate, someone taking a rigorous approach will not discover any reason to treat escalation as a phenomenon that gets going on its own, or to use the intransitive verb *escalate* to the relative exclusion of the transitive one.

18. Kahn, *On Escalation*, p. 3.

19. *Gradualist* is the term Sallagar uses at times in *Road to Total War*. For a reference to this kind of escalation, see for instance p. 156. *Graduated* is Alexander George's term. However, in "Some Thoughts on Graduated Escalation" and elsewhere, George seems to lean to a stepped view similar to what will be proposed here.

20. Here is a list of events in the U. S. air war against North Vietnam in 1965:

7 February   First air strike against North Vietnam (except for the one-shot Gulf of Tonkin raids), with U. S. Air Force (USAF) and Republic of Vietnam Air Force (RVNAF) planes attacking North Vietnamese targets "in reprisal" (it is declared) for a Viet Cong attack on a major U. S. Army base at Pleiku the previous day. Principal, and northernmost, target is Dong Hoi, about 50 miles north of the demilitarized zone (DMZ), and a major Viet Cong (VC) staging area for infiltration. Forty-nine planes take part.

8 February   Twenty-four RVNAF bombers, with USAF fighter escort, bomb the Vinh Linh area, near the DMZ.

11 February   Another major reprisal raid, following a VC attack on an important U. S. Army billet. More than a hundred USAF planes strike again near Dong Hoi. Fifty-six USAF and RVNAF planes strike Chop Le, near the DMZ in the North Vietnam.

Raids on North Vietnam are suspended during the latter half of February because of the 19 February coup in Saigon. Marshall Ky later says that a major joint strike had been planned for the 19th, which would not have been called a reprisal strike.

2 March   More than 160 U. S. and South Vietnamese planes strike Quang Khe naval base, 65 miles north of the DMZ. The declaration connected with this strike does not assert that it is in reprisal for a specific VC action but rather "to make clear to Hanoi that North Vietnam will be held fully accountable for continuing aggression against South Vietnam."

15 March   Over a hundred U. S. planes strike Phu Qui, 180 miles north of the DMZ and 100 miles south of Hanoi.

19 March   More than 120 U. S. planes raid North Vietnamese targets in the area of Phu Van, 160 miles north of the DMZ.

22 March   First armed reconnaissance strikes by U. S. aircraft.

26 March   Forty U.S. aircraft, not including fighter escort, strike targets approximately 50 miles south of Hanoi.

29 March   Forty-two U. S. aircraft again strike the same targets.

3 April   Bridges and roads, the first targets not obviously military, are struck. One bridge is 65 miles south of Hanoi.

4 April   The same targets are struck again, plus a power station about 65 miles south of Hanoi. After 4 April, air strikes on North Vietnam are stepped up in frequency to almost daily. (From here on, this summary will mention only strikes thrusting further north or adding new targets.)

14 April   Large numbers of propaganda leaflets are dropped over North Vietnam for the first time.

23 April   Over 200 U. S. and RVNAF aircraft strike numerous targets in North Vietnam, up to about 60 miles south of Hanoi.

22 May   A North Vietnamese Army barracks 55 miles south of Hanoi is struck.

18 June   First raid north of Hanoi. An army barracks at Son La is struck—110 miles northwest of Hanoi and 80 miles from the Chinese border.

2 July   An oil-storage depot 40 miles from Hanoi is struck.

21-23 August   Five raids are made over a period of two days on the Ban Thach dam and hydroelectric station, about 80 miles from Hanoi—the first strike on this kind of target.

15-20 December   U. S. aircraft strike the Uong Bi thermal power station, 14 miles from Haiphong. This station produces 15 percent of North Vietnam's electric power, including most power for the Hanoi-Haiphong area. U. S. spokesmen declare that this, the first raid on a target of major industrial importance, is in reprisal for a Viet Cong attack on a U. S. billet in Saigon in early December.

(Source: *Keesing's Contemporary Archives* for the period covered.)

This chronology raises a number of interesting issues. A principal one, and a controversial one at the time, concerns the steady progression of events. In all significant aspects, the principle of gradualism holds: in the number of planes taking part in raids, in the frequency of raids, in the geographic portion of North Vietnam coming under attack, in the categories of targets struck, and even in whether the raid was declaratively linked as a reprisal to a specific action of the Viet Cong. This pattern of gradualism continued to hold long after it was clear that air raids over the North were to be general policy and were not specific reprisals.

21. In terms of classical (Aristotelian) epistemology, what we have done is this: we have rejected both "escalation as a very small number of large steps" and "escalation as a continuous process," because in both cases the "genus" is too narrow; hence the concept must be incomplete. We have rejected "escalation as both or either" because, while the genus is wide enough, there is no "differentia"; hence, there is no way of distinguishing

escalation from any other kind of increase. The criterion of "a step crossing a saliency" provides the needed differentia.

Clearly for some special applications, definition by the criteria of absolute size or kind could be appropriate. An investigation of the consequences of an escalation to the use of nuclear weapons obviously defines this escalation in terms of a size or kind of step. Even here, though, a consideration of the consequences in terms of additional escalation steps probable or possible will want to revert to general, contextual criteria.

22. Kahn, p. 214; and p. vi of the preface to the original RAND version of Sallagar's *Road to Total War*. Similar thoughts, but not I believe just this phrase, appear in the later book version.

23. A few formalities: I have stated earlier that this study restricts itself to actual warfare between nation-states and to escalation in the sense of means or activities. When escalation in a diplomatic crisis or escalation in the sense of ends or objectives is meant, this will be explicitly indicated. The major variables in the formal definition have constituted the subject matter of this chapter and the previous one: saliencies, their definition of the limits of war, and action-reaction and the interaction of succeeding steps. The actor, depending on context and immediate purpose, may be taken to be the nation-state, an institution thereof, or an individual or group of individuals. The opponent is to be taken in the same senses. These definitions may be employed at any level of analysis.

Bibliography for Chapter 2 - The Many Meanings of Escalation

Aron, Raymond. "The Evolution of Modern Strategic Thought." In *Problems of Modern Strategy*, pt. 1. Adelphi Paper No. 54, pp. 1-17. London: International Institute of Strategic Studies, 1969.

Barringer, Richard E. *War: Patterns of Conflict.* Cambridge, Mass.: MIT Press, 1972.

Boulding, Kenneth E. "Toward a Pure Theory of Threat Systems." *American Economic Review, Papers and Proceedings* 53 (1963):424-434.

Deutsch, Karl W. *The Analysis of International Relations.* Englewood Cliffs, N.J.: Prentice-Hall, 1968.

Etzioni, Amitai. *The Hard Way to Peace.* New York: Collier Books, 1962.

Ferguson, Allen R. "Tactics in a Local Crisis." RAND RM-3034-ISA. Santa Monica, Calif.: RAND Corp., September 1962.

George, Alexander L. "Some Thoughts on Graduated Escalation." RAND P-3169. Santa Monica, Calif.: RAND Corp., May 1965.

Halperin, Morton H. *Limited War in the Nuclear Age.* New York: John Wiley & Sons, 1963.

Jervis, Robert. *Perception and Misperception in International Politics.* Princeton, N. J.: Princeton University Press, 1976.

Jones, W. M. "A Framework for Exploring Escalation Control." RAND

R-1536-RC. Santa Monica, Calif.: RAND Corp., June 1974.

Kahn, Herman. *On Escalation: Metaphors and Scenarios.* Rev. ed. Baltimore, Md.: Penguin Books, 1968.

Kaufmann, William W. "Limited Warfare." In William W. Kaufmann, ed., *Military Policy and National Security.* Princeton, N. J.: Princeton University Press, 1956.

——— "The Crisis in Military Affairs." *World Politics* 10 (1958):579-603.

Milburn, Thomas. "The Concept of Deterrence: Some Logical and Psychological Considerations." *Journal of Social Issues* 17 (1961):3-11.

Nitze, Paul. "Symmetry and Intensity of Great Power Involvement in Limited Wars." In Washington Center of Foreign Policy Research, *Military Policy Papers,* December 1958, 52-62.

Osgood, Charles. *An Alternative to War or Surrender.* Urbana, Ill.: University of Illinois Press, 1962.

Quester, George. *Deterrence Before Hiroshima.* New York: John Wiley & Sons, 1966.

Rapoport, Anatol. *Strategy and Conscience.* New York: Harper & Row, 1964.

Sallagar, Frederick M. *The Road to Total War.* New York: Van Nostrand Reinhold, 1976. First published as *The Road to Total War: Escalation in World War II.* RAND R-465-PR. Santa Monica, Calif.: RAND Corp., 1969.

Schelling, Thomas C. *The Strategy of Conflict.* Cambridge, Mass.: Harvard University Press, 1960.

——— *Arms and Influence.* New Haven, Conn.: Yale University Press, 1966.

Siegler, Miriam, and Humphry Osmond. *Models of Madness, Models of Medicine.* New York: Macmillian Co., 1974.

Singer, J. David. "Threat Perception and the Armament-Tension Dilemma." *Journal of Conflict Resolution* 2 (1959):90-105.

——— *Deterrence, Arms Control, and Disarmament.* Columbus, Ohio: Ohio State University Press, 1962.

Wharton School of Business, University of Pennsylvania. *The Escalation and De-escalation of Conflict.* Report prepared for the U. S. Arms Control and Disarmament Agency (ACDA-ST-149). Philadelphia: University of Pennsylvania, 1969.

Notes to Chapter 3 - One Approach to Control

1. This observation has been made especially forcefully by Rosenau in both "Moral Fervor" and *In Search of Global Patterns.*

2. This term is used, for instance, in George and Smoke, *Deterrence in American Foreign Policy.* In "Case Study and Theory in Political Science," Eckstein uses the term *disciplined configurative* for what is essentially the same method, deployed to a somewhat different purpose. Other writers

have used this approach, as discussed in Appendix B, without giving it a proper name.

3. Scholars and others interested in seeing the links between the research questions and the case study material developed in response thereto are referred to my earlier version of this study, "Control of Escalation." There this linkage is performed explicitly, and many of the conclusions are organized under the headings provided by the research questions. Here they are not.

4. The late 1960s and the 1970s have witnessed a movement among scholars studying international affairs and foreign policy in the direction of emphasizing bureaucratic politics and institutional processes, and de-emphasizing what may have been, during the previous ten or fifteen years, somewhat overabundant attention to the logic of the strategic interactions among players presumed to be single, unitary entities. The premier statements to date of the intragovernmentalist cause are Allison's *Essence of Decision* and Halperin's *Bureaucratic Politics and Foreign Policy*. Their joint paper, "Bureaucratic Politics," may be taken as the authoritative summary of this movement's theme.

Advocates of the bureaucratic politics perspective have drawn, in turn, on an earlier generation of scholars, including Charles Lindblom, Warner Shilling, Paul Hammond, Samuel Huntington, Herbert Simon, Roger Hilsman, and perhaps especially, Richard Neustadt, Richard Cyert, and James March. Recently, the bureaucratic politics movement has received some criticism; see, for instance, Art, "Bureaucratic Politics"; Rothstein, *Planning, Prediction and Policymaking*; and Krasner, "Are Bureaucracies Important?"

Related to, but distinguishable from, the above movement is a rising interest among some international relations scholars in psychological perspectives on cognitive processes and on group dynamics. Aspects of this theme will be taken up later.

5. For instance, Brodie has written that "with the advent of nuclear weapons the entire value of past military experience as a guide to the future was called basically into question" (*Strategy in the Missile Age*, p. 149). But note also his chapter in Knorr, *Historical Dimensions*.

6. Holsti, *Crisis Escalation War*, esp. chaps. 1, 5, and 8.

7. Schelling, *Arms and Influence*, p. 117.

8. Additional arguments against this approach should be noted. Aside from the question of nuclear weapons, the disadvantages of using pre—Cold War cases seem to be three:

First, with the exceptions of the Second World War and, in part, the First World War and the interwar period, such cases usually must restrict themselves to escalation by means of widening the geographic scope of the conflict or by bringing in new belligerents. Escalation by introducing new categories of weapons generally is not significant. (It is not clear, though, that in any postwar case the introduction of new weapons into a conflict has had much escalatory pressure. I am not aware of any escalation literature that seriously discusses the introduction of new weapons—save, of course, nuclear weapons.)

Second is the existence of advanced *conventional* technology, especially in communications and transportation. What seems to be the greatest technological difference between, say, the Near East crises of 1854 and 1958 is not the extent of their escalatory potential, for both could have become major strategic wars of devastating consequences. Rather, it seems to be the speed and volume of communications surrounding the respective crises —and hence the speed of decision-making—and, secondarily, the speed with which sizable forces were potentially transportable into the crisis area.

The third major difference is systemic alteration in the general context of international relations. In the eighteenth century and at least the earlier portion of the nineteenth, limits in the marginal economic power that could be mobilized placed constraints on military options. Limits of technology restricted the destructive power of forces. Prior to the French Revolution and possibly later, there were distinct limits on the manpower demands states could make of their citizens. Familial relationships among the heads of state of different powers, and conceptions such as the Concert of Europe, may have also limited conflict.

These general contextual differences will not be analyzed in detail here. All but one of our selected cases is recent enough that most of these factors do not appear too serious, and the single case from the eighteenth century will be interesting in spite of them. In my judgment the much greater speed of events in the contemporary era is the most significant difference. Some of its implications are mentioned in Part Three.

Valuable discussions of systemic differences in war in different eras may be found in a number of sources. One of the most useful is Osgood, *Limited War*, pt. 2. Kaufmann discusses the matter in "Limited Warfare." Brodie is somewhat briefer in *Strategy in the Missile Age*. Lengthier treatments may be found in Dorn, *Competition for Empire*, and in the more technical military literature such as Fuller's *The Conduct of War*, and Earle's *Makers of Modern Strategy*.

9. A recent (1974) bibliography of the principal literature on the Cuban missile crisis appears following chap. 15 of George and Smoke, *Deterrence in American Foreign Policy*.

10. The selection of these five cases from the very large number potentially available proved a challenging problem. Even if we assume right off that usable data would be available only from about the seventeenth century on, and only from among the important European and North American powers, the number of possible cases is still enormous. In *A Study of War* (app. 20), Wright lists no less than 277 wars involving these powers

between about 1600 and World War II. Further constraints were therefore introduced.

The exclusion of minor colonial actions reduced the total considerably. Some preliminary research suggested that the adequacy of the relevant information begins to fall off as one goes back before the early 1700s. It also indicated cases since that date which could be immediately dismissed as uninteresting because they evidently lacked escalation situations meeting the two criteria. At this point some 23 wars remained, containing a somewhat larger number of potentially interesting escalation situations. In addition to those finally selected, these were the following:

> The War of the Austrian Succession (1740-1748)
> The War of the Bavarian Succession (1778)
> The American Revolutionary War (1776-1783)
> The Russo-Turkish War of 1790-1792
> The Austro-French Wars of 1791 and 1792
> The Wars of the French Revolution (1793-1801)
> The Napoleonic Wars (1802-1814)
> The American War of 1812
> The Russo-Turkish War of 1828-1829
> The Mexican War (of the United States) (1845-1848)
> The Russo-Turkish War of 1877
> The Boer War (1899-1905)
> The Russo-Japanese War (1905)
> The Balkan Wars of 1912-1913
> The outbreak of World War I
> The Mexican "War" of 1916
> The Western interventions in the Soviet Union, post World War I
> The Russo-Finnish War (1939-1940) (the "Winter War").

Some additional research on each of these indicated, with moderate (but only moderate) confidence, which of them met the two criteria best and were most readily researchable. Some of these conflicts, like the War of the Bavarian Succession, were, in Kaufmann's phrase, "neat, bloodless quadrilles," where the rather special limitation of not wishing to deflate the value or grandeur of the contested throne forbade much scope for escalation. Others, like the Russo-Japanese War, threatened the analyst with serious problems of how to research them. Others, such as the Napoleonic Wars and the Wars of the French Revolution, presented an image of extreme complexity. Others, such as the Balkan Wars of 1912-1913, might have served as readily as those actually chosen.

World War I was excluded from this study, not because it fails to meet the criterion of a conflict that ought to have stayed under control, but simply because it has already been researched in depth by a team led by Robert North of Stanford University and in subsequent studies by individuals who had been part of that project. Holsti's *Crisis Escalation War* is a spin-off from that project. Other publications flowing directly or indirectly from it, for the most part less policy oriented than Holsti's book, are cited and reviewed, in *Contemporary Research in International Relations* by Zinnes, another of the researchers involved in the "outbreak" project.

Sources employed in my preliminary research were Albrecht-Carrie, *Concert of Europe* and *A Diplomatic History of Europe;* Earle, *Makers of Modern Strategy;* Falls, *Hundred Years of War;* Fuller, *Conduct of War* and *Military History of the Western World;* Hart, *Strategy;* Montross, *War Through the Ages;* Oman, *History of War in the Middle Ages* and *History of War in the Sixteenth Century;* Osgood, *Limited War;* Petrie, *Diplomatic History* and *Earlier Diplomatic History;* Spaulding and Wright, "Warfare in Modern Times"; Taylor, *Struggle for Mastery in Europe;* Turner, *History of Military Affairs;* Wright, *Study of War;* and *Encyclopedia Britannica.*

11. The two German wars are close together in time, and we shall discover that they resemble each other in their main outlines, although not in many important details. I have included them both, mainly to be able to make a detailed comparison between two generally similar situations. The other cases are quite diverse, in fact none of the conflicts strongly resemble any of the others, except for the pair of German wars. In one instance (the portion of the Seven Years War escalation sequence we shall study) the actual or potential escalation takes the form of more violent tactics, troop deployments, and the like. In two instances (the pair of German wars) it takes the form of other nations becoming involved. In the other two instances it includes both. In two of these cases (the Spanish Civil War and the portion of the Seven Years War), the conflict was essentially a proxy battle for most or all of the escalation sequence. In the other three cases, the conflict was a direct one among great powers, competing without benefit of proxy (except, in a marginal sense, in aspects of the Crimean War escalation sequence).

For these reasons and others, there is necessarily some variation in the way the case studies are presented. Where the time periods involved are short, or where the escalation situation is very complicated, I have used a chronological format. Otherwise I have employed an analytical format.

It is only coincidental that the three cases studied entirely or primarily as instances of escalation controlled are the three most recent, and the two studied as instances of uncontrolled escalation are slightly more distant.

It is always possible to argue that my treatment has overestimated the extent to which things could have been different, particularly in the three cases where I claim there was a very real danger of a much bigger war growing out of the original conflict. There is no way to settle such questions, since perceptions of historical inevitability always contain subjective components. In this context I lean toward a behavioralist viewpoint, emphasizing that it was the judgment of well-informed observers at the time that the danger was a serious one. More important, the question of the probability of events flowing in a different pattern does not, within a significant range, affect seriously the kinds of conclusions arrived at by this study.

Bibliography for Chapter 3 - One Approach to Control

Albrecht-Carrie, Rene. *A Diplomatic History of Europe Since the Congress of Vienna.* New York: Harper and Bros., 1958.

—— *The Concert of Europe.* New York: Harper Torchbooks, 1968.

Allison, Graham T. *Essence of Decision.* Boston: Little, Brown and Co., 1971.

—— and Morton H. Halperin, "Bureaucratic Politics: A Paradigm and Some Policy Implications." In Richard H. Ullman and Raymond Tanter, eds., *Theory and Practice in International Relations.* Princeton, N. J.: Princeton University Press, 1972. Originally published in *World Politics* 24, supplement (1972):40-79.

Art, Robert J. "Bureaucratic Politics and American Foreign Policy: A Critique." *Policy Sciences* 4 (1973):467-490.

Brodie, Bernard. *Strategy in the Missile Age.* Princeton, N. J.: Princeton University Press, 1959.

Dorn, Walter L. *Competition for Empire, 1740-1763.* New York: Harper and Bros., 1940.

Earle, Edward Meade. *Makers of Modern Strategy.* Princeton, N. J.: Princeton University Press, 1941.

Eckstein, Harry. "Case Study and Theory in Political Science." In Fred I. Greenstein and Nelson W. Polsby, eds., *Handbook of Political Science,* vol. 7. Reading, Mass.: Addison-Wesley Publishing Co., 1975.

Falls, Cyril. *A Hundred Years of War.* London: Gerald Duckworth and Co., 1953.

Fuller, J. F. C. *A Military History of the Western World.* New York: Funk and Wagnalls Co., 1954.

—— *The Conduct of War 1789-1961.* New Brunswick, N. J.: Rutgers University Press, 1961.

George, Alexander L., and Richard Smoke. *Deterrence in American Foreign Policy: Theory and Practice.* New York: Columbia University Press, 1974.

Halperin, Morton H. *Bureaucratic Politics and Foreign Policy.* Washington, D. C.: Brookings Institution, 1974.

Hart, B. F. Liddell. *Strategy.* New York: Praeger Publishers, 1954.

Holsti, Ole R. *Crisis Escalation War.* Montreal: McGill-Queens University Press, 1972.

Kaufmann, William W. "Limited Warfare." In William W. Kaufmann, ed.,

Military Policy and National Security. Princeton, N. J.: Princeton University Press, 1956.

Knorr, Klaus. *Historical Dimensions of National Security Problems*. Princeton, N. J.: Princeton University Press, 1976.

Krasner, Stephen D. "Are Bureaucracies Important? (or Allison Wonderland)." *Foreign Policy* 7 (1972):159-179.

Montross, Lynn. *War Through the Ages*. New York: Harper and Bros., 1944.

Oman, Charles W. C. *A History of the Art of War in the Sixteenth Century*. London: Methuen Co., 1937.

——— *A History of the Art of War in the Middle Ages*. 2nd ed., revised. New York: B. Franklin, 1959.

Osgood, Robert E. *Limited War*. Chicago: University of Chicago Press, 1957.

Petrie, Charles. *Diplomatic History 1713-1933*. London: Hollis & Carter, 1947.

——— *Earlier Diplomatic History, 1492-1713*. London: Hollis & Carter, 1949.

Roseneau, James N. "Moral Fervor, Systematic Analysis, and Scientific Consciousness in Foreign Policy Research." In Austin Ranney, ed., *Political Science and Public Policy*. Chicago: Markham Press, 1968.

——— *In Search of Global Patterns*. New York: Free Press, 1977.

Rothstein, Robert. *Planning, Prediction and Policymaking in Foreign Affairs: Theory and Practice*. Boston: Little, Brown and Co., 1972.

Schelling, Thomas C. *Arms and Influence*. New Haven, Conn.: Yale University Press, 1966.

Smoke, Richard. "The Control of Escalation: An Historical Analysis." Unpublished Ph.D. dissertation, MIT, December 1971.

Spaulding, Oliver L., and John W. Wright. "Warfare in Modern Times." In Oliver L. Spaulding, Hoffman Nickerson, and John W. Wright, *Warfare*. New York: Harcourt Brace, 1925.

Taylor, A. J. P. *The Struggle for Mastery in Europe 1848-1918*. Oxford: Clarendon Press, 1954.

Turner, Gordon B., ed. *A History of Military Affairs in Western Society Since the 18th Century*. Ann Arbor, Mich.: Edwards Bros., 1952.

Wright, Quincy. *A Study of War*. 2nd ed. Chicago: University of Chicago Press, 1965.

Zinnes, Dina A. *Contemporary Research in International Relations: A Perspective and a Critical Appraisal*. New York: Free Press, 1976.

Notes to Chapter 4 - The Spanish Civil War

1. The causes and sources of the Spanish Civil War are exceedingly complicated and can barely be alluded to here. In the English language, the two best general treatments of the conflict are the books by Thomas (*Span-*

ish Civil War) and by Broué and Temine (Revolution and Civil War in Spain), the latter recently translated. This section of the chapter and the next two draw principally upon these sources. The Broué and Temine volume may be somewhat more revealing with respect to internal political developments within republican Spain; the Thomas may be better balanced between the two sides in its sympathies and coverage, and is more comprehensive.

2. Van der Esch, Prelude to War, p. 29. Hitler later claimed that his transport aircraft won the war for Franco. Thomas suggests (p. 612) that one cannot be certain of this, but that the dispatch of the planes "was a really decisive moment." High-level Italians had already reached an agreement with many of the military conspirators in March 1934.

3. Thomas, pp. 260-261.

4. Van der Esch, p. 43; Thomas, pp. 292-310; and Broué and Temine, pp. 245-251. About two thousand Soviet tankmen, technicians, and officers were committed (van der Esch, p. 45). The large quantities of arms, ammunition, and other materiel sent to the republican forces by the Comintern, apart from the Russian materiel sent directly by Moscow, are detailed in Thomas (p. 636). There were also foreigners who volunteered to fight on the Nationalist side (p. 635).

5. Thomas, pp. 316, 333, and 634-635.

6. Van der Esch, pp. 41-42; and Thomas, p. 337.

7. Cattell, Soviet Diplomacy, pp. 32-37; Toynbee, Survey of International Affairs, 1937, pp. 194-201.

8. Broué and Temine, pp. 336-343; Thomas, pp. 394-395; and van der Esch, pp. 77-78. The control plan has been widely discussed in literature on the international aspects of the civil war. See especially Padelford's "Non-Intervention Agreement" and Wilcox's "Localization of the Spanish War."

9. Van der Esch, p. 84; and Thomas, pp. 395, 510, and 552.

10. Thomas, pp. 332-333 and 407-411. In April 1937 British ships carrying foodstuffs to the republican port of Bilbao were halted, but this time the blockade was found to be "paper" and the ships received protection from the Royal Navy. Franco did not wish to offend London unnecessarily and declined to press the point; Bilbao fell to his forces a few months later anyway. In the spring of 1938 Nationalist and Italian airmen bombarded British ships in republican waters and ports; on this occasion London did nothing.

The details of the highly complex story of the Nationalist blockade and ship seizures are outside the scope of this work. I have drawn summary information from Padelford, "Foreign Shipping," "International Law and the Spanish Civil War," and International Law and Diplomacy.

11. At its height Italian involvement comprised more than 60,000 infantry organized in four regular divisions, some 750 aircraft and 5,700 officers and men of the Italian air force, and about 90 warships, including

submarines, of the Italian navy (Thomas, p. 535). The figure for aircraft includes Italian planes given to the Nationalists, but mostly piloted by Italians. Thomas in his appendix 3 gives the figures for all foreign involvement.

12. Thomas, 467-482; and Toynbee, *Survey, 1937*, pp. 339-352.

13. Thomas, pp. 523-524, 540, and 573.

14. Ibid., pp. 522-523, 534, 537, 556-557, and 612; and van der Esch, pp. 45-46.

15. Broué and Temine, p. 510; and Thomas, pp. 556 and 566. The arms shipment included a full month's total German production of machine guns, as well as artillery and other equipment and materiel. More was not required of Germany because the forces of the republic, now many months with hardly any outside aid, were running short on supplies and materiel. Furthermore, they were exhausted and discouraged.

Weinberg, in *Foreign Policy of Hitler's Germany*, does not discuss German policy toward Spain near the end of the civil war; in a single sentence he indicates that he thinks the negative objective did not change (p. 299). Thomas, on the other hand, points out explicitly that Hitler reversed that policy in the autumn of 1938 (pp. 612-613). Weinberg does not analyze the events of the period and may underestimate the significance of the final massive German aid. It strains plausibility to imagine that Berlin did not calculate what effect this critically timed assistance would have on the progress of the war. And we know that Hitler expected Franco to join him in European wars that he anticipated in the near future. On these grounds, the inference that Berlin intended a decisive escalation seems not merely plausible but compelling.

16. Broué and Temine (pp. 549-561) give a useful chronology of significant international events and actions of foreign powers relevant to the civil war. Toynbee's *Survey, 1937* presents an excellent résumé of the general motives, interests, and objectives of the major European powers.

The United States declared itself neutral and embargoed arms deliveries to either Spanish belligerent for the duration of the war. This act, plus the obvious isolationist sentiment of America in that era, made it clear that no European power had to concern itself with any intercession by the United States in Spanish events. Mexico alone among the Latin American nations sent the legal government of Spain war materiel, in moderate quantity.

17. Broué and Temine, p. 485; and Thomas, p. 535. In such an event the republicans, tying down major Italian and some German forces, could expect the British and French immediately to offer alliance.

18. High-level civil policy-makers of the republic twice vetoed actions proposed by their military commanders that might have generated a wider war: once a proposed retaliation against the German fleet for the bombardment of Almería, and once a proposed air raid on Rome in retaliation for

Italian air force bombing of republican cities (Broué and Temine, p. 485; and Thomas, pp. 441-442).

19. The only deviations from these limits were an abortive republican attack on Nationalist Majorca early in the war, which quickly failed; and the Nationalists' capture of Minorca, previously Loyalist, at their leisure near the end of the war. Both campaigns, being insular, were also territorially confined.

20. German policy toward Spain early in the war is discussed in Weinberg, pp. 284-299. Hitler's first gift of transport planes to Franco, to ferry African troops across the straits to the Iberian peninsula, was made in the expectation that this would probably ensure a prompt Nationalist victory. When, thanks to the aid the republic received from the USSR, it did not, Hitler quickly realized the advantages to Germany of a drawn-out Spanish war. In addition to Spanish mineral rights, these included (as Weinberg discusses) distraction of the West from Germany's own rearmament and an inevitable *approchement* between Rome and Berlin—already an objective of German foreign policy. Hitler's interests in Spain are also discussed in Toynbee, *Survey, 1937*, pp. 185-194; van der Esch, pp. 11-14; and Thomas, pp. 228-230. Hitler naturally expected Franco to ally Spain with Germany in World War II and was enraged when he did not (van der Esch, p. 12).

The inference presented earlier, that the dispatch of the Condor Legion was in response to Soviet aid to the republic, may never be completely demonstrated by surviving documents. Weinberg speculates (pp. 294-295) that it was merely to accelerate the Nationalist cause generally and to aid in the capture of Madrid particularly. It is true that the decision in Berlin was made toward the end of October, exact date unclear, and the first Soviet-supplied tanks and aircraft were not employed in battle by the republic until October 29th. The hypothesis that the two events were not directly linked is therefore a possible one. However, German intelligence in Spain at this time was good, and it strains credulity to imagine that Berlin did not know at least generally of the massive Russian and Comintern supplies that were arriving in the republic throughout October, or that this knowledge did not play a role in the decision to form the Condor Legion.

21. The USSR is an exception to the generalization of the previous chapter that in pre-World War II cases the motivation and utility calculi of decision-makers on all sides of the conflicts are open to us. The preceding paragraphs have attempted to summarize what may reasonably be inferred about the roots of the Soviet role in the Spanish Civil War. Remarks are drawn mainly from Cattell, especially chaps. 4 and 5 of *Soviet Diplomacy*; Jackson, pp. 423-424; Toynbee, *Survey, 1937*, pp. 194-201; Thomas, pp. 214-215; and van der Esch, pp. 20-21.

Stalin radically disagreed with French and British policy-makers on the general strategy for preventing a new European war. He believed that Hitler and Mussolini (whom, unlike most English decision-makers, he lumped together) could not be appeased and could only be faced down while their military strength was less than that of Britain, France, and Russia combined. He therefore favored a vigorous and aggressive use of deterrence strategies. In the Nonintervention Committee and in other diplomacy surrounding the civil war, Soviet representatives were constantly encouraging showdowns with the fascist powers over their violations of the agreement, and seeking backing from London and Paris for such confrontations. Without this kind of support, Stalin lacked some requirements for credible diplomacy or deterrent threats that might have halted aid to the Nationalists; he therefore fell back on giving aid to the republic as he could—a poor second-best from his viewpoint because of the difficulties involved, which became increasingly serious.

22. On Italian policy in Spain see van der Esch, pp. 14-15; Toynbee, *Survey, 1937*, pp. 177-184; Thomas, pp. 226-227; and Broué and Temine, pp. 346-349. The latter make what I feel is a real mistake in asserting that Mussolini's ideological goals were only a facade. With many others, I believe that in fact they were a central, although not the sole, factor in his motivation.

23. On French policy in Spain see van der Esch, pp. 15-16; Toynbee, *Survey, 1937*, pp. 138-151; Broué and Temine, pp. 327-331; and Thomas, pp. 213 and 258-259. Werth's *Twilight of France* gives an evocative impression of the atmosphere as well as the substance of French policy in this period. On British policy in Spain see Jackson, *Spanish Republic and Civil War*, pp. 424-427; van der Esch, pp. 16-17; Toynbee, *Survey, 1937*, pp. 151-177; and Thomas, pp. 219-223. For the viewpoint of the Spanish republic on French and British policy, see Puzzo, *Spain and the Great Powers*, chap. 4.

24. Thomas, pp. 258-259.

25. An insightful analysis of calculated and noncalculated factors in making foreign policy appears in May's essay, "The Nature of Foreign Policy."

26. Note again the important role of what earlier was called the definitional phase of the war when initial limits were crystallizing. *Before* the close of the phase, Paris and London could not be sure that the modest intercession represented by the open frontier might not involve France in a rapid and dangerous escalation sequence. Much later in the war, when many of its limits were well-established, the same act carried a much lower perceived risk.

27. It can be argued that in small ways British policy was pro-Nationalist from the first. Searchlights from British Gibralter aided the Nationalists in bringing their troops across from Africa, and later some British officials quietly helped the Nationalists locate unregistered ships. These

and other small indications undoubtedly added to the expectation in Rome and Berlin that the Conservative government in London would not take amiss a Franco victory and might not react too strenuously to moderate escalations on Franco's behalf (private communications from Gabriel Jackson, January 1973).

28. Quoted in Toynbee *Survey, 1937*, p. 162. The parliamentary debate from which this especially crisp statement is drawn occurred on 21 December 1937, but similar remarks were being made by the same government fifteen and more months previously (ibid., pp. 157-162).

29. Lord Vansittart, *Mist Procession*, p. 516.

30. Italian caution was inspired more by fear of a French military reaction to their escalations in Spain than by fear of a British one. In this period leaders in Rome (and also Berlin) underestimated the degree to which French policy was, in effect, being determined in London. The Italian testing strategy is discussed further below.

31. I have discovered no indication of any such threats delivered by private channels, although it is possible that a search of the Nazi and Italian archives would uncover one. Such a threat delivered against the USSR would likely have been noncredible, because Moscow well understood the fascist powers' desire not to provoke Britain and France. Soviet assistance to republican Spain was declining after the early months of the war in any case.

32. It may also be true that the French and British would have reacted more vigorously in 1936 or 1937 to curb fascist escalations than they would have or did in 1938: that is, that French and British risk aversion was increasing over time. However, Berlin and Rome almost certainly underestimated the true Western risk aversion to some degree during the first year and a half of the war.

33. I have deliberately separated this discussion from the earlier one concerning the territorial limits on the Spanish arena. Two related but distinct topics are involved: one is the degree to which an arena is clearly defined; the other is the nature and extent of the lines of communication between the arena, however defined, and the zones of interior of the great powers potentially and actually involved in the arena. Discontinuities in these lines of communication generally *can* be leapfrogged by nations who simply want to escalate; the focus here is on their role in restraining escalation when the involved nations hope to avoid an uncontrolled sequence.

34. That the motives in Spain of Hitler's Germany were not primarily ideological is emphasized by Toynbee, *Survey, 1937* (pp. 185-187), which contrasts them directly with the quite ideological motives of Mussolini's Italy. On the ideological motives of the French government in power, see for instance Thomas, pp. 213-214 and 259.

35. This is in part why the Blum and Daladier governments went no farther in the spring of 1938 than opening the border and transmitting

supplies, despite the critical prognosis for the republic. Interestingly, the other contiguous nation, Portugal, did commit a substantial number of "volunteers" to the Nationalists, but as noted earlier the Portuguese border was protected by a wide belt of surrounding Nationalist territory. Since Portugal was not the close ally of any great power, a republican attack on her would not have raised the serious threat of an uncontrolled escalation sequence.

36. Russian crews did not themselves always man the republic's tanks (van der Esch, p. 45), but sometimes they did (Thomas, p. 316).

Bibliography for Chapter 4 - The Spanish Civil War

Askew, William C. "The Italian Intervention in Spain: The Agreement of March 31, 1934 with the Spanish Monarchist Parties." *Journal of Modern History* 24 (1952):181-183.

Blythe, Henry. *Spain Over Britain: A Study of the Strategical Effect of the Italian Intervention on the Defense of the British Empire.* London: Routledge & Sons, 1937.

Braidsford, H. N. "Britain Blunders in Spain." *Current History* 47 (1937): 40-44.

Broué, Pierre, and Emile Temine. *The Revolution and the Civil War in Spain.* London: Faber and Faber, 1972.

Buckley, Henry. *Life and Death of the Spanish Republic.* London: Hamish Hamilton, 1940.

Carr, E. H. *International Relations Between the Two World Wars.* London: Macmillan and Co., 1965.

Carr, Raymond. *Spain, 1808-1939.* Oxford: Clarendon Press, 1966.

Cattell, David T. *Communism and the Spanish Civil War.* Berkeley, Calif.: University of California Press, 1955.

_____ *Soviet Diplomacy and the Spanish Civil War.* Berkeley, Calif.: University of California Press, 1957.

Churchill, Winston S. *The Gathering Storm.* Boston: Houghton Mifflin Co., 1948.

Ciano, Count Galeazzo. *Ciano's Diaries, 1939-1943.* Garden City, New York: Doubleday & Co., 1946.

_____ *Ciano's Hidden Diary 1937-1938.* New York: E. P. Dutton & Co., 1953.

DeWilde, John C. "The Stuggle Over Spain." In *Foreign Policy Reports.* New York: Foreign Policy Association, April 1938.

Eden, Sir Anthony (Earl of Avon). *Facing the Dictators.* London: Cassell & Co., 1962.

Esch, P. A. M. van der. *Prelude to War.* The Hague: Martinus Nijhoff, 1951.

Feis, Herbert. *The Spanish Story.* New York: Alfred A. Knopf, 1948.

Fernsworth, Lawrence. "Twentieth-Century Piracy." *Current History* 47 (1937):59-64.

Genet, Raoul. "Charge of Piracy in the Spanish Civil War." *American Journal of International Law* 32 (1938):253-263.

Guttmann, Allen. *The Wound in the Heart.* New York: Free Press of Glencoe, 1962.

Hamilton, Thomas J. *Appeasement's Child.* New York: Alfred A. Knopf, 1943.

Jackson, Gabriel. *The Spanish Republic and the Civil War, 1931-1939.* Princeton, N. J.: Princeton University Press, 1965.

Loveday, Arthur F. *World War in Spain.* London: John Murray, 1939.

May, Ernest R. "The Nature of Foreign Policy: the Calculated versus the Axiomatic." *Daedalus* 91 (fall 1962):652-667.

Muggeridge, Malcolm. *The Thirties.* London: William Collins Sons & Co., 1940.

Namier, L. B. *Diplomatic Prelude, 1938-39.* London: Macmillan and Co., 1948.

——— *Europe in Decay.* London: Macmillan and Co., 1950.

New Statesman and Nation. "Is It the End of Piracy?" 14 (1937):396-397.

Padelford, Norman J. "International Law and the Spanish Civil War." *American Journal of International Law* 31 (1937):226-243.

——— "Non-Intervention Agreement and the Spanish Civil War." *American Journal of International Law* 31 (1937):578-603.

——— "Foreign Shipping During the Spanish Civil War." *American Journal of International Law* 32 (1938):264-279.

——— *International Law and Diplomacy in the Spanish Civil Strife.* New York: Macmillan Co., 1939.

——— and Henry G. Seymour. "Some International Problems of the Spanish Civil War." *Political Science Quarterly* 52 (1937):364-380.

Payne, Stanley G. *Politics and the Military in Modern Spain.* Stanford, Calif.: Stanford University Press, 1967.

Peers, Allison E. *The Spanish Tragedy 1930-36.* New York: Oxford University Press, 1936.

Phillips, Paul D. "French Position and Policy in the Mediterranean 1919-1939." Unpublished master's thesis, University of California, Berkeley, August 1941.

Puzzo, Dante A. *Spain and the Great Powers 1936-1941.* New York: Columbia University Press, 1962.

Richards, V. *Lessons of the Spanish Revolution.* London: Freedom Press, 1953.

Salter, Cedric. *Try-Out in Spain.* New York: Harper & Bros., 1943.

Simon, Yves R. *The Road to Vichy 1918-1938.* New York: Sheed and Ward, 1942.

Temperley, Maj. Gen. A. C. "Military Lessons of the Spanish War." *Foreign Affairs* 16 (1937):34-43.

Thomas, Hugh. *The Spanish Civil War.* London: Eyre and Spottiswoode, 1961.

Toynbee, Arnold J., ed. *Survey of International Affairs, 1937.* Vol. 2, *The International Repercussions of the War in Spain (1936-37).* London: Oxford University Press, 1938.

Vansittart, Lord Robert. *The Mist Procession.* London: Hutchinson & Co., 1958.

Weinberg, Gerhard L. *The Foreign Policy of Hitler's Germany.* Chicago: University of Chicago Press, 1970.

Werth, Alexander. *The Twilight of France 1933-1940.* New York: Harper & Bros., 1942.

Whitaker, Arthur P. *Spain and the Defense of the West.* New York: Harper & Bros., 1961.

Wilcox, Francis O. "The Localization of the Spanish War." *American Political Science Review* 32 (1938):237-260.

Wolfers, Arnold. *Britain and France Between Two Wars.* New York: Harcourt Brace & Co., 1940.

Notes to Chapter 5 - The Austro-Prussian War

1. Compensation was often used as a device for providing a nation with some gain, such as a small piece of territory, to offset and equalize a roughly equivalent gain being made by another nation with competing interests. A similar device was retorsion, which justified a nation seizing an equivalent value when compensation had not been received. The doctrine of reprisal justified one nation coercively imposing a limited penalty on another, as retribution for a loss sustained. The principle underlying these devices, and underlying most activities at the congresses, was that marginal changes should be made along cleavages in the international system sufficiently often and sufficiently flexibly that grievances and tensions would not accumulate.

2. The general information on this and the next few pages is drawn from several sources. Valuable brief accounts of the political and diplomatic events surrounding the war are found in Taylor's *Struggle for Mastery in Europe*, chap. 8, and in Joll, "Prussia and the German Problem." The definitive accounts of the politics and diplomacy surrounding the war are Clark's *Franz Joseph and Bismarck* and Friedjung's *Struggle for Supremacy in Germany*.

3. Falls summarizes the military events of the war in *A Hundred Years of War*, chap. 5. Craig's *Battle of Königgrätz* presents that battle vividly and the preceding smaller engagements more briefly. Hozier's *Seven Weeks War* recounts the military events in great detail.

4. At this time Bismarck's title was minister-president, a post compara-

ble to but slightly less powerful than the position of chancellor, which he created and occupied in the governments of the North German Confederation (1866-1871) and the Second Reich. The minister-president carried the foreign minister's portfolio and therefore, in common with many historians, I shall sometimes refer to Bismarck as the foreign minister.

5. This discussion of Bismarck's preconditions is drawn mainly from Clark and from Friedjung. The problem of convincing an absolute monarch that one's nation is acting "defensively" may seem somewhat obsolete, until one reflects that it may resemble the problem of convincing a cabinet or a politburo or a bureaucracy or even public opinion of the same thing. On Bismarck's overall objective, see Darmstaedter, p. 268.

6. Although the intensification of diplomatic crises in general is excluded from the subject matter of this study, in this case we must devote a few pages to prewar diplomacy crucial in the definition of the initial war context. Information in the table and in the discussion immediately following is derived principally from Clark, chaps. 11 and 12, and from Taylor, *Struggle*, chap. 8.

7. On the perceptions and actions of Prussian policy-makers toward the Russians, see Mosse, *The European Powers*, pp. 218-220, 222-226, and 233-238; Friedjung, p. 86; and Clark, p. 347.

8. Taylor, *Struggle*, p. 156.

9. Darmstaedter, p. 287; on Biarritz, see also Taylor, *Struggle*, pp. 158-160, and *Bismarck*, pp. 80-81; and Clark, pp. 343-344.

10. Pflanze, *Bismarck and the Development of Germany*, p. 287; Clark, pp. 343-344; and Taylor, *Struggle*, pp. 160-162.

11. Decision-makers in many of the smaller states decided to follow the lead of Bavaria, but Bavarian policy vacillated through the spring, as first Berlin and then Vienna sent Munich threats and inducements. Finally Bavaria mobilized after Prussia did, whereupon some of the other states followed suit. Still the Prussians flooded them all with carrots and sticks, designed to overwhelm the smaller states' decision-making capacities, leading to delay, disunity, and indecision. No contingency plans for this situation had been made, even though nearly all the smaller states had traditionally professed to fear Prussian aggression. "These problems taxed Austrian diplomacy to the utmost, and in the end they were even less satisfactorily solved than the Vienna statesmen, in their pessimism, had anticipated" (Clark, p. 445). Some of the states surrendered to Prussia at once; others failed to unite their armies and surrendered in July. Von Moltke had counted upon the lesser German states to prove ineffectual, had based his military plans on that supposition, and—with assistance from the foreign ministry—had been proved right. See Clark, pp. 390-402 and 445-454; Friedjung, pp. 206-208 and 278; and Falls, pp. 72-75.

12. Friedjung, pp. 111-114, 117, and 190-192; Oncken, *Napoleon III and the Rhine*, pp. 58-59; Pflanze, pp. 297-302; and Clark, pp. 344-345. Prus-

sian mobilization was "a triumph" of planning, and Prussian intelligence was excellent (Hozier, pp. 22 and 28).

13. Clark, p. 351.

14. Ibid., pp. 333 and 337; and Friedjung, p. 102.

15. Friedjung, pp. 93-94 and 97-100; and Clark, pp. 403-408.

16. Clark, pp. 407-408.

17. The quotation is from Friedjung, pp. 183-184. Material elsewhere in this paragraph is from Clark, pp. 433-441, and Friedjung, pp. 180-184.

18. This decision had other motives, too complicated to analyze in detail here: briefly, to preserve and enhance Austria's moral position and to consolidate the political support of the middle and small German states behind the Austrian position. See Clark, pp. 349-363.

19. Pflanze, p. 289; Friedjung, pp. 133-136; and Clark, pp. 379-387. The Austrian decision was made in one day, although there was no military necessity for such haste.

20. Taylor, *Struggle*, p. 162.

21. Ibid., pp. 164-165; and Clark, pp. 428-433.

22. Friedjung, pp. 187-189; and Clark, pp. 456-466.

23. Clark, p. 489; and Friedjung, p. 54.

24. Clark, pp. 491-492 and 514; Friedjung, pp. 64 and 97-98; and Taylor, *The Hapsburg Monarchy*, chap. 9.

A good example of the emperor's appointments is General Benedek, a commander experienced on the Italian front who knew, he said, "every tree as far as Milan," but who was utterly ignorant of the Austrian Empire's northern frontier area. Franz Joseph insisted upon his taking command on the northern front; he placed Archduke John, the other available ranking commander (who knew Germany well), in command on the Italian front because the archduke, as a member of the House of Hapsburg, could not be exposed to possible defeat at the hands of the Prussians. Victory on the Italian front was considered certain in any case, and for the archduke to command there would reflect credit on the dynasty. See Redlich, *Emperor Francis Joseph*, pp. 323-325.

25. On the Prussian general staff system see Craig, *Politics of the Prussian Army*, esp. chap. 4. Liddell-Hart discusses it briefly in his essay, "Armed Forces and the Art of War" (pp. 310-311).

26. Two other factors were the personality and modest abilities of the emperor (discussed, for example, by Redlich in his chap. 4) and the atmosphere in Vienna of "historical pessimism," as it might be called. Taylor gives an instance of this, remarking that "the real director of policy, Maurice Esterhazy, was a despairing conservative who believed that Austria was doomed and should therefore perish honorably" (*Struggle*, p. 156). These and other elements of the Austrian failure are discussed by Clark at some length (pp. 484-497 and 511-518).

27. Craig, *Königgrätz*, chaps. 1 and 8; and Friedjung, pp. 234-235.

28. Friedjung, chaps. 16 and 17; and Craig, *Politics of the Prussian Army*, pp. 198-204.

29. Friedjung, p. 214.

30. Darmstaedter, pp. 298-301; and Friedjung, pp. 266-275.

31. Robertston, *Bismarck*, p. 216. At this time Napoleon was suffering from a painful illness, which some historians have judged to be an important reason for the comparative passivity in French policy (see Clark, p. 473, and Friedjung, p. 270).

32. Mosse, pp. 239-249.

33. The remainder of the discussion in this section is drawn, except as otherwise indicated, from Craig, *Politics of the Prussian Army*, pp. 198-204; Friedjung, chaps. 14, 16, and 17; Darmstaedter, pp. 290-305; and Bismarck, *Memoirs*, vol. 2, pp. 38-42.

34. Quoted from Generaladjutant von Boyen, in Craig, *Politics of the Prussian Army*, p. 202.

35. Quoted in Friedjung, p. 287.

36. A dramatic rendition of these events is given by Bismarck, vol. 2, pp. 36-54. Commentary on Bismarck's account and more sober versions are presented in many sources; particularly useful are Friedjung, pp. 286-289; Taylor, *Bismarck*, pp. 84-87; and Eyck, *Bismarck and the German Empire*, pp. 132-133. The crown prince at this time was commander of one of the two major Prussian armies invading Austria, and held military rank inferior only to that of the king himself.

37. See note 33.

38. In this discussion I have deliberately emphasized Bismarck's convictions concerning the great uncertainties associated with a wider war. It is also true, however, as Robertson points out, that under certain circumstances Bismarck might have accepted those risks. Rather than submit to Napoleon's original terms of Schleswig-Holstein only as Prussia's gains, Bismarck might have gambled on a general war (Robertson, pp. 213 and 215). The point is somewhat academic, since King Wilhelm would never have tolerated such small gains in any case.

Bismarck's time-span was even longer than I have argued here, in that almost immediately after Königgrätz, and perhaps even before, he was already looking ahead to the time when Austria would be Prussia's ally. "The task now," Bismarck wrote, "is to win back the old friendship with Austria" (quoted in Robertson, p. 212). "We shall need Austria's strength in the future for ourselves" (Bismarck, vol. 2, p. 42).

Bibliography for Chapter 5 - The Austro-Prussian War

Beust, Count Friederich von. *Memoirs.* 2 vols. London: Remington & Co., 1887.

Bismarck, Otto von. *Memoirs.* Translated by A. J. Butler. 2 vols. New York: Harper & Bros., 1899.

Clark, Chester W. *Franz Joseph and Bismarck*. Cambridge, Mass.: Harvard University Press, 1934.

Craig, Gordon A. *The Politics of the Prussian Army, 1640-1945*. New York: Oxford University Press, 1955.

────── *The Battle of Königgrätz*. Philadelphia: J. B. Lippincott Co., 1964.

Darmstaedter, F. *Bismarck and the Creation of the Second Reich*. London: Methuen & Co., 1948.

Eyck, Erich. *Bismarck and the German Empire*. London: Allen & Unwin, 1950.

Falls, Cyril. *A Hundred Years of War*. London: Gerald Duckworth & Co., 1953.

Fletcher, W. A. *The Mission of Vincent Benedetti to Berlin 1864-1870*. The Hague: Martinus Nijhoff, 1965.

Friedjung, Heinrich. *The Struggle for Supremacy in Germany, 1859-1866*. New York: Russell & Russell, 1966. (First published in German in 1897 and in English in 1935.)

Goerlitz, Walter. *History of the German General Staff 1657-1945*. New York: Praeger Publishers, 1953.

Hozier, H. M. *The Seven Weeks War*. London and New York: Macmillan and Co., 1872.

Joll, James. "Prussia and the German Problem 1830-66." In *New Cambridge Modern History*, vol. 10, pp. 493-521. Cambridge: Cambridge University Press, 1960.

Liddell-Hart, B. H. "Armed Forces and the Art of War: Armies." In *New Cambridge Modern History*, vol. 10, pp. 302-330. Cambridge: Cambridge University Press, 1960.

Macartney, C. A. *The Hapsburg Empire, 1790-1918*. London: Weidenfeld and Nicolson, 1968.

Mosse, W. E. *The European Powers and the German Question 1848-1871*. Cambridge: Cambridge University Press, 1958.

Oesterreichs Kampfe in Jahre 1866. 2 vols. Vienna: Verlag des k.k. Generalstabes, 1868.

Oncken, Hermann. *Napoleon III and the Rhine*. New York: Alfred A. Knopf, 1928.

────── ed. *Die Rheinpolitik Kaiser Napoleons III von 1863 bis 1870*. 2 vols. Osnabruck: Biblio Verlag, 1967.

Pflanze, Otto. *Bismarck and the Development of Germany*. Princeton, N. J.: Princeton University Press, 1963.

Redlich, Joseph. *Emperor Francis Joseph of Austria*. New York: Macmillan Co., 1929.

Robertson, C. Grant. *Bismarck*. New York: Henry Holt & Co., 1919.

Sybel, Heinrich von. *The Founding of the German Empire*, vols. 4 and 5. New York: Crowell, 1891.

Taylor, A. J. P. *The Hapsburg Monarchy*. London: Macmillan and Co., 1941.

———— *The Struggle for Mastery in Europe, 1848-1918*. Oxford: Clarendon Press, 1954.

———— *Bismarck, the Man and the Statesman*. New York: Alfred A. Knopf, 1955.

Notes to Chapter 6 - The Franco-Prusssian War

1. Bismarck was to claim afterward that he "laid a trap" for Napoleon III, but the prevailing opinion among historians is that the great raconteur was embellishing his story. It is more likely that he expected merely a diplomatic crisis, which would be useful in reducing pro-French sentiment in the South German states—sentiment that would have to be reduced if the gradual movement toward their union with the North German Confederation was to continue. However, Bismarck almost certainly appreciated that a war was possible, and at this point had no reason to avoid it. See Pflanze, *Bismarck and the Development of Germany*, pp. 438-457; Foot, "Origins of the Franco-Prussian War"; and Taylor, *Bismarck*, pp. 115-118. For a detailed account of the Hohenzollern crisis, see Steefel, *Bismark*.

Material in the opening section of this chapter is drawn from Pflanze and from Foot; from Howard, *Franco-Prussian War*; and from Taylor, *Struggle for Mastery in Europe*, chap. 10.

Following common usage, I shall usually refer to the German side as "Prussia," since all German decisions discussed in this case study were made by the Prussian government. Technically, the German side was made up of the North German Confederation, wholly dominated by Prussia, in military alliance with the independent states of South Germany—Bavaria, Baden, Württemberg, and Hesse.

2. Since this was the crucial French diplomatic error of the Hohenzollern crisis, blame for it subsequently was shifted around by the parties involved, and by later historians. As Pflanze points out (pp. 449-450), the French foreign minister, Gramont, was given to hasty and belligerent action during this crisis. On the other hand, there is good evidence that Napoleon himself put the foreign minister up to this particular blunder. See *France, Ministry of Foreign Affairs*, vol. 28, pp. 260-61, document number 8436.

3. The most useful book-length account of the military events of the war is undoubtedly that of Howard. Falls gives a summary in his *Hundred Years of War*, chap. 6.

4. Taylor, *Struggle*, p. 212.

5. Taylor, "International Relations," p. 542.

6. The war between the French guerrillas and the German counterin-

surgency forces (as they would be called today) recieves very little attention in the immense literature on the Franco-Prussian War, surprisingly
little from the late twentieth-century viewpoint. The sole major study in
English of which I am aware is Hale's *"Peoples' War" in France,* and this
book lacks a bibliography.

7. The regimes of Austria-Hungary and Russia, both conservative and
antidemocratic, were not sympathetic to the question of popular involvement in France. British opinion favored the French and gradually inclined
more toward them as the war progressed. See Raymond, *British Policy and
Opinion,* chaps. 11-14. Other reasons why the British government remained aloof are taken up below.

8. Bismarck was active in preparing the crisis, in that he energetically
promoted Leopold's candidacy to King Wilhelm and within the Hohenzollern family. Except for some communications with the Spanish emissaries,
however, there was little activity on the international scene. See Pflanze,
pp. 438-449.

The analysis in the text depends upon the consensus of most historians
that Bismarck did not, in fact, intend the Hohenzollern candidacy itself to
create a war or even necessarily a crisis. If one accepts the alternative view
advanced by Bismarck in his memoirs, that the policy of promoting the
candidacy was intended to lead the French into beginning a war, then analytically one must conclude that the crisis of June 1870 was not merely exploited, but actively created and controlled by Bismarck in a manner very
similar to his policy in the causal crisis of the 1866 war.

9. Pflanze, p. 371; and Foot, p. 599. Baden, which was predominantly
pro-Prussian in this period, may have been a partial exception to this generalization.

10. Howard, pp. 58-59; and Foot, p. 599.

11. Robertson, *Bismarck,* pp. 253-254, 268, and 272; and Pflanze, pp.
480-481. There were, in addition, some indications that the South German
states might be drifting away from the Prussian orbit; these provided Bismarck with an additional incentive to accept a crisis earlier rather than
later.

12. Robertson, pp. 254-256; and Pflanze, pp. 372-383. At this time, too,
Bismarck had not given up on more peaceable ways of uniting the South
German states with the North German Confederation. Indeed, characteristically, he was pursuing several complementary strategies to this end right
up to the outbreak of the Franco-Prussian War. See Pflanze, pp. 383-384.

13. Millman, *British Foreign Policy,* esp. p. 198.

14. On Austro-Hungarian behavior at this point see Taylor, *Struggle,*
pp. 208-209; and Pflanze, pp. 419-432.

15. Taylor, *Struggle,* p. 201.

16. Liddell-Hart, "Armed Forces and the Art of War," p. 306; and Howard, pp. 5-6.

17. Liddell-Hart, p. 307; and Howard, p. 36.

18. Extract from a telegram from Ambassador Lyons to Foreign Secretary Granville, quoted and cited by Millman (p. 186). This and a similar report shortly thereafter came a few days before full mobilization had been ordered on either side, but while both sides were taking premobilization preparatory actions, the performance of which greatly influenced the speed and efficiency of subsequent mobilization. Ambassador Lyons' observation applies equally well to the days following the midmonth decision of both sides to mobilize. On the superiority of Prussian intelligence see Steefel p. 238; also Bismarck, *Memoirs*, vol. 2, p. 92.

19. Howard, pp. 44-48 and 67-71. A reform of some aspects of the French army had begun in 1868 but was only partial and, in 1870, still incomplete (Foot, pp. 584-585).

20. Taylor, *Struggle*, p. 210.

21. Eyck (pp. 154-155) points out that publication of the previously secret treaties "was understood as a warning to France that she would have to deal with a united Germany should war break out over the Luxembourg question." Nothing had happened in the three-year interim that would have changed the terms of the conventions or the circumstances under which they could be activated.

22. Robertson, p. 270. See also Pflanze, pp. 424-432, 449, and 460; and Taylor, *Struggle*, 208-209.

23. Taylor, *Struggle*, p. 209; see also p. 203.

24. Foot, pp. 577-578; and Taylor, *Struggle*, chap. 9.

25. Robertson, p. 268.

26. Millman, pp. 200-201; and Raymond, pp. 88-92. The treaty had indeed been proposed by the French, but in August 1866. Bismarck tried to create the impression that it was a recent proposal.

27. Mosse, pp. 306-307; and Clark, "Bismarck, Russia and Origins," pp. 200-203. The Austrian preparations included the construction and repair of fortifications and the purchase of horses—two "long-lead-time items" in today's jargon—and a partial call-up of reservists.

Taylor takes the position (*Struggle*, p. 207) that the threat of the 300,000 Russian troops is a myth. There is documentary evidence for it, however; Mosse (p. 306) explicitly refutes Taylor's view.

28. Mosse presents this story in detail (pp. 306-312 and 317-328).

29. There was one minor exception. Early in the war the French navy shelled a part of the North Sea coast of Germany and threatened to land troops. But the mounting defeats on the French frontier caused this operation to be canceled. The Prussians had deployed a division in the area against this hazard, and there was little military risk to Germany. More serious was the possibility of involving Denmark in the conflict, which in turn might have threatened the standing Russian interest in free passage through the channels to the Baltic. The Russians made strong representa-

tions in Paris, therefore, on the subject of keeping Denmark out of the war. See von Moltke, *The Franco-German War*, pp. 3, 5, 8, and 413; also *Moltke's Military Correspondence*, p. 51, telegram #61.

30. Taylor, *Struggle*, p. 210.

31. Ibid., p. 212.

32. Millman, chap. 11. Militarily the British were unprepared to intervene on the continent. Their naval supremacy was absolute, and absolutely irrelevant to the ongoing war. Their army at this point being small, except for forces in India, a vigorous intervention in force would have required a potential Continental ally; as long as the Russians and Austro-Hungarians remained uninvolved, such an ally did not exist.

33. Almost every historian of the war discusses this problem, some at length. Conclusive evidence is lacking, so that scholars must fall back on interpretations based upon partial evidence. In the discussion that follows, I have relied particuarly on Pflanze, pp. 473-479; Howard, pp. 227-228; and Robertson, pp. 288-289.

34. Quoted by Pflanze, p. 475. Twelve or fifteen times was an exaggeration, but not a gross one. Taylor dismisses the significance, for Bismarck, of the military argument, but here I have followed the more recent and much more extensive discussion by Pflanze.

35. Robertson, pp. 277-278.

36. Rose, "Mission of M. Thiers" and Taylor, *Struggle*, pp. 212-214.

37. Bismark, vol. 2, pp. 109-110; Darmstaedter, *Bismarck and the Second Reich*, p. 369; and Washburne, *Franco-German War*, pp. 48-49, n. 49.

38. From the very outset of the war Bismarck undertook a long process of secret diplomacy aimed at arousing this Russian interest (Mosse, pp. 334-338).

Bibliography for Chapter 6 - The Franco-Prussian War

Benedetti, Vincent. *Ma Mission en Prusse*. Paris: H. Plon, 1871.

Benjamin, H. C. "Official Propaganda and the French Press during the Franco-Prussian War." *Journal of Modern History* 4 (1932):214-230.

Beust, Count Friedrich von. *Memoirs*. 2 vols. London: Remington & Co., 1887.

Bismarck, Otto von. *Memoirs*. Translated by A. J. Butler. 2 vols. New York: Harper & Bros., 1899.

———— *Bismarck's Letters to His Wife from the Seat of War, 1870-71*. London: Jarrold & Sons, 1915.

Bonnin, G., ed. *Bismarck and the Hohenzollern Candidature for the Spanish Throne: The Documents in the German Diplomatic Archives*. London: Chatto & Windus, 1957.

Busch, Moritz. *Bismarck in the Franco-German War*. 2 vols. New York: Charles Scribner's Sons, 1879.

———— *Bismarck, Some Secret Pages of His History*. 2 vols. New York: Macmillan Co., 1898.

Clark, Chester W. "The Foreign Policy of Prussia, 1858-1871." *Journal of Modern History* 6 (1934):444-450.

——— "Bismarck, Russia, and the Origins of the War of 1870." *Journal of Modern History* 14 (1942):195-208.

Correspondence of Wilhelm I and Bismarck. 2 vols. New York: Stokes, 1903.

Craig, Gordon A. *The Politics of the Prussian Army 1640-1945.* New York: Oxford University Press, 1955.

Darmstaedter, F. *Bismarck and the Creation of the Second Reich.* London: Methuen & Co., 1948.

Eyck, Erich. *Bismarck and the German Empire.* London: Allen & Unwin, 1950.

Falls, Cyril. *A Hundred Years of War.* London: Gerald Duckworth & Co., 1953.

Fletcher, Willard A. *The Mission of Vincent Benedetti to Berlin 1864-1870.* The Hague: Martinus Nijhoff, 1965.

Foot, Michael. "The Origins of the Franco-Prussian War and the Remaking of Germany." In *New Cambridge Modern History,* vol. 10. pp. 577-602. Cambridge: Cambridge University Press, 1960.

France, Ministry of Foreign Affairs. *Les Origines diplomatiques de la guerre de 1870-71.* Paris: G. Ficker, Imprimerie Nationale, 1910-1927.

Fuller, J. F. C. *A Military History of the Western World,* vol. 3. New York: Funk & Wagnalls Co., 1956.

Germany, Military History Section of the General Staff. *Der Deutsch-Französische Krieg, 1870-71.* 5 vols. Berlin: E. S. Mittler und Sohn, 1872-1881.

Giesberg, Robert Irwin. *The Treaty of Frankfort.* Philadelphia: University of Pennsylvania Press, 1966.

Hale, Lonsdale A. *The "People's War" in France 1870-71.* London: H. Rees, 1904.

Howard, Michael. *The Franco-Prussian War.* London: Rupert Hart-Davis, 1961.

Jerrold, William Blanchard. *The Life of Napoleon III.* 4 vols. London: Longmans, Green & Co., 1882.

Kissinger, Henry. "The White Revolutionary: Reflections on Bismarck." *Daedalus* 97 (summer 1968):888-924.

Liddell-Hart, B. H. "Armed Forces and the Art of War: Armies." In *New Cambridge Modern History,* vol. 10, pp. 302-330. Cambridge: Cambridge University Press, 1960.

Lord, R. H. *The Origins of the War of 1870: New Documents from the German Archives.* Cambridge, Mass.: Harvard University Press, 1924.

Macartney, C. A. *The Hapsburg Empire 1790-1918.* London: Weidenfeld and Nicolson, 1968.

Millman, Richard. *British Foreign Policy and the Coming of the Franco-Prussian War.* Oxford: Clarendon Press, 1965.

Mitchell, Allan. *Bismarck and the French Nation 1848-1890.* New York: Bobbs-Merrill Co., 1971.

Moltke, Count Helmuth von. *The Franco-German War of 1870-71.* 2 vols. New York: Harper & Bros., 1893.

——— *Moltke's Military Correspondence 1870-71.* Oxford: Clarendon Press, 1923.

Mosse, W. E. *The European Powers and the German Question 1848-1871.* Cambridge: Cambridge University Press, 1958.

Ollivier, Emile. *The Franco-Prussian War and its Hidden Causes.* Boston: Little, Brown & Co., 1912.

Pflanze, Otto. *Bismarck and the Development of Germany.* Princeton, N. J.: Princeton University Press, 1963.

Raymond, Dora Neill. *British Policy and Opinion During the Franco-Prussian War.* New York: Columbia University Press, 1921.

Robertson, C. Grant. *Bismarck.* New York: Henry Holt & Co., 1919.

Rose, Holland. "The Mission of M. Thiers to the Neutral Powers in 1870." *Transactions of the Royal Historical Society*, ser. 3, vol. 11 (1917):35-60.

Steefel, Lawrence D. *Bismarck, the Hohenzollern Candidacy, and the Origins of the Franco-German War of 1870.* Cambridge, Mass.: Harvard University Press, 1962.

Sybel, Heinrich von. *The Founding of the German Empire,* vols. 6 and 7. New York: Crowell, 1891.

Taylor, A. J. P. *The Struggle for Mastery in Europe 1848-1918.* Oxford: Clarendon Press, 1954.

——— *Bismarck, the Man and the Statesman.* New York: Vintage, 1955.

——— "International Relations" In *New Cambridge Modern History*, vol. 11, pp. 542-566. Cambridge: Cambridge University Press, 1960.

The Times (London). "Proposed Treaty between France and Prussia." 25 July 1870, p. 9.

Verdy du Vernois, Julius von. *With the Royal Headquarters in 1870-71.* London: Kegan Paul, Trench, Trulner & Co., 1897.

Washburne, E. B. *The Franco-German War and the Insurrection of the Commune: Correspondence of E. B. Washburne, Ambassador of the United States to France.* Washington, D. C.: U. S. Government Printing Office, 1878.

Notes to Chapter 7 - The Crimean War

1. Ramm and Sumner, "Crimean War," p. 468.

2. Falls, *Hundred Years of War*, p. 21.

3. An exception to the generalization about nineteenth-century diplomacy was the Congress of Vienna in 1814-1815, but this lasted only a few months. The diplomacy directly involved with the Crimean War extends over a period of more than four years. The extremely terse and compact

treatment of this period in the *New Cambridge Modern History* takes up twenty-two pages.

4. Falls provides a brief account of the military events of the Crimean War; Vulliamy's *Crimea* is a book-length treatment. The significance of the war in military history is summarized by Liddell-Hart in his essay, "Armed Forces and the Art of War."

5. One of the major consequences of the Crimean War, and hence of the escalation sequence that led to it, was a drastic reduction in the usefulness of the Concert of Europe system, which had been reasonably successful in maintaining the peace of Europe since 1815. But the technique of calling emergency international conferences in times of crisis, and other aspects of the Concert, were not invoked during the events that led to the Crimean War. Thereafter the Concert was taken less seriously. Three major wars were fought in Europe during the fifteen years following the end of the Crimean War, whereas there had been none for thirty-five years previously. Craig discusses this in his "System of Alliances and the Balance of Power," pp. 267-273. It is also a theme of Schroeder's *Austria, Great Britain, and the Crimean War.*

6. Marriott, *Eastern Question,* chap. 9; and Puryear, *England, Russia, and the Straits Question,* chaps. 1-4.

7. Marriott, chap. 9; Taylor, *Struggle for Mastery,* pp. 49-51; and Schmitt, "Diplomatic Preliminaries," p. 41.

8. Mange, *Near Eastern Policy of Napoleon III,* pp. 7-24; Gooch, "A Century of Historiography," p. 37; Marriott, pp. 252-254; Puryear, pp. 197-208; and Taylor, *Struggle,* pp. 48-49. Napoleon also thought that the regime of his predecessor, Louis Philippe, had fallen because of a lackluster foreign policy.

9. Temperley, *England and the Near East,* pp. 308-329; and Ramm and Sumner, p. 473.

10. Schmitt, p. 41; Gooch, pp. 38-39; Temperley, pp. 303-310; Ramm and Sumner, pp. 470-471. That Nesselrode did not know the full scope of Menshikov's instructions is indicated by Schmitt, p. 47; also Vitzthum von Eckstaedt, *St. Petersburg and London,* vol. 1, p. 38; and Maxwell, *Life and Letters of Clarendon,* vol. 2, p. 9.

11. From a dispatch from the British chargé in Constantinople to John Russell, at that time (December 1852) foreign minister in London. Quoted in Taylor, *Struggle,* p. 49.

12. Schmitt, pp. 45-47. Czar Nicholas had been considering a descent on Constantinople; the Menshikov mission may have been proposed to him by his foreign minister as a more pacific substitute (Ramm and Sumner, pp. 470-471).

13. Taylor, *Struggle,* pp. 53-54; Marriott, p. 266; Puryear, pp. 254, 267, and 281-283; and Gooch, p. 57.

14. Taylor, *Struggle,* pp. 51-52.

15. Ibid. That the czar's action was somewhat hasty is suggested by Temperley, p. 469.

16. Puryear, p. 244.

17. Material in this and the previous three paragraphs is drawn from Marriott, pp. 256-259; Ramm and Sumner, p. 476; Puryear, pp. 210-215 and 223-232; Temperley, pp. 299-300; Taylor, *Struggle,* pp. 50-51; and Gooch, pp. 54-55. As Gooch points out, the czar did not understand that an agreement he had made with Lord Aberdeen in 1844 would not necessarily bind the very different cabinets of 1853 and 1854.

St. Petersburg's impression of being able to rely on Britian was further enhanced by reports at the end of January that the English were preparing for the possibility of a direct attack from France, in the event of an Anglo-French crisis. Anglo-French cooperation in the Near East then would be unthinkable (Puryear, pp. 222-223). Schmitt argues (p. 58) that a stronger British move in the spring, as Palmerston wanted, would have shown the czar that English policy was changing.

18. Gooch, pp. 56-57; Mange, p. 24; Schmitt, p. 57; Schroeder, p. 42; and Vitzthum von Eckstaedt, vol. 1, p. 66.

19. The problem of "commitments" in deterrence, and some conventional misunderstandings thereof, are discussed in George and Smoke, *Deterrence in American Foreign Policy,* chaps. 3 and 19.

20. The extent to which Stratford Canning acted in ways calculated to make war more probable (and in ways that exceeded his instructions) on this and many other occasions is a matter of controversy among historians. It is certain that he disliked Russia intensely, and he may have welcomed a war against her by the time it was actually imminent; still, this is not the same as saying that he tried during 1853 to create a war. Some historians (Puryear, for example) argue that he cynically manipulated events in Constantinople to bring the great powers to war and that he must bear primary responsibility for the Crimean conflict. Many others (such as Temperley and Taylor) argue that Canning behaved judiciously and even tried to prevent war as best he could, but was later made into a scapegoat when the conflict proved costly to England. The question probably cannot be settled decisively, because too much of what occurred in Constantinople was never documented. It is true, at a minimum, that Aberdeen, Clarendon, and certain other members of the cabinet in London distrusted Canning (Temperley, p. 348; and Marriott, p. 263).

21. French policy of this time is discussed by Mange, pp. 28-30; Puryear, pp. 236-241; Taylor, *Struggle,* p. 53; and Fowler, *History of the War,* pp. 1-9.

22. Puryear, p. 244. Material in this paragraph and the one preceding is drawn mainly from Puryear, pp. 242-250.

23. The immediate motive for the decision was fear of a possible Rus-

sian surprise strike against Constantinople and, to quote Foreign Minister Clarendon, that it seemed "the least measure that will satisfy public opinion" (Schmitt, p. 55). Material in this paragraph is drawn also from Mange, pp. 29-30; and Puryear, pp. 268-277.

24. "That the British cabinet . . . acted precipitately . . . is shown by the fact that no opportunity was given Russia to make explanations as to why Menshikov had severed relations" (Puryear, p. 275).

25. The Russian occupation was the more inflexible of the two rigidities. As November approached, the Besika Bay squadrons might possibly have been divided, some of the ships advancing and others retreating. With an appropriate declaratory policy this might have had little effect, although the Russians were to complain sharply about the few ships that did proceed to Constantinople seriatim in this period. The principalities, however, were either completely occupied effectively or they were not; the action was not decomposable.

26. Schmitt, pp. 52 and 57-58; see also Puryear, pp. 232-233.

27. Since many of the Ottoman governmental organizations and officials left inadequate records or none at all, it is impossible to be certain what the full reasons for policy outcomes were. Events in Constantinople during this period are discussed by Temperley, pp. 339-342.

28. On the sources of Austrian policy see Schroeder, chap. 1; also Taylor, *Struggle*, p. 55; Schmitt, pp. 65-67; and Henderson, "Diplomatic Revolution of 1854," pp. 25-26.

29. Temperley, pp. 350-352; and Puryear, pp. 292-293.

30. Quoted by Temperley, p. 354.

31. The riots and their effect in London are discussed in detail by Temperley, pp. 350-358. See also Lane-Poole, *Life of Stratford Canning*, vol. 2, p. 307. The impact on this situation of the need to move the fleets out of Besika Bay before winter is discussed by Puryear, pp. 291-292, and by Taylor, *Struggle*, pp. 56-57, Puryear argues vehemently (pp. 292-295) that Stratford Canning was conspiring to enflame the Turks by bringing up a few of the fleet's minor vessels, but I have followed the majority opinion among historians and rejected this interpretation. Canning had full authority to bring up the entire fleet if he wished, indeed had been so ordered. If he was trying to enflame the Turks, why did he not do so?

32. The order to the Turkish forces to advance and engage the Russian enemy was sent from Constantinople late on the 18th or early on the morning of the 19th, so the entrance of the British squadron into the Dardanelles was not the literal signal for opening hostilities. But practically speaking, it was. The sultan and his principal advisers and subordinates learned on the 15th that Stratford Canning was calling the squadron to Constantinople.

Earlier the Turks had sent a message to Gorchakov, the general in command in the principalities, that demanded a Russian withdrawal. The

Turkish commander in the vicinity, who did not yet know that the Western squadrons would be arriving in Constantinople, interpreted Gorchakov's response as pacific. Ottoman policy-makers in the capital, who did know, interpreted the response as bellicose—or said they did. Their reply was the order to attack (Temperley, pp. 363-365).

33. Ramm and Sumner, p. 476; and Mange, p. 32. The Russian government made an official denial of its "violent interpretation" of the Vienna Note, but with its private document actually public knowledge, this denial could not be very credible (Schmitt, p. 38; and Temperley, p. 355).

34. Taylor, *Struggle*, pp. 57-58. On the English reaction see also Temperley, pp. 355-356.

35. Temperley, pp. 352-357; and Ramm and Sumner, p. 476. Schroeder (pp. 64-65) argues that the fleet would have been advanced even without the leaking of the "violent interpretation." Possibly so, but the timing was significant, and it seems likely that the leaked Russian document at least accelerated this decision.

36. Taylor, *Struggle*, p. 59.

37. Ibid., p. 57; and Puryear, p. 326.

38. Ramm and Sumner, p. 475; and Puryear, p. 273.

39. See George, Hall, and Simons, *Limits of Coercive Diplomacy*, chap. 5; also George and Smoke, pp. 561-565. An exception to the generalization in the text occurs when a deterring or coercing state has military options for exerting pressure on the same opponent at different points.

40. Taylor, *Struggle*, pp. 58-59; Temperley, pp. 366-367; Ramm and Sumner, p. 477; Puryear, p. 326; and Schroeder, p. 84.

41. Fowler, pp. 62-73.

42. Ibid., pp. 73-76; Temperley, pp. 368-371; and Ramm and Sumner, p. 477.

43. Ramm and Sumner, p. 477; and Fowler, pp. 73-76. The Turkish flotilla was inside Sinope harbor (Temperley, p. 371). The popular outcry over Sinope in the West was increased by the apparent excessive brutality of the operation, the Russians having shot Turkish survivors swimming toward shore, for instance; and by the fact that huge celebrations were promptly held in Russia.

44. Temperley, p. 375. The Western reaction to Sinope is discussed by Temperley, pp. 371-378; Ramm and Sumner, p. 477; and Mange, pp. 34-35.

45. Quoted by Temperley, p. 378.

46. Ramm and Sumner, pp. 477-478.

47. This is not to suggest that such a policy would have been either easy or certain. By January 1854 the British and French could not have acted with complete impartiality; they were too deeply convinced of the injustice of Russian actions and goals. Furthermore, as Schroeder points out (chaps.

5 and 6), the intracabinet politics in London were very intricate. Obtaining a sufficent consensus on *any* policy decision was a struggle in this period.

Yet a "mixed role" might have been feasible for the British. If skillfully handled, there was no necessary incompatibility between a policy of assisting the Ottomans (by means short of providing British troops) to regain their principalities but nothing more, and a policy of sealing the conflict into the limits of the principalities. By removing the Black Sea from the conflict and by preventing the Turks from renewing operations on the Caucasus front when spring came, the British and French might have succeeded in delimiting the conflict. Even a serious effort in this direction might have convinced the Russians, who still did not want a great-power war, that there were other possible outcomes to the situation. It might also have brought the Austrians into the problem with the active policy they were, in fact, to pursue shortly.

48. Temperley, pp. 381-383.

49. Mange, pp. 37-38; and Schmitt, pp. 52-53. In this period it was not the French, but some English cabinet members, notably Palmerston and Clarendon, who most favored a vigorous policy (Schroeder, pp. 128-136). Even Palmerston, however, thought that the Russians would "become reasonable" and reopen negotiations (Temperley, p. 382). Other principal cabinet members also believed at this time that peace could be preserved (Maxwell, vol. 2, p. 40).

50. Schroeder, pp. 164-168 and 178-181; and Ramm and Sumner, pp. 471-479. The initial objective of the allied expeditionary force was to protect Constantinople; an advance into the principalities would come only later. Hence, although Britain and France were "theoretically at war, they were a long way from fighting" (Taylor, *Struggle*, p. 63). Again there might have been time and opportunity to reopen negotiations, but now there was less inclination to do so because policy-makers in London, Paris, and St. Petersburg were expecting a "test of capabilities within very restrictive ground rules" (Alexander George's name for one kind of politico-military strategy: *Limits of Coercive Diplomacy*, chap. 1).

51. Taylor, *Struggle*, pp. 32-33; and Puryear, p. 331.

52. Henderson, p. 24; Ramm and Sumner, p. 479; Taylor, *Struggle,* pp. 49-51, 57, 60, and 64; Gooch, p. 41; and Marriott, p. 261.

53. Henderson, pp. 27-28; and Schroeder, pp. 187, 189-190, and 192.

54. Schroeder, pp. 183, 187-188, 193-194, and 203-204; and Maxwell, vol. 2, p. 41.

55. Liddell-Hart, p. 322; Schroeder, p. 205; and Mange, p. 40. An additional reason for moving quickly was that cholera was beginning to ravage the troops (Ramm and Sumner, p. 479). However, this would have been at least as good an argument in the other direction: for canceling the amphibious operation entirely and settling for naval actions.

56. Ramm and Sumner, p. 479. The Anglo-French troops could move faster by sea on troopships than the defending troops could march on land, and only a very few points were significantly garrisoned.

Bibliography for Chapter 7 - The Crimean War

Anderson, Olive. *The Liberal State at War: English Politics and Economics during the Crimean War.* New York: St. Martin's Press, 1967.

Ashley, Evelyn. *The Life of Viscount Palmerston.* London: Bentley & Sons, 1879.

Binkley, Robert C. *Realism and Nationalism.* New York: Harper & Bros., 1935.

Byrne, Leo G. *The Great Ambassador.* Columbus, Ohio: Ohio State University Press, 1964.

Caldwell, Robert G. "The Peace Congresses of the 19th Century." *Rice Institute Pamphlets*, vol. 5, no. 2 (April 1918).

Chesney, Kello. *Crimean War Reader.* London: Frederick Muller, 1960.

Craig, Gordon. "The System of Alliances and the Balance of Power." In *New Cambridge Modern History*, vol. 10, pp. 246-273. Cambridge: Cambridge University Press, 1960.

Falls, Cyril. *A Hundred Years of War.* London: Gerald Duckworth & Co., 1953.

Fowler, George. *A History of the War.* 2nd ed. London: Sampson Low & Co., 1855.

George, Alexander L., and Richard Smoke. *Deterrence in American Foreign Policy: Theory and Practice.* New York: Columbia University Press, 1964.

————, David K. Hall, and William E. Simons. *The Limits of Coercive Diplomacy.* Boston: Little, Brown & Co., 1971.

Gooch, Brison D. "A Century of Historiography on the Origins of the Crimean War." *American Historical Review* 62 (October 1956):33-58. Reprinted as *Publications in the Humanities*, no. 25. Cambridge, Mass.: MIT Press, n.d.

Gooch, G. P. "The Problem of the Near East." *Lectures on the History of the 19th Century.* F. A. Kirkpatrick, ed. Cambridge: Cambridge University Press, 1904.

Hamley, Edward. *The War in the Crimea.* London: Seely & Co., 1891.

Henderson, Gavin B. "The Diplomatic Revolution of 1854." *American Historical Review* 43 (1937):22-50.

———— *Crimean War Diplomacy and Other Historical Essays.* Glasgow: Jackson, Son & Co., 1947.

Kinglake, Alexander W. *The Invasion of the Crimea.* Edinburgh: William Blackwood & Sons, 1863.

Lane-Poole, Stanley. *The Life of the Right Honourable Stratford Canning.* 2 vols. London: Longmans, Green and Co., 1888.

Liddell-Hart, B. H. "Armed Forces and the Art of War: Armies." In *New Cambridge Modern History*, vol. 10, pp. 302-330. Cambridge: Cambridge University Press, 1960.

Mange, Alyce Edythe. *The Near Eastern Policy of the Emperor Napoleon III*. Urbana, Ill.: University of Illinois Press, 1940.

Marriott, John. *The Eastern Question*. 4th ed. Oxford: Clarendon Press, 1958.

Maxwell, Herbert. *The Life and Letters of George William Frederick Fourth Earl of Clarendon*. 2 vols. London: Edward Arnold, 1913.

Pemberton, Baring W. *Battles of the Crimean War*. London: Balsferd, 1962.

Puryear, Vernon J. *England, Russia, and the Straits Question 1844-1856*. Berkeley, Calif.: University of California Press, 1931.

Ramm, Agatha, and B. H. Sumner. "The Crimean War." In *New Cambridge Modern History*, vol. 10, pp. 468-492. Cambridge: Cambridge University Press, 1960.

Rodkey, Frederick S. "Lord Palmerston and the Rejuvenation of Turkey, 1830-41." *Journal of Modern History* 2 (1930):193-225.

Schmitt, Bernadotte E. "The Diplomatic Preliminaries of the Crimean War." *American Historical Review* 25 (1919):36-67.

Schroeder, Paul W. *Austria, Great Britain and the Crimean War*. Ithaca, N.Y.: Cornell University Press, 1972.

Southgate, Donald. *"The Most English Minister," The Policies and Politics of Palmerston*. New York: Macmillan Co. and St. Martin's Press, 1966.

Taylor, A. J. P. *Rumours of Wars*. London: Hamish Hamilton, 1952.

———— *The Struggle for Mastery in Europe 1848-1918*. Oxford: Clarendon Press, 1954.

Temperley, Harold. *England and the Near East: The Crimea*. London: Longmans, Green and Co., 1936.

Vitzthum von Eckstaedt, Count Carl. *St. Petersburg and London in the Years 1852-1864*. 2 vols. London: Longmans, Green and Co., 1887.

Vulliamy, C. E. *Crimea: The Campaign of 1854-56*. London: Jonathan Cape, 1939.

Woodham-Smith, Cecil. *The Reason Why*. New York: McGraw-Hill, 1953.

Notes to Chapter 8 - The Seven Years War

1. This is the title of chapter 18 of Savelle, *Origins of American Diplomacy.*

2. Dorn, *Competition for Empire*, p. 281.

3. Savory, *His Brittanic Majesty's Army in Germany*, p. i.

4. Quoted by Parkman, *Battle for North America*, p. 471.

5. A comprehensive study of escalation in this war should include at-

tention to the later accession to the conflict of Spain and Portugal. This aspect is excluded here, however, to avoid a cumbersome case history and because the decisions by Madrid and Lisbon depended heavily upon considerations of little relevance today.

Charles III, King of Spain, was a Bourbon and hence related by blood to Louis XV, the Bourbon king of France. This fact had not been sufficient to bring Spain into the war at once, but by 1761 the Spaniards were becoming concerned about the potential threat that British victories in the Caribbean and North America might pose to the Spanish Empire in the Americas. In addition, there were several long-standing grievances against the English, and a large number of fresh ones: British privateers, for example, enforcing the blockade of France, had taken goods from Spanish merchantmen in European waters and even seized whole ships. These factors, added to the dynastic link, were sufficient to cause the Spaniards to sign the so-called Family Compact in August 1761. Under its terms the French agreed not to terminate the war until Spanish objectives had been met.

For many decades friendship between Portugal and England, waxing periodically into military alliance, had been traditional for a number of reasons, notably a mutually profitable trade arrangement. When Spain allied with France, the two powers sought to wage economic warfare by closing as many European ports as possible to English commerce; to this end they ordered the Portuguese to cease trade with Britain. The Portuguese declined, were attacked across the Spanish frontier, and invoked the traditional alliance with Britain.

6. The following account of the perceptions in London and Paris of the origins of the conflict, and of events early in the process of intensification, is drawn mainly from Parkman, pp. 471-500; Dorn, pp. 281-288; and Gipson, *British Empire*, vol. 5, chaps. 10 and 11.

7. From Dinwiddie's message to the French of December 1753, quoted in Parkman, p. 488.

8. Parkman, p. 500.

9. Higonnet, "Origins of the Seven Years' War," pp. 68-69; Gaxotte, *Louis XV and His Times*, p. 193. The French were also in possession of a copy of the surrender document from Fort Necessity, signed by Washington, which confessed to the "assassination" of a French military officer. Washington, who knew no French, thought he had merely admitted killing the officer.

10. Osgood, *American Colonies*, pp. 356-357. This and the next three paragraphs are drawn mainly from Dorn, pp. 287-290; Gipson, vol. 6, pp. 54-60; Corbett, *England in the Seven Years War*, vol. 1, chap. 2; and Charteris, *William Augustus Duke of Cumberland*, chaps. 9-12.

11. Corbett, vol. 1, p. 31; Braddock's orders are described on pp. 25-26. On French policy at this point, see Higonnet, pp. 81-83.

12. Corbett, vol. 1, pp. 41-50. As late as February, policy-makers in

London and Paris almost unanimously expected no war (Higonnet, pp. 71 and 82-83). London underestimated the strength of the force that the French would commit and initially sent Boscawen west to wait for it with a squadron weaker then the French fleet that actually sailed. When the size of the flotilla departing Brest was discovered, the admiralty quickly sent Boscawen reinforcements.

13. Gipson provides a dramatic account of the details of Boscawen's mission and encounter with the French (vol. 6, pp. 101-104). See also Corbett, vol. 1, pp. 53-56.

14. Gaxotte, p. 193; Dorn, pp. 289-290; and Corbett, vol. 1, pp. 63-67.

15. Thistlethwaite, "Rivalries in America," p. 538; Wrong, *Rise and Fall of New France*, vol. 2, p. 761; and Dorn, pp. 290-291.

16. Dorn lucidly explains the somewhat complicated Diplomatic Revolution of 1756 in *Competition for Empire* (chap. 7). On the penalty for offensive action see, for instance, Corbett, vol. 1, pp. 20, 23, and 41.

17. Corbett, vol. 1, p. 27.

18. "Before the crisis of the summer of 1754, Newcastle and his colleagues would have liked to limit the action of the mother country to two well-defined objectives: financing the building and maintenance of a fort at the forks of the Ohio and encouraging a union of the colonies that would have made it possible for them to resist Canadian offensives" (Fregault, *Canada*, p. 75).

19. Dorn, pp. 286-287; Cobban, *History of Modern France*, vol. 1, p. 69; Savelle, "Diplomatic Preliminaries," p. 20; and Thistlethwaite, p. 530.

20. For instance, see Gaxotte, pp. 192-193.

21. Thistlethwaite, p. 537.

22. Charteris, pp. 121-122; Corbett, vol. 1, p. 16; and Higonnet, p. 72.

23. Gaxotte, pp. 193-194; Savelle, *Origins*, pp. 399-400, and "Diplomatic Preliminaries," p. 20.

24. Dorn, pp. 251-268; Gipson, vol. 5, pp. 31-32, and vol. 6, pp. 15-16.

25. Savelle, "Diplomatic Preliminaries," p. 125; Higonnet, p. 72; Parkman, pp. 472-473; Fregault, p. 20; and Charteris, p. 125.

26. Fregault, pp. 31, 69-70, and 76. In addition, the French sought to protect their access to an important settlement of theirs in what is now Illinois, which they perceived the English to be threatening (Thistlethwaite, p. 531).

27. Charteris, p. 125; and Higonnet, pp. 60-65 and 84.

28. This is the title of John Tebbel's condensation of Parkman's multivolume *France and England in North America*.

29. Dorn, p. 287. See also Corbett, vol. 1, p. 31. The British, for their part, offered several negotiating proposals to the French, that would have denied the Ohio territory to the English Americans for an indefinite time. See also Higonnet, p. 71.

30. Corbett, vol. 1, p. 26; Higonnet, p. 68.

31. On the commission, see Gipson, vol. 6, chap. 10; and Savelle, *Origins*, pp. 391-395, and "Diplomatic Preliminaries," pp. 22-25. The commission was briefly revived again later at French insistence, with no significant result. For most of its life, one of the British commissioners was William Shirley, governor of the colony of Massachusetts and one of the most aggressive of the English Americans; one of the French commissioners was Marquis La Jonquièrre, ex-governor of New France and one of the fathers of the scheme for fortifying the Ohio. Their failure to come to a meeting of minds is scarcely surprising. At the same time, neither they nor anyone else involved with the commission had first-hand knowledge of the Ohio area, nor much of the other disputed territories. On the lack of any felt need for urgency, see Higonnet, p. 68.

32. See Gipson, vol. 5, chap. 10.

33. Savelle, *Origins*, pp. 395-399; and Gipson, vol. 5, chap. 10.

34. Higonnet, pp. 81-89; and Savelle, *Origins*, pp. 399-418. The month, almost, between the death of Albemarle and the return of Mirepoix to London, during which neither power had an ambassador in the other capital, was a particularly critical month during which negotiation should have been pressed (Higonnet, p. 69).

35. Corbett, vol. 1, p. 16. Newcastle's hope was not an unreasonable one. After learning of Duquesne's high level of activity in the Ohio region in 1753, but before the battles of 1754, Versailles decided to dismiss Duquense for going too far (Higonnet, p. 67).

36. Savelle, *Origins*, pp. 406-407; and Gipson, vol. 6, pp. 335-338. Gipson, who discusses the plan in some detail, concludes that it "might have given the [American] continent a long period of peace" (p. 335).

37. Corbett, vol. 1, pp. 41-42.

38. The likelihood of this sequence is argued by Higonnet (pp. 87-88). He also presents evidence (pp. 85-86) that during the previous month (February) policy-makers in both capitals, because of certain false information, had temporarily become overoptimistic about the prospects of a peaceful resolution through diplomacy and hence did not negotiate as energetically as the situation in fact demanded.

39. Fregault, pp. 36-41; and Thistlethwaite, p. 536.

40. Wrong, vol. 2, pp. 741, 745, and 750; and Parkman, p. 477.

41. Gipson, vol. 5 chap. 11; and Charteris, pp. 127-128.

42. Charteris, pp. 118 and 134. The British expected that the Braddock mission would not ignite a general war, but there is no evidence that they gave much consideration to French options for a *limited* military response.

43. Fregault, pp. 63 and 95; Parkman, pp. 507 and 518-519.

44. Corbett, vol. 1, pp. 42-43.

45. Gipson, vol. 5, pp. 335-338; Dorn, pp. 284-285; and Wrong, vol. 2, p. 745.

46. Parkman, pp. 472-473.

47. Higonnet makes the same point (p. 65).

48. Robson, "Armed Forces and the Art of War," p. 173; and Parkman, pp. 513-522.

49. An obvious counterpart is the American decision to send quantities of regular forces to Southeast Asia in the mid-1960s.

50. Corbett, vol. 1, p. 67; and Fregault, p. 89.

51. Corbett, vol. 1, pp. 37-39. Another ingredient of this expectation was the cabinet's belief at this time that Britain's alliance relationships with other European powers were improving and that therefore it was less likely that the French would find it advantageous to begin a war.

52. Gipson, vol. 6, p. 117; and Corbett, vol. 1, pp. 57-59. Corbett also points out the failure of the cabinet to give Admiral Boscawen more careful orders.

53. Corbett, vol. 1, pp. 60-62.

54. Higonnet, p. 59. There was a somewhat similar alarmist report from Dinwiddie at about the same time (pp. 72-73).

55. Ibid., p. 74; see also pp. 69 and 73.

56. Ibid., p. 77.

57. Cobban, vol. 1, chaps. 1 and 2; Dorn, pp. 23-25; and Higonnet, pp. 73, 75, 81, and 83.

58. To repeat again a phrase employed by several historians, the reputation of Newcastle has been handed down from generation to generation in a blaze of derision. Universally he is considered one of the least able prime ministers Great Britain has ever had. The diplomatic policies of his cabinet, however, have been judged less inept than those of Louis XV's regime in this period. See Lecky, *History of England*, vol. 2, pp. 345-351; Corbett, vol. 1, pp. 62-68; and Dorn, pp. 293-294.

Bibliography for Chapter 8 - The Seven Years War

Bird, Harrison. *Battle for a Continent.* New York: Oxford University Press, 1965.

Butterfield, Herbert. *The Reconstruction of an Historical Episode: The History of the Enquiry into the Origins of the Seven Years War.* Glasgow: Jackson, Son & Co., 1951.

Charteris, Evan. *William Augustus Duke of Cumberland and the Seven Years War.* London: Hutchinson & Co., 1925.

Cobban, Alfred. *A History of Modern France.* Vol. 1, *1715-1799.* London: Penguin Books, 1957.

Corbett, Julian. *England in the Seven Years War.* 2 vols. London: Longmans, Green and Co., 1907.

Dorn, Walter L. *Competition for Empire.* New York: Harper & Bros., 1940.

Fregault, Guy. *Canada: The War of the Conquest.* Translated by Margaret Cameron. Toronto: Oxford University Press, 1969.

Gaxotte, Pierre. *Louis XV and His Times.* Translated by J. Lewis May. Philadelphia: J. B. Lippincott Co., 1934.

Gipson, Lawrence Henry. *The British Empire Before the American Revolution.* Vol. 5, *Zones of International Friction.* New York: Alfred A. Knopf, 1942.

———— *The British Empire Before the American Revolution.* Vol. 6, *The Great War for the Empire: The Years of Defeat, 1754-1757.* New York: Alfred A. Knopf, 1946.

Hamilton, Edward P. *The French and Indian Wars.* Garden City, N.Y.: Doubleday & Co., 1962.

Higonnet, Patrice L. R. "The Origins of the Seven Years' War." *Journal of Modern History* 40 (1968):57-90.

Kaplan, Herbert H. *Russia and the Outbreak of the Seven Years War.* Berkeley, Calif.: University of California Press, 1968.

Lecky, William. *A History of England in the Eighteenth Century.* 8 vols. New York: Appleton, 1878.

Lokke, Carl L. *France and the Colonial Question.* New York: Columbia University Press, 1924.

Namier, L. B. *England in the Age of the American Revolution.* London: Macmillan Co., 1930.

Osgood, Herbert. *The American Colonies in the Eighteenth Century.* New York: Columbia University Press, 1924.

Parkman, Francis. *The Battle for North America.* Abridged and edited by John Tebbell from the works of Francis Parkman. Garden City, N. Y.: Doubleday & Co., 1948.

Petrie, Charles. *Diplomatic History, 1713-1933.* New York: Macmillan Co., 1949.

Robson, Eric. "Armed Forces and the Art of War." In *New Cambridge Modern History,* vol. 7, pp. 163-190. Cambridge: Cambridge University Press, 1957.

Samuel, Sigmund. *The Seven Years War in Canada.* Toronto: Ryerson, 1934.

Savelle, Max. "Diplomatic Preliminaries of the Seven Years War in America." *Canadian Historical Review* 20 (1939):17-36.

———— *The Origins of American Diplomacy: The International History of Anglo-America, 1492-1763.* New York: Macmillan Co., 1967.

Savory, Reginald. *His Britannic Majesty's Army in Germany During the Seven Years War.* Oxford: Clarendon Press, 1966.

Sherrad, O. A. *Lord Chatham; Pitt and the Seven Years War.* London: Bodley Head, 1955.

Thistlethwaite, Frank. "Rivalries in America: The North American Continent." In *New Cambridge Modern History,* vol. 7, pp. 500-513. Cambridge: Cambridge University Press, 1957.

Wood, William. *The Fight for Canada.* London: Archibald Constable, 1904.

Wrong, George M. *The Rise and Fall of New France.* 2 vols. New York: Macmillan Co., 1928.

Notes to Chapter 9 - On the Assessment of Conflicts

1. *Parametric variables* might be a more precise, or at least more formal, term. I avoid it because *parameter* has lost some of its original meaning and become something of an all-purpose jargon word.

In addition to the two aspects of escalation mentioned here, decisions about escalations are made through complex policy-making processes. This aspect will be taken up later.

2. *Strategy of Conflict*, pp. 3-4.

3. The extent to which decision-makers are or need to be *consciously aware* of the bargaining aspect of war limitation and escalation is a slightly ambiguous area in Schelling's theory of limited war. To the extent that the theory is viewed as prescriptive, clearly they must be quite consciously aware. To the extent that it is viewed as descriptive, the issue is a little more complicated.

Presumably the process of selecting saliencies as limits occurs about as readily among those who do not realize that this is their criterion of selection as among those who do. If only a single saliency is available, one does not need to know the principle to be likely to hit on the saliency. If, as is usual, multiple saliencies are available, it is not clear that players who attempt to coordinate their behavior consciously by that criterion will do a great deal better than those who attempt to coordinate their behavior without any conscious criteria. In its general form Schelling's saliency principle, as he points out, is a psychological hypothesis about subconscious pattern recognition, of a type familiar to gestalt psychologists.

The way belligerent nations maneuver for advantageous ground rules in war can be usefully analyzed as a tacit bargaining process, whether or not decision-makers are highly conscious of this process. And determining empirically in any particular past case how conscious of it policy-makers actually were is difficult. Both in the interpretation of historical documents and in the interviewing of still-living policy-makers, the exact definition and wording of the research questions are likely to have a considerable effect on whether one reaches a generally affirmative or generally negative conclusion. Certainly a great many diplomats and other policy-makers in the pre-World War II eras understood that both the limitation and the expansion of armed conflicts required maneuvering in a context that included elements of conflict and of cooperation (tacit, or even sometimes explicit). But they would not have used, as Schelling does, the words *tacit bargaining*, or even *bargaining*, and of course never *nonzero sum game.*

The specific component in the tacit bargaining that Schelling calls *manipulation of risk*, however, must be mostly or entirely conscious. If one is not conscious of it, one may still escalate in order (among other goals) to increase the enemy's risks. But the deliberate heightening of a *shared* risk for its deterrent and compellent value, and as a way of demonstrating resolve and commitment, must be conscious. Again, many policy-makers of the pre-World War II eras were aware of this aspect of strategy, nonverbally or in different language, and usually without bothering to isolate this aspect of their policy decisions for special attention in documentation.

The risk being manipulated and exploited certainly does not have to be a hazard to ultimate survival, as Schelling points out with his example from classical Greece, cited earlier. One does not need global holocaust as the hazard for the logic of risk manipulation to function. At most times in history there has been a possible danger, if wars got far enough out of hand, of very great destruction to the polity. Even the personal danger to policy-makers themselves—that if a war goes badly they may be overthrown either by the enemy or by a disgusted domestic populace—is probably enough to bring the logic of risk manipulation into play in the dynamics of escalation. The manipulation of risk, then, is potentially an explanatory factor throughout the period embraced by the case studies in this book.

Since, historically, decision-makers rarely have singled this factor out for special mention, the researcher must deduce its presence or absence from the language they did employ and from context. The deliberate heightening of a shared risk for its bargaining value was unquestionably part of the Anglo-French strategy in the step-by-step advancement of their fleets in 1853. Mussolini was prepared through most of the Spanish Civil War to accept substantially higher risks of a European war than Hitler was, or than the British and French were. Exploiting this, he sharply escalated the Italian involvement in Spain in the expectation—which proved correct—that he could win a competition in risk-taking. The fascist powers' later interventions in the Spanish Civil War, after Mussolini and Hitler reassessed downward the British and French risk acceptance, also involved risk manipulation—at least in the sense that these interventions included the kind of pre-emptive deterrence associated with risk manipulation. They were steps that deterred Western response because the only feasible counterreactions would generate a greater shared risk of world war than the British and French would accept. However, the escalation sequence leading to the Seven Years War did not include much risk manipulation in Schelling's sense, although it was heavily demonstrative, because until about the time Admiral Boscawen sailed, both sides assessed the probability of a general war as fairly low.

4. Nor did French policy-makers attempt, except perhaps marginally, to exploit the change in tenor of French feeling for demonstrative or risk-

manipulative purposes, perhaps because they recognized that the German commitment, motivation, or will was just as great and was ample to continue the war even with its changed character.

It might appear that because the escalations were the consequence of the German demand and the French refusal, they involved bargaining, after all, over the terms of peace. However, this is to confuse bargaining in a wider sense, that involves explicit negotiation to end wars, with the narrower and more technical sense of bargaining meant by Schelling and employed in this book—tacit, coercive bargaining to find and impose advantageous yet probably stable limits to ongoing wars.

The German siege of Paris, incidentally, was intended as sheer coercion to compel a French surrender on German terms, not as a strategic heightening of risk; and not, except marginally, as a demonstration of motivation and will.

5. May, "Nature of Foreign Policy." The significance of latent objectives in escalation processes is also discussed by Fairbanks in "War Limiting."

6. The U. S. decision to elevate its war objectives in the Korean conflict in the autumn of 1950 is analyzed in some detail in George and Smoke, *Deterrence in American Foreign Policy* (chap. 7). On that decision see also, in particular, Neustadt, *Presidential Power*; Lichterman, "To the Yalu and Back"; and Spanier, *Truman-MacArthur Controversy*. The judgment that the United Nations could have obtained somewhat better terms in the autumn of 1950 than it eventually did cannot, of course, be proved but is widely held.

7. In the sequence leading to the Seven Years War, decision-makers on both sides held graduated objectives and had important perceptions of the opponent's minimum and maximum objectives. Bismarck's objectives were somewhat less graduated, but not unitary: in 1866, a minimum of Schleswig-Holstein and a maximum of North German hegemony (and after Königgrätz, slightly more); in 1870, a minimum of German victory that would go far toward unifying the military alliance in a new Reich and a maximum of creating the Reich during the war. In addition, Bismarck in 1870 may well have entertained territorial aims at French expense as part of his maximal objectives from the first.

8. The national interest is a complicated concept, because it involves both relatively objective relationships and values, comparatively unchanging in the short run, and quite subjective evaluations of those relationships and values by policy-makers, alterable at will.

Indeed, it is even more complicated than this implies. Consider, for instance, one historian's interesting summary of British policy during the Franco-Prussian War: "The Government had successfully defended Britain's interests on the Continent by restricting their scope" (Millman, *British Foreign Policy*, p. 218). The extent to which national interests may be threatened by a crisis or war abroad is not only a matter for interpretation by policy-makers but something that can actually be adjusted by them, within limits. How different might have been the history of recent U. S. foreign affairs if in the mid-1960s Washington had adopted a policy of "defending American interests in Southeast Asia by restricting their scope!"

There has not yet been a fully adequate analysis of the complications that the difficult but unavoidable concept of national interest poses for policy-makers. A recent brief overview of the question is "The Concept of National Interest" by George and Keohane. Other treatments appear in appendix A of Rostow's *United States in the World Arena*, in Bloomfield's *United Nations and U. S. Foreign Policy*, in the Sprouts' *Foundations of International Politics*, and in Brodie's essay, "Vital Interests."

"The" national interest as a general organizing principle for the explanation of international politics is the centerpiece of the so-called Realist school in international relations theory. But here the concept has remained, on the whole, abstract and nonoperationalized. The Realist school has not yet succeeded in providing many useful criteria for policy-makers' assessment of national interests in specific contexts. See Wolfers' essay "National Security as an Ambiguous Symbol," in his book, *Discord and Collaboration*.

9. Under certain circumstances the perceived legitimacy or illegitimacy of some step may be important. In the Franco-Prussian War, for instance, the siege of Paris was generally perceived as legitimate and did not increase the danger of outside intervention. Under other circumstances the overall simplicity of an escalation pattern may be important. The complexity of the Crimean escalation, for instance, hindered sound decision-making.

In arena wars, sealing off combustible material and preventing escalation along lines of connection are two elements that help control escalation. Two others are suggested by the case studies. Policy-makers evidently need to feel that they can bring to bear within the arena sufficient capabilities to give reasonable prospect of attaining their objectives. None of the interveners found Spain too distant to be able to deliver and employ forces there in the hopes of attaining their objectives. But in the Seven Years War the British considered themselves militarily unable to recapture the Ohio region if the French reinforced Canada; intercepting those reinforcements or abandoning the objective therefore became the only two options available. In the Crimean War, it was *after* the Western expeditionary force had gotten bogged down on the Crimean peninsula that the British and French tried hardest to expand the war to the Baltic with a Swedish involvement; earlier they had expected a prompt victory in the original arena.

Secondly, it appears that the geography should embrace the belligerents' significant objectives, as well as provide the arena for their fighting. In the Spanish Civil War and both Prussian wars it did. In the Crimean War the original arenas of hostilities did not include the Russian naval bases that became the primary Anglo-French objective. In the 1750s the minimum objectives of the French and British were confined to the Ohio area but their maximum ones were not, and each increasingly saw the other as pursuing maximum objectives.

Incidentally, all four of these "prerequisites" were fulfilled in the Korean and Vietnam wars and in the Arab-Israeli wars of 1956, 1967, and 1973.

10. After listing some five or six other reasons why the Paris Peace Conference of 1919 was substantially a failure, from the long-term Western point of view, Kennan observes that "all this operated against the background of a great and pervasive conceptual error, which was the inability to assess correctly the significance and the consequences of the war in which Europe had just been engaged" (*Russia and the West*, p. 149). One of Kennan's other reasons, incidentally, also comes under the heading of conceptual failure as I use it here—what he calls "being able to envisage and apprehend the spirit of another society" (p. 148).

Joseph de Rivera also uses the term *conceptual failure* and quotes this passage in his book, *The Psychological Dimension of Foreign Policy* (chap. 3), as part of a valuable discussion of such failures and some conditions that tend to discourage them.

11. Closest to straightforward intelligence failures in a simple sense were the very poor estimates the Austrians made before June 1866 of Prussian (and also French) military power, and the inadequate evaluations by the French before July 1870 of certain Prussian military capabilities, notably artillery and logistics. Even in these cases, the most important source of the intelligence failures lay in conceptual lapses in Vienna and Paris—policy-makers' inability or unwillingness to challenge their own sanguine assumptions. In both the Austrian and French cases, some intelligence reports that might have given warning of the true situation were available. One very accurate set of reports was ignored by the French government before 1870. Various reports received by the Austrians before 1866 and pointing, at least, in the right direction were the source of a mounting anxiety in some Austrian military circles—an anxiety, however, that had not yet reversed the confident expectations of victory entertained by the government as a whole.

12. Many scholars, analysts, and experienced policy-makers have pointed out the importance of adequate images, models, or perceptions of other nations' behavior and its sources, to sound decision-making in foreign and military policy. In particular, ingredients similar to those listed in Table 7 are discussed analytically by Wohlstetter, "Cuba and Pearl Harbor;" Jervis, *Perception and Misperception* and "Hypotheses on Misperception"; Pruitt, "Definition of the Situation"; Rothstein, *Planning, Prediction, and Policymaking*, chap. 4; and de Rivera, *Psychological Dimension of Foreign Policy*, chaps. 2 and 3.

Some of the ingredients listed here are also mentioned in George and Smoke (see especially the table of components in U. S. intelligence failures, pp. 584-585).

13. In the months preceding the outbreak of the Austro-Prussian War, Austrian policy-makers almost certainly could have made better decisions had they had more time. On the other hand, the Prussians had exactly as much or as little time, and their policy-making was highly successful. This instance, therefore, should really be laid at the door of the more general analytic failures and the pathological policy-making processes in Vienna, not at the door of the time factor.

In the late fall of 1853, British policy-makers were pressed by time in making a decision on their response to Sinope. Even so, several weeks passed between the arrival of the battle news in England and the transmission of orders to the squadrons to enter the Black Sea, time in which analytic factors discussed in the case study could have received recognition and did not. Officials in London, though, undoubtedly felt a real sense of urgency during those weeks.

One of the many advantages of studying cases dating from before World War II rather than more contemporary ones is that, with some important exceptions like the outbreak of World War I, time pressures generally were much less in earlier eras. With judicious selection, then, this element can be largely factored out; other aspects of escalation dynamics will then be more visible.

14. Such a review, drawing on literature current through 1974, appears in George et al., "The Use of Information."

It is impossible to do justice, in exploratory research such as this, to all the factors that can come into play in decision-making, or to the relevant literature. In this note I give only a sampling of representative sources that discuss impediments to the adequate use of information. Wohlstetter's *Pearl Harbor: Warning and Decision* is a classic analysis of foreign and military policy-makers' failure to recognize and act on available information, and she shows that a number of elements were involved: among them intraservice and interservice rivalries, personalities, "noise," and organizational problems in the management of highly sensitive information. She also emphasizes, as does Schelling in his introduction to the book, what she calls "the very human tendency to pay attention to the signals that support current expectations" (p. 392).

Many writers have pointed out the significance of individuals' prior beliefs, and the inertia of their basic assumptions, to their recognition or nonrecognition of information. In the foreign policy-making context, this has been addressed in particular by Jervis in both his books; by May, *"Lessons" of the Past*; by Rothstein, chap. 4; and by Wohlstetter, "Cuba and Pearl Harbor." Receptivity to indicators of imminent crisis or attack is a theme of the latter article, and of chap. 20 of George and Smoke. Deutsch

mentions "the rejection of information that does not fit accepted preconditions" in his discussion of escalation and its control in *The Analysis of
International Relations* (p. 148). The psychological tendency to try to
maintain "cognitive consistency" will be taken up in the next chapter. In a
very different way, the problem that rigid assumptions may pose to the
interpretation of other states' behavior is a theme of Allison's *Essence of
Decision.*

15. The argument presented here is a somewhat delicate one, because if
slightly oversimplified in one direction it appears to be very obvious, and if
slightly oversimplified in another direction it appears to be clearly false.

I am not advancing the very obvious idea that policy errors occur because human beings make mistakes; and after all, governments are made
up of human beings. In this chapter, and in a different way in the next, I
am trying to identify closely the particular classes of analytic errors that are
most significant in failure to control escalation.

I am also not advancing the clearly false notion that hindrances in policy-
making caused by bureaucratic politics, organizational procedures, and
the like are easily reduced to very modest levels if only high-level policy-
makers want badly enough to reduce them. There is a whole body of literature, previously referred to and partially cited, which demonstrates in
depth that these aspects of decision-making are deeply imbedded in governmental processes and that reducing their malevolent effect is always
difficult, sometimes almost impossible.

At the same time, it is perfectly plain that in some times and places these
malevolent effects are very much less than in other times and places. The
reasons for comparative improvement include specially able personnel, an
elusive but real quality that can be called management skill, good luck,
learning by trial and error, and sometimes in recent decades the application
of knowledge from the political and management sciences. Another reason,
which may be particularly relevant in the context of controlling escalation,
is effort on the part of responsible officials to be more than ordinarily demanding and imaginative about analytical possibilities, followed by more
than ordinarily active effort to find or tap information relevant to those
possibilities.

The idea that a conceptual failure is involved when the "full extent of the
processes' malevolent consequences [is] not comprehended until they
materialize" is, in a sense, the premise underlying efforts by many students
of bureaucratic politics to convince decision-makers of the central importance of governmental processes, and to find tools to give them for
improving the processes. (See, for instance, the recommendations of Allison and Halperin in "Bureaucratic Politics.") The entire effort to identify
and elucidate "Models Two and Three" might also be said to be itself a
"rational," hence in a sense "Model One," activity.

16. On Roosevelt's technique, see Neustadt, pp. 157-158. For a valuable

assessment of the strengths and weaknesses of the competitive approach to policy-making, consult Johnson, *Managing the White House.*

President Kennedy's encouragement of diverse opinions among his advisers during the Cuban missile crisis has been widely noted, usually with approval. See, for instance, Johnson's book, Janis' *Victims of Groupthink* (chap. 6), and George's "The Case for Multiple Advocacy." The degree of competitiveness may vary. As an example, Johnson distinguishes between a highly competitive decision-making system and a somewhat different system that involves moderate competitiveness (which he terms collegial).

17. Allison and Halperin, "Bureaucratic Politics"; Halperin, *Bureaucratic Politics and Foreign Policy;* George, "The Case for Multiple Advocacy."

18. Steinbruner, *Cybernetic Theory of Decision.*

19. Lindblom, "The Science of Muddling Through." For broader applications of incrementalism in political decision-making, see also Lindblom's *Intelligence of Democracy* and Braybrooke and Lindblom, *A Strategy of Decison.*

20. Coulam, *Illusions of Choice.*

21. Introductions to systems thinking include Laszlo, *Systems View of the World;* Churchman, *The Systems Approach;* and Emery, *Systems Thinking.*

22. The U. S. intelligence and analytic failure in the period just preceding the Cuban missile crisis is discussed at greater length in George and Smoke (chap. 15). The brief treatment here is drawn from that discussion.

Bibliography for Chapter 9 - On the Assessment of Conflicts

Allison, Graham T. *Essence of Decision.* Boston: Little, Brown and Co., 1971.

———— and Morton Halperin. "Bureaucratic Politics: A Paradigm and Some Policy Implications." In Richard H. Ullman and Raymond Tanter, eds., *Theory and Practice in International Relations.* Princeton, N. J.: Princeton University Press, 1972. Originally published in *World Politics* 24, supplement, spring 1972, 40-79.

Bloomfield, Lincoln. *The United Nations and U. S. Foreign Policy.* Boston: Little, Brown and Co., 1960.

Braybrooke, David, and Charles E. Lindblom. *A Strategy of Decision.* New York: Free Press, 1963.

Brodie, Bernard. "Vital Interests: By Whom and How Determined?" In Frank Trager and Philip Kronenberg, eds., *National Security and American Society.* Lawrence, Kans.: University Press of Kansas, 1973.

Churchman, C. West. *The Systems Approach.* New York: Dell Books, 1968.

Coulam, Robert. *Illusions of Choice.* Princeton, N. J.: Princeton University Press, 1977.

de Rivera, Joseph H. *The Psychological Dimension of Foreign Policy.* Columbus, Ohio: Charles E. Merrill Books, 1968.

Deutsch, Karl W. *The Analysis of International Relations.* Englewood Cliffs, N. J.: Prentice-Hall, 1968.

Emery, F. E. *Systems Thinking.* Harmondsworth, U. K.: Penguin Books, 1969.

Fairbanks, Charles. "War-Limiting, an Historical Analysis." In Klaus Knorr, ed., *Historical Dimensions of National Security Problems.* Princeton, N. J.: Princeton University Press, 1976.

George, Alexander L. "The Case for Multiple Advocacy in Making Foreign Policy." *American Political Science Review* 66 (1972):751-785.

—— and Robert Keohane. "The Concept of National Interest: Uses and Limitations." In Alexander L. George et al., "The Use of Information." Appendix D, Report of the Commission on the Organization of the Government for the Conduct of Foreign Policy (Murphy Commission). Washington, D. C.: U. S. Government Printing Office, 1975 and 1976.

—— and Richard Smoke. *Deterrence in American Foreign Policy: Theory and Practice.* New York: Columbia University Press, 1974.

—— et al. "The Use of Information." Appendix D, Report of the Commission of the Organization of the Government for the Conduct of Foreign Policy (Murphy Commission). Washington, D. C.: U. S. Government Printing Office, 1975 and 1976.

Halperin, Morton. *Bureaucratic Politics and Foreign Policy.* Washington, D. C.: Brookings Institution, 1974.

Janis, Irving. *Victims of Groupthink.* Boston: Houghton Mifflin Co., 1972.

Jervis, Robert. "Hypotheses on Misperception." *World Politics* 20 (1968): 454-479.

—— *The Logic of Images in International Relations.* Princeton, N. J.: Princeton University Press, 1970.

—— *Perception and Misperception in International Relations.* Princeton, N. J.: Princeton University Press, 1976.

Johnson, Richard T. *Managing the White House.* New York: Harper & Row, 1974.

Kennan, George F. *Russia and the West Under Lenin and Stalin.* Boston: Little, Brown and Co., 1960.

Laszlo, Ervin. *The Systems View of the World.* New York: George Braziller, 1972.

Lichterman, Martin. "To the Yalu and Back." In Harold Stein, ed., *American Civil-Military Decisions: A Book of Case Studies.* Tuscaloosa, Ala.: University of Alabama Press, 1963.

Lindblom, Charles E. "The Science of Muddling Through." *Public Administration Review* 19 (1959):79-88.

—— *The Intelligence of Democracy.* New York: Free Press, 1965.

May, Ernest R. "The Nature of Foreign Policy: The Calculated versus the

Axiomatic." *Daedalus* (fall 1962), 653-667.

———— "Lessons" of the Past. New York: Oxford University Press, 1974.

Millman, Richard. *British Foreign Policy and the Coming of the Franco-Prussian War*. Oxford: Clarendon Press, 1965.

Neustadt, Richard E. *Presidential Power*. New York: John Wiley & Sons, 1960.

Pruitt, Dean G. "Definition of the Situation as a Determinant of International Action." In Herbert C. Kelman, *International Behavior*. New York: Holt, Rinehart and Winston, 1965.

Rostow, W. W. *The United States in the World Arena*. New York: Harper & Bros., 1960

Rothstein, Robert L. *Planning, Prediction and Policymaking in Foreign Affairs*. Boston: Little, Brown and Co., 1972.

Schelling, Thomas C. *The Strategy of Conflict*. Cambridge, Mass.: Harvard University Press, 1960.

———— *Arms and Influence*. New Haven, Conn.: Yale University Press, 1966.

Spanier, John W. *The Truman-MacArthur Controversy and the Korean War*. Cambridge, Mass.: Harvard University Press, 1959.

Sprout, Harold, and Margaret Sprout. *Foundations of International Politics*. Princeton, N. J.: Van Nostrand Co., 1962.

Steinbruner, John D. *The Cybernetic Theory of Decision*. Princeton, N. J.: Princeton University Press, 1974.

Wohlstetter, Roberta. *Pearl Harbor: Warning and Decision*. Stanford, Calif.: Stanford University Press, 1962.

———— "Cuba and Pearl Harbor: Hindsight and Foresight." *Foreign Affairs* 43 (1965):707-723.

Wolfers, Arnold. *Discord and Collaboration*. Baltimore, Md.: Johns Hopkins University Press, 1962.

Notes to Chapter 10 - The Heart of Escalation Dynamics

1. Some of these limitations will be discussed shortly. For more systematic treatments see Jervis, *Logic of Images, Perception and Misperception*, and "Hypotheses on Misperception"; and de Rivera, *Psychological Dimension of Foreign Policy* (esp. chaps. 2 and 3). See also the references in note 12 to Chapter 9.

In this chapter I shall give more emphasis to the subjectivity of decision-makers' perceptions and expectations than is necessary for some readers; this book is intended for several different audiences, not all of whom will find this idea equally familiar. I shall also emphasize it because I am concerned not only with relatively specifiable perceptions, but also with vaguer, more diffuse notions, including "images" about plausible futures which may be semiconscious and perhaps even unconscious (although in no sense is this a psychoanalytic assessment).

2. I do not mean to imply that all expectations therefore are equally

plausible—clearly not. Nevertheless their "real" plausibility cannot be checked until the future arrives. (On the checking of perceptions see the three Jervis works.)

This line of approach employs a moderately objective meaning for the term *plausibility*. An alternative way is to employ a more subjective meaning for the term, in which case my immediate theme, the subjectivity of expectations, is more obvious. Either way, there is a relative difference between the confirmability of perceptions about the present and expectations about the future.

3. In "When the Fighting Has to Stop." See also Iklé's book, *Every War Must End.*

4. On prediction and forecasting in foreign policy-making, see Choucri and Robinson, *Forecasting in International Relations;* and Rothstein, *Planning, Prediction and Policymaking in Foreign Affairs* (esp. chap. 4).

5. "Wars of attrition" and "tests of capabilities within very restrictive ground rules" are two of the four main strategies for the use of force discussed by George in chap. 1 of *The Limits of Coercive Diplomacy.* The other two are "quick, decisive military strategy" and "coercive diplomacy." Policy-makers may, of course, find themselves unintentionally shifting from one to another if, for example, an attempted quick, decisive stroke becomes bogged down in a war of attrition.

6. Something that looks like a one-shot action which might fall in this category of exceptions is the reprisal—generally an operation undertaken to punish the opponent for some action he has committed and to warn him not to repeat it. An example is the German shelling of the Spanish republic seacoast town of Almería during the Spanish Civil War, in reprisal for a republican attack on the German warship *Deutschland.* If a reprisal succeeds in its intentions (as this one did), neither it nor the action that provoked it are repeated, and expectations about the progress and outcome of the war are in many respects unchanged. Still, everyone's expectations have been modified about what kinds of operations and policies are and are not likely to be carried out successfully. The side taking the original action now knows something it did not about the opponent's response thresholds and about the costs a certain strategy is likely to incur. The side taking the reprisal action has won a test of wills and strengthened its bargaining position. Or, should the reprisal fail, there may be a series of actions by the first side, each receiving the same inadequate reprisal, which amounts to a reciprocal escalation and counterescalation generating a new level of violence in the war. There is also the possibility of counterreprisal by the first side; if a sequence of counterreprisals and counter-counter-reprisals continues, it will quickly lose its reprisal character and become simply a cyclical escalation sequence.

7. Schelling, *Strategy of Conflict,* chap. 3, and *Arms and Influence,* chaps. 3 and 4.

8. The distance between Minorca and Majorca, which had long been

401

held by the Nationalist side, is comparable to the distance between Spain and Spanish Morocco. But Majorca was garrisoned mainly by the Italians, and Generalissimo Franco gave a commitment that he would occupy Minorca only with Spanish forces (Thomas, *Spanish Civil War*, p. 580).

9. In this and later discussion I am deliberately leaving out, for simplicity, the important fact that various decision-makers or groups within a single government may have somewhat different expectations about the progress and outcome of a war. Someone else's escalation, therefore, may greatly change the expectations of one set of policy-makers (and perhaps lead them to urge a counterescalation) but not those of another set.

10. For a list of principal events early in the U. S. gradualist escalation against North Vietnam, see note 20 to Chapter 2.

11. The extent to which expectations vary among policy-makers in different warring nations is a variable, not a constant. The frequency of extremely dissimilar expectations, or of very similar expectations, might be a suitable topic for research, particularly research aimed at identifying the circumstances that tend to favor each pattern. (See Appendix B for more about research of this nature.)

12. This appears to be the implicit model employed in many discussions about escalation. It is stated explicitly in, for example, Jones' "Framework for Exploring Escalation Control."

13. It is true that policy-makers can have partly, perhaps entirely, unconscious motives and goals in warfare. Usually, however, these occur in the form of latent motives for selecting explicit war objectives, objectives for which there are manifest motives as well. Fairly explicit objectives, at least in a military sense, are a prerequisite for military planning.

14. The maintenance of consistency is one of the fundamental findings of cognitive psychology. See Festinger, *A Theory of Cognitive Dissonance;* Abelson et al., *Theories of Cognitive Consistency;* Feldman, *Cognitive Consistency;* and Festinger, *Conflict, Decision and Dissonance.* (The word *conflict* in the last title refers to conflict within the subjective universe, not conflict between persons or states.) A useful summary of cognitive consistency to the context of foreign policy-making is found in Steinbruner, *Cybernetic Theory of Decision* (pp. 97-100).

15. The reality-simplifying effect of stress on cognitive consistency is discussed in, for example, Lazarus, *Psychological Stress and the Coping Process.* For purposes of this analysis I have oversimplified the role of stress considerably. For example, mild stress of a kind that increases motivation may lead to the creation of a richer and more comprehensive "cognitive map" of a situation, compared to the casual observations characteristic of very relaxed states. Reality-simplifying sets in only as stress mounts higher.

Stress has a variety of other effects on decision-making performance besides those involving cognitive consistency. The general effects of stress are discussed in Holsti and George, "Effects of Stress on Performance"; and George, "Adaptation to Stress." They are summarized more briefly in Milburn, "Management of Crises" and in Hermann and Hermann, "Maintaining the Quality of Decision-Making." Janis discusses the effects of stress in increasing "groupthink" in *Victims of Groupthink*.

16. Holsti, "The 1914 Case" and *Crisis Escalation War*.

17. For other discussions of this theme, see for example Hermann, "International Crisis as a Situational Variable" and *Crises in Foreign Policy*. As in note 15, see also Milburn, Holsti and George, and George.

18. Technically, this response is still to stress; not to crisis stress, but to a more mental or subjective kind of stress. This is one kind of stress as psychologists use the term, but it is not what government officials usually mean by the word. Stress in governmental usage generally refers to the effect of time pressure or other kinds of nonsubjective external pressure: the kind of stress found especially during intense crises.

Although there has been considerable experimentation with the psychological effects of threat, I am not aware of experimentation testing the hypothesis presented here: that in conflict situations a series of hostile steps back and forth, sequentially placing more and more important stakes at risk, invokes the reality-simplifying effect of cognitive consistency through the creation of anxiety and a sense of being seriously threatened. The hypothesis seems well worth testing if an adequate experiment can be designed. There appears to be a definite ethical issue involved relating to experimentation with human subjects, since cognitive consistency is invoked significantly only by threatening really serious values.

This ethical issue might be sidestepped and the hypothesis tested at least partially by simulation and gaming experiments, in which the players may temporarily identify so completely with a fictional entity that serious threats to that entity invoke the psychological mechanisms. Simulations and gaming experiments to date tend, on the whole, to lend plausibility to the hypothesis without, I think, having adequately tested it. Citations to some particularly relevant examples appear in note 20. The simulation and gaming literature to 1972 is reviewed in Shubik, Brewer, and Savage, "Literature of Gaming, Simulation and Model-Building."

19. *Escalation and the Nuclear Option*, p. 119.

20. There is a sizable literature reporting research on the perception of threats, and decision-making in response, carried out by psychologists, political scientists, and others interested in social conflict in general, as well as in the simulation of international conflict. Some of the literature most relevant to escalation dynamics includes the following: North, Brody, and Holsti, "Some Empirical Data on the Conflict Spiral"; Rapoport and Chammah, *Prisoner's Dilemma*; Rapoport, "Additional Experimental Findings on Conflict and Games" and "Prospects for Experimental Games"; Nardin, "Communication and the Effects of Threats;" Ogley, "Investigating the

Effects of Threats"; Deutsch, "Bargaining, Threat and Communication"; Brody, Benham, and Milstein, "Hostile International Communication"; and Sisson and Ackoff, "Toward a Theory of the Dynamics of Conflict." Two of the pioneering theoretical statements were Boulding, "Towards a Pure Theory of Threat Systems," and Singer, "Inter-Nation Influence."

Although substantial research has been done in this area, the psychological assessment of escalation dynamics is certainly not yet fully developed, and in my opinion considerable important research remains to be done. Much of the work to date is pitched at the level of attempting to simulate a rise in tensions, or in hostilities, in international relations *in general*, and does not focus upon the special properties of escalation dynamics involving military action. Thus, for instance, much of this work investigates the perception of, and response to, messages that communicate a "threat." This is more directly relevant to the question of how crises may intensify than to the problem of military escalation where deeds, not messages, carry the threat and the communication is mostly tacit. As mentioned in note 18, research thus far also does not focus upon the mounting sense of being deeply threatened because of the rising stakes, which is a central feature of escalation. In addition, much of the research to date has employed the repetitive play of the Prisoner's Dilemma game and variations upon it. But repetitive play of *one* interaction (or any small number), though valuable in other ways, is not an adequate simulation of an escalation sequence with its series of *shifting* interactions.

Despite these considerations, existing results are certainly relevant to the dynamics of military escalation; though not without some ambiguities, they tend to support the hypothesis stated in the text—that a sequence of hostile behavior back and forth tends to reinforce and confirm each side's perceptions of the other as a hostile opponent, perceptions that lead to hostile responses and thus continue the cycle.

One of the lines along which valuable additional research could be done is testing the more specific hypothesis that such reinforcement cycles invoke the reality-simplifying effect of cognitive consistency. It is useful to distinguish this mechanism (presuming it exists) from the shifting perceptions that could be argued to follow rationally (at least in some sense of the term) from hostile behavior by the other side.

21. This theme is addressed at greater length in George and Smoke, *Deterrence in American Foreign Policy* (chap. 19).

22. The Crimean is a case where the transition from peace to war was fairly distinct, since the original Russian occupation of the principalities was not considered an act of war. Legal as well as practical war between the Russians and the Turks began when the Turks attacked in October to try to regain Moldavia and Wallachia. One can dimly perceive the tenuous outlines of what could have become a definitional phase immediately following, in which the conflict was defined as another Russo-Turkish War

not involving the Western powers directly. After the first few weeks, indeed, that conflict would have simmered at a very low level for some six months because of weather; then the French and British, if they had not yet advanced their fleets to the Dardanelles or taken equivalent action elsewhere, might well have remained only peripherally involved or uninvolved. As events actually developed, there was no period during which expectations of a purely Russo-Turkish War coud crystallize. The fleet advancement to Constantinople, the Sinope massacre and Western reaction to it, and subsequent movement of ships into the Black Sea kept the escalation in motion and did not allow initial limits to remain stable for any length of time.

Bibliography for Chapter 10 - The Heart of Escalation Dynamics

Abelson, Robert, et al., eds. *Theories of Cognitive Consistency: A Sourcebook.* Chicago: Rand McNally & Co., 1968.

Boulding, Kenneth E. "Towards a Pure Theory of Threat Systems." *American Economic Review* 53, supplement (1963):424-434.

Brodie, Bernard. *Escalation and the Nuclear Option.* Princeton, N. J.: Princeton University Press, 1966.

Brody, Richard A., Alexandra H. Benham, and Jeffrey S. Milstein. "Hostile International Communication, Arms Production, and Perception of Threat: A Simulation Study." *Peace Research Society (International) Papers* 7 (1967):15-40.

Choucri, Nazli, and Thomas Robinson. *Forecasting in International Relations: Theory, Method, Problem and Prospects.* San Francisco: W. H. Freeman, 1975.

de Rivera, Joseph H. *The Psychological Dimension of Foreign Policy.* Columbus, Ohio: Charles E. Merrill Books, 1968.

Deutsch, Morton. "Bargaining, Threat, and Communication: Some Experimental Studies." In Kathleen C. Archibald, ed., *Strategic Interaction and Conflict.* Berkeley, Calif.: Institute of International Studies, 1966.

Feldman, Shel, ed. *Cognitive Consistency: Motivational Antecedents and Behavioral Consequents.* New York: Academic Press, 1966.

Festinger, Leon. *A Theory of Cognitive Dissonance.* Evanston, Ill.: Row, Peterson & Co., 1957.

——— et al. *Conflict, Decision and Dissonance.* Stanford, Calif.: Stanford University Press, 1964.

George, Alexander L. "Adaptation to Stress in Political Decision-Making." In George V. Coelho, David A. Hamburg, and John E. Adams, eds., *Coping and Adaptation.* New York: Basic Books, 1974.

——— and Richard Smoke. *Deterrence in American Foreign Policy: Theory and Practice.* New York: Columbia University Press, 1974.

———, David K. Hall, and William E. Simons. *The Limits of Coercive Diplomacy.* Boston: Little, Brown and Co., 1971.

Hermann, Charles F. *Crises in Foreign Policy: A Simulation Analysis.* Indianapolis, Ind.: Bobbs-Merrill Co., 1969.

───── "International Crisis as a Situational Variable." In James N. Rosenau, ed., *International Politics and Foreign Policy.* Rev. ed. New York: Free Press, 1969.

Hermann, Margaret G., and Charles F. Hermann. "Maintaining the Quality of Decision-Making in Foreign Policy Crises: A Proposal." In Alexander L. George et al., "The Use of Information." Appendix D, Report of the Commission on the Organization of the Government for the Conduct of Foreign Policy (Murphy Commission). Washington, D. C.: U. S. Government Printing Office, 1975 and 1976.

Holsti, Ole R. "The 1914 Case." *American Political Science Review* 59 1965):365-378.

───── *Crisis Escalation War.* Montreal: McGill-Queens University Press, 1972.

───── and Alexander L. George. "The Effects of Stress on Performance of Foreign Policy-Makers." In C. P. Cotter, ed., *Political Science Annual,* vol. 6. Indianapolis, Ind.: Bobbs-Merrill Co., 1975.

Iklé, Fred C. "When the Fighting Has to Stop: The Arguments About Escalation." *World Politics* 19 (1967):692-707.

───── *Every War Must End.* New York: Columbia University Press, 1971.

Janis, Irving. *Victims of Groupthink.* Boston: Houghton Mifflin Co., 1972.

Jervis, Robert. "Hypotheses on Misperception." *World Politics* 20 (1968): 454-479.

───── *The Logic of Images in International Relations.* Princeton, N. J.: Princeton University Press, 1970.

───── *Perception and Misperception in International Politics.* Princeton, N. J.: Princeton University Press, 1976.

Jones, W. M. "A Framework for Exploring Escalation Control." RAND R-1536-RC. Santa Monica, Calif.: RAND Corporation, 1974.

Lazarus, Richard S. *Psychological Stress and the Coping Process.* New York: McGraw-Hill, 1966.

Milburn, Thomas W. "The Management of Crises." In Charles F. Hermann, ed., *International Crises: Insights from Behavioral Research.* New York: Free Press, 1972.

Nardin, Terry. "Communication and the Effects of Threats in Strategic Interaction." *Peace Research Society (International) Papers* 9 (1968): 69-86.

North, Robert C., Richard A. Brody, and Ole R. Holsti. "Some Empirical Data on the Conflict Spiral." *Peace Research Society (International) Papers* 16 (1970):61-93.

Rapoport, Anatol. "Additional Experimental Findings on Conflict and Games." *Peace Research Society (International) Papers* 5 (1966):87-98.

———— "Prospects for Experimental Games." *Journal of Conflict Resolution* 12 (1968):461-470.

———— and Albert M. Chammah. *Prisoner's Dilemma: A Study of Conflict and Cooperation.* Ann Arbor, Mich.: University of Michigan Press, 1965.

Schelling, Thomas C. *The Strategy of Conflict.* Cambridge, Mass.: Harvard University Press, 1960.

———— *Arms and Influence.* New Haven, Conn.: Yale University Press, 1966.

Shubik, Martin, Garry Brewer, and E. Savage. "The Literature of Gaming, Simulation and Model-Building: Index and Critical Abstracts." RAND R-620-ARPA. Santa Monica, Calif.: RAND Corporation, 1972.

Singer, J. David. "Inter-Nation Influence: A Formal Model." *American Political Science Review* 57 (1963):420-430.

Sisson, Roger L., and Russell L. Ackoff. "Toward a Theory of the Dynamics of Conflict." *Peace Research Society (International) Papers* 5 (1966): 183-197.

Steinbruner, John. *The Cybernetic Theory of Decision.* Princeton, N. J.: Princeton University Press, 1976.

Thomas, Hugh. *The Spanish Civil War.* London: Eyre & Spottiswoode, 1961.

Notes to Appendix B - The Research Methodology:
Presuppositions and Rationale

1. A much more technical approach to the issues treated in this appendix, and related issues, is taken in Smoke and George, "Theory for Policy in International Affairs." Most of what appears in that article will not be repeated here.

Also overlapping the material in this appendix are two of my recent articles, "Policy-applicable Theory" and "Theory for and about Policy." These, in turn, draw heavily on earlier work by George, notably the introduction to his book with Hall and Simons, *The Limits of Coercive Diplomacy*, and several unpublished papers.

2. Lippmann's use of this tripartite distinction, which may have been the first published use of it, is described and elaborated upon by Thompson in his essay, "Toward a Theory of International Politics" (essentially a report of a conference attended by Lippmann and other theorists). Hoffmann includes this paper in his book, *Contemporary Theory in International Relations*, and repeats the trichotomy approvingly in his covering essay.

3. Some specialists employ the term *scientific theory*, or *scientific study*, in the context of international relations research, as synonymous with what J. David Singer has termed *QIP*—quantitative international politics. That is, the terms refer to research that employs quantitative data

and mathematical and statistical methods. This is a narrower use of the term *science* than the meaning many specialists give it or than I give it here. On QIP see, for instance, Zinnes, "Research Frontiers."

4. In addition to the peace research movement, there are other isolated streams of thought and opinion that are part of the moral approach to world politics. Traditional Idealism, which has now largely died out, is one. The small world federalist movement is another. Still another is the "alternative world orders" presently being paid attention by some futurists and other specialists.

The variety of opinions and perspectives that exist in this area have not yet begun to be integrated into a wider theoretical framework that embraces philosophical, ethical, and even spiritual questions as well as technical and narrowly political problems in the evolution of the world system. It is not sufficient to create models and hypotheses about alterations in the international system, or even strategies in a narrow political sense for how these might be accomplished. Such work seems likely to remain isolated and fragmentary until it can be placed in a larger conceptual context, one that gives it coherence and persuasiveness. For example, theory is needed to cope with the difficult intellectual issues raised by the concept of value and its operationalization in the context of international affairs and foreign policy. It is necessary, as part of this formulation, to identify the role of values in foreign policy and foreign policy-making; and to discover how values may be ordered and systematized for application in international affairs, as well as rendered convincing and practical in both the long-term and short-term senses. The ultimate goal in the development of normative theory would appear to be an integrated and analytically reasonable, yet inspiring, vision-cum-theory of the evolution and transformation of the world political system to an entirely new historical level: a level appropriate for the twenty-first century and characterized, probably, not by full political union on the models of the twentieth century and earlier, still less by totalitarian uniformity, but by some version of unity-in-diversity.

One result of the general lack of theory in this area is that the credibility of the few normative ideas that do exist is low. Many college and graduate school courses in international relations, for instance, pay little serious attention to normative issues in international politics. Values have relatively little influence upon policy-making in the West, on the whole, except insofar as they become translated via political machinery and movements into political pressure on decision-makers. In recent times perhaps only two government leaders in the West, John F. Kennedy and Charles de Gaulle, have brought with them into office a personal vision of the improvement of the world political system. This quality is not generally looked for in political candidates, and probably will not be until a coherent and inspiring conception exists of the desirable and feasible future of the international system. Such a conception must embrace the level of fundamental values if it is to have the necessary influence, although at some

408

stage it must be translated into more political strategies as well. One discussion, unfortunately a somewhat isolated one, that seems to be pitched at this fundamental level is Niebuhr's *The Children of Light and the Children of Darkness* (chap. 5).

5. May's *"Lessons" of the Past* attempts to come to grips with one important aspect of officials' images of the significance of events and of the basic goals of other states: the use of historical analogies. A different aspect of decision-makers' images of international reality is emphasized in the "operational code" method, pioneered by Nathan Leites and developed by Alexander George ("The 'Operational Code' ") and others. Design theory and the other aspects of policy theory are discussed in Simon, *Science of the Artificial*; Rosenau, "Moral Fervor"; Bobrow, *International Relations*; and the special issue devoted to this subject of *Policy Sciences*, vol. 4 (December 1973).

6. A good deal of material that is generally regarded as part of the literature on the decision-making process, or on policy instruments like deterrence, is essentially descriptive. Such material can be considered policy relevant, but is not often applicable operationally to new policy problems. Many scholars address themselves to current foreign policy issues, and explicitly or implicitly offer substantive recommendations. Such literature is not operationally applicable in the analytical sense being developed here, although of course authors hope decision-makers will apply their prescriptions. In addition, many scholars refer to essentially empirical theorization about, say, the dynamics of arms races as policy relevant, even where conclusions that could be applied operationally are mostly or entirely absent.

7. Suggestions are made, for example, in Allison and Halperin, "Bureaucratic Politics," and in Halperin's *Bureaucratic Politics and Foreign Policy*.

8. Steinbruner briefly discusses the operational applicability of the theory of decision-making he calls cybernetic in *The Cybernetic Theory of Decison*. The operational applicability of this theory is also discussed in Coulam, *Illusions of Choice*.

9. The low applicability to operational planning of deterrence research is one of the main themes of George and Smoke, *Deterrence in American Foreign Policy* (chaps. 3 and 16 especially).

Our discussion here will not pursue further the topic of research on the policy-making process. With the exception of Chapter 10, this study has given only peripheral attention to the process. The psychological mechanisms hypothesized in that chapter must be considered part of the decision-making process, broadly conceived. However, they are not included in what many political scientists usually mean by the phrase "the decision-making process": the interpersonal, interoffice, and interagency flow of information, opinion, decisions, instructions, and orders.

A useful review of the literature (current to 1974) on the making of foreign policy and the efforts of scholars to render theorization about it useful to decision-makers is Bloomfield's "Foreign Policy Process." Two relatively recent books on this process, both of which take a comprehensive approach, are Hilsman, *Politics of Policy-Making,* and Rothstein, *Planning, Prediction and Policymaking.*

10. There is also a paragraph of factors "militating against" escalation, of which two out of five are the mirror images of two of the factors quoted in the text. I have omitted this subsequent paragraph for reason of space and because it does not change my assessment.

11. Barringer also describes types of de-escalation. As with Wright, I have omitted this description for reason of space and because it does not change the assessment.

12. When analysts in the field of national security affairs introduced systems analysis in the late 1950s and early 1960s as a way of improving national security policy-making, this development was *not* received with criticism because of its quantitative nature. The subsequent controversy was over the number and variety of fields to which the technique could be applied, and within the government came as a result of bureaucratic and institutional resistance to the policy implications. It was not a product of any philosophical animus against quantitative methods.

Another assessment, consistent with mine but in greater depth, appears in O'Leary et al., "Quest for Relevance." A particularly interesting recent analysis of the debate between the quantitativists and nonquantitativists is Lijphart's "Structure of the Theoretical Revolution." Lijphart, however, does not treat the particular needs and demands of theory intended to be operationally applicable.

13. In some cases the change in decision-makers' policy may be left partially implicit. For example, Barringer's conclusions about escalation may be expressed in the form, "If conditions *a, b, c, . . .* are present in a situation of description *x*, then Type Three escalation is probable." (This terminology and form differ somewhat from Barringer's own.) What policies should be adopted upon recognition of these conditions are not fully explicated in Barringer's discussion. However, appropriate measures could often be specified with only a slight extension of his analysis.

In this discussion I have avoided reference to dependent and independent variables, because which is which can change, depending on the research design. O'Leary and colleagues employ this terminology in their "Quest for Relevance." In the more technical paper from which this appendix is partially drawn, decision-makers' "calculations about the meaning of the situation" are referred to as "diagnoses"; their "calculations about their own strategy" are referred to as "contingent predictions" (of one type); and both are discussed in more detail (Smoke and George, sec. 3).

14. The exceptions are instances where the technique is employed as a means of testing the validity or importance of a limited number of hypoth-

eses in a limited range of circumstances or situations. Young's *Politics of Force* and Holsti's *Crisis Escalation War* fall into this category. With only a few such exceptions, the comparison of case studies cannot be used for rigorous testing of the general frequency with which any particular hypothesis occurs, because normally the sample of cases is neither exhaustive nor necessarily representative. Conclusions based on frequency, therefore, are not possible (except that one knows that the frequency is not zero; the hypothesized combination of variables *can* occur). For this reason, conclusions such as those suggested in Chapter 10 must be hypotheses whose general validity is yet to be established. From the empirical viewpoint, indeed, the comparative case study method is most often useful as a generator of hypotheses, not as a tester of them.

However, the comparative method can also be used as a means of extending and refining hypotheses, because the technique is a useful one for identifying the conditions that cancel, mediate, enlarge, or otherwise modify the validity of a hypothesis. In somewhat different ways Eckstein ("Case Study and Theory"), Russett ("International Behavior Research"), and Verba ("Some Dilemmas in Comparative Research") all have pointed out this merit, as well as the exploratory value, of the comparative case study approach.

Bibliography for Appendix B - The Research Methodology:
Presuppositions and Rationale

Allison, Graham, and Morton H. Halperin. "Bureaucratic Politics: A Paradigm and Some Policy Implications." In Richard H. Ullman and Raymond Tanter, eds., *Theory and Practice in International Relations.* Princeton, N. J.: Princeton University Press, 1972. Originally published in *World Politics* 24, supplement (1972):40-79.

Barringer, Richard E. *War: Patterns of Conflict.* Cambridge, Mass.: MIT Press, 1972.

Bloomfield, Lincoln P. "The Foreign Policy Process: Making Theory Relevant." Sage Professional Papers in International Studies, vol. 3, no. 02-028. Beverly Hills, Calif.: Sage Publications, 1974.

———— and Amelia C. Leiss. *Controlling Small Wars.* New York: Alfred A. Knopf, 1969.

Bobrow, Davis. *International Relations: New Approaches.* New York: Free Press, 1972.

Clark, Grenville, and Louis Sohn. *World Peace Through World Law.* Cambridge, Mass.: Harvard University Press, 1960.

Coulam, Robert. *Illusions of Choice*, Princeton, N. J.: Princeton University Press, 1977.

Eckstein, Harry. "Case Study and Theory in Political Science." In Fred I. Greenstein and Nelson W. Polsby, eds., *Handbook of Political Science*, vol. 7. Reading, Mass.: Addison-Wesley Publishing Co., 1975.

George, Alexander L. "The 'Operational Code': A Neglected Approach to the Study of Political Leaders and Decision-making." *International Studies Quarterly* 13 (1969):190-222.

———— and Richard Smoke. *Deterrence in American Foreign Policy: Theory and Practice.* New York: Columbia University Press, 1974.

————, David K. Hall, and William E. Simons. *The Limits of Coercive Diplomacy.* Boston: Little, Brown and Co., 1971.

Halperin, Morton H. *Bureaucratic Politics and Foreign Policy.* Washington, D. C.: Brookings Institution, 1974.

Hilsman, Roger. *The Politics of Policy-Making in Defense and Foreign Policy.* New York: Harper & Row, 1971.

Hoffmann, Stanley. *Contemporary Theory in International Relations.* Englewood Cliffs., N. J.: Prentice-Hall, 1960.

Holsti, Ole R. *Crisis Escalation War.* Montreal: McGill-Queens University Press, 1972.

Janis, Irving. *Victims of Groupthink.* Boston: Houghton Mifflin Co., 1972.

Kant, Immanuel. *Perpetual Peace.* Translated by Lewis W. Beck, New York: Bobbs-Merrill Co., 1957.

Lijphart, Arend. "The Structure of the Theoretical Revolution in International Relations." *International Studies Quarterly* 18 (1974):41-74.

May, Ernest R. *"Lessons" of the Past.* New York: Oxford University Press, 1973.

Nicolson, Harold. *Diplomacy.* 3rd ed. Oxford: Oxford University Press, 1963.

Niebuhr, Reinhold. *The Children of Light and the Children of Darkness.* New York: Charles Scribner's Sons, 1960.

O'Leary, Michael K., William D. Coplin, Howard B. Shapiro, and Dale Dean. "The Quest for Relevance: Quantitative International Relations Research and Government Foreign Affairs Analysis." *International Studies Quarterly* 18 (1974):211-237.

Paige, Glenn. "Comparative Case Analysis of Crisis Decisions: Korea and Cuba." In Charles Hermann, ed., *International Crises: Insights from Behavioral Research.* New York: Free Press, 1972.

Rosenau, James N. "Moral Fervor, Systematic Analysis, and Scientific Consciousness in Foreign Policy Research." In Austin Ranney, ed., *Political Science and Public Policy.* Chicago: Markham Press, 1968.

Rothstein, Robert L. *Planning, Prediction and Policymaking in Foreign Affairs: Theory and Practice.* Boston: Little, Brown and Co., 1972.

Russett, Bruce M. "International Behavior Research: Case Studies and Cumulation." In Michael Haas and Henry S. Kariel, eds., *Approaches to the Study of Political Science.* Scranton, Penn.: Chandler Publishing Co., 1970.

Simon, Herbert. *The Science of the Artificial.* Cambridge, Mass.: Harvard University Press, 1969.

Smoke, Richard. "Policy-applicable Theory." In Alexander L. George et al., "The Use of Information." Appendix D, Report of the Commission on the Organization of the Government for the Conduct of Foreign Policy (Murphy Commission). Washington, D. C.: U. S. Government Printing Office, 1975 and 1976.

———— "Theory for and about Policy." In James N. Rosenau, ed., *In Search of Global Patterns*. New York: Free Press, 1977.

———— and Alexander L. George. "Theory for Policy in International Relations." *Policy Sciences* 4 (1973):387-413. (A shorter version appears as the appendix in George and Smoke, *Deterrence in American Foreign Policy*.)

Steinbruner, John D. *The Cybernetic Theory of Decision*. Princeton, N. J.: Princeton University Press,1974.

Thompson, Kenneth W. "Toward a Theory of International Politics." *American Political Science Review* 49 (1955):733-746.

Verba, Sidney. "Some Dilemmas in Comparative Research." *World Politics* 20 (1967):111-127.

Wright, Quincy. "The Escalation of International Conflicts." *Journal of Conflict Resolution* 9 (1965):434-449.

Young, Oran R. *The Politics of Force*. Princeton, N. J.: Princeton University Press, 1968.

Zinnes, Dina A. "Research Frontiers in the Study of International Politics." In Fred I. Greenstein and Nelson W. Polsby, eds. *Handbook of Political Science*, vol. 8. Reading, Mass.: Addison-Wesley Publishing Co., 1975.

Notes to Appendix C - The Italian Submarine Campaign in the Spanish Civil War

1. Where not otherwise specified, the information in this section is drawn from *Ciano's Hidden Diary*, pt. 1; from Puzzo, *Spain and the Great Powers*, pp. 195-200; from Toynbee, *Survey of International Affairs, 1937*, pp. 185 and 339-352; from the editorial in the *A.J.I.L.*; and from Thomas, *Spanish Civil War*, pp. 467-482. The information in Table 6 is taken primarily from Toynbee, *Survey, 1937*, pp. 340-341, and from the editorial, pp. 659-660. The Italian ship was presumably attacked in error.

2. *Strategic warning* is intelligence of a general character that another nation may be likely soon to launch a new line of action; it is contrasted with *tactical warning*, intelligence of specific actions that are imminent.

Naturally it is impossible to be certain that no attention was given to Mussolini's options anywhere within the British or French governments. But there is no indication of this in the available sources, and the sluggish policy response suggests there had been no preparation. See also the comments to follow about the failure to attempt deterrence.

3. It is not necessary to assume that decision-makers in Rome were highly conscious of this purpose in advance and ordered the escalation

413

with that thought uppermost. Once taken, the steps could be employed to draw appropriate conclusions regarding the prospects for additional steps. Thus a sequence of unilateral escalations can and often does serve as a testing strategy, whether or not decision-makers launch the sequence with that purpose specifically in view.

4. In January 1938 the Nyon submarine patrols were reduced in view of the absence of attacks. Immediately, submarine attacks on non-Spanish ships resumed. Rather than bring the patrols back to their previous level, Britain and France, with the sanction of the Nyon signatories, announced that forthwith any submerged submarine in the Mediterranean would be attacked, whether near a sunk merchantman or not. The submarine attacks again ceased. For the details of these events, see Toynbee, *Survey, 1938*, vol, 1, pp. 364-367.

5. The concept of compellence is introduced and discussed by Schelling in *Arms and Influence*. The similar concept of coercive diplomacy is the subject of *The Limits of Coercive Diplomacy* by George, Hall, and Simons.

6. Except for special actions like commando raids, ground forces possess and control the territory they are on. To free an area from their control requires them to pull back; it requires compellence. Air forces are entirely nonterritorial; they fly over territory to strike a point or a set of points. With a few exceptions, more relevant to peacetime than wartime, they do not cruise; if they are denied a point to strike, they stay at home on their bases and do nothing. Such a denial is therefore also a kind of compellence. Naval forces, on the other hand, cruise territory without controlling or possessing it. One can deny them the use of their weapons and still allow them to cruise; they are still active. If this is compellence at all, it is a much weaker form of it, and the requirements for it are more easily satisfied.

Bibliography for Appendix C - The Italian Submarine Campaign in the Spanish Civil War

Ciano, Count Galeazzo. *Ciano's Hidden Diary 1937-1938*. New York: E. P. Dutton & Co., 1953.

Editorial. "Piracy in the Mediterranean." *American Journal of International Law* 31 (1937):659-665.

George, Alexander L., David K. Hall, and William E. Simons. *The Limits of Coercive Diplomacy*. Boston: Little, Brown and Co., 1971.

Puzzo, Dante A. *Spain and the Great Powers 1936-1941*. New York: Columbia University Press, 1962.

Schelling, Thomas C. *Arms and Influence*. New Haven, Conn.: Yale University Press, 1966.

Thomas, Hugh. *The Spanish Civil War*. London: Eyre and Spottiswoode, 1961.

Toynbee, Arnold J., ed. *Survey of International Affairs, 1937*. Vol. 2, *The International Repercussions of the War in Spain (1936-37)*. London: Oxford University Press, 1938.

——— *Survey of International Affairs, 1938*, vol. 1. London: Oxford University Press, 1941.

Index

NOTE: Not included are individuals, events, and places mentioned in the historical chapters; with few exceptions, the text gives only fragmentary information about them. Appendix A is not included because it is already a form of conceptual index to the study.

417